MATERNAL EMPLOYMENT AND CHILDREN'S DEVELOPMENT
Longitudinal Research

PLENUM STUDIES IN WORK AND INDUSTRY

Series Editors:
Ivar Berg, *University of Pennsylvania, Philadelphia, Pennsylvania*
and Arne L. Kalleberg, *University of North Carolina, Chapel Hill, North Carolina*

WORK AND INDUSTRY
Structures, Markets, and Processes
Arne L. Kalleberg and Ivar Berg

ENSURING MINORITY SUCCESS IN CORPORATE MANAGEMENT
Edited by Donna E. Thompson and Nancy DiTomaso

INDUSTRIES, FIRMS, AND JOBS
Sociological and Economic Approaches
Edited by George Farkas and Paula England

MATERNAL EMPLOYMENT AND CHILDREN'S DEVELOPMENT
Longitudinal Research
Edited by Adele Eskeles Gottfried and Allan W. Gottfried

WORKERS, MANAGERS, AND TECHNOLOGICAL CHANGE
Emerging Patterns of Labor Relations
Edited by Daniel B. Cornfield

MATERNAL EMPLOYMENT AND CHILDREN'S DEVELOPMENT
Longitudinal Research

Edited by

Adele Eskeles Gottfried
California State University, Northridge
Northridge, California

and

Allen W. Gottfried
California State University, Fullerton
Fullerton, California

PLENUM PRESS • NEW YORK AND LONDON

Library of Congress Cataloging in Publication Data

Maternal employment and children's development.

(Plenum studies in work and industry)
Bibliography: p.
Includes index.
1. Working mothers—United States—Longitudinal studies. 2. Mother and child—United States—Longitudinal studies. 3. Mothers—Employment—United States—Longitudinal studies. 4. Child development—United States—Longitudinal studies. I. Gottfried, Adele Eskeles. II. Gottfried, Allen W. III. Series.
HQ759.48.M35   1988   306.8'7   88-15167
ISBN 0-306-42867-9

This limited facsimile edition has been issued
for the purpose of keeping this title available
to the scientific community.

10 9 8 7 6 5 4 3 2

© 1988 Plenum Press, New York
A Division of Plenum Publishing Corporation
233 Spring Street, New York, N.Y. 10013

All rights reserved

No part of this book may be reproduced, stored in a retrieval system, or transmitted in any form or by any means, electronic, mechanical, photocopying, microfilming, recording, or otherwise, without written permission from the Publisher

Printed in the United States of America

Dedicated to
Michael and Jeffrey

Contributors

Kay Bathurst, Department of Psychology, University of California, Los Angeles, Los Angeles, California

Martha J. Cox, Timberlawn Psychiatric Research Foundation, Dallas, Texas

Debra DeMeis, Department of Psychology, Hobart and William Smith Colleges, Geneva, New York

M. Ann Easterbrooks, Department of Child Study, Tufts University, Medford, Massachusetts

Nancy L. Galambos, Department of Psychology, University of Victoria, Victoria, British Columbia, Canada

Ellen Galinsky, Bank Street College of Education, New York, New York

Wendy A. Goldberg, Program in Social Ecology, University of California, Irvine, Irvine, California

Adele Eskeles Gottfried, Department of Educational Psychology, California State University, Northridge, Northridge, California

Allen W. Gottfried, Department of Psychology, California State University, Fullerton, Fullerton, California

Ellen Hock, Department of Family Relations and Human Development, Ohio State University, Columbus, Ohio

Diane Hughes, Bank Street College of Education, New York, New York

Kathleen Lenerz, Department of Education, University of California, Los Angeles, Los Angeles, California

Jacqueline V. Lerner, College of Human Development, Pennsylvania State University, University Park, Pennsylvania

Susan McBride, Graduate School, Wheelock College, Boston, Massachusetts

Margaret Tresch Owen, Timberlawn Psychiatric Research Foundation, Dallas, Texas

Anne C. Petersen, Department of Human Development and Family Studies, Pennsylvania State University, University Park, Pennsylvania

Foreword

In a review written in 1979, I noted that there was a paucity of research examining the effects of maternal employment on the infant and young child and also that longitudinal studies of the effects of maternal employment were needed (Hoffman, 1979). In the last 10 years, there has been a flurry of research activity focused on the mother's employment during the child's early years, and much of this work has been longitudinal. All of the studies reported in this volume are at least short-term longitudinal studies, and most of them examine the effects of maternal employment during the early years.

The increased focus on maternal employment during infancy is not a response to the mandate of that review but rather reflects the new employment patterns in the United States. In March 1985, the Bureau of Labor Statistics reported that 49.4% of married women with children less than a year old were employed outside the home (Hayghe, 1986). This figure is up from 39% in 1980 and more than double the rate in 1970. By now, most mothers of children under 3 are in the labor force. This new pattern of employment among mothers of preschoolers has stimulated research partly because it is viewed as a social problem, just as employment of mothers of school-aged children once was, and there is considerable public concern as well as scientific interest in understanding its significance for children's development. Partly, however, the new research thrust also reflects the increased availability of subject populations. Two decades ago, mothers of infants who were employed were hard to find, and, when samples of sufficient sizes could be located, they were so special—financially destitute or extremely committed to their professions—that it was difficult to sort out the effects of employment from the special characteristics of the sample. In some of the studies reported in this book, such as the one by Hock, DeMeis, and McBride, subjects are recruited directly from the maternity ward. Even 15 years ago, it would have been impossible to recruit an adequate sample of mothers planning to return to work within a year by this procedure.

The increased prevalence of longitudinal research is, to some extent, a natural outcome of this new interest in infancy. How do you assess the effects of maternal employment on infants? The behavioral repertoire of infants is limited. The best measures must rely on inferences from a very narrow range of behavior. The infant development scales have only moderate predictive value. There are no preschool measures of cognitive ability that predict well to later IQ scores. In the emotional domain, Mary Ainsworth's strange situation measure of the security of the toddler's attachment has proven useful with some populations in predicting to early childhood behavior (Sroufe, Fox, & Pancake, 1983), but even its validity has been questioned when it is used with infants who have had extensive experience with nonmaternal care (Clarke-Stewart, 1984). Is the situation really "strange" when the baby has been accustomed to new settings and substitute caretakers? Is independence in an infant sometimes mistaken for insecure-avoidant behavior (Hoffman, 1984)? Thus, in studying the effects of maternal employment on infants, it is quite possible that there are effects that are not manifest until the child is older and also that there are apparent effects in infancy that wash out with maturation. It is only through longitudinal investigations that these issues can be addressed.

For older children also, however, the importance of longitudinal research has become apparent. What was once called child psychology is now more commonly referred to as developmental psychology, reflecting the increased sensitivity to the process of maturation and the changes that occur with growth. The child who seems well-adjusted according to his or her fifth-grade teacher ratings may appear quite different in the ninth grade when adolescent peer pressures and new academic demands may threaten previous self-esteem. Academic conformity in elementary school does not necessarily predict adult achievement patterns. A stress in childhood that is mastered may become a source of strength when the child is an adult (Elder, 1984). Thus, even when the dimension of interest can be adequately tapped in the child, it is important to know what its significance is in the course of development.

A major advantage of the longitudinal approach in maternal employment studies, then, is that it makes it possible to observe both the disappearance of early empirical relationships and the emergence of new ones at a later point. Goldberg and Easterbrooks, in Chapter 5, for example, found that maternal employment during toddlerhood predicted to certain maternal attitudes at that stage but no longer characterized these mothers when their children were of kindergarten age. On the other hand, although employment status did not relate to attachment security at toddlerhood, the number of hours the mother worked at that time did relate to separation anxiety scores obtained 4 years later (positively for boys, negatively for girls). On the whole, however, few sleeper effects emerged in these studies. Even where a wide span of years was considered, as in the Lerner and Galambos chapter, latent patterns did not emerge.

Another advantage of the longitudinal design is the opportunity to examine change *per se*. Goldberg and Easterbrooks, for example, found that children's ego resiliency was higher if the mother did not change her labor force activity over the years. In general, however, the studies in this volume did not make their major focus change in work status. In fact, a major advantage of longitudinal designs in maternal employment studies that has been cited over the years is the opportunity to tap the family situations and the child's behavior patterns before the mother enters the labor force and then observe the changes that follow this event. The idea here, of course, is to separate employment status effects from mother's predispositions. This advantage could not be realized in the present book because most of these investigations were looking at new mothers and the onset of employment during the child's infancy.

In addition to sharing the longitudinal method, the studies reported in this book also share an awareness that maternal employment is not so robust a variable that it can be linked directly to a child characteristic. Maternal employment operates through its effects on the family environment and on the child care arrangements. This is perhaps clearest in the research reported in Chapter 2 by A. E. Gottfried, A. W. Gottfried, and K. Bathurst. Maternal employment status is found to be related to certain aspects of the home environment and these, in turn, relate to child qualities. For example, these researchers find that the father's involvement in child care is likely to be higher when the mother is employed. The father's involvement is positively related to the child's social competence at 6 years of age. Thus, to the extent that a mother's employment increases the father's involvement, as it often but not always does, it has an indirect positive effect on the child's competence. In the Owen and Cox study, the data indicate that mothers who are employed more than 40 hours weekly show a higher level of anxiety, and this, in turn, is seen as affecting their interaction with the child. Very few of the many analyses reported in this volume show direct effects of employment status. It is clear in all of this research also that the nature of any effects vary depending on the timing, stability, and extent of the employment; the temperament and attitudes of the various family members; the stability of the nonmaternal care; and a host of other variables. Finally, these studies indicate that research which focuses exclusively on the potential negative outcomes of maternal employment is very limited. The data reported here suggest many positive effects for both sons and daughters, particularly in the form of ego enhancement.

One of the variables that is considered throughout the book for its conditioning influence is the sex of the child. Previous research has suggested that maternal employment has a different effect on sons than on daughters. Where data have indicated differences between the children of employed and nonemployed mothers, they have generally shown the daughters of the employed mothers to be higher on cognitive ability, achievement, and mental health, whereas the pattern for sons has been more ambiguous. There have been several different interpretations of these results: (a) sex differences in temperament make girls more compatible with maternal employment than boys; (b) for daughters, the employed mother is a more competent and timely role model than the nonemployed mother; (c) the tendency to overprotect daughters in the traditional family is avoided in the employed-mother family because of the greater encouragement of independence, whereas this pattern may lead to the overgranting of autonomy to boys; and (d) the lesser traditonalism in the employed mother family is a particular benefit to daughters (Hoffman, 1980; 1984a,b). In the studies reported here, sex differences are not prominent. Owen and Cox did find that when the infants were 3 months old, though not later, employed mothers of girls and nonemployed mothers of boys were the most satisfied, a finding that matches previous results in studies of preschoolers (Bronfenbrenner & Crouter, 1982; Hoffman, 1984a,b). However, there is no evidence here for lower cognitive performance by the middle-class sons of employed mothers sometimes reported in prior research. In fact, Goldberg and Easterbrooks found that in kindergarten, the most ego-resilient children were boys with employed mothers and girls with nonemployed mothers. The previous generalizations about sex differences in the effects of maternal employment seem, on the basis of this volume, to need reevaluation and new empirical empirical investigation. Because of the significance of adolescence for achievement patterns, ego development, and self-esteem, it would be interesting to reexamine these relationships for older children, and, ideally for these same children when they are older.

In this volume, the editors have brought together six independent longitudinal investigations that pertain to the consequences for children of the mother's employment. The authors not only describe their own empirical findings, but each chapter also reviews the previous relevant literature. Scientifically sound studies in this area, however, never produce unequivocal conclusions. In addition to limitations of design, measurement, and samples that are inescapable in real-life research, studies of maternal employment, if they are honest, must face the multidimensional qualities of the independent variable and the complexities of individual temperament, the family system, and the surrounding environment. These authors have done a solid job of reviewing the previous work and reporting their own findings and, as a result, there are no clear-cut, neatly packaged conclusions. Instead, there are valuable insights, important new data, and serious challenges to previous ideas. There is also reconfirmation of earlier conclusions, stengthened now by longitudinal data. *Maternal Employment and Children's Development: Longitudinal Research* is a valuable addition to the research literature.

Lois Wladis Hoffman

Ann Arbor, Michigan

REFERENCES

Bronfenbrenner, U., & Crouter, A. C. (1982). Work and family through time and space. In S. G. Kamerman & C. D. Hayes (Eds.), *Families that work: Children in a changing world* (pp. 39–84). Washington, DC: National Academy Press.

Clarke-Stewart, A. (1984). Day care: A new context for research and development. In M. Perlmutter (Ed.), *Parent-child interaction, Minnesota Symposium Series* (Vol. 17, pp. 61–100). Hillsdale, NJ: Erlbaum Press.

Elder, G. (1984). Families, kin, and the life course: A sociological perspective. In R. R. Parke (Ed.), *The family: Review of child development research* (Vol. 7, pp. 223–282). Chicago: University of Chicago Press.

Hayghe, H. (1986). Rise in mothers' labor force activity includes those with infants. *Monthly Labor Review, 109*(2), 43–45.

Hoffman, L. W. (1979). Maternal employment: 1979. *American Psychologist, 34*(10), 859–865.

Hoffman, L. W. (1980). Effects of maternal employment on children's academic motivations and performance. *School Psychology Review, 9*(4), 319–335.

Hoffman, L. W. (1984a). Maternal employment and the young child. In M. Perlmutter (Ed.), *Parent-child interaction, Minnesota Symposium Series* (Vol. 17, pp. 101–127). Hillsdale, NJ: Erlbaum Press.

Hoffman, L. W. (1984b). Work, family, and the socialization of the child. In R. D. Parke (Ed.), *The family: Review of child development research* (Vol. 7, pp. 223–282). Chicago: University of Chicago Press.

Sroufe, L. A., Fox, N. E., & Pancake, V. R. (1983). Attachment and dependency in developmental perspective. *Child Development, 54*, 1615–1627.

Preface

Maternal employment has been referred to as a "social revolution" that has profound implications for the family and workplace (Kamerman & Kahn, 1981). Additionally, work and family are viewed as interrelated (Mortimer & London, 1984). The inclusion of *Maternal Employment and Children's Development: Longitudinal Research* in the Plenum Studies in Work and Industry series provides an opportunity to address the interrelation of work and family roles, specifically with regard to the effects of maternal employment on children's development. Although work certainly has profound impact on the family, the family has an impact on the workplace as well. The workplace will need to become increasingly responsive to family issues as mothers continue to enter the work force. Fathers' increasing family responsibilities in the wake of maternal employment will also influence the need for family-oriented policies and programs in the workplace.

In this book, mothers' employment status, the extent of their employment (e.g., hours of weekly employment), part- versus full-time employment, their pattern of employment stability, their occupational status, and their work-related attitudes are examined as to their contemporaneous and longitudinal impact on a wide variety of children's developmental outcomes. Implications for corporate programs and policies, and for social policy, are advanced. A conclusion which emerges is that maternal employment is not only a gender issue but one that provides new challenges for the family, the workplace, and society as a whole.

Gratitude is extended to all the contributors for their efforts. Special thanks go to Lois Hoffman for kindly agreeing to write the Foreword. We are pleased to have Professor Hoffman contribute the Foreword. She has been a forerunner in the field of maternal employment research particularly as it pertains to children's development.

We would like to acknowledge California State universities, Northridge and Fullerton, the Thrasher Research Fund, and the Spencer Foundation for supporting various phases of our research.

Adele Eskeles Gottfried
Allen W. Gottfried

Northridge, California

REFERENCES

Kamerman, S. B., & Kahn, A. J. (1981). *Child care, family benefits, and working parents: A study in comparative policy.* New York: Columbia University Press.

Mortimer, J. T., & London, J. (1984). The varying linkages of work and family. In P. Voydanoff (Ed.), *Work and family: Changing roles of men and women* (pp. 20–35) Palo Alto, CA: Mayfield Publishing Co.

Contents

PART I. INTRODUCTION

Chapter 1

**Maternal Employment and Children's Development:
An Introduction to the Issues** 3

    Adele Eskeles Gottfried

PART II. LONGITUDINAL STUDIES

Chapter 2

**Maternal Employment, Family Environment, and Children's
Development: Infancy through the School Years** 11

    Adele Eskeles Gottfried, Allen W. Gottfried, and
    Kay Bathurst

  I. Introduction and Conceptualization 11
 II. Method 14
    A. Subjects 14
    B. Procedure 15
    C. Measures 16
    D. Cognitive Functioning 16
    E. Academic Achievement 16
    F. Temperament and Social Competence 17
    G. Behavioral Adjustment 17
    H. Home and Family Environment 18
    I. Maternal Employment and Attitudes 20

III. Results	21
A. Descriptive Analyses	23
B. Relationships between Maternal Employment, Children's Development, and Home Environment: Contemporaneous Analyses	25
C. Prospective Analyses	33
D. Consistency Analyses	47
E. Maternal Occupation, Hours of Work, and Attitudes: Relationships with Development and Environment	49
IV. Summary	51
V. Discussion	52
References	56

Chapter 3

The Influences of Maternal Employment across Life: The New York Longitudinal Study   59

Jacqueline V. Lerner and Nancy L. Galambos

I. Introduction	59
II. The New York Longitudinal Study (NYLS)	60
III. The NYLS Data Set	62
A. Childhood Ratings	62
B. Adolescent Ratings	65
C. Early Adult Ratings	65
D. Maternal Variables	66
E. Contextual Variables	67
F. Mother–Child Interaction Variables	68
IV. Approach to Data Analysis— The "Process of Influence" Model	69
A. Direct Effects: Analyses and Results for the First 5 Years	70
B. Relationships among Contextual, Maternal, Mother–Child Interaction, and Child Variables	73
C. Testing the "Process of Influence" Model	76
D. Findings from Adolescence and Early Adulthood	79
V. Summary, Conclusions, and Directions for Future Research	80
References	82

Contents

Chapter 4

Maternal Employment and the Transition to Parenthood 85

Margaret Tresch Owen and Martha J. Cox

- I. Rationale for the Present Study 88
  - A. Employment, Attitudes, and Psychological Functioning 88
  - B. Employment and Mother–Infant Interaction 90
  - C. Employment and Infant–Mother Attachment 91
  - D. Employment and the Sex of the Infant 91
- II. Method 92
  - A. Subjects 92
  - B. Procedures 93
  - C. Measures 95
- III. Results 103
  - A. Maternal Attitudes regarding Employment 104
  - B. Maternal Psychological Health 105
  - C. Maternal Investment in Parenthood 106
  - D. Mother–Infant Interaction and Ratings of the Home Environment 107
  - E. Maternal Employment and the Quality of Infant–Mother Attachment 108
  - F. Relations between Attachment and Correlates of Maternal Employment..................................... 109
- IV. Discussion 111
  - A. Processes of Maternal Employment's Influence in Infancy 111
  - B. Role Satisfaction and Maternal Employment during the Infancy Period 113
  - C. Conclusions 114
- V. Summary 116
- References 117

Chapter 5

Maternal Employment When Children Are Toddlers and Kindergartners 121

Wendy A. Goldberg and M. Ann Easterbrooks

- I. Introduction: Maternal Employment When Children Are Young 121

II. Our Research 125
   A. Sample 126
   B. Procedures 128
   C. Measures 129
III. Results 134
   A. Mothers' Reasons for Working or Not Working outside the Home 134
   B. Relation of Maternal Employment to Children's Socioemotional and Socio-Personality Development 135
   C. Relation of Maternal Employment to Children's Social-Cognitive Development 139
   D. Relation of Maternal Employment to Parental Attitudes, Behavior, and Emotions 140
   E. Sleeper Effects of Maternal Employment on Children's Development 142
   F. Stability and Change in Maternal Employment from Toddlerhood to Kindergarten 144
IV. Summary 145
V. Discussion 147
   References 151

Chapter 6

Maternal Employment and Sex Typing in Early Adolescence: Contemporaneous and Longitudinal Relations 155

Nancy L. Galambos, Anne C. Petersen, and
Kathleen Lenerz

I. The Life-Span Developmental Perspective 156
II. The Influences of Maternal Employment on Sex Typing in Adolescents: A Review 158
   A. Direct Links 159
   B. Processes of Influence 163
III. The Early Adolescence Study 167
   A. Plan of the Study 167
   B. Features of the Sample and the Data 168
IV. Analyses 175
   A. Cross-Sectional Results 175
   B. Longitudinal Results 180
V. Summary 182
   References 185

Chapter 7

Maternal Separation Anxiety: Its Role in the Balance of Employment and Motherhood in Mothers of Infants 191

Ellen Hock, Debra DeMeis, and Susan McBride

   I. Introduction 191
  II. The Importance of Maternal Separation Anxiety 193
     A. The Sociocultural Influence 194
     B. The American Situation: Maternal Employment 195
     C. Maternal Employment: Conflicts about Separation 196
     D. The Development of the Maternal Separation Anxiety Scale 197
 III. The Importance of Employment Preference 199
 IV. Maternal Separation Anxiety and Employment Preference 202
     A. Purpose 202
     B. Instruments 202
     C. Procedure 205
     D. Subjects 206
     E. Results 208
     F. Discussion 213
  V. Maternal Separation Anxiety and Choices regarding Nonmaternal Care 216
     A. Purpose 216
     B. Procedures 218
     C. Subjects 218
     D. Results 219
     E. Discussion 223
 VI. Summary 225
     References 227

PART III. MATERNAL EMPLOYMENT: INTEGRATION OF FINDINGS, CORPORATE APPLICATIONS, AND SOCIAL POLICIES

Chapter 8

Balancing Work and Family Lives: Research and Corporate Applications 233

Diane Hughes and Ellen Galinsky

   I. Changing Demographics 233

II. Overview of the Literature 234
   A. Job Conditions 235
   B. Family Conditions 239
III. The Corporate Work and Family Life Study 240
   A. Procedures 241
   B. Sample 242
   C. Measures 242
   D. Methods of Analyses 247
   E. Results 248
   F. Discussion 253
   G. Summary 255
IV. Corporate Work—Family Programs 256
   A. Work Hours Programs 257
   B. Work Location Programs 258
   C. Benefit Programs 259
   D. Family Responsive Services 260
   E. Child Care Support and Services 261
   F. Training Programs 262
V. Conclusions 263
   References 264

Chapter 9

Maternal Employment and Children's Development: An Integration of Longitudinal Findings with Implications for Social Policy 269

Adele Eskeles Gottfried and Allen W. Gottfried

I. Contemporaneous and Long-Term Relationships between Maternal Employment Status and Children's Development 269
II. Relationships between Maternal Employment Status and Family Environment 272
III. Effects of Consistency of Maternal Employment Status on Children's Development 275
IV. Child's Gender and Maternal Employment Status 275
V. Schedules of Employment and Maternal Occupation 276
VI. Maternal Attitudes, Role Satisfaction, and Stress 278
VII. Other Influential Variables 282
VIII. General Conclusions and Future Research 283
IX. Implications for Social Policy 284
   References 286

Index **289**

MATERNAL EMPLOYMENT AND CHILDREN'S DEVELOPMENT

I
INTRODUCTION

1

Maternal Employment and Children's Development

An Introduction to the Issues

Adele Eskeles Gottfried

The majority of mothers are now employed, and projections are for this trend to continue (Hayghe, 1982). Women's roles have changed both within and outside the family. These changes have raised questions regarding the impact of maternal employment on children's development. Investigating this issue has become increasingly important for social scientists, developmental psychologists, professionals working with families, employers, and policymakers. It is apparent that maternal employment has profound implications for our society.

The role of maternal employment in children's development continues to be an unresolved issue, and, up until the publication of the present volume, there has been little systematic research regarding the long-term effects of maternal employment on children. The focus of this book concerns longitudinal investigations of the impact of maternal employment on children's development, and this impact is investigated within the context of family processes.

Early research on maternal employment tended to use a univariate or direct-effect approach, that is, differences between children of employed and nonemployed mothers were examined without considering

---

Adele Eskeles Gottfried • Department of Educational Psychology, California State University, Northridge, Northridge, California 91330.

the complexity of other factors that might mediate the effects of maternal employment. Further, the body of existing data has focused almost entirely upon contemporaneous effects. Recently there has been a call by eminent researchers (e.g., Hoffman, 1984) to study the long-term effects of maternal employment in the context of family processes and employment-related variables (e.g., role satisfaction, attitudes) and to control for extraneous variables that may confound the maternal employment variable (e.g., socioeconomic status).

In part, the conceptualization of this book emerged not only from previous literature on maternal employment as it relates to children's development but from our own longitudinal research program (A. W. Gottfried & A. E. Gottfried, 1984). As our longitudinal research on the relationships between maternal employment and children's development progressed, it became evident that the potential impact of maternal employment could best be understood within the family context and across time.

Additionally, we felt the necessity to compare findings across longitudinal studies of maternal employment and children's development. This is essential to determine the generality and uniqueness of findings across different samples, different ages, and varied developmental domains. Hence, what became apparent to us was the need for a book focusing on longitudinal studies, investigating the relationship between maternal employment and children's development.

In this volume, contemporaneous and long-term relationships between maternal employment and children's development are addressed, particularly in the first five longitudinal studies presented (A. E. Gottfried, A. W. Gottfried, & K. Bathurst; Lerner & Galambos; Owen & Cox; Goldberg & Easterbrooks; and Galambos, Petersen, & Lenerz). By comparing the contemporaneous and long-term relationships between maternal employment and children's development, the magnitudes, patterns, and consistency of these relationships over time, across ages, and across developmental domains can be determined.

Another issue examined in the present volume (in chapters by A. E. Gottfried *et al.*, Goldberg & Easterbrooks; and Galambos, *et al.*) is whether patterns of maternal employment over time have differential effects on children's development. Analyses in these chapters address the question of whether consistency versus inconsistency of employment status (stability versus instability) over time differentially relates to children's development.

The need to study maternal employment within the family context has been identified as an important issue (e.g., Bronfenbrenner & Crouter, 1982). By using longitudinal methodology, the network of family

An Introduction to the Issues

and work variables and their interrelatedness can be studied with regard to their short- as well as long-term impact on children. For example, although it is known that home environment bears significant and long-term relationships to children's development (A. W. Gottfried & A. E. Gottfried, 1984), what has not been clear previous to this volume is whether maternal employment bears a long-term relationship to children's home environment. Moreover, do differences in the home environment that may be attributable to maternal employment relate to children's development over a longitudinal period, and, if so, to which areas of development? In this book, longitudinal studies are presented that examine the impact of maternal employment on children through its relationship to family environmental processes.

Another area that has assumed great importance concerns maternal employment-related and role satisfaction attitudes as intermediary processes that may serve to relate, on the one hand, to maternal employment, and, on the other hand, to children's development (Hoffman, 1984). The longitudinal studies presented here address relationships between maternal employment status, mothers' employment-related and role satisfaction attitudes, and children's development. The longitudinal, and in some instances, causal impact of such attitudes on development are examined. Maternal employment-related attitudes are also examined longitudinally as an important construct for mothers of infants and preschoolers (Hock, DeMeis, & McBride), and the relationship of such attitudes to child care choices is examined as well.

Maternal employment has been recognized as a multidimensional variable (Bronfenbrenner & Crouter, 1982). For example, employed mothers differ with regard to their occupations, the number of weekly hours worked, full- or part-time employment status, and timing and stability of employment. These factors are examined in the present volume with regard to their contemporaneous and long-term impact on children's development.

The purpose of this book is to provide a comprehensive analysis and integration of findings concerning the role of maternal employment in children's development based exclusively on longitudinal research. This book comprises the first compendium of longitudinal research specifically examining the role of maternal employment in children's development. This in itself is a significant contribution. The studies in this volume examine constructs and processes involved in the relationship of mothers' employment to children's development. These research findings provide a foundation for social policies that are advanced in the final chapter.

In the present book, although each investigation covers specific aspects of children's development, collectively the studies span a wide range both in terms of children's ages and developmental domains examined. The book as a whole presents analyses for children ranging in age from early infancy through adolescence and deals with significant developmental areas (e.g., cognitive, affective, social, academic, and behavioral).

The following specific issues are addressed in this book:

1. The role of maternal employment status (including both employment and nonemployment) in children's development is examined from 3 months of age through adolescence (adult children are examined in one study). Developmental trends concerning the effects of maternal employment status on children of different ages are examined.

2. An extensive array of developmental domains is studied. These include infant developmental status, attachment, temperament, cognitive and language development, intellectual performance, social reasoning, social development, sex role development, behavioral adjustment, academic performance, and school motivation and adjustment. The impact of maternal employment status across these different areas of development is investigated.

3. The role of home environment as a mediator in the relationship between maternal employment status and children's development is examined. The cognitive and social-emotional stimulation available in the home, parent–child interactions, family social-emotional climate, and the degree of fathers' involvement are studied as family process variables.

4. The mothers' own attitudes regarding the dual demands of parenthood and employment and the issue of mothers' role satisfaction are examined both in relation to children's development as well as phenomena in and of themselves. Maternal separation anxiety is examined as a developmental parenting construct through the early childhood period. Other sources of maternal stress and anxiety, both in the family and on the job, are studied.

5. Maternal employment status is analyzed in the context of other potentially influential variables. For example, appropriate controls for socioeconomic status, or family size, are included in a number of the studies reported. Both main effects of maternal employment status and effects mediated by other processes are examined in multivariate, and, in some instances, causal analyses.

6. Contemporaneous and long-term effects of maternal employment on children's development are studied. The timing of mothers' employment and the consistency and duration of mothers' employment

An Introduction to the Issues

are examined in relation to children's current and subsequent development.

7. Maternal employment is differentiated into full- and part-time employment, and the number of hours employed per week is also investigated. The relationship of maternal occupational status to children's development is investigated.

8. The impact of maternal employment status is examined in relation to children's genders.

9. Conditions in the workplace are presented as issues affecting employed parents.

10. The implications of this research for business and social policy are advanced.

The studies in this book have all investigated the role of maternal employment in a wide range of middle-class families. The high degree of maternal employment in these middle-class families is itself a phenomenon because these mothers might have fewer "survival" reasons for employment compared to single mothers or mothers in low-income families. It may also be that the accessibility and relative stability of these families permitted the collection of longitudinal data.

This book is organized into two main sections. The first main section presents the longitudinal studies (A. E. Gottfried et al.; Lerner & Galambos; Owen & Cox; Goldberg & Easterbrooks; Galambos et al.; and Hock et al.) These were selected for inclusion because all researchers conceptualized maternal employment as a complex variable and examined its impact through its relation to mediating attitudinal and/or family processes. In addition, all studies used a multivariate approach.

The second main section concerns the role of maternal employment in the larger context of business and society (Hughes & Galinsky; A. E. Gottfried & A. W. Gottfried). In the Hughes and Galinsky chapter, research is presented concerning work and family factors influencing parents' ability to balance the demands of these dual responsibilities. The authors also advance specific family responsive programs and policies used in corporations. The final chapter, by A. E. Gottfried and A. W. Gottfried, presents an integration of results across studies, and an assessment of the generalizability of these findings, to determine the impact of maternal employment on children's development. Findings unique to particular studies are highlighted as well. Social policy implications of the research are advanced in this chapter.

Studying the role of maternal employment in children's development is important for theoretical and applied reasons. Theoretically, investigating the impact of maternal employment on children's development within the family context allows for the investigation of fundamental questions regarding how family roles influence the child's environment and development. Potential applications that may be based upon the results of this research are far-reaching. Research results must be disseminated to the public so that families can make decisions about maternal employment based on scientific knowledge. Moreover, programs and policies need to be developed and implemented, taking into account scientific findings, to enhance the quality of life for all children and families.

REFERENCES

Bronfenbrenner, U., & Crouter, A. C. (1982). Work and family through time and space. In S. B. Kamerman & C. D. Hayes (Eds.), *Families that work: Children in a changing world* (pp. 39–83). Washington, DC: National Academy Press.

Gottfried, A. W., & Gottfried, A. E. (1984). Home environment and cognitive development in young children of middle-socioeconomic-status families. In A. W. Gottfried (Ed.), *Home environment and early cognitive development: Longitudinal research* (pp. 57–115). New York: Academic Press.

Hayghe, H. (1982). Dual-earner families: Their economic and demographic characteristics. In J. Aldous (Ed.), *Two paychecks: Life in dual-earner families* (pp. 27–40). Beverly Hills, CA: Sage Publications.

Hoffman, L. W. (1984). Maternal employment and the young child. In M. Perlmutter (Ed.), *Parent-child interaction and parent-child relations in child development: The Minnesota Symposia on Child Psychology* (Vol. 17, pp. 101–127). Hillsdale, NJ: Lawrence Erlbaum.

# II
LONGITUDINAL STUDIES

The longitudinal studies presented in this part provide the data concerning contemporaneous and long-term effects of maternal employment on children's development. The first two chapters span the widest age ranges. Children in the A. E. Gottfried, A. W. Gottfried, and Bathurst chapter are studied from ages 1 to 7 years. Lerner and Galambos present data from the New York Longitudinal Study in which children were followed from early childhood through adulthood. Each of the following chapters deals with a more specific developmental period. The Owen and Cox study concerns maternal employment during infants' first year of life. Goldberg and Easterbrooks concentrate on maternal employment during children's toddler and kindergarten years. Galambos, Petersen, and Lenerz present research on sixth- through eighth-grade adolescents. The research by Hock, DeMeis, and McBride focuses on mothers' own anxieties regarding separation from their infants and the relation of maternal separation anxiety to child care choices during the children's first 3.5 years.

Together, these studies examine a wide range of child developmental outcomes across the ages studied. Home environment and family processes as well as maternal attitudes are examined as variables that mediate between maternal employment status, on the one hand, and child developmental outcomes, on the other. Conclusions based on an integration of findings across chapters are presented in Part III.

2

Maternal Employment, Family Environment, and Children's Development
Infancy through the School Years

Adele Eskeles Gottfried, Allen W. Gottfried, and Kay Bathurst

I. INTRODUCTION AND CONCEPTUALIZATION

Family patterns are undergoing rapid change in our society, in part a consequence of maternal employment. The proportion of employed mothers with children under 18 has shown a steady increase from 1940 to the present (Hoffman, 1984b), and projections are for this trend to continue (Hayghe, 1982). Two-earner families are now prevalent due to the increase of mothers' employment (Hayghe, 1982). As a result of employment of both husbands and wives, family roles of men and women are changing as well (Hoffman, 1984b; Lamb & Sagi, 1983; Pleck, 1985). It is therefore reasonable to expect that home environments in dual- and single-earner families differ. The goal of this research is to

---

Adele Eskeles Gottfried • Department of Educational Psychology, California State University, Northridge, Northridge, California 91330.   Allen W. Gottfried • Department of Psychology, California State University, Fullerton, Fullerton, California 92634.   Kay Bathurst • Department of Psychology, University of California, Los Angeles, Los Angeles, California 90024.

determine how maternal employment relates to home environment and children's development in a longitudinal study from infancy through the early school years.

The effect of maternal employment on children's development continues to be an area of great significance. The literature has produced discrepant results, with reports of detrimental, favorable, and nonsignificant effects of maternal employment on children's development (Hoffman, 1984a,b, 1985). Numerous differences between studies in methodology, samples employed, measures used, and inclusion of adequate controls further complicate the issue. At present, there is no theoretical or empirical explanation for divergent findings. It is our view that discrepant findings regarding the effects of maternal employment on children's development can be explained by differences in children's home environments. Our view emerges both from the literature on maternal employment and results of our prior research (A. W. Gottfried & A. E. Gottfried, 1984).

The prior body of literature on the effects of maternal employment on children's development points to several conclusions: (1) Family processes that mediate the influence of maternal employment must be studied (Bronfenbrenner & Crouter, 1982); (2) fathers' roles in families must be studied in relationship to maternal employment (Bronfenbrenner, 1986; Hoffman, 1984a); (3) research must take a longitudinal and multivariate focus to study the long-term impact of maternal employment and take account of timing and stability of employment (Bronfenbrenner, 1986; Heyns, 1982; Hoffman, 1984a); (4) studies of simple comparisons between employed and nonemployed mothers are inadequate because potential confounding factors (e.g., SES, marital status) remain uncontrolled (Hoffman, 1984a); and (5) maternal employment variables should also include mothers' occupational status, hours of employment, employment attitudes, and stress (Bronfenbrenner & Crouter, 1982; Hoffman, 1984a). The present research reports such a study.

In this research we examine family environmental processes and children's development as related to maternal employment. We take the position that if maternal employment status has any effect on children's development, it is due to the proximal home environment rather than due to employment status *per se*. Proximal home environment comprises the cognitive, social-emotional, and physical stimulation available to children in the home, as well as family interpersonal relationships. Our perspective is guided by the following rationale. First, in our prior work on home environment and young children's cognitive development (A. W. Gottfried & A. E. Gottfried, 1984), we distinguished between distal variables of home environment (e.g., SES) that provide little by way of explaining children's development and proximal variables of home environment that provide detailed measurement of actual environmental stimuli and processes available to children. We conceptualize maternal employment similarly. Maternal employment status itself is a distal variable. It categorizes mothers on the basis of employment or nonemployment. Such categorization gives no information regarding the quality of home environment provided to children. Additionally, maternal occupation, attitudes, and number of hours employed may vary within the employed group of mothers, which may moderate the nature of the proximal home environment. Hence, to understand the effects of maternal employment on children, one must examine the proximal home environment and its relationship to both maternal employment and children's development. A reported positive or negative effect of maternal employment on children's development may result from differences in the proximal home environment.

Second, our work (A. W. Gottfried & A. E. Gottfried, 1984; A. E. Gottfried, A. W. Gottfried, & Guerin, 1986) has shown that children's cognitive, academic, and social developments from infancy through the school years are positively related to children's proximal home environment. There is a substantial body of research also supporting this from infancy through adolescence (A. W. Gottfried, 1984; Marjoribanks, 1979). However, the prior maternal employment research has failed to examine the relationship between maternal employment and home environment over a long-term period. Evidence indicates that home environment is sensitive to family structural variables (Cotterell, 1986; A. W. Gottfried & A. E. Gottfried, 1984). Thus the relationship of maternal employment to home environment requires extensive examination.

This research is unique in that it presents an extensive, longitudinal, multivariate analysis of maternal employment as related to the proximal home environment. Moreover, both maternal employment and home environment are examined in relation to children's development from 1 to 7 years of age over a wide array of developmental domains. Also examined is the relationship of maternal employment to fathers' family involvement. Fathers' involvement is conceptualized as an aspect of the proximal home environment. Mothers' attitudes toward employment, weekly hours of employment, occupational status, and stress are included to determine how these variables relate to both children's development and proximal environment.

Because this is a longitudinal study, we examine both the immediate and long-term impact of maternal employment on children's development and home environment. Studying the impact of maternal employment on children's development contemporaneously and longitudinally is, in itself, a significant issue (Hoffman, 1984b). Further, having collected maternal employment data from ages 1 through 7, the consistency and inconsistency of employment patterns as well as the timing of employment will be examined. The developmental outcomes include infant developmental status, children's cognitive development, social development, behavioral adjustment or problems, and academic achievement and motivation. In addition, we have continuously collected data on SES, marital status, and number of children in the family. These variables, as well as child's gender, are controlled throughout the study so that it can be determined if maternal employment has any effects independent of these variables.

The major issues addressed in this research are the following:

1. Is maternal employment status independently related to proximal home environment and children's development contemporaneously from infancy through the early school years?
2. Is there a long-term effect of maternal employment on children's development and home environment from infancy through the early school years?
3. Is consistency versus inconsistency of maternal employment status related to home environment and children's development?
4. Do mothers' occupations, hours of employment, or employment attitudes relate to children's development and home environment?

II. METHOD

A. Subjects

In the fall of 1979, a longitudinal investigation of children's development was initiated. One hundred and thirty 1-year-olds and their families were selected from birth notifications of hospitals surrounding California State University, Fullerton. The only selection criteria were that infants had no neurological or visual abnormalities (A. W. Gottfried & Gilman, 1983). All infants were full-term and of normal birth weight. Additionally, all families spoke English.

Of the 130 infants recruited at 1 year, 68 were male, 62 were female, 117 were white, and 13 were from other racial groups. The sample represented a wide range of middle-class families as measured by the Hollingshead Four Factor Index of Social Status (Hollingshead, 1975). Other major contemporary socioeconomic indicators corroborated this appraisal. However, the Hollingshead was used in our analyses because it incorporates occupation of employed mothers into its computation of family social status (A. W. Gottfried, 1985). Throughout the study, virtually all fathers were employed. Employment of mothers showed a progressive increase. At the outset of the investigation, 36.2% were employed, and when the children reached 7 years of age, 64.2% of the mothers were employed. For both mothers and fathers, there was a full range of occupational ratings (Hollingshead scale) ranging from semiskilled workers to professionals. Virtually all parents graduated from high school with the majority having some college or more. There was a negligible change in their educational achievement by the time the children were age 7. On the average, parents were in their late 20s when the study children were born. Fifty-five percent of the children were firstborns and 45% were second- through fifthborns. The number of children in the homes averaged around two. Throughout the study thus far, 78% of the families remained intact (i.e., not separated or divorced). At any specific assessment period, 89 to 94.1% of the parents were married. Characteristics of the sample are presented in Table 2. Further demographic information may be found in A. W. Gottfried and A. E. Gottfried (1984).

B. Procedure

Beginning at age 1 year, the children were tested every 6 months until they reached 3.5 years of age. They were tested again at 5, 6, and 7 years of age. Hence, there were a total of nine laboratory evaluations. Throughout the course of investigation, the return rate of the study population has been high with 99% (128), 95% (123), 94% (122), 92% (119), 91% (118), 85% (111), 81% (105), and 82% (106) returning at 1.5, 2, 2.5, 3, 3.5, 5, 6, and 7 years, respectively. Discontinuation of families in the project was primarily the result of relocation. At each laboratory assessment, which consumed a single 1.5-hour session, a battery of psychological tests was administered to the child. Because the focus of this investigation was on individual differences, all tests were administered to all children in exactly the same sequence. The amount of missing data was minimal because every attempt was made to completely test all children at all ages (see Bathurst & A. W. Gottfried, 1987).

Direct home assessments have been conducted at 2 ages thus far. At 15 months and 2 years later at 39 months, the homes of the children were visited. Of the 130 children originally in the sample, 99% (129) and 89% (116) had their homes visited at these two ages, respectively. Of the 119 children returning for the 3-year laboratory assessment, 97%

had their homes visited at 39 months. Each home assessment typically involved 1 hour and was conducted with the mother and study child present.

To collect contemporaneous information on family demographics and monitor the quality of family relationships and changes in family structure, mothers completed a series of questionnaires and standardized inventories at the laboratory assessments. Questionnaires regarding their work status and attitudes were also filled out. Additionally, mothers as well as the children's teachers completed standardized scales pertaining to the children's behavioral functioning.

C. Measures

Throughout the course of this longitudinal investigation, numerous tasks evaluating a variety of aspects of development were conducted. However, only the major measures bearing on the issues put forth in this research are presented. Multiple measures were used to assess the developmental and environmental domains. When available, contemporary standardized tests were selected to be included in the psychological test battery.

D. Cognitive Functioning

At each laboratory evaluation, children's intellectual performance was assessed. The children were administered the Mental Scale of the Bayley Scales of Infant Development (Bayley, 1969) at 1, 1.5, and 2 years of age, McCarthy Scales of Children's Abilities (McCarthy, 1972) at 2.5, 3, and 3.5 years, Kaufman Assessment Battery for Children (KABC) (Kaufman & Kaufman, 1983) at 5 years, and Wechsler Intelligence Scale for Children-Revised (WISC-R) (Wechsler, 1974) at 6 and 7 years. At the 39-month home assessment, the children were given the Test of Early Language Development (TELD) (Hresko, Reid, & Hammill, 1981).

E. Academic Achievement

Beginning at age 5 years, the children were evaluated on academic skills. At 5 years, the Achievement Scale of the KABC was administered. Performance on this scale involved children's knowledge in the areas of naming well-known faces and places, arithmetic, riddles, and reading/decoding. The four subtests result in a summary standard score. The Wide Range Achievement Test-Revised (WRAT-R) (Jastak & Jastak, 1984) was given at 6 years. Academic performance in the areas of reading, arithmetic, and spelling are appraised. The Woodcock-Johnson Psycho-Educational Battery was employed at 7 years. The battery evaluates children's achievement in reading, mathematics, written language, and academic knowledge (science, social studies, and the humanities). At this age, teacher grade ratings (reading, math, and spelling) were used from the teacher version of the Child Behavior Checklist (Achenbach & Edelbrock, 1986). Also at age 7 years, the children were administered a downward extension of the Children's Academic Intrinsic Motivation Inventory (CAIMI) (A. E. Gottfried, 1985, 1986). The downward extension of this reliable and valid inventory assesses children's enjoyment of learning in the subject areas of reading and math.

F. Temperament and Social Competence

A set of temperament inventories was completed by mothers. The Infant Characteristics Inventory (Bates, Freeland, & Lounsbury, 1979) was filled out at 1.5 years, Toddler Temperament Scale (Fullard, McDevitt, & Carey, 1978) at 2 years, and Behavior Styles Questionnaire (McDevitt & Carey, 1975) at 3, 3.5, and 5 years of age. At 3.5 years, children were given the Preschool Interpersonal Problem Solving Test (PIPS) (Shure & Spivach, 1974). This test assesses children's ability to generate alternative social solutions to interpersonal conflict situations involving a mother and child or between children. A summary score indicates the total number of different solutions generated across both conflict situations. The Kohn Social Competence Scale-Revised (Kohn, Parnes, & Rosman, 1979) was completed by teachers when the children were 5 and 6 years old. This inventory evaluates children's classroom social competence in the areas of interest-participation and cooperation-compliance. Also at age 6 years, the Vineland Adaptive Behavior Scales (Sparrow, Balla, & Cicchetti, 1984) were administered to mothers via a semistructured interview. These scales measure the personal and social sufficiency of children in the areas of communication, daily living skills, and socialization. There is also a summary score of these three domains as well as an adaptive behavior composite score.

G. Behavioral Adjustment

A series of behavior problem checklists were administered beginning in the preschool period to assess children's behavioral adjustment and problems. During the 39-month home visit, the Eyberg Child Behavior Inventory (Robinson, Eyberg, & Ross, 1980) was filled out by mothers. Two scores are derived: an intensity score (frequency of problems) and a problem score (number of problems for mother). At the 3.5-year assessment, mothers completed the Preschool Behavior Questionnaire (Behar & Stringfield, 1974). A single score, designating the total number of problems, was used. The parent version of the Child Behavior Checklist (Achenbach & Edelbrock, 1983) was administered at 4, 5, 6, and 7 years. At the latter three ages, mothers filled out the checklist during the laboratory assessment. At age 4 years, the information was collected via mail. At ages 6 and 7 years, teachers completed the teacher version of the Child Behavior Checklists (Achenbach & Edelbrock, 1986). Analyses on the parent and teacher Child Behavior Checklists included the externalizing and internalizing broad-band syndrome scores as well as the total behavior problem score.

H. Home and Family Environment

Because the study of environment-development relationships has been a major focus of our investigation, (A. W. Gottfried, 1984; A. W. Gottfried & A. E. Gottfried, 1984, 1986; A. E. Gottfried, A. W. Gottfried, & Guerin, 1986), a variety of ongoing environmental assessments were conducted. At the 15- and 39-month home visits, the infant and preschool versions of the HOME (Home Observation for Measurement of the Environment) were administered (Caldwell & Bradley, 1984). This inventory was designed to measure the social-emotional and cognitive supports made available to young children. The infant version of the HOME contains 45 items divided into six subscales and has a total score based on all items. The six subscales are I. Emotional and Verbal Responsivity of Mother; II. Avoidance of Restrictions and Punishment; III. Organization of the Physical and Temporal Environment; IV. Provision of Appropriate Play Materials; V. Maternal Involvement with the Child; and VI. Opportunities for Variety in Daily Stimulation. The preschool version of the HOME contains 55 items forming eight subscales and a total score. The eight subscores are I. Stimulation through Toys, Games, and Reading Materials; II. Language Stimulation; III. Physical Environment: Safe, Clean, and Conducive to Development; IV. Pride, Affection, and Warmth; V. Stimulation of Academic Behavior; VI. Modeling and Encouragement of Social Maturity; VII. Variety of Stimulation; and VIII. Physical Punishment. During the 15-month home visit, the physical section of the Purdue Home Stimulation Inventory (PHSI) (Wachs, 1976) was administered. The PHSI contains 30 items (27 used in our study) focusing on specific physical characteristics of the environment.

At the 39-month home visit and 5-year laboratory assessment, mothers filled out the Variety of Experience Checklist (VEC) (see A. W. Gottfried & A. E. Gottfried, 1984). Mothers checked off the type of experiences their children had outside of the home in the past year on three categories: travel—types of vehicle; entertainment; and visits to geographic areas. The score on this checklist was the total number of different experiences the child had received.

To monitor the quality of family relationships, mothers completed the Family Environment Scale (FES) (Moos & Moos, 1981) at 3, 5, and 7 years. This scale evaluates the social climate of the family along 10 dimensions: cohesion, intellectual-cultural, active-recreational, expressiveness, conflict, moral-religious, control, organization, independence, and achievement orientation. Our factor analysis (using a varimax rotation) of this scale (Bathurst, A. W. Gottfried, & Nordquist, 1987) yielded the same 2-factor solution at each age. The first factor, labeled Positive Family Involvement, comprised the first five dimensions. The second factor, named Family Regulation, included the next three dimensions. The last two dimensions did not load on these factors and were not used.

At the 5- and 7-year follow-up, mothers filled out the Home Environment Survey (HES) (developed by the authors). Factor analyses of the surveys (using varimax rotation) resulted in three factors at each age. At age 5 years, 12 items formed three factors: Mother Provides Educational Stimulation (3 items), Educational Attitudes (4 items), and Provision of Learning Materials (5 items). Examples of items are taking child to library and time spent reading to child for the first factor; mothers' educational expectations for child (high school through professional), has own real musical instrument, and amount of TV viewing, for the second factor; and provision of activity books and availability of electronic teaching aids and personal computer in home for the third factor. At age 7 years, 12 items formed three factors: Mother Provides Educational Stimulation (5 items), Maternal Involvement (3 items), and Educational Attitudes (4 items). Examples of items are taking child to library, time spent reading to child, time spent daily working on academic skills with child, and child has subscription to a magazine or book club for the first factor; hours spent taking care and doing things with child (average schoolday) and frequency of discussions of school activities in a given week for the second factor; and mothers' educational expectation for child, child receives private lessons, and amount of TV watching for the third factor.

To gather information on fathers' participation in raising the children, mothers completed the Father Involvement Checklist (developed by the authors) when the children were ages 6 and 7 years. Mothers filled out the checklist so as to obtain an independent appraisal of the fathers' roles in children's development. The checklist comprises 29 items pertaining to caretaking, nurturing, and intellectually stimulating activities that the father is involved in on a regular weekly basis. The score on this checklist is the total number of activities the father is involved in with the child. The 1-year cross-time consistency of mothers' reports on this checklist was substantial with a correlation of .67, $p = .001$.

Interobserver reliabilities were conducted on the developmental tests and home environment inventories at every assessment. The use of a pilot longitudinal sample helped to establish a high degree of interobserver agreement just prior to each assessment period. Furthermore, continuous interobserver reliabilities were conducted on the actual study sample. In the study sample, all reliabilities exceeded .92 for the developmental tests and 91% agreement for the HOME and PHSI.

I. Maternal Employment and Attitudes

At each laboratory assessment, a maternal employment survey was completed by mothers. Data on employment status (full-time, part-time, or not employed) and maternal occupation were collected. Maternal occupation was scored according to the occupational scale of the Hollingshead Four-Factor Index of Social Status (Hollingshead, 1975).

At the 5- and 7-year assessments, maternal attitudes were assessed as well as hours per week worked. At age 5, employed mothers were asked to answer items using a 5-point rating scale regarding their satisfaction with their employment, reasons for employment (income, personal satisfaction), perception of the influence of their employment on their children's development, stress with their child, and ability to coordinate family and work responsibilities. A 12-item scale was developed, yielding substantial internal consistency reliability (coefficient alpha = .80). Higher scores on this scale indicate more favorable attitudes toward employment, greater personal satisfaction, more favorable view of the effect of employment on their children's development, more job flexibility, better ability to coordinate work and family responsibilities, and less stress and less emphasis on income as a reason for employment.

At the 7-year assessment, the attitudinal measures for employed mothers were expanded to tap psychological spillover from job to family and related stress. In addition to developing our own items, we included nine items used by Galinsky in her work on corporate employment (Galinsky, 1985). Because the items included were designed to tap different areas, a factor analysis with varimax rotation was conducted yielding three factors: Maternal Availability and Confidence, Perceptions of Dual Responsibilities, and Satisfaction with Employment. The first factor included six items dealing with mothers' ability to attend school-related events and take child to appointments, worry about child while at work, and job flexibility. Higher factor scores indicate higher maternal availability, job flexibility, and less worry. The second factor consisted of six items dealing with being tired, stressed, and irritable with child because of events at work and ability to coordinate dual responsiblities. Higher scores indicate more favorable perceptions, (i.e., less stress and irritability) and more ability to handle dual responsibilities. The third factor included three items dealing with satisfaction with employment. Higher scores indicate higher satisfaction.

In addition, at the 7-year assessment, all mothers answered role satisfaction items: I am satisfied with my role as a parent; I am not currently employed, but I would like to be; I am currently employed, but I would prefer not to work. All items were responded to on a 5-point scale. Across all attitude items used at ages 5 and 7, scores were appropriately reversed where necessary so that higher scores indicate more favorable perceptions.

A table of sample means and standard deviations for the major measures are presented in Table 1.

III. RESULTS

Multivariate data analyses were the predominant techniques employed. These included multivariate analyses of variance (MANOVA) and multiple regressions. Use of these analyses permitted us to control for variables that may have influenced the relationship between maternal employment and pertinent outcomes and to control for chance findings when multiple dependent variables were used. Other analyses were also used to answer specific questions. Initial analyses were conducted in which Maternal Employment Status was divided into three categories: not employed, employed part-time, and employed full-time. These analyses were compared with identical analyses in which the part-time and full-time employed categories were combined. Results of these analyses were the same, regardless of considering maternal employment as divided into part- and full-time or combining across these categories. Hence, part- and full-time employment statuses were combined, and, for all analyses reported here, maternal employment status consists of nonemployed and employed mothers (coded as 1 = nonemployed and 2 = employed). Because certain points in time were used for some anal-

Table 1. Means and Standard Deviations on Major Outcome Variables[a]

Variable	Means (standard deviations)
1 year Bayley	113.3 (10.3)
1.5 years Bayley	113.4 (16.6)
1.5 years Temperament Difficulty Score	3.2 (0.7)
2 years Bayley	115.0 (20.3)
2 years Temperament Difficulty Score	2.1 (1.0)
2.5 years McCarthy General Cognitive Index	112.2 (13.9)
3 years McCarthy General Cognitive Index	108.3 (13.0)
3 years Temperament Difficulty Score	2.0 (0.9)
39 months TELD	9.7 (5.2)
39 months Eyberg Intensity	112.6 (21.0)
39 months Eyberg Problem	5.5 (4.8)
3.5 years McCarthy General Cognitive Index	112.4 (10.7)
3.5 years Temperament Difficulty Score	2.0 (1.0)
3.5 years PIPS	2.7 (1.9)
3.5 years Preschool Behavior Questionnaire	15.8 (5.8)
5 years KABC Mental Processing	113.3 (12.1)
5 years KABC Achievement	111.5 (11.5)
5 years Kohn Interest	152.4 (19.2)
5 years Kohn Cooperation	84.8 (14.6)
5 years Temperament Difficulty Score	2.0 (1.0)
6 years WISC Full Scale	114.5 (12.6)
6 years WRAT Reading	100.7 (16.6)
6 years WRAT Spelling	98.4 (14.9)
6 years WRAT Arithmetic	100.4 (15.6)
6 years Kohn Interest	154.7 (17.6)
6 years Kohn Cooperation	87.6 (12.9)
6 years Vineland Summary	291.7 (33.6)
6 years Vineland Adaptive Composite	95.7 (13.5)
7 years WISC Full Scale	116.5 (13.3)
7 years Woodcock-Johnson Reading	68.1 (24.7)
7 years Woodcock-Johnson Math	72.4 (23.6)
7 years Woodcock-Johnson Written Language	71.1 (24.5)
7 years Woodcock-Johnson Knowledge	65.6 (25.4)
7 years Teachers' Ratings of Achievement-Reading	3.6 (1.0)
7 years Teachers' Ratings of Achievement-Math	3.6 (0.8)
7 years Teachers' Ratings of Achievement-Spelling	3.6 (0.9)
7 years CAIMI Reading	26.7 (4.0)
7 years CAIMI Math	25.9 (4.0)
4 years Achenbach—Parent total	
Boys	30.2 (17.2)
Girls	28.5 (15.8)
5 years Achenbach—Parent total	
Boys	23.9 (14.0)
Girls	22.9 (14.6)
6 years Achenbach—Parent total	
Boys	24.7 (15.7)
Girls	21.5 (16.6)

Table 1. *(Continued)*

Variable	Means (standard deviations)
6 years Achenbach—Teacher total	
Boys	18.8 (17.6)
Girls	13.7 (14.0)
7 years Achenbach—Parent total	
Boys	23.6 (16.8)
Girls	23.0 (18.1)
7 years Achenbach—Teacher total	
Boys	16.3 (20.2)
Girls	11.7 (11.8)
15 months HOME Total Score	36.4 (3.7)
39 months HOME Total Score	42.8 (5.9)
39 months VEC	12.7 (3.8)
5 years VEC	11.0 (3.5)
6 years Father Involvement Checklist	15.0 (6.3)
7 years Father Involvement Checklist	15.5 (6.2)

[a] FES and HES factor scores each have a mean of 0.0 and a standard deviation of 0.9.

yses (e.g., for prospective and consistency analyses), some variables had to be analyzed at the closest time frame relative to the actual point at which they were collected.

A. Descriptive Analyses

Families of employed and nonemployed mothers were compared on demographic factors including socioeconomic status (SES), fathers' occupation, number of children, mothers' and fathers' educational level, marital status, and sex of the child. Fathers' occupation was compared, as well as SES, because the inclusion of mothers' occupation was expected to lower the family SES for the employed mother group because mothers' occupations tend to be of lower status than fathers'. Comparisons using *t*-tests are presented in Table 2. Across all ages, no significant differences in fathers' occupation were obtained. However, as expected, SES was significantly different but predominantly in the infancy and preschool years. Where significant, families in which the mother was employed had lower SES than families in which the mother was not employed. Mothers tended to take jobs at lower occupational levels than their husbands, resulting in lower SES compared to the SES of families in which mothers do not work. Data in Table 2 indicate that mothers' occupational level increased as the children became older.

Table 2. Comparison of Demographic Variables by Maternal Employment Status[a]

Age of child and demographic factors	Maternal employment status Nonemployed	Employed	t	df
1 year				
SES	47.2 (12.0)	43.0 (10.6)	2.01*	124
Fathers' occupation	6.2 (2.0)	6.0 (2.1)	.58	123
Mothers' occupation		4.9 (1.9)		
Number of children	1.8 (.9)	1.5 (.8)	1.66	128
Mothers' education	14.2 (2.1)	14.0 (2.1)	.41	128
Fathers' education	15.1 (2.4)	14.4 (2.4)	1.44	128
Mothers' age	29.1 (3.9)	27.8 (4.6)	1.68	127
Fathers' age	31.8 (5.2)	30.8 (5.0)	1.02	127
1.5 years				
SES	46.4 (12.6)	44.0 (9.4)	1.13	125
Fathers' occupation	6.1 (2.1)	6.0 (2.2)	.23	124
Mothers' occupation		5.1 (1.6)		
2 years				
SES	47.5 (13.2)	42.8 (10.6)	2.19*	121
Fathers' occupation	6.3 (2.3)	5.6 (2.1)	1.69	119
Mothers' occupation		5.3 (1.6)		
2.5 years				
SES	47.9 (13.6)	43.0 (9.3)	2.68**	115
Fathers' occupation	6.6 (2.3)	6.0 (1.8)	1.49	115
Mothers' occupation		4.9 (1.7)		
3 years				
SES	49.6 (13.6)	43.9 (9.3)	2.68**	114
Fathers' occupation	6.6 (2.3)	6.0 (1.8)	1.49	114
Mothers' occupation		5.3 (1.7)		
Number of children	2.2 (.9)	1.8 (1.0)	2.03*	117
Mothers' education	14.5 (2.5)	14.1 (2.4)	1.04	117
Fathers' education	15.8 (2.5)	14.6 (2.4)	2.56**	116
3.5 years				
SES	49.7 (11.6)	45.7 (9.2)	2.04*	112
Fathers' occupation	6.5 (2.0)	6.3 (1.9)	.38	113
Mothers' occupation		5.6 (1.6)		
5 years				
SES	49.4 (12.8)	46.7 (8.5)	1.36	108
Fathers' occupation	6.7 (1.8)	6.4 (1.8)	.80	105
Mothers' occupation		5.7 (1.6)		
Number of children	2.7 (1.0)	2.0 (.9)	3.74**	107
Mothers' education	14.1 (1.9)	14.7 (1.9)	−1.60	108
Fathers' education	15.5 (2.5)	15.4 (4.0)	.20	105
6 years				
SES	49.7 (11.4)	47.4 (8.2)	1.20	99
Fathers' occupation	6.7 (1.4)	6.7 (1.8)	.12	97
Mothers' occupation		5.5 (1.5)		
Number of children	2.6 (1.1)	2.2 (1.0)	2.08*	100
Mothers' education	13.8 (1.8)	14.6 (2.0)	−2.16*	100
Fathers' education	15.4 (2.8)	15.0 (2.1)	.72	99

Table 2. (*Continued*)

Age of child and demographic factors	Maternal employment status		t	df
	Nonemployed	Employed		
7 years				
SES	51.6 (11.4)	47.8 (8.3)	1.96[b]	104
Fathers' occupation	6.9 (1.7)	6.6 (1.7)	.91	101
Mothers' occupation		6.0 (1.4)		
Number of children	2.6 (1.2)	2.2 (.9)	2.43*	107
Mothers' education	14.3 (1.9)	14.6 (1.9)	−.45	107
Fathers' education	15.7 (2.7)	14.7 (2.1)	1.92	106

[a] Standard deviations are presented in parentheses. All *t*-tests are two-tailed.
[b] Borderline significance, $p = .053$.
* $p \leq .05$.   ** $p \leq .01$.

Regarding mothers' educational level, there were no significant differences between employed and nonemployed mothers, except at age 6. Regarding fathers' education, there were also no significant differences except at 3 years.

Chi-squares with Yates correction were conducted to examine the association between marital status (married vs. not married) and maternal employment status. There was no significant association between these variables at any age. Chi-squares were also conducted between maternal employment status and child's sex. Significant χ^2's were obtained at 30 months, $\chi^2 (1) = 5.62$, $p = .02$; 36 months $\chi^2 (1) = 5.50$, $p = .02$, and 42 months $\chi^2 (1) = 5.10$, $p = .02$. At these ages, mothers of boys were less likely to be employed, and mothers of girls were more likely to be employed. Mothers of boys appeared to be more invested in the parental role than mothers of girls.

B. Relationships between Maternal Employment, Children's Development, and Home Environment: Contemporaneous Analyses

The first central question addressed was whether maternal employment relates to both children's development and home environment contemporaneously. Further, although we were interested in the main effects of maternal employment on children's development and home environment, we were also interested in whether maternal employment related to developmental outcomes and environment above and beyond other potentially influential variables. Hence, two types of analyses were employed. First, we examined the main effects of maternal employment by using MANOVAs. On all dependent measures, a Maternal Employment Status × Sex MANOVA was conducted. Multiple dependent variables were grouped according to the category to which they belonged and entered into the MANOVA. For variables that did not have multiple dependent measures, univariate ANOVA was conducted. Significant multivariate effects, tested with Wilks Lambda, were followed up with univariate ANOVA. MANOVA was conducted on the following sets of developmental variables: McCarthy scales (2.5, 3, and 3.5 years), Temperament scales (1.5, 2, 3, 3.5, and 5 years), Eyberg scales (3 years), Kohn scales (5 and 6 years), Vineland scales (6 years), WRAT scales (6 years), WISC Verbal and Performance scales (6 and 7 years), Woodcock-Johnson scales (7 years), CAIMI Reading and Math scales (7 years), and teacher ratings of academic achievement (7 years). ANOVA was conducted on Bayley (1, 1.5, and 2 years), McCarthy General Cognitive Index (2.5, 3, and 3.5 years), overall Difficulty Score of Temperament (1.5, 2, 2.5, 3, 3.5, and 5 years), TELD (3.5 years), PIPS (3.5 years), Preschool Behavior Questionnaire (3.5 years), KABC Mental Processing Score, and KABC Achievement Score (5 years), Summary Scores of the Vineland (6 years), Full Scale IQ of the WISC (6 and 7 years), and total problem score of the Achenbach Child Behavior Checklist, parent report (4, 5, 6, and 7 years) and teacher report (6 and 7 years). For ease of presentation, all significant F's presented are the univariates. Because of sex differences in the Internal and External categories on the Child Behavior Checklist, we analyzed these variables for the sexes separately using Hotelling T^2 with Maternal Employment as the grouping factor.

Across all child development outcomes at all ages, maternal employment proved to be nonsignificant as a main effect, and there were no reliable significant interactions between Maternal Employment and Sex across any of the variables. There were few significant Sex effects across the variables studied. These are presented in the multiple regressions table (Table 3).

MANOVAs and ANOVAs were also conducted on the measures of home environment. MANOVA was computed on the subscales of the HOME (15 and 39 months), items of the Purdue Home Stimulation Inventory (15 months), factors of the FES (3, 5, and 7 years), factors of the Home Stimulation Survey (5 and 7 years). ANOVA was conducted on the total HOME score, Variety of Experience Checklist score (39 months and 5 years), and the Father Involvement Checklist score (6 and 7 years). Significant main effects for Maternal Employment were obtained on the following variables: Purdue Home Stimulation Inventory, the Home Environment Survey at age 5, the Variety of Experience Checklist at age 5, and the Father Involvement Checklist at age 6. There were no reliable significant interactions between Maternal Employment Status and Sex or significant main effects for sex.

The findings for the Purdue showed that, in the homes of employed mothers, there were significantly more adults in the home, $F(1,124) = 4.47$, $p = .04$; more adults caring for the child $F(1,124) = 14.64$, $p < .001$; more attempts at training toileting and dressing skills $F(1,124) = 10.19$ and 8.44, $p < .01$, respectively; nonemployed mothers were more likely to visit neighbors $F(1,124) = 7.58$, $p < .01$; and children of nonemployed mothers were more likely to have a regular naptime $F(1,124) = 5.01$, $p = .03$. At the 5-year assessment, employed mothers scored higher on the Educational Attitudes factor of the Home Environment Survey $F(1,86) = 6.88$, $p = .01$, indicating higher educational aspirations for the child and less TV viewing. Children of employed mothers were exposed to a greater diversity of experience on the Variety of Experience Checklist, $F(1,106) = 4.14$, $p = .04$. On the Father Involvement Checklist at age 6, fathers were significantly more involved when mother was employed, $F(1,87) = 4.33$, $p = .04$. There were no significant differences in the home environments of employed and nonemployed mothers as measured by the HOME and FES at any age.

Our next analyses entailed multiple regressions to determine the contributions of maternal employment to children's development and environment relative to other variables. For analyses of developmental outcomes, variables included in the multiple regressions, in addition to maternal employment status, were SES, sex of child, marital status, number of children, and concurrent environmental measure. This latter variable was chosen due to our research showing the significant role of environment in children's development. At each age, the contemporaneous measure of each of these variables was included in the regression. For example, for 1-year developmental outcome (criterion variable), independent variables (predictors) were 1-year maternal employment status, 1-year SES, 1-year marital status, number of children in the home at 1 year, sex of child, and the 15-month HOME total score. Maternal employment status was entered first hierarchically (forced entry) in each regression because we sought to determine how much variance it would account for before and after the entry of other variables. The remaining variables were entered stepwise. Summary scores were used for measures with subscales because the results of MANOVA indicated no differences in results for subscales as for summary scores. This was the procedure for all analyses to be reported henceforth. For example, the McCarthy General Cognitive Index was used, not the subscales. Interactions between Maternal Employment Status and Sex were not included in the regressions because the MAN-

OVAs showed nonsignificant interactions, and our preliminary analyses showed that the interaction was nonsignificant when it was included in the regressions (A. E. Gottfried, A. W. Gottfried, & Bathurst, 1985). Further, Maternal Employment Status × Marital Status interactions were also not included because MANOVAs with these factors on the dependent variables showed nonsignificant interactions.

Results of these multiple regressions are presented in Table 3. As can be readily seen, maternal employment status was not a significant predictor of children's development. A number of variables did show consistent relationship to children's development. These were SES, children's environment, and, to a lesser extent, child's sex and number of children.

Multiple regressions on the environmental variables were similar to those conducted on the developmental variables. The outcome (criterion) variables were the environmental measures, and the predictors were maternal employment status (forced entry), SES, marital status, sex of child, and number of children (entered stepwise). Two regressions indicated significant independent effects for maternal employment status. Maternal employment status significantly and postively predicted the Educational Attitudes factor of the Home Environment Survey at ages 5 and 7 years, independent of any other factor. Employed mothers had higher scores, indicating that they held higher educational aspirations for their children, both they and their children engaged in less TV viewing, and children received more out-of-school lessons. Results for the regressions on environmental variables are presented in Table 4.

Regarding the results presented in Tables 3 through 6, all significant R^2's were tested with critical values developed by Wilkinson to control for Type 1 error (Tabatchnick & Fidell, 1983). In Table 3, results are presented for regressions in which the HOME and the Home Environment Survey were included as the environmental measure because there were pervasive significant results obtained with these measures. At age 6, results for the Father Involvement Checklist are reported because this was the only environmental measure at that age. Regressions not reported in Table 3 had also been conducted using the FES (at 3, 5, and 7 years), Father Involvement Checklist (7 years), and the Variety of Experience Checklist (39 months and 5 years) as predictors for the concurrent developmental outcomes. Results showed that the FES (Positive Family Involvement factor) significantly predicted the McCarthy General Cognitive Index (3 years), Difficulty Temperament score (3 years), Eyberg Intensity Scale, Achenbach Parent total (boys at 5 and 7 years), CAIMI Math score (7 years), and Teacher rating of spelling (7 years).

Table 3. Multiple Regressions for Contemporaneous Analyses: Developmental Variables

	Predictors[a,b]		
Age and outcome variables	Maternal employment	Other significant predictors	Total regression $R(R^2)$
1-year			
Bayley	NS	Sex**	.26(.07)**
1.5 years			
Bayley	NS	SES**	.27(.07)**
Temperament Difficulty Score	NS	SES*	NS
2-years			
Bayley	NS	SES***	.41(.17)***
Temperament Difficulty Score	NS	NS	NS
2.5 years			
McCarthy General Cognitive Index	NS	SES***	.32(.11)**
3 years			
McCarthy-General Cognitive Index	NS	HOME total***	.47(.22)***
Temperament Difficulty Score	NS	NS	NS
39 months			
TELD	NS	HOME total*** Marital status*(−)	.41(.17)***
Eyberg Intensity	NS	HOME total**(−)	.29(.08)**
Eyberg Problem	NS	HOME total**(−) Sex*(−)	.31(.09)**
3.5 years			
McCarthy General Cognitive Index	NS	HOME total*** SES** Sex**	.59(.34)***
Temperament Difficulty Score	NS	HOME total**(−)	.27(.08)**
PIPS	NS	HOME total*	NS
Preschool Behavior Questionnaire	NS	HOME total**(−) Sex*(−)	.37(.13)**
5 years			
KABC Mental Processing	NS	HES Educational Stimulation* Educational Attitudes*	.33(.11)*
KABC Achievement	NS	SES*** HES Educational Stimulation**	.49(.24)***
Kohn Interest	NS	SES*	NS
Kohn Cooperation	NS	Number of children*	NS
Temperament Difficulty Score	NS	HES Educational Attitudes*(−)	NS

(continued)

Table 3. (Continued)

Age and outcome variables	Maternal employment	Other significant predictors	Total regression $R(R^2)$
6 years			
WISC-Full Scale	NS	SES***	.40(.16)***
WRAT-Reading	NS	SES***	.32(.10)**
WRAT-Spelling	NS	Sex** SES**	.42(.18)***
WRAT-Arithmetic	NS	SES** Sex*	.33(.11)*
Kohn Interest	NS	NS	NS
Kohn Cooperation	NS	NS	NS
Vineland Summary	NS	Sex*** Marital status** (−) Father Involvement Checklist**	.53(.28)***
Vineland Adaptive Composite	NS	Sex*** Marital status** (−) Father Involvement Checklist**	.53(.28)***
7 years			
WISC-Full Scale	NS	SES***	.46(.21)***
Woodcock-Johnson			
Reading	NS	HES Educational Stimulation** SES**	.45(.20)***
Math	NS	SES***	.33(.11)**
Written Language	NS	SES** HES Educational Stimulation* Maternal Involvement*	.50(.25)***
Knowledge	NS	SES** HES Educational Stimulation** Maternal Involvement*	.50(.25)***
Teachers' Ratings of Achievement			
Reading	NS	HES Educational Stimulation** SES*	.46(.21)***
Math	NS	SES*	.27(.08)*
Spelling	NS	HES Educational Stimulation*** Sex*	.52(.27)***
CAIMI			
Reading	NS	NS	NS
Math	NS	NS	NS

Table 3. (Continued)

Age and outcome variables	Predictors[a,b] Maternal employment	Other significant predictors	Total regression $R(R^2)$
Achenbach Child Behavior Checklist[c]			
4 years			
Parent total			
Boys	NS	SES** (−)	.43(.19)**
Girls	NS	NS	NS
5 years			
Parent total			
Boys	NS	SES*** (−)	.48(.23)**
Girls	NS	NS	NS
6 years			
Parent total			
Boys	NS	SES*** (−)	.45(.20)**
Girls	NS	SES** (−)	.42(.18)*
Teacher total			
Boys	NS	SES** (−)	.38(.14)*
Girls	NS	NS	NS
7 years			
Parent total			
Boys	NS	SES** (−)	.41(.17)***
Girls	NS	HES Educational Attitudes**(−)	.46(.21)**
Teacher total			
Boys	NS	HES Maternal Involvement*(−)	NS
Girls	NS	NS	NS

[a] Predictors included in this table are maternal employment status regardless of significance and all others that significantly contributed to the regression. The total set of predictors included maternal employment status, SES, sex of child, marital status, number of children, and pertinent environmental measure. Predictors are listed in descending order of significance. Coded values for categorized predictors are Maternal Employment Status (1 = nonemployed, 2 = employed); Sex (1 = male, 2 = female), Marital Status (1 = married, 2 = not married). Continuous variables are SES, Number of children, and environment scores. Higher scores indicate higher values on the continuous variables.
[b] Negative beta weights are indicated in the table in parentheses next to the significant predictor. These refer to inverse relationships between the predictor and outcome variable. Variables with no parentheses indicate positive beta weights and refer to positive relationships between the predictor and outcome variable.
[c] Results for the Child Behavior Checklist are presented separately by sex.
* $p \leq .05$.   ** $p \leq .01$.   *** $p \leq .001$.   NS = not significant.

Table 4. Multiple Regressions for Contemporaneous Analyses: Environmental Variables

Age and outcome variables	Maternal employment	Other significant predictors	Total regression $R(R^2)$
15 months			
HOME total	NS	Number of children***(−) SES**	.41(.17)***
39 months			
HOME total	NS	Number of children***(−) SES***	.47(.22)***
3 years			
FES			
Positive Involvement	NS	SES***	.32(.10)**
Family Regulation	NS	Number of children*** Marital status*	.36(.13)**
VEC	NS	SES***	.34(.11)**
5 years			
HES			
Educational Stimulation	NS	NS	NS
Educational Attitudes	**	SES** Sex*	.45(.20)***
Learning Materials	NS	SES**	.32(.10)**
FES			
Positive Involvement	NS	SES**	.30(.09)**
Family Regulation	NS	NS	NS
VEC	NS	SES*** Number of children**(−)	.47(.22)***
6 years			
Father Involvement Checklist	NS	NS	NS
7 years			
HES			
Educational Stimulation	NS	SES***	.37(.14)***
Educational Attitudes	**	SES***	.46(.22)***
Maternal Involvement	NS	NS	NS
FES			
Positive Involvement	NS	SES***	.32(.10)**
Family Regulation	NS	NS	NS
Father Involvement Checklist	NS	NS	NS

[a] Predictors included in this table are maternal employment status regardless of significance and all others that significantly contributed to the regression. The total set of predictors included maternal employment status, SES, sex of child, marital status, and number of children. Predictors are listed in descending order of significance. Coded values for categorized predictors are Maternal Employment status (1 = nonemployed, 2 = employed); Sex (1 = male, 2 = female), Marital status (1 = married, 2 = not married). Continuous variables are SES, Number of children. Higher scores indicate higher values on the continuous variables.

[b] Negative beta weights are indicated in the table in parentheses next to the significant predictor. These refer to inverse relationships between the predictor and outcome variable. Positive beta weights are not indicated and refer to positive relationships between the predictor and outcome variable.

* $p \leq .05$.   ** $p \leq .01$.   *** $p \leq .001$.   NS = not significant.

Higher cohesiveness, expressiveness, intellectual-cultural orientation, active recreation, and less conflict were related to higher cognitive scores, fewer reported problems, and higher math motivation. Father involvement (7 years) was a significant predictor of WISC Full Scale IQ, and Woodcock-Johnson Knowledge score. Greater father involvement was related to higher IQ and achievement. The Variety of Experience Checklist was not a significant predictor. Maternal employment was nonsignificant in these regressions.

C. Prospective Analyses

The next issue addressed was whether there were any longitudinal or long-term effects of maternal employment on development or environment. Several ages were selected as important developmental periods to examine. These were early infancy (1 year); end of infancy (2 years); preschool (3.5 years); kindergarten entry (5 years); school entry (6 years); and the current last data point (7 years). Maternal employment status and other independent variables at each of these ages (up to age 6) were used to predict developmental and environmental outcomes at each of the later ages up to age 7. For example, for predictions to subsequent developmental variables from 1 year of age, independent variables were the 1-year assessments of maternal employment status, SES, marital status, sex of child, number of children, and the HOME total score. Predictions were made to developmental outcomes at 2, 3.5, 5, 6, and 7 years. For the environmental variables, the predictors were the same except for the exclusion of earlier environmental measures. Outcome measures were the environmental variables assessed at 3.5, 5, 6, and 7 years. This same analysis strategy was used for predictions made from 2, 3.5, 5, and 6 years to each subsequent age up to 7. Results are presented in Table 5 for the developmental outcomes and Table 6 for the environmental outcomes. For developmental variables, the predominant finding was that of nonsignificance for maternal employment status. Although there were some scattered significant findings, there were no consistent trends. Hence there was no evidence for long-term or "sleeper" effects of maternal employment status across cognitive, academic, and social and behavioral developmental domains from infancy throughout the school years.

For the environmental measures, several significant findings were obtained. Maternal employment status was significantly and positively associated with the Educational Attitudes factor of the Home Environment Survey for the child at age 7. This emerged as a consistent longitudinal trend, beginning with assessment of maternal employment

Table 5. Multiple Regressions for Prospective Analyses: Developmental Variables

Age and outcome variables	Maternal employment	Other significant predictors	Total regression $R(R^2)$
Predictors[a,b]			

Predictions from 1-year maternal employment and other variables to later outcomes at 2, 3.5, 5, 6, and 7 years

Age and outcome variables	Maternal employment	Other significant predictors	Total regression $R(R^2)$
2 years			
Bayley	NS	SES***	.42(.18)***
Temperament Difficulty Score	NS	NS	NS
3.5 years			
McCarthy General Cognitive Index	NS	SES***	.47(.22)***
		Sex**	
		HOME total*	
Temperament Difficulty Score	NS	NS	NS
PIPS	NS	SES*	NS
Preschool Behavior Questionnaire	NS	HOME total*(−)	.45(.20)***
		Sex**(−)	
		SES*(−)	
5 years			
KABC Mental Processing	NS	SES**	.39(.15)***
		Number of children**(−)	
KABC Achievement	NS	SES***	.52(.27)***
		Number of children**(−)	
Kohn Interest	NS	NS	NS
Kohn Cooperation	NS	NS	NS
Temperament Difficulty Score	NS	SES*(−)	.24(.06)*
6 years			
WISC—Full Scale	NS	SES***	.40(.16)***
WRAT—Reading	NS	SES***	.44(.20)***
		Number of children**(−)	
		Sex*	
WRAT—Spelling	NS	Sex***	.46(.22)***
		SES*	
		HOME total*	
WRAT—Arithmetic	NS	SES***	.38(.14)***
		Sex**	
Kohn Interest	NS	NS	NS
Kohn Cooperation	NS	NS	NS
Vineland Summary	NS	Sex***	.38(.14)**
		SES*	
Vineland Adaptive Composite	NS	Sex***	.41(.17)***
		SES**	
7 years			
WISC—Full Scale	NS	SES***	.51(.26)***
		Number of children***(−)	

Table 5. (Continued)

	Predictors[a,b]		Total regression $R(R^2)$
Age and outcome variables	Maternal employment	Other significant predictors	

Predictions from 1-year maternal employment and other variables to later outcomes at 2, 3.5, 5, 6, and 7 years (continued)

Age and outcome variables	Maternal employment	Other significant predictors	Total regression $R(R^2)$
Woodcock-Johnson			
Reading	NS	HOME total*	.34(.12)**
		Number of children*(−)	
Math	NS	SES**	.33(.11)**
Written Language	NS	SES**	.40(.16)***
		Number of children**(−)	
Knowledge	NS	SES***	.55(.30)***
		Number of children***(−)	
Teachers' Rating of Achievement			
Reading	NS	SES***	.52(.27)***
		Number of children***(−)	
Math	NS	SES**	.32(.11)**
Spelling	NS	Number of children*(−)	NS
CAIMI			
Reading	NS	NS	NS
Math	NS	NS	NS
Achenbach Child Behavior Checklist[c]			
4 years			
Parent total			
Boys	NS	SES**(−)	.44(.19)**
Girls	NS	NS	NS
5 years			
Parent total			
Boys	NS	SES**(−)	.43(.18)**
Girls	NS	NS	NS
6 years			
Parent total			
Boys	NS	SES*(−)	.36(.13)*
Girls	NS	SES**(−)	.50(.25)**
Teacher total			
Boys	NS	NS	NS
Girls	NS	NS	NS
7 years			
Parent total			
Boys	NS	SES**(−)	.46(.21)**
		Number of children*	
Girls	NS	SES**(−)	.40(.16)*
Teacher total			
Boys	NS	Number of children***	.62(.39)***
		Marital status**	
Girls	NS	NS	NS

(continued)

Table 5. (Continued)

Age and outcome variables	Predictors[a,b] Maternal employment	Other significant predictors	Total regression $R(R^2)$
Predictions from 2-year maternal employment and other variables to later outcomes at 3.5, 5, 6, and 7 years			
3.5 years			
McCarthy General Cognitive Index	NS	SES*** Sex** HOME total*	.44(.19)***
Temperament Difficulty Score	NS	NS	NS
PIPS	NS	NS	NS
Preschool Behavior Questionnaire	NS	HOME total***(−) Sex**(−)	.41(.17)***
5 years			
KABC Mental Processing	NS	HOME total**	.24(.06)*
KABC Achievement	*(−)	SES*** Number of children**(−)	.49(.24)***
Kohn Interest	NS	NS	NS
Kohn Cooperation	NS	NS	NS
Temperament Difficulty Score	NS	NS	NS
6 years			
WISC—Full Scale	NS	SES** HOME total*	.39(.15)***
WRAT—Reading	NS	SES*** Number of children**(−) Sex**	.49(.24)***
WRAT—Spelling	NS	Sex*** SES*** Number of children**(−)	.49(.24)***
WRAT—Arithmetic	NS	SES*** Sex**	.39(.15)***
Kohn Interest	NS	Sex*	NS
Kohn Cooperation	NS	NS	NS
Vineland Summary	NS	Sex*** SES*	.40(.16)***
Vineland Adaptive Composite	NS	Sex*** SES**	.42(.18)***
7 years			
WISC—Full Scale	NS	SES*** Number of children**(−)	.42(.17)***
Woodcock-Johnson Reading	*(−)	Number of children**(−) SES*	.42(.17)***

Table 5. (*Continued*)

	Predictors[a,b]		
Age and outcome variables	Maternal employment	Other significant predictors	Total regression $R(R^2)$
Predictions from 2-year maternal employment and other variables to later outcomes at 3.5, 5, 6, and 7 years (continued)			
Math	NS	SES*	.31(.09)**
Written Language	***(−)	Number of children***(−) SES**	.50(.25)***
Knowledge	NS	Number of children***(−) SES***	.49(.24)***
Teachers' Ratings of Achievement			
Reading	NS	Number of children***(−) SES**	.49(.24)***
Math	NS	Number of children*(−)	NS
Spelling	NS	Number of children**(−)	.34(.12)*
CAIMI			
Reading	NS	NS	NS
Math	NS	SES*	NS
Achenbach Child Behavior Checklist			
4 years			
Parent total			
Boys	NS	SES**(−)	.40(.16)**
Girls	NS	NS	NS
5 years			
Parent total			
Boys	NS	SES**(−)	.37(.13)**
Girls	NS	NS	NS
6 years			
Parent total			
Boys	NS	SES*(−)	.33(.11)*
Girls	NS	SES*(−)	.42(.17)**
Teacher total			
Boys	NS	NS	NS
Girls	NS	NS	NS
7 years			
Parent total			
Boys	NS	SES**(−)	.35(.12)*
Girls	NS	NS	NS
Teacher total			
Boys	NS	Number of children***	.50(.25)***
Girls	NS	NS	NS

(*continued*)

Table 5. (*Continued*)

Age and outcome variables	Predictors[a,b] Maternal employment	Other significant predictors	Total regression $R(R^2)$
Predictions from 3.5-year maternal employment and other variables to later outcomes at 5, 6, and 7 years			
5 years			
KABC Mental Processing	NS	HOME total**	.31(.10)**
KABC Achievement	NS	HOME total***	.59(.35)***
		SES***	
Kohn Interest	NS	NS	NS
Kohn Cooperation	NS	NS	NS
Temperament Difficulty Score	NS	NS	NS
6 years			
WISC—Full Scale	NS	HOME total**	.48(.23)***
		SES**	
WRAT—Reading	NS	HOME total***	.53(.28)***
		SES*	
		Sex*	
WRAT—Spelling	NS	HOME total***	.56(.31)***
		Sex***	
		SES**	
WRAT—Arithmetic	NS	HOME total**	.45(.21)***
		Sex**	
		SES*	
Kohn Interest	NS	Sex*	NS
Kohn Cooperation	NS	NS	NS
Vineland Summary	NS	HOME total***	.54(.29)***
		Sex***	
Vineland Adaptive Composite	NS	HOME total***	.55(.31)***
		Sex***	
7 years			
WISC—Full Scale	NS	HOME total***	.51(.26)***
		SES**	
Woodcock-Johnson			
Reading	NS	HOME total***	.49(.24)***
		Marital status*(−)	
Math	NS	HOME total***	.42(.17)***
Written Language	NS	HOME total**	.46(.21)***
		SES**	
Knowledge	NS	HOME total***	.51(.26)***
		SES*	
Teachers' Ratings of Achievement			
Reading	NS	HOME total***	.56(.31)***
		SES**	

Table 5. (*Continued*)

	Predictors[a,b]		Total regression $R(R^2)$
Age and outcome variables	Maternal employment	Other significant predictors	

Predictions from 3.5-year maternal employment and other variables to later outcomes at 5, 6, and 7 years (continued)

Math	NS	HOME total***	.37(.14)**
Spelling	NS	SES**	.31(.10)*
CAIMI			
Reading	NS	NS	NS
Math	NS	NS	NS
Achenbach Child Behavior Checklist			
5 years			
Parent total			
Boys	NS	SES**(−)	.39(.16)**
Girls	NS	NS	NS
6 years			
Parent total			
Boys	NS	SES**(−)	.36(.13)*
Girls	NS	SES**(−)	.43(.19)*
Teacher total			
Boys	*	NS	.29(.08)*
Girls	NS	NS	NS
7 years			
Parent total			
Boys	NS	SES**(−)	.40(.16)**
Girls	**(−)	SES**(−)	.47(.22)**
Teacher total			
Boys	NS	HOME total**(−)	.42(.18)**
Girls	NS	NS	NS

Predictions from 5-year maternal employment and other variables to later outcomes at 6 and 7 years

6 years			
WISC—Full Scale	NS	HES Educational Stimulation*** SES**	.49(.24)***
WRAT—Reading	NS	HES Educational Stimulation*** Educational Attitudes**	.47(.22)***

(*continued*)

Table 5. (*Continued*)

Age and outcome variables	Predictors[a,b] Maternal employment	Other significant predictors	Total regression $R(R^2)$

Predictions from 5-year maternal employment and other variables to later outcomes at 6 and 7 years (*continued*)

6 years (*continued*)			
WRAT—Spelling	NS	HES Educational Stimulation*** SES*** Sex**	.58(.34)***
WRAT—Arithmetic	NS	HES Educational Stimulation* SES* Sex*	.39(.15)**
Kohn Interest	NS	NS	NS
Kohn Cooperation	*	NS	.25(.06)*
Vineland Summary	NS	HES Educational Stimulation*** Educational Attitudes** Sex** Marital status**(−)	.62(.38)***
Vineland Adaptive Composite	NS	HES Educational Stimulation*** Educational Attitudes*** Sex** Marital status**(−)	.62(.38)***
7 years			
WISC—Full Scale	*	HES Educational Stimulation*** SES***	.52(.27)***
Woodcock-Johnson			
Reading	NS	SES*** HES Educational Stimulation*	.43(.17)***
Math	NS	HES Educational Attitudes** Educational Stimulation* SES*	.47(.23)***

Table 5. (Continued)

Age and outcome variables	Maternal employment	Other significant predictors	Total regression $R(R^2)$

Predictors[a,b]

Predictions from 5-year maternal employment and other variables to later outcomes at 6 and 7 years (continued)

Written Language	NS	SES***	.43(.18)***
Knowledge	NS	SES***	.35(.12)**
Teachers' Ratings of Achievement			
Reading	NS	SES***	.39(.16)**
Math	NS	SES**	.31(.09)*
Spelling	NS	NS	NS
CAIMI			
Reading	NS	NS	NS
Math	NS	NS	NS
Achenbach Child Behavior Checklist			
6 years			
Parent total			
Boys	NS	SES**(−)	.38(.14)*
Girls	NS	HES Educational Attitudes**(−)	.45(.21)*
Teacher total			
Boys	NS	NS	NS
Girls	NS	NS	NS
7 years			
Parent total			
Boys	NS	SES**(−)	.39(.15)*
Girls	*(−)	SES**(−)	.49(.24)**
Teacher total			
Boys	NS	SES**(−)	.41(.17)*
Girls	NS	NS	NS

Predictions from 6-year maternal employment and other variables to later outcomes at 7 years

7 years			
WISC—Full Scale	NS	SES***	.46(.21)***
Woodcock-Johnson			
Reading	NS	SES**	.31(.09)**
Math	NS	SES**	.31(.09)**
Written Language	NS	SES***	.37(.14)**
Knowledge	NS	SES***	.40(.16)**

(continued)

Table 5. *(Continued)*

	Predictors[a,b]		
Age and outcome variables	Maternal employment	Other significant predictors	Total regression R(R²)

Predictions from 6-year maternal employment and other variables to later outcomes at 7 years

7 years *(continued)*			
Teachers' Ratings of Achievement			
Reading	NS	SES**	.43(.19)**
		Number of children*(−)	
Math	NS	SES**	.35(.12)**
Spelling	NS	NS	NS
CAIMI			
Reading	NS	Father Involvement Checklist**	.28(.08)*
Math	NS	NS	NS
Achenbach Child Behavior Checklist			
Parent total			
Boys	NS	SES***(−)	.52(.27)***
Girls	NS	SES*(−)	NS
Teacher total			
Boys	NS	SES*(−)	NS
Girls	NS	NS	NS

[a] Predictors included in this table are maternal employment status regardless of significance and all others that significantly contributed to the regression. The total set of predictors included maternal employment status, SES, sex of child, marital status, number of children, and pertinent environmental measure. Predictors are listed in descending order of significance. Coded values for categorized predictors are Maternal Employment Status (1 = nonemployed, 2 = employed); Sex (1 = male, 2 = female), Marital Status (1 = married, 2 = not married). Continuous variables are SES, Number of children, and environment scores. Higher scores indicate higher values on the continuous variables.
[b] Negative beta weights are indicated in the table in parentheses next to the significant predictor. These refer to inverse relationships between the predictor and outcome variable. Variables with no parentheses indicate positive beta weights and refer to positive relationships between the predictor and outcome variable.
[c] Results for the Child Behavior Checklist are presented by sex.
*$p \leq .05$. **$p \leq .01$. ***$p \leq .001$. NS = not significant.

status at 3.5 years, and for each assessment thereafter. These findings were in accord with the results of the contemporaneous MANOVAs and multiple regressions.

Maternal employment status at 5 years was positively and significantly predictive of fathers' involvement at age 6. Fathers in the employed mother families were significantly more involved. This finding was consistent with the contemporaneous ANOVA findings at age 6.

Table 6. Multiple Regressions for Prospective Analyses: Environmental Variables

Age and outcome variables	Maternal employment	Other significant predictors	Total regression $R(R^2)$

Predictors[a,b]

Predictions from 1-year maternal employment and other variables to later outcomes at 3.5, 5, 6, and 7 years

Age and outcome variables	Maternal employment	Other significant predictors	Total regression $R(R^2)$
3.5 years			
HOME total[c]	NS	SES***	.55(.30)***
		Number of children***(−)	
FES[c]			
Positive Involvement	NS	SES**	.32(.10)**
		Number of children**(−)	
Family Regulation	NS	Number of children***	.37(.14)***
VEC[c]	NS	SES**	.36(.13)**
		Marital status*(−)	
5 years			
HES			
Educational Stimulation	NS	NS	NS
Educational Attitudes	NS	SES***	.45(.21)***
		Sex**	
		Number of children*(−)	
Learning Materials	NS	SES**	.37(.14)**
		Number of children*	
FES			
Positive Involvement	NS	SES*	.24(.06)*
Family Regulation	NS	Number of children**	.25(.06)*
VEC	NS	SES*	.30(.09)*
		Number of children*(−)	
6 years			
Father Involvement Checklist	NS	NS	NS
7 years			
HES			
Educational Stimulation	NS	SES***	.36(.13)***
Maternal Involvement	NS	NS	NS
Educational Attitudes	NS	SES***	.33(.11)**
FES			
Positive Involvement	NS	SES***	.39(.15)***
		Number of children**(−)	
Family Regulation	NS	NS	NS
Father Involvement Checklist	NS	NS	NS

Predictions from 2-year maternal employment and other variables to later outcomes at 3.5, 5, 6, and 7 years

Age and outcome variables	Maternal employment	Other significant predictors	Total regression $R(R^2)$
3.5 years			
HOME total[c]	NS	SES***	.49(.24)***
		Number of children**(−)	

(continued)

Table 6. (*Continued*)

Age and outcome variables	Maternal employment	Other significant predictors	Total regression $R(R^2)$
Predictors[a,b]			

Predictions from 2-year maternal employment and other variables to later outcomes at 3.5, 5, 6, and 7 years (*continued*)

3.5 years (*continued*)
FES[c]

Positive Involvement	NS	Number of children**(−) SES*	.34(.11)**
Family Regulation	NS	Number of children***	.38(.14)***
VEC[c]	NS	SES***	.34(.12)***

5 years
HES

Educational Stimulation	NS	NS	NS
Educational Attitudes	NS	SES** Sex** Number of children*(−)	.45(.20)***
Learning Materials	NS	SES**	.29(.08)*

FES

Positive Involvement	NS	SES**	.26(.07)*
Family Regulation	NS	Number of children**	.25(.06)*
VEC	NS	SES** Number of children*(−)	.33(.11)**

6 years

Father Involvement Checklist	NS	NS	NS

7 years
HES

Educational Stimulation	NS	SES**	.30(.09)**
Maternal Involvement	NS	NS	NS
Educational Attitudes	NS	SES***	.35(.12)**

FES

Positive Involvement	NS	SES** Number of children**(−)	.38(.14)***
Family Regulation	NS	NS	NS
Father Involvement Checklist	NS	NS	NS

Predictions from 3.5-year maternal employment and other variables to later outcomes at 5, 6, and 7 years

5 years
HES

Educational Stimulation	NS	SES*	.30(.09)*
Educational Attitudes	NS	SES** Sex*	.35(.12)**
Learning Materials	NS	SES**	.33(.11)**

Infancy through the School Years

Table 6. (*Continued*)

Age and outcome variables	Maternal employment	Other significant predictors	Total regression $R(R^2)$
Predictions from 3.5-year maternal employment and other variables to later outcomes at 5, 6, and 7 years (*continued*)			
FES			
Positive Involvement	NS	SES**	.29(.09)**
Family Regulation	NS	SES*(−)	.32(.10)**
		Number of children*	
VEC	NS	Number of children**(−)	.40(.16)***
		SES**	
6 years			
Father Involvement Checklist	NS	NS	NS
7 years			
HES			
Educational Stimulation	NS	SES***	.46(.21)***
Maternal Involvement	NS	Marital Status*(−)	.24(.06)*
Educational Attitudes	**	SES**	.34(.11)**
FES			
Positive Involvement	NS	SES***	.43(.19)***
		Marital Status*(−)	
Family Regulation	NS	NS	NS
Father Involvement Checklist	NS	Marital Status*(−)	NS
Predictions from 5-year maternal employment and other variables to later outcomes at 6 and 7 years			
6 years			
Father Involvement Checklist	*	NS	.22(.05)*
7 years			
HES			
Educational Stimulation	NS	SES***	.35(.12)**
Maternal Involvement	*	Marital status*(−)	.26(.07)*
Educational Attitudes	**	SES***	.39(.15)***
FES			
Positive Involvement	NS	SES***	.41(.17)***
Family Regulation	NS	NS	NS
Father Involvement Checklist	NS	NS	NS
Predictions from 6-year maternal employment and other variables to later outcomes at 7 years			
7 years			
HES			
Educational Stimulation	NS	SES**	.36(.13)**
Maternal Involvement	NS	NS	NS
Educational Attitudes	***	SES***	.45(.21)***

(*continued*)

Table 6. (*Continued*)

	Predictors[a,b]		
Age and outcome variables	Maternal employment	Other significant predictors	Total regression R(R²)

Predictions from 6-year maternal employment and other variables to later outcomes at 7 years (*continued*)

7 years (*continued*)
 FES
  Positive Involvement | NS | SES*** | .34(.12)**
  Family Regulation | NS | NS | NS
  Father Involvement Checklist | NS | NS | NS

[a] Predictors included in this table are maternal employment status regardless of significance and all others that significantly contributed to the regression. The total set of predictors included maternal employment status, SES, sex of child, marital status, and number of children. Predictors are listed in descending order of significance. Coded values for categorized predictors are Maternal Employment Status (1 = nonemployed, 2 = employed); Sex (1 = male, 2 = female), Marital Status (1 = married, 2 = not married). Continuous variables are SES, Number of children. Higher scores indicate higher values on the continuous variables.
[b] Negative beta weights are indicated in the table in parentheses next to the significant predictor. These refer to inverse relationships between the predictor and outcome variable. Positive beta weights are not indicated and refer to positive relationships between the predictor and outcome variable.
[c] These measures were collected during the child's third year, and are listed in this table as 3.5-year outcome variables.
*$p \leq .05$. **$p \leq .01$. ***$p \leq .001$. NS = not significant.

Maternal employment at age 5 was also positively and significantly associated with the Maternal Involvement factor on the Home Environment Survey at age 7. Employed mothers were more involved in discussing school activities, caring for, and doing things with the child.

Table 5 reports the prospective regressions to later developmental outcomes, using either the HOME total score or the factors of the Home Environment Survey (whichever was measured at the appropriate age) as the environmental predictors. These are reported because of the pervasive significance obtained for these measures. The Father Involvement Checklist is reported for the 6-year regressions in Table 5 because it was the only environmental measure at that age. Regressions not reported in Table 5 were also conducted using the FES factors (ages 3.5 and 5 years), and the Variety of Experience Checklist (ages 3.5 and 5 years). These regressions resulted in nonsignificant effects for maternal employment status. The FES Positive Family Involvement factor (3.5-year regression) was significantly and positively predictive of KABC Achievement, Kohn Cooperation Scale (6 years), Vineland Summary and Adaptive Scores, WRAT Spelling and Arithmetic Achievement, WISC Full

Scale IQ (7 years), and the Parent total on the Child Behavior Checklist (boys at age 5). The FES Positive Family Involvement factor (5 years) was positively and significantly predictive of Vineland Summary and Adaptive Scores, and WRAT achievement in all areas, and it was negatively and significantly related to Parent total on the Child Behavior Checklist (boys at ages 6 and 7). The FES Family Regulation factor (3.5-year regression) was negatively and significantly predictive of WRAT Reading achievement, teachers' ratings of reading achievement (age 7), and parent total on the Child Behavior Checklist (girls at age 5); and positively related to parent total of the Child Behavior Checklist (boys at age 7). The FES Family Regulation factor (5 years), and the Variety of Experience Checklist (all ages) did not significantly relate to developmental outcomes. Hence, greater family cohesiveness, intellectual-cultural orientation, active recreation, and lower conflict were generally associated with more favorable outcomes, while greater emphasis on rules, organization, and moralistic beliefs tended to be associated with lower performance where significance occurred.

Across analyses, significant predictors of development included environment, SES, and to a lesser extent, child's sex and number of children in the home. More stimulating environments and higher SES were associated with more favorable developmental outcomes. SES was the major longitudinal predictor of environmental variables. Higher SES was associated with higher environmental scores.

D. Consistency Analyses

The next issue examined was whether the pattern of mothers' employment (i.e., consistency or inconsistency across time) was related to development or environment. This issue was analyzed by examining patterns of employment at the following periods: through the end of infancy (2 years); the preschool period (3.5 years); kindergarten entry (5 years); school entry (6 years); and our most recent assessment (7 years). At each of these ages, mothers' employment status was designated as consistently not employed, consistently employed, or inconsistently employed. Mothers' consistency-of-employment status was assessed from the maternal employment status data collected at each assessment during the entire period.

The following measures were analyzed with either MANOVA or ANOVA using the following factors: Consistency of Employment Status (consistently not employed, inconsistently employed, consistently employed) × Child Sex.

2 years: ANOVA: Bayley MDI, Temperament Difficulty Score, HOME total score (15-months)

3.5 years: MANOVA: FES scales; ANOVA: McCarthy General Cognitive Index, PIPS, Temperament Difficulty Score, Preschool Behavior Questionnaire, HOME total score (39 months), Variety of Experience Checklist, parent total of the Child Behavior Checklist (4 years).

5 years: MANOVA: Home Environment Survey Factors, FES factors, Kohn factors; ANOVA: KABC Mental Processing, KABC Achievement, Temperament Difficulty Score, parent total of the Child Behavior Checklist, Variety of Experience Checklist.

6 years: MANOVA: WRAT Scales, Kohn Scales; ANOVA: WISC-Full Scale, Vineland Summary and Adaptive Composite, parent and teacher totals on the Child Behavior Checklist, Father Involvement Checklist.

7 years: MANOVA: Woodcock-Johnson Scales; Teachers' achievement ratings, CAIMI scales, Home Environment Survey factors; FES factors; ANOVA: WISC-Full Scale, parent and teacher totals of the Child Behavior Checklist, Father Involvement Checklist.

Results showed a preponderance of nonsignificant findings for the Consistency of Employment Status factor and for the Consistency × Sex interaction across all ages. There were two significant main effects for the Consistency factor: KABC Achievement, $F(2,104) = 3.77, p = .03$; and WISC Full Scale IQ at age 6, $F(2,96) = 3.95, p = .02$. *Post-hoc* analyses showed that children of inconsistently employed mothers had significantly higher achievement and IQ scores compared to children of either consistently employed or not employed mothers, whereas these two latter groups did not differ.

Although analyses on the FES factors yielded no significant multivariate effects, the univariate F for the Family Regulation factor was significant at every age assessed: 3.5 years, $F(2,111) = 3.90, p = .02$; 5 years, $F(2,102) = 3.09, p = .05$; and 7 years, $F(2,102) = 3.33, p = .04$. Due to this consistent finding at all three ages, *post-hoc* analyses were conducted. Results at all ages showed that the lowest scores on this factor were obtained by the inconsistently employed mothers, whereas the consistently employed and nonemployed mothers did not differ. The homes of inconsistently employed mothers were characterized by less rule orientation and control.

Overall, consistency or inconsistency in maternal employment patterns bore little relationship to either development or environment throughout the course of the study. No reliable interactions between Consistency of Employment × Sex were obtained.

E. Maternal Occupation, Hours of Work, and Attitudes: Relationships with Development and Environment

Across the correlations reported next, findings for the sexes were not significantly different as determined by comparing the correlations of boys and girls using Fisher r to z transformations. Fewer significant differences between the sexes were obtained than would be expected by chance. Hence, the data are presented for boys and girls combined.

1. Occupation

At every age, maternal occupation was correlated with development and environment partialling fathers' occupation (SES was not partialed from these correlations because maternal occupation is a component of SES). Most correlations were not significant across age, developmental domain, and environmental variables. For developmental variables, where significance occurred, higher occupational levels were associated with higher cognitive development (Bayley at 2 years, McCarthy at 3.5 years, and WISC IQ at 6 and 7 years), higher achievement (WRAT Reading and Woodcock-Johnson Knowledge), and more mature social adaptiveness (Vineland Summary and Adaptive Composite). The significant r's ranged from .23 to .30, p's <.05 to .01.

For environmental variables, where significance occurred, there was a trend for higher occupational status to be positively associated with teaching child to wash and keeping toys in one place (Purdue), more positive family involvement (FES at 3 and 7 years), and the Educational Attitudes factor on the Home Environment Survey (5 and 7 years). Significant r's ranged from .23 to .49, p's <.03 to .001.

2. Hours

The number of hours mothers were employed per week was correlated with developmental and environmental measures partialling family SES. The mean number of hours and standard deviations were 32 (11.3), 31 (12.7), and 31 (12.4) at ages 5, 6, and 7, respectively. Where significant, more hours of employment were negatively related to KABC achievement, Teacher ratings of reading achievement, and the Educational Stimulation factor on the Home Environment Survey (7 years). Hours of employment were positively related to Family Regulation on the FES at 5 years, and Educational Attitudes on the Home Environment Survey (7 years). Significant r's ranged from −.22 to .41, p's <.05 to .001. Given the large number of nonsignificant correlations, there is not strong support for number of hours of employment being a significant factor in either children's development or home environment.

3. Attitudes

Correlations between maternal attitudes toward employment (when children were 5 and 7), and development and environment were computed partialling family SES.

Most correlations were nonsignificant across development and environment. At age 5, where significant results emerged, they showed that when the mother has more positive attitudes toward employment and the dual roles of career and family, children have higher interest and participation in school (Kohn), and fewer reported behavior problems (parent total of the Child Behavior Checklist). More positive attitudes were related to higher Educational Stimulation on the Home Environment Survey, and more positive family involvement on the FES. Significant r's ranged from $-.23$ to $.28$, p's $<.05$.

At age 7, the Maternal Availability and Confidence factor showed some significant correlations with developmental and environmental outcomes. When the mother was more available and confident, children had higher intrinsic motivation in reading (CAIMI), and Educational Stimulation and Maternal Involvement on the Home Environment Survey were higher, although Educational Attitudes were lower. Significant r's ranged from $-.22$ to $.32$, p's $<.05$ to $.01$.

Correlations between the Perception of Dual Responsibilities factor and developmental and environmental outcomes showed that more favorable attitudes (and less stress) regarding dual responsibilities were related to higher school achievement (Woodcock-Johnson Reading and Writing, Teachers' ratings of math achievement), intrinsic motivation in reading (CAIMI), fewer reported behavior problems (Parent and the Teacher totals on the Child Behavior Checklist), more maternal involvement with the child (Home Environment Survey), and more democratic family regulation (FES). Significant r's ranged from $-.36$ to $.27$, p's $< .05$ to $.01$. The Maternal Satisfaction with Employment factor was unrelated to any outcome.

4. Role Satisfaction

At age 7, employed and nonemployed mothers completed items regarding role satisfaction. Nonemployed mothers responded to: I am not currently employed, but I would like to be (1 = *strongly agree*, 5 = *strongly disagree*). No reliable significant correlations, partialling SES, were obtained. The same was true for correlations of role satisfaction for employed mothers, who responded to: I am currently employed, but I would prefer not to work (1 = *strongly agree*, 5 = *strongly disagree*).

All mothers responded to: I am satisfied with my role as a parent (1 = *strongly agree*, 5 = *strongly disagree*). For nonemployed mothers, parental satisfaction showed little relationship to either development or environment. For employed mothers, more satisfaction was related to higher reading and writing achievement on the Woodcock-Johnson, higher teacher ratings of reading achievement, more educational stimulation and maternal involvement (Home Environment Survey), and more positive family involvement (FES). Significant r's ranged from $-.20$ to $-.43$, p's $<.05$ to $.001$.

IV. SUMMARY

Two consistent trends emerged from the present research. First, maternal employment status proved to be nonsignificant in its relationship to children's development from infancy through the school-entry years. This was found across a wide array of developmental domains, both in the contemporaneous and prospective analyses. The few significant effects obtained were sporadic, with no consistency across age or type of analysis. Given the large number of analyses conducted, these few significant findings pale in comparison to the overwhelming pattern of nonsignificance. Major significant predictors of children's development were SES, home environment, and, to a lesser extent, number of children in the family. Developmental measures were positively related to SES and environmental variables and were inversely related to number of children.

The second trend obtained was for maternal employment status to be significantly, positively, and independently related to educational attitudes at ages 5 and 7. Employed mothers held higher educational aspirations for their children, had children in more out-of-school lessons, and both they and their children watched less TV than the children of nonemployed mothers. These results were independent of SES, marital status, number of children, and child's gender. The relationship of educational attitudes to maternal employment status was a longitudinal trend that emerged when the child was 3.5 years. From that age on, maternal employment status was a predictor of later educational aspirations. These findings were corroborated by the contemporaneous and prospective regressions, and by the MANOVA's.

Other findings are summarized here:

1. *Contemporaneous analyses.* Employed mothers encouraged developmental advance in infancy to a greater extent, exposed children to a greater variety of experience at age 5, and fathers were significantly more involved at age 6.
2. *Longitudinal analyses.* Maternal employment status at age 5 positively predicted fathers' involvement at age 6 and maternal involvement at age 7.
3. *Consistency of employment.* The consistency or inconsistency of maternal employment status bore little relationship to either development or environment from infancy on.
4. *Maternal occupation, hours of employment, and attitudes.* Overall, occupation, hours, and attitudes did not show strong relationships to development or environment either by pattern or magnitude of correlations. Occupational status and maternal perceptions of dual responsibilities showed the most consistent trends with more favorable child outcomes for mothers of higher occupational level and for those with more favorable perceptions of dual responsibilities (less stress).

Occupation. Mothers of higher occupational status had children with higher achievement and IQ, had higher educational attitudes themselves, and their families were characterized as having more positive involvement.

Attitudes. At age 5, when the mother had more positive attitudes toward employment as well as the dual roles of employment and parenting, children had more interest in school, fewer reported behavior problems, and there was more positive family involvement. At age 7, when mothers were more available and had more confidence in their dual roles, children had higher intrinsic motivation in reading, and mothers provided higher educational stimulation and involvement. Less stress due to dual roles was related to children's higher reading intrinsic motivation, higher achievement, fewer reported behavior problems, and less rule orientation and control.

V. DISCUSSION

The results clearly show that from infancy through the early school years, children of employed versus nonemployed mothers do not differ in development, whether this is considered contemporaneously, prospectively, or by consistency of employment. There is simply *no negative effect* of maternal employment status. This is true for boys as well as girls. A hypothesis regarding the increased vulnerability of middle-class boys to maternal employment (Bronfenbrenner, 1986; Hoffman, 1984b) was not supported across age or developmental domain. Neither was the environment provided for children of employed versus nonemployed mothers different for the sexes.

Hoffman (1984b) proposed the need to study maternal employment over a longitudinal period from infancy to later years to determine if there are any long-term effects of maternal employment that are not apparent during the infancy period. Our findings indicated no such sleeper effects. Children of employed versus nonemployed mothers were not differentially affected by employment status *per se* from infancy throughout the course of the study.

Maternal employment status did have a significant, independent impact on educational attitudes, fathers' involvement, and maternal involvement, with the most pervasive effect having been obtained for educational attitudes. Maternal employment status is advantageous with regard to these variables, with higher educational attitudes, more father involvement, and greater maternal involvement obtained for employed compared to nonemployed mothers.

Our data show that not only do employed mothers hold higher educational attitudes for their children, but higher educational attitudes are related to higher cognitive development, academic achievement, social development, and fewer reported occurrences of behavior problems in girls. These are particularly intriguing findings because the children of employed mothers may ultimately show enhanced development compared to the children of nonemployed mothers due to the long-term impact of higher educational aspirations. Seginer (1986) recently reported that mothers' educational aspirations were causally related to sons' achievement (daughters were not included in her study) through the mediation of achievement-related behaviors in the home, with an advantage for sons whose mothers had higher aspirations. We propose that whereas maternal employment plays no direct role in children's development, it is through the provision of differential proximal home environments that children's development is influenced. In this case, educational aspirations may ultimately play a mediational role between maternal employment status and eventual developmental outcomes in children.

This view may also relate to other findings. In the present research, the fathers in families with employed mothers show more involvement, and this is consistent with prior literature (Hoffman, 1985). What is novel about our data is that we have also found fathers' involvement to be positively and independently related to some aspects of children's development. As reported before, fathers' involvement at age 6 was related to more maturity in children's social development, and, at age 7, more father involvement was related to higher IQ and achievement. In addition, in other findings at age 6 (A. E. Gottfried, A. W. Gottfried, & Bathurst, 1987), fathers' involvement was positively correlated with children's IQ and WRAT achievement, partialling fathers' occupation. Hence, an indirect relationship may exist between children's development and maternal employment status as mediated through fathers' involvement.

Maternal employment status at age 5 predicted higher maternal involvement on the Home Environment Survey at age 7. Higher maternal involvement was also related to higher achievement for boys and girls and to fewer behavior problems for boys. Here again, we believe we have a foundation for hypothesizing an indirect link between maternal employment status and development, through the proximal home environment.

Consistency or inconsistency of employment played little role in either the development of children or environment provided for them. In contrast to the view that inconsistent maternal employment patterns are potentially detrimental to children (e.g., Bronfenbrenner, 1986), the present data show that inconsistent employment patterns do not result in any detrimental differences with regard to the child or the home environment. On the contrary, some positive outcomes were associated with the inconsistent employment pattern. In view of our perspective, we assert that it is not the consistency of employment *per se* that influences children. Rather, it is the extent to which consistency of employment is associated with environmental influences that would affect children. Again, we speculate that employment consistency would need to be mediated by home environment to have any impact on children's development. This view is also supported by Baker and Mednick (1984) who assert that any impact on children of maternal employment consistency or inconsistency is mediated through family stability or instability.

Our findings overwhelmingly show that children's development is pervasively related to proximal home environmental variables above and beyond SES. These results are consistent with out previous findings through the early childhood years (A. E. Gottfried, A. W. Gottfried, & Guerin, 1986; A. W. Gottfried, 1984; A. W. Gottfried & A. E. Gottfried, 1984, 1986), and with the contemporary literature (A. W. Gottfried & A. E. Gottfried, 1986).

A prior cross-sectional study (MacKinnon, Brody, & Stoneman, 1982) reported little difference in preschoolers' home environments, measured by the HOME, comparing employed versus nonemployed mothers in intact families. Our findings also showed maternal employment status was not related to HOME scores. Though our analyses showed some significant differences in home environment during infancy on the Purdue, most of our findings with regard to maternal employment and environment occurred during the kindergarten and early school years, with maternal employment status during preschool predictive of later environment. There may be a developmental trend in which the contemporaneous environments provided to infants and preschoolers of employed and nonemployed mothers do not differ. However, as children enter kindergarten, home environments relevant to education may differ in relation to maternal employment status.

As cited in the introduction, there have been divergent findings with regard to the effects of maternal employment on children's development. It is our contention that divergent findings will become consistent with one another when investigators take into account home environment. Differences in the proximal home environments within particular studies and samples can contribute to positive and negative effects of maternal employment. When environment remains unmeasured, it is potentially an unaccounted confounding variable. The long-term implications of our findings and conceptualization are significant. If maternal employment continues to be favorably related to proximal home environment, then children's development may be favorably influenced, albeit indirectly. We would expect this influence to increase as children progress through the school years because there is reliable evidence showing continuity of environmental stimulation and experience over time (A. W. Gottfried, 1984; A. W. Gottfried & A. E. Gottfried, 1986). Further, educational aspirations of children may be influenced by their mothers' aspirations, and this may have significant impact on their later development and academic functioning. By continuing our research, we hope to study the long-term impact of maternal employment and home environment on children.

Maternal occupation, hours of employment, and attitudes showed either nonsignificant correlations or generally low correlations with development and environment. However, where significance occurred, the trends showed more favorable developmental or environmental outcomes to be associated with higher maternal occupational status, more favorable attitudes, and higher maternal availability and less stress due to dual responsibilities. Consistent with our view, we propose that, to the extent that these variables are components of the proximal home environment or influence the home environment, they may affect children's development. Investigation of how these variables moderate each other and their causal directions is clearly the next step.

The purpose of this research was to determine the role of maternal employment in children's development and environment, *not* to prescribe decisions regarding maternal employment. Our data indicate that maternal employment status *per se* has no direct impact on children's development. Rather, the quality of the home environment is of great significance to children's development for those whose mothers are employed or nonemployed. We believe that any family can provide a favorable environment for children's development regardless of mothers' employment status. This does not mean that families need not work hard to provide a quality environment. Quite the contrary, across a wide range of middle-class families, whatever efforts or accomodations need to be made to provide an environment that facilitates children's development, it is apparent that employed mothers and their families are certainly meeting the demands.

Acknowledgments

This research was supported by grants from the Thrasher Research Fund, Spencer Foundation, and California State Universities at Fullerton and Northridge. Deepest appreciation is extended to the families who participated in the longitudinal study. We thank Connie Meyer, Diana Guerin, Gigi Nordquist, and Pamela DiBello for their help in various aspects of this research.

REFERENCES

Achenbach, T. M., & Edelbrock, C. (1983). *Manual for the Child Behavior Checklist and Revised Child Behavior Profile*. Burlington, VT: University of Vermont Department of Psychiatry.

Achenbach, T. M., & Edelbrock, C. (1986). *Manual for the Teacher's Report Form and Teacher Version of the Child Behavior Profile*. Burlington, VT: University of Vermont Department of Psychiatry.

Baker, R. L., & Mednick, B. R. (1984). *Influences on human development: A longitudinal perspective*. Hingham, MA: Kluwer Academic Publishers.

Bates, J. E., Freeland, C. B., & Lounsbury, M. L. (1979). Measurement of infant difficulty. *Child Development, 50*, 794–803.

Bathurst, K., & Gottfried, A. W. (1987). Untestable subjects in child development research: Developmental implications. *Child Development, 58*, 1135–1144.

Bathurst, K., Gottfried, A. W., & Nordquist, G. (1987, April). *Confirmatory factor analysis of the Family Environment Scale using structural equation modeling*. Paper presented at the annual convention of the Western Psychological Association, Long Beach, CA.

Bayley, N. (1969). *Bayley Scales of Infant Development: Birth to two years.* New York: Psychological Corporation.
Behar, L., & Stringfield, S. (1974). *Preschool Behavior Questionnaire, scale and manual.* Durham: Learning Institute of North Carolina.
Bronfenbrenner, U. (1986). Ecology of the family as a context for human development: Research perspectives. *Developmental Psychology, 22,* 723–742.
Bronfenbrenner, U., & Crouter, A. C. (1982). Work and family through time and space. In S. B. Kamerman & C. D. Hayes (Eds.), *Families that work: Children in a changing world* (pp. 39–83). Washington, DC: National Academy Press.
Caldwell, B. M., Bradley, R. H. (1984). *HOME observation for measurement of the environment.* Little Rock, AR: University of Arkansas at Little Rock.
Cotterell, J. L. (1986). Work and community influences on the quality of child rearing. *Child Development, 57,* 362–374.
Fullard, W., McDevitt, S. C., & Carey, W. B. (1978). *Toddler Temperament Scale.* Unpublished manuscript, Temple University, Philadelphia.
Galinsky, E. (1985). *The Work and Family Life Questionnaire.* Bank Street College of Education, Unpublished manuscript.
Gottfried, A. E. (1985). Academic intrinsic motivation in elementary and junior high school students. *Journal of Educational Psychology, 77,* 631–645.
Gottfried, A. E. (1986). *Children's Academic Intrinsic Motivation Inventory.* Odessa, FL: Psychological Assessment Resources.
Gottfried, A. E., Gottfried, A. W., & Bathurst, K. (1985, August). *Maternal employment and children's development: A longitudinal study.* Paper presented at the annual convention of the American Psychological Association, Los Angeles.
Gottfried, A. E., Gottfried, A. W., & Bathurst, K. (1987, April). *Fathers' involvement, maternal employment, and young children's cognitive, academic, and social development.* Paper presented at the annual convention of the American Educational Research Association, Washington, DC.
Gottfried, A. E., Gottfried, A. W., & Guerin, D. (1986, April). *Environmental predictors of cognitive development and early school success: A longitudinal study.* Paper presented at the annual convention of the American Educational Research Association, San Francisco.
Gottfried, A. W. (Ed.) (1984). *Home environment and early cognitive development: Longitudinal research.* New York: Academic Press.
Gottfried, A. W. (1985). Measures of socioeconomic status in child development research: Data and recommendations. *Merrill-Palmer Quarterly, 32,* 85–92.
Gottfried, A. W., & Gilman, G. (1983). Development of visual skills in infants and young children, *Journal of the American Optometric Association, 54,* 541–544.
Gottfried, A. W., & Gottfried, A. E. (1984). Home environment and cognitive development in young children of middle-socioeconomic-status families. In A. W. Gottfried (Ed.), *Home environment and early cognitive development: Longitudinal research* (pp. 57–115). New York: Academic Press.
Gottfried, A. W., & Gottfried, A. E. (1986). Home environment and children's development from infancy through the school entry years: Results of contemporary longitudinal investigations in North America. *Children's Environments Quarterly, 3,* 3–9.
Hayghe, H. (1982). Dual-earner families: Their economic and demographic characteristics. In J. Aldous (Ed.), *Two paychecks: Life in dual-earner families* (pp. 27–40). Beverly Hills, CA: Sage.
Heyns, B. (1982). The influence of parents' work on children's school achievement. In S. B. Kamerman & C. D. Hayes (Eds.), *Families that work: Children in a changing world* (pp. 229–267). Washington, DC: National Academy Press.

Hoffman, L. W. (1984a). Maternal employment and the young child. In M. Perlmutter (Ed.), *Parent-child interaction and parent-child relations in child development: The Minnesota Symposia on Child Psychology, Vol. 17.* (pp. 101–127). Hillsdale, NJ: Lawrence Erlbaum.

Hoffman, L. W. (1984b). Work, family, and the socialization of the child. In R. D. Parke (Ed.), *Review of child development research, Vol. 7, The family* (pp. 223–282). Chicago: University of Chicago Press.

Hoffman, L. W. (1985, August). *Work, family, and the child.* Paper presented as part of the Master Lecture Series at the annual meeting of the American Psychological Association, Los Angeles.

Hollingshead, A. B. (1975). *Four factor index of social status.* Unpublished manuscript, Yale University (available from Department of Sociology).

Hresko, W. P., Reid, D. K., & Hammill, D. D. (1981). *The Test of Early Language Development.* Austin, TX: Pro-ed.

Jastak, J. F., & Jastak, S. (1984). *The Wide Range Achievement Test* (rev. ed.). Wilmington, DE: Jastak Associates.

Kaufman, A. S., & Kaufman, N. L. (1983). *Kaufman Assessment Battery for Children.* Circle Pines, MN: American Guidance Service.

Kohn, M., Parnes, B., & Rosman, B. L. (1979). *A rating and scoring manual for the Kohn Problem Checklist and Kohn Social Competence Scale* (rev. ed.). Unpublished manuscript, The William Alanson White Institute of Psychiatry, Psychoanalysis, and Psychology, New York, NY.

Lamb, M. E., & Sagi, A. (Eds.). (1983). *Fatherhood and family policy.* Hillsdale, NJ: Lawrence Erlbaum.

MacKinnon, C. E., Brody, G. H., & Stoneman, Z. (1982). The effects of divorce and maternal employment on the home environments of preschool children. *Child Development, 53,* 1392–1399.

Marjoribanks, K. (1979). *Families and their learning environments.* London: Routledge & Kegan Paul.

McCarthy, D. (1972). *McCarthy Scales of Children's Abilities.* New York: Psychological Corporation.

McDevitt, S. C., & Carey, W. B. (1975). *Behavior Style Questionnaire.* Unpublished manuscript, Temple University, Philadelphia.

Moos, R. H., & Moos, B. S. (1981). *Family Environment Scale manual.* Palo Alto, CA: Consulting Psychologists Press.

Pleck, J. H. (1985). *Working wives/working husbands.* Beverly Hills, CA: Sage.

Robinson, E. A., Eyberg, S. M., & Ross, A. W. (1980). The standardization of an inventory of child conduct problem behaviors. *Journal of Clinical Child Psychology, 9,* 22–28.

Shure, M. B., & Spivack, G. (1974). *The PIPS test manual.* Unpublished manuscript, Hahnemann Medical College and Hospital, Philadelphia.

Seginer, R. (1986). Mothers' behavior and sons' performance: An initial test of an academic achievement path model. *Merrill-Palmer Quarterly, 32,* 153–166.

Sparrow, S. S., Balla, D. A., & Cicchetti, D. V. (1984). *Vineland Adaptive Behavior Scales.* Circle Pines, MN: American Guidance Service.

Tabachnick, B. G., & Fidell, L. S. (1983). *Using multivariate statistics.* New York: Harper & Row.

Wachs, T. D. (1976). *Purdue Home Stimulation Inventories* (Sections I, II, and III). Unpublished manual, Purdue University.

Wechsler, D. (1974). *Manual for the Wechsler Intelligence Scale for Children-Revised.* New York: Psychological Corporation.

3

The Influences of Maternal Employment across Life
The New York Longitudinal Study

Jacqueline V. Lerner and Nancy L. Galambos

I. INTRODUCTION

The fact that the majority of mothers will enter or return to the work force shortly after the birth of their child is not a new phenomenon. Today, nearly half of the mothers of infants are employed and are expected to remain employed throughout their child's life (Hayghe, 1986). The increase in maternal employment has been evident for the past two decades and has been coupled with an increasing concern over how maternal employment affects the lives and development of children. Although researchers to date conclude that the effects of maternal employment on children need to be studied longitudinally, the existence of long-term studies is rare. The New York Longitudinal Study (NYLS) is a 30-year-old study of the development of 133 white, middle- to upper-middle-class children. Although the focus of the NYLS was not on maternal employment *per se*, extensive information exists on the mother's employment history and child development outcomes. Thus we are able

---

Jacqueline V. Lerner • College of Human Development, Pennsylvania State University, University Park, Pennsylvania 16802. **Nancy L. Galambos** • Department of Psychology, University of Victoria, Victoria, British Columbia, Canada V8W 2Y2.

to look at the influences of the mother's employment on selected aspects of her child's development from infancy through young adulthood.

In this chapter, we will first present descriptive information on the NYLS regarding sample characteristics, type of data available, and the historical period during which the data were collected. Second, we will present findings from three age periods—childhood (ages 3–5), adolescence (14–18), and early adulthood (19–22). Finally, we will summarize our findings and discuss directions for future research.

II. THE NEW YORK LONGITUDINAL STUDY (NYLS)

The NYLS was begun in 1956 by Alexander Thomas and Stella Chess (Thomas & Chess, 1977, 1980; Thomas, Chess, & Birch, 1968). The major sample is composed of 133 children (66 males, 67 females). The families of this sample are of middle- to upper-middle-class backgrounds and are 78% Jewish, 7% Catholic, and 15% Protestant, with 40% of the mothers and 60% of the fathers having both college educations and postgraduate degrees. Demographic characteristics of the sample are presented in Table 1. Although twice as many employed as nonemployed mothers hold postgraduate degrees, another recent study with this sample, revealed that the mother's educational level did not explain a significant proportion of variance in labor force participation rates (Galambos & Lerner, 1987).

The prestige of the father's occupations is high, with most fathers holding highly prestigious jobs (e.g., medical doctors, university professors). In turn, there is considerable homogeneity in the socioeconomic status of the total sample (middle to upper middle class). It is likely, therefore, that the employed mothers were employed for reasons of personal fulfillment rather than economic need. We are aware of the fact that homogeneity of the sample limits the generalizability of the results to other groups of lower SES, where many mothers may be employed for economic reasons. However, all major, long-term longitudinal studies in the United States have nonrepresentative samples (e.g., the Berkeley/Oakland data sets, the Fels data set), and, although sampling bias may impose limitations in making generalizations about mean levels or possibly, variability, it does not necessarily constrain generalizations about structural patterns within or across time (Jessor, 1982). In this regard, Eichorn (1984) indicated that no finding derived from a major longitudinal study has been concluded to be incorrect on the basis of subsequent cross-sectional research with more representative samples.

Table 1. Demographic Characteristics of the NYLS Sample

Gender	Females = 67
	Males = 66
Socioeconomic status	Middle to upper middle class
Ethnicity	78% Jewish
	7% Catholic
	15% Protestant
Mean age of mothers at birth of target child	31.6 years
Mean age of fathers at birth of target child	36.4 years
Mean prestige scores for father's occupation when child was 3 years old	65 (range = 20–82)[a]
Mean prestige scores for mothers who were employed when their child was age 3	58 (range = 20–82)[a]
Father's educational level when child was age 3	100%—high school degree
	40%—college degree
	60%—postgraduate degree
Mother's educational level when child was age 3	100%—high school degree
	44%—college degree
	36%—postgraduate degree
Marital status when child was age 3	98%—nonemployed mothers—married
	84%—employed mothers—married
Mother's employment status when child was age 1	24%—employed (17% part-time)
	(7% full-time)
Employment status when child was age 3	36%—employed (25% part-time)
	(11% full-time)
Mother's employment status when child was age 5	42%—employed (30% part-time)
	(12% full-time)
Mother's employment status when child was between ages 6–16	65%—employed (28% part-time)
	(37% full-time)

[a] Occupational prestige scores based on those of the National Opinion Research Center (NORC) rankings (Davis, 1980).

As detailed before, the NYLS sample is a very homogeneous one. Most of the parents had attained a high level of education and were in very prestigious occupations. In addition, the historical era of the late 1950s and early 1960s was unlike that of today with respect to maternal employment. The employment of mothers of infants and preschoolers was far from the norm; indeed, it was rather rare for a mother to resume work soon after the birth of her child. However, 38% of the mothers of the sample children resumed work within the first 3 years of their child's life, many doing so in the first and second years. In some respects, these mothers are like many middle-class mothers today—they pursue a higher education, hold high-status jobs, and resume work soon after their child is born. On the other hand, the social atmosphere and attitudes toward employed mothers has changed significantly over the last two decades—employed mothers are accepted much more today than they were 30 years ago. So, although the NYLS sample mothers may be similar in some respects to the middle-class mothers of today, the differences in social and individual attitudes of the two eras may indeed represent different sources of influence on the mothers and their children. We feel that it is important to keep these issues in mind when interpreting and generalizing the results of our analyses.

III. THE NYLS DATA SET

A. Childhood Ratings

A longitudinal study that has extended over the course of more than a quarter of a century has a considerable amount of data. We will discuss those data that are pertinent to the present chapter. Upon entry into the study, demographic information about the parents and family was obtained. This information included the educational and employment history and status of the parents, the structure of the family, and the type of residence wherein the family resided. Families, recruited into the study during the end of pregnancy or shortly after the birth of the child, also made available the mother's obstetrical history (e.g., complications during pregnancy), birth information (e.g., use of medications), and neonatal information (e.g., weight and length).

Because the NYLS was begun as a study of temperament, or behavioral style, detailed measures exist on each child's temperamental attributes, as well as whether they were considered to be "easy" or "difficult." Temperament, as defined by Thomas and Chess (1977) is the *how* of behavior; not *what* a person does, but how he or she goes about doing it. The nine attributes of temperament conceptualized by Thomas and Chess are activity level—level, tempo, and frequency of motor behavior present in a person's functioning; rhythmicity—degree of regularity in biological functions such as eating, sleeping, and elimination; approach/withdrawal—the person's initial reaction to any new stimulus such as food, people, places, toys, or routines; adaptability—the sequential course of responses a child makes to new or altered situations; intensity of reaction—the energy content of a response irrespective of its direction; threshold of responsiveness—the level of extrinsic stimulation that is necessary to evoke a response; quality of mood—the amount of pleasant, joyful, friendly behavior as contrasted with unpleasant, crying, unfriendly behavior; distractibility—the effectiveness of extraneous environmental stimuli interfering with, or altering, the direction of an ongoing behavior; and, attention span and persistence—attention span refers to the length of time a particular activity is pursued; persistence refers to the person's maintenance of an activity in the face of obstacles to its continuation.

In the NYLS sample, some of the attributes tended to cluster in some of the children. For example, the attributes of low rhythmicity, negative mood, slow adaptability, high intensity of response, and frequent withdrawal responses tended to go together in some children. These children tended to have difficulty in interactions, had adjustment problems, and thus were labeled as *difficult* children. On the other hand, *easy* children had a temperamental constellation characterized by high rhythmicity, high adaptability, positive mood, frequent approach behaviors, and moderate intensity of responses. These children were labeled as *easy* because caring for them and interacting with them involved fewer problems than did interacting with difficult children. These children were also found to be better adjusted in childhood than were difficult children.

Starting in the first few months of life, parents were interviewed periodically (e.g., every 3 months in the child's first year of life) about the child's behaviors in numerous content areas (e.g., sleep, feeding, bathing, toileting, mobility, social responsibility, and sensory functioning). Along with their responses to this interview, the parents' responses were elicited to questions pertaining to responsibilities for the daily care of the baby and to details of daily living. As the child became older, data collection was expanded to include the other contexts within which the child interacted. These interviews were open-ended and probed several areas of the child's functioning. As the child grew older, the open-ended interviews were supplemented by short checklists on which parents rated the problem behaviors of their children. As a child entered nursery school or elementary school, detailed teacher interviews were conducted about the adaptation and overall functioning of the child, and classroom observations of the child were made; both interviews and observations were conducted throughout the school years. As was done with the parents, the teacher interviews were open-ended and were supplemented with checklists regarding the child's behavior at school. The same questionnaires and interviews were used with all subjects' parents and teachers. In addition, psychometric measures (e.g., IQ tests such as the Stanford-Binet and the WISC) of cognitive functioning, standardized achievement test scores (e.g., California Achievement

Test, Iowa Test of Basic Skills), and school grades were also obtained throughout the school years.

The range of data obtained from these parent interviews in the child's early years has made it possible to develop rating schedules for the child's overall behavioral adjustment. Ratings of problem behaviors on a 5-point scale in 11 areas were obtained at ages three and five. They are sleep (i.e., rituals, night waking, nightmares); eating (i.e., spitting food, disruptive at table, finicky); elimination (i.e., enuresis and encopresis, withholding); sex (i.e., masturbation, sex preferences); fears, tics, and rituals (i.e., expresses fears of animals, people, exhibits tics, turns routines into rituals); speech and communication (i.e., talks excessively, incoherent speech, immature speech); motor activity (i.e., clumsy, poor fine motor activity); relationship with parents (i.e., clings to parents, makes unnecessary demands, prefers one parent to other); discipline (i.e., rude, talks back, tantrums, disobedient, and noncompliant); relationships with sibs (i.e., quarrels with and hurts sib(s), preoccupied with sib(s); and nonfamily relationships (i.e., timid with other adults, too friendly with strangers, fights with peers). Two other categories were added to the 5-year interview: relationship to school (i.e., resists entering classroom, disobeys teacher) and coping and task mastery (i.e., negative, withdraws from tasks when frustrated, acts out when frustrated). A similar rating scale, with appropriate modifications, was developed for the 5-year teacher interview. For the 3-year parent data, interrater reliability ranged from .64 to .94 on the 11 categories, except for .32 for coping. For the 5-year parent and teacher data, the reliabilities were significantly higher, all being above .88. Global adjustment scores were then calculated by adding up the scores for each category and dividing by the number of categories.

When the children were approximately 3 years of age, 100 of the mothers and 93 of the fathers were interviewed about their child care practices, parental attitudes, parental and spouse roles, and the effects of the child on them as individuals and as a family. Each parent was interviewed independently by two interviewers who had no prior information about the family. All interviews were audiotaped. The interview obtained information pertinent to parental permissiveness, consistency of rules, and discipline strategies. This interview also assessed parental warmth for and approval of the child. In addition, questions about the marital relationship, attitudes toward the spouse, and attitudes toward the parental role were included. Finally, as a means to obtain additional data relevant to the effects of the child on the family context, the parents were questioned about their expectations for the child as well as the concrete effects the child was seen to have had on the family milieu.

B. Adolescent Ratings

When the subjects were 16 to 17 years old, semistructured open-ended interviews were conducted with 107 subjects. This interview covered such areas as self-evaluation (subject asked to evaluate himself/herself), medical history (significant medical events that occurred since last interview, health status), life goals (plans for future, career, goals, long-term plans), immediate goals (plans for the near future), daily routines (day-to-day routines, habits), biological functions (daily habits in waking, eating), athletic activity (participation in sports in or out of school), special interests or hobbies (pursuits not academically related), relations with family, school, work (how subject gets along with people in these contexts), social and sexual functioning (problems with same- or opposite-sexed peers in social or sexual situations), expressiveness and communication (ability to relate to and communicate with others), adaptive patterns (patterns of coping with daily life), substance use (use of tobacco, alcohol, marijuana, or hard drugs), psychological and psychosomatic symptoms (presence of psychological or psychosomatic problems). Primarily, those not interviewed were from the youngest age group of the sample. The same interview protocol was used for separate interviews with the parents.

Because of the limitation of resources at the time, a number of the adolescent interviews were time-limited and the data relatively skimpy, as compared with the interviews obtained later in early adulthood. For this reason, ratings from the adolescent protocols were based on a combination of the subject and parent interviews. Global adaptation scores were derived by averaging all areas; interrater reliability was .85. The interview data were adequate for rating temperament in 85 of the 107 subject–parent interviews. Interrater reliability ranged from .14 for intensity to .82 for approach/withdrawal. For the other three categories comprising the easy/difficult constellation, interrater reliability was .70 for rhythmicity, .47 for adaptability, and .76 for quality of mood. Difficult temperament scores were calculated for the adolescent period (DIFADOL). Also obtained was a clinical problem score (CLIN15) indicating whether the subject had received a clinical psychiatric diagnosis by age 15.

C. Early Adult Ratings

Out of the total sample of 133 original subjects, 132 were interviewed at 18 to 22 years. In approximately 60% of the cases, there was one interviewer; in the other 40%, there were two interviewers, each of whom made independent ratings. Of the 132 subject interviews, 50 were rated by three raters, 29 by two, and 53 by one.

The early-adult interviews were open-ended and covered in detail the same areas as did the adolescent interview: self-evaluation, medical history, life goals, immediate goals, daily routines, biological functions, athletics, special interests and hobbies, relations with family, school, and work, social and sexual functioning, expressiveness and communication, adaptive patterns, substance use and psychological and psychosomatic symptoms.

Each rater scored the subjects for each of these areas on a 7-point scale, ranging from excellent to poor. An overall global adaptation score on a 9-point scale and ratings for each of our nine temperament categories on a 7-point scale were also obtained from the interview data. Psychiatric diagnoses where indicated were also made by each rater. Interrater reliabilities for the global adaptation scores were high, ranging from .82 to .87. For the dimensions of temperament, the reliabilities were lower, being above .60 in only four categories. Difficult temperament scores were calculated for the early adult period (DIFADULT). A clinical psychiatric score for adulthood (CLINADUL) was also used.

D. Maternal Variables

This section will detail the various measures we have obtained that pertain to the mother and her job (if she was employed). These variables were maternal role satisfaction; satisfaction with husband's contributions to the household; whether or not the mother's job accommodates her parental role; maternal role strain; and maternal employment status (nonworking, full-time, part-time) for each of the child's first 5 years. In addition, the mother's educational level was also coded. With the exception of maternal employment status, all of these variables were coded from the interviews conducted with the mothers when their children were 3 years old. Trained raters listened to audiotapes in order to make these assessments. Interrater reliabilities were obtained for 20% of the sample and ranged from .88 to 1.00. Maternal employment status was retrieved from the interviews conducted regularly throughout the child's life and from the 3-year parent interview. The definitions of the variables we coded follow.

1. Maternal Role Satisfaction

This measure refers to the mother's feelings about being an employed or nonemployed mother. Responses ranged from 1 = *very negative* to 5 = *very positive*.

2. Satisfaction with Husband's Contributions

Mothers were also asked how satisfied they were with their husband's contributions to houshold help and child care. Again, responses were rated on a 5-point scale with 1 = *very dissatisfied* to 5 = *very satisfied*.

3. Accommodation of Job

If the mother was employed, an inquiry was made as to how accommodating her job was to her parental role; that is, was it possible to rearrange her work hours around the needs of the child? Responses ranged from 1 = *not accommodating* to 3 = *very accommodating*.

4. Maternal Role Strain

Although this was not directly probed in the interviews, it was possible to rate each employed mother with respect to the amount of role strain she seemed to be experiencing. That is, audiotapes were reviewed in order to rate how much strain resulted from balancing the demands of work and family life. Ratings were coded as 1 = *significant role strain*, 2 = *moderate role strain*, and 3 = *no apparent role strain*.

5. Maternal Employment Status

Mother's work status was coded from interviews with the mother for each of the first 5 years of the child's life. A rating scale of 0, 1, or 2 represents nonworking, part-time (5–29 hours a week), or full-time (30 or more hours a week), respectively.

6. Mother's Education

Mother's educational level was rated on a 5-point scale as follows: 1 = high school graduate, 2 = some college or technical school, 3 = college graduate, 4 = some graduate school (MA, MS, or equivalent), and 5 = advanced graduate degree (PhD, MD, law degree).

E. Contextual Variables

In addition to mother and child variables, it was possible to obtain measures of several other aspects of the context that were relevant for the model we were testing. These variables were amount of help with housework and child care, father's attitudes about the mother's role, and the number of children in the family under 6 years of age. These variables were also coded from the 3-year interview.

1. Amount of Help with Housework and Child Care

The amount of outside help that the mother received with housework and child care was coded on a 4-point scale as follows: 1 = *no help*, 2 = *part-time days*, 3 = *full-time days*, and 4 = *lives in home*. These ratings were made for help with housework and child care separately.

2. Father's Attitudes about Mother's Work

Father's attitudes toward his wife's working or not was rated on a 5-point scale from 1 = *very negative* to 5 = *very positive*. It should be noted that these attitudes were based on the mother's reports.

3. Number of Children under Age 6

Because the number of young children in the family was thought to be a contribution to role strain, it was of interest to us. We noted how many children were under the age of 6 when the sample child was age 3 (at the time of the parent interview).

F. Mother–Child Interaction Variables

The focused interview, as noted previously, was administered when the sample children were approximately 3 years old and covered a variety of parenting-related topics such as degree of parental conflict, degree of warmth, protectiveness, and permissiveness directed toward the child, and the degree and forms of discipline. A rater from the original NYLS research team (Thomas & Chess, 1977) coded each set of parents on a wide variety of such variables and obtained 99 items of information. Cameron (1977) selected 70 items that met statistical criteria for use in correlation analyses. Only mother's responses were used because, in the majority of cases, both parents provided identical responses. These 70 items were then subjected to a cluster analysis using the Tryon (Tryon & Baily, 1966) system. Eight oblique parental clusters resulted from the 70-item matrix. We chose three of these clusters that seemed to us to be the most directly relevant to mother–child interaction to use in our analyses. They were (a) parental disapproval, intolerance, and rejection, with high scores indicating high intolerance and little feeling for the child; (b) the degree of restrictiveness and strictness of discipline when dealing with the child; and (c) inconsistent discipline reflecting the relationship between the frequency of disciplinary issues in a home and the number of conflicts that arise around discipline. We labeled these three clusters *maternal rejection, limit setting,* and *inconsistent disciplinary style.*

IV. APPROACH TO DATA ANALYSIS—THE "PROCESS OF INFLUENCE" MODEL

Our goal in data analysis was to identify relevant and timely research questions that could be approached with our data. Recent empirical work seemed to be striving toward an illumination of the processes by which child development is influenced by maternal employment. A key component of one developmental process that has been emphasized in recent years is the mediating variable of maternal role satisfaction. Recent evidence suggests that the mother's role satisfaction may be more important than working or not working *per se* (Hock, 1978, 1980); however, the studies that suggest the importance of this variable fail to specify and document the overall developmental process of influence by which maternal employment operates to affect child development. Some studies link role satisfaction directly to child development outcomes (Farel, 1980; Hock, 1978, 1980; Hoffman, 1963a; Williamson, 1970; Woods, 1972), whereas others link role satisfaction to parental functioning (Stuckey, McGhee, & Bell, 1982; Yarrow, Scott, DeLeeuw, & Heinig, 1962). Yet only one, to our knowledge, attempts to empirically tie these pieces together. We (Lerner & Galambos, 1985) have made a preliminary attempt to do this, using the data from the NYLS. We have investigated how maternal role satisfaction influences parent–child interaction and how this, in turn, influences child development.

Our view with respect to what types of parent–child interactions are optimal is consistent with those of other researchers. Berndt (1983), for example, notes that the parental characteristics of warmth and acceptance (as opposed to hostility and rejection), firm but not excessive control, disciplinary techniques based on reasoning rather than force, and verbal interaction designed to stimulate a child's cognitive development are viewed as defining good parent–child relationships in most psychological writings.

It is our belief that parent–child interaction, or specifically, mother–child interaction, is influenced directly by the mother's overall feelings and satisfaction with her roles. In turn, we believe that variables from

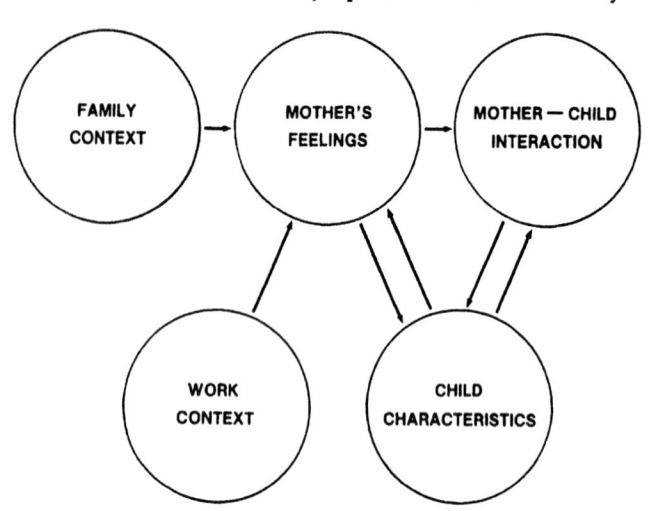

Figure 1. A general model of maternal employment in context.

the mother's family and work context will influence her satisfaction with her role and her attitudes regarding employment. A simplified illustration of this general model of viewing maternal employment in context is represented in Figure 1. An important feature of this model is that of the bidirectional effects that can occur between mother's attitudes and child characteristics and between mother–child interaction and child characteristics. That is, a mother's attitudes, values, and satisfaction can both influence and be influenced by her child's characteristics; in the same way, the quality of mother–child interactions can both influence and be influenced by her child's characteristics.

We have been able to test a part of this model using maternal role satisfaction; mother–child interaction characteristics such as rejection, inconsistent disciplinary style and limit setting; and the child's characteristic of "difficult" temperament. The results of this investigation (Lerner & Galambos, 1985) are described in detail later and support the notion that role satisfaction is indeed an important mediator variable in the process linking mother's satisfaction and child outcomes. Before we present the results of the "process" analysis, we will summarize the results that looked at "direct" effects: Does employment status discriminate among the children?

A. Direct Effects: Analyses and Results for the First 5 Years

During the child's first 5 years of life, mothers could have worked part-time, full-time, or both. Maternal employment was assessed during each year. For the first 5 years, 24% of the mothers were employed full- or part-time during the first year, 30% during the second year, 36% during the third year, 39% during the fourth year, and 42% during the child's fifth year.

To examine if there were differences among the maternal and child variables outlined here for part-time versus full-time versus nonemployed mothers, mothers also received a comprehensive work score to indicate the "degree" (ranges from 0 = *did not work at all*, to 2 = *always worked full-time*) of her employment status for the first 3 years and first 5 years of the child's life. The child outcome variables of interest for these analyses are listed in Table 2 along with the means and standard deviations for these variables. Table 3 lists the maternal and contextual variables used in the analyses with their means and standard deviations.

Our first step in data analysis was to look at various direct effects of maternal employment. Although we have argued here that a focus on "direct" effects alone ignores the influences of possible important "mediating" variables, we used it as a first step for comparison with other studies.

Multivariate analyses of variance with the independent variable of comprehensive employment status at ages 3 and 5 (ranging from *did not work at all* to *always worked full-time*) and the mother–child interaction variables of maternal rejection, limit setting, and inconsistency as dependent variables indicated no significant differences for the total sample [$L = .96$, $F(3,101) = 1.44$, $p > .23$], and there was no effect for sex [$L = .96$, $F(3,101) = 1.12$, $p > .34$]. When the age 3 and 5 adjustment variables presented in Table 2 were used in the MANOVA as the set of dependent variables, again no significant differences emerged for employment status using the total sample [$L = .95$, $F(3,88) = 1.36$, $p > .25$] and no sex effect [$L = .97$, $F(3,88) = .87$, $p > .46$]. When the difficult child scores for ages 3, 4, and 5 were used as the dependent variables, a significant employment effect was found, indicating that mothers who had scored higher on the comprehensive employment status score had temperamentally "easier" children ($L = .84$, $F(3,86 = 5.29$, $p < .002$). Scoring higher on the comprehensive employment score means that overall, for the years summed, mothers worked more hours. It does not necessarily mean that a high score indicates that the mother always worked full-time. Again, no sex differences emerged in this analysis [$L = .95$, $F(3,86) = 1.44$, $p > .23$], nor were there significant interactions.

Therefore, when we look at the direct effects of maternal employment in the NYLS sample, we find that the children of employed and nonemployed mothers do not differ on the various child adjustment measures except for the easy/difficulty temperament measure.

Table 2. Means and Standard Deviations for Child Outcome Variables

Variable	Mean	Standard deviation
Age 3[a]		
Sleep	1.9	.21
Eating	1.8	.19
Elimination	2.4	.30
Sex	1.2	.17
Fears, tics, rituals	1.6	.20
Speech and communication	1.3	.16
Motor activity	1.2	.14
Relationship with parents	1.7	.20
Discipline	1.8	.21
Relationships with sibs	1.9	.19
Nonfamily relationships	1.7	.18
IQ	123.11	16.13
Difficult child rating age 3	1.79	.95
Difficult child rating age 4	1.30	.76
Difficult child rating age 5	1.26	1.05
Age 5[b]		
Sleep	1.1	.14
Eating	1.3	.17
Elimination	1.2	.16
Sex	1.4	.15
Fears, tics, rituals	1.6	.19
Speech and communication	1.6	.20
Motor activity	1.4	.21
Relationship with parents	1.3	.21
Relationships with sibs	1.2	.17
Nonfamily relationships	1.3	.18
Relationship to school	1.6	.19
Coping and task mastery	1.8	.17

[a] Variables sleep through nonfamily relationships coded on a 1–5 point scale with 1 = *no problems* and 5 = *significant problems*; difficult child score = high score is more difficult, range = 0–8.
[b] All variables coded on a 1–5 point scale with 1 = *no problems* to 5 = *significant problems*.

In terms of IQ scores at ages 3 and 6 and achievement scores for grades 1 through 6, a MANOVA indicated that again, the children did not differ on these measures when grouped by employment status (comprehensive score at ages 3 and 5) [$L = .96$, $F(3,86) = 1.21$, $p > .23$]. Thus, except when we look at temperament, our findings concur with those of some other studies that report no differences between employed and nonemployed groups (Brookhart & Hock, 1976; Farran & Ramey, 1977; Maccoby & Feldman, 1972; Rubenstein, Howes, & Boyle, 1981;

Table 3. Means and Standard Deviations for Maternal and Contextual Variables

Variable	Mean	Standard deviation
Maternal role satisfaction	3.8	.80
Satisfaction with husband's contributions	4.2	.76
Accommodation of job (employed mothers only)	2.05	.69
Maternal role strain	2.6	.66
Mother's education	3.96	1.11
Father's attitudes about mother's work	4.0	.98
Maternal rejection	49.5	9.32
Limit setting	50.21	7.41
Inconsistent disciplinary style	50.49	8.92

Schacter, 1981). What can we conclude about our finding that temperamentally "easy" children were more likely to have mothers who were employed? It would be plausible to contend that the mothers of "difficult" children might work more because of the problems and stress experienced in the parent–child relationship—the mother may look for refuge in employment. On the other hand, based on our finding, we may propose that "easy" children allow mothers to return to work because they adjust easily to alternative care arrangements and are pleasant and predictable; they thus make the mother's role easier and probably allow her to feel she is doing the right thing.

We can say further that because of the mother's perception of the child's "easiness," her role satisfaction and personal fulfillment may be increased, and, along the lines of our argument for a "process of influence" model, we may contend that these increases lead to more optimal child outcomes. We will examine this proposition later through the use of path analysis when we directly test our proposed "process of influence" model.

B. Relationships among Contextual, Maternal, Mother–Child Interaction, and Child Variables

Our next step in data analysis was to examine the relationships among the various maternal, contextual, child, and mother–child interaction variables through the use of a series of stepwise multiple regression analyses. The results of these analyses are detailed in Table 4. No significant relationships were found when contextual variables such as amount of help with housework and child care, father's attitudes

Table 4. Multiple Regression Results

Dependent variable	Predictors	R	R^2	p
Global adjustment, age 3	Household help Flexibility of job Childcare help Father's attitudes Maternal employment, age 3 (comprehensive score), $N = 91$	.157	.02	NS
Global adjustment, age 5	Household help Flexibility of job Childcare help Father's attitudes Maternal employment, age 5 (comprehensive score), $N = 91$	.344	.118	NS
Role strain	Household help** Flexibility of job** Number of children** under age 6, $N = 87$	.45	.20	<.002
Maternal rejection	Father's attitudes* Mother's role satisfaction,* $N = 93$	.39	.15	<.02
Limit setting	Mother's role strain* Father's attitudes,* $N = 87$	.43	.18	<.001
Global adjustment, age 3	Mother's role satisfaction Maternal rejection Limit setting Father's attitudes Mother's employment status—age 3 (comprehensive score) Mother's employment status—age 5 (comprehensive score) $N = 88$	.06	.003	NS
Child difficulty, age 3	Mother's employment** status—age 3 (comprehensive score) Mother's employment** status—age 5 (comprehensive score), $N = 84$	.63	.39	<.001
Child difficulty, age 4	Mother's role* satisfaction Mother's employment** status—age 3 (comprehensive score) Maternal rejection,* $N = 87$	.53	.28	<.001

[a] NS = not statistically significant.
* = $p < .05$. ** = $p < .01$.

about the mother's role, and the number of children in the family under 6 years of age were used to predict the child outcome variables of global adjustment at aged 3 and 5 and difficult temperament at ages 3, 4, and 5. Sex of subject was used as a predictor, but no significant effects emerged.

Several significant relationships were obtained, however, when we used contextual variables to predict maternal variables, when we used contextual and maternal variables to predict mother–child interactions, and when we used maternal and mother–child interaction variables to predict child outcomes.

We have noted before that maternal role strain is of considerable interest for us because of its possible influence on role satisfaction and parenting variables, which, according to the "process" model detailed here, may further influence child outcomes. For the employed mother, role strain may arise from the duties that she must perform at home, including child care and household work, in addition to the hours that she spends in paid employment away from home.

We sought to explore the relationships among the contextual variables of help with household work and child care, number of young children present, whether the mother's job accommodates her parenting role, and role strain. Because ratings of role strain were obtained only for employed mothers, our sample size for these analyses was 48. Specifically, we used the contextual variables to predict role strain and found that the combination of three of them significantly predicted role strain—help with housework, whether or not her job was accommodating to the mother's parental role, and the number of children in the family under age 6. These variables accounted for a significant proportion of the variance in role strain ($R^2 = .20$, $p < .002$). Those employed mothers who had the most outside help with their housework, had jobs that best accommodated their parental roles, and had the fewest number of children under age 6 showed the least amount of role strain. This finding is consistent with our view that specific contextual factors may influence the mother's feelings—in this case, her perceived role strain. However, role strain was not directly related to any of the child outcome measures.

In the prediction of mother–child interaction variables, several contextual and maternal variables accounted for significant proportions of the variance. Fathers' attitudes about mothers' role and mothers' role satisfaction accounted for 15% of the variance ($p < .02$) in maternal rejection. That is, mothers felt that when fathers were not positive about the mothers' roles and when mothers were not satisfied with their roles, higher amounts of maternal rejection of the children were present for the total sample. In addition, role strain and fathers' attitudes about mothers' roles accounted for 18% of the variance ($p < .01$) in the parenting variable of limit setting. That is, for the employed mother sample, high role strain and negative feelings by the father with regard to the mother's role were associated with higher amounts of limit setting on the child.

In a final set of multiple regression analyses, we used mother's role satisfaction, maternal rejection, limit setting, father's attitudes about mother's role, and mother's comprehensive work status scores (at ages 3 and 5) to predict the child outcomes of global home and school adjustment at ages 3 and 5, and difficult temperament at ages 3, 4, and 5. Again, global adjustment scores were not significantly predicted by any of the variables. Consistent with our other findings of direct effects, child difficulty at ages 3, 4, and 5 was significantly predicted by some of the maternal, contextual, and mother–child interaction variables.

Specifically, 39% of the variance ($p < .001$) in child difficulty at age 3 was accounted for by mother's comprehensive work score at age 3, a result consistent with our finding that mothers of "easy" children work more; in addition, age-3 difficulty was predicted by maternal rejection (higher rejection was related to higher difficulty scores). Second, 28% of the variance ($p < .001$) in child difficulty at age 4 was accounted for by mother's role satisfaction (higher satisfaction was related to less difficulty), mother's comprehensive work score at age 3 (again, mothers who worked more up to age 3 had easier children at age 4, and maternal rejection (higher amounts of rejection were associated with higher difficulty scores at age 4). Inconsistent disciplinary style did not significantly contribute to the prediction of child outcomes.

These results support our ideas about the importance of addressing the child's context when exploring the relationship between maternal employment and child outcomes. That is, our results are consistent with our prediction and the findings of other studies that maternal employment status *per se* is not linked to child outcomes. However, what is linked to child outcomes is both maternal role satisfaction and mother–child interaction (maternal rejection). Although significant relationships were found through the use of multiple regression analyses, these analyses were unable to take complete advantage of the longitudinal nature of the data and to allow for an adequate test of the "process of influence" model of maternal role satisfaction—mother–child interaction—child outcome.

C. Testing the "Process of Influence" Model

To test this proposed "process of influence" model, we investigated, through the use of path analytic models, the relationships among early child difficulty (age 2), maternal role satisfaction, mother–child interaction, and later child difficulty. Because of the longitudinal nature of the data set, this analysis was able to include an early measure of child difficulty (age 2) in order to investigate the effect that the child's early temperament may have on the mother's role satisfaction and on later child difficulty (age 4). The inclusion of this "difficulty" measure at age 2 was to investigate the possible bidirectional effects of child on mother and mother on child. This issue was raised earlier with respect to the notion that the mother's satisfaction influences her interactions with her child and her child's subsequent adjustment and that the child (in this case, his or her "difficulty") can exert an equally strong influence upon the mother's satisfaction. Maternal role satisfaction was only measured at age 3, because it was derived from the detailed parental interviews.

It was hypothesized that a stronger relationship would exist for the indirect path—from role satisfaction—mother–child interaction—child difficulty (age 4)—than for the direct paths—of child difficulty (age 2)—child difficulty (age 4); role satisfaction—child difficulty; early child difficulty—role satisfaction; or early child difficulty—mother–child interaction.

A path analytic model was tested that included the direct paths from child difficulty (age 2)—role satisfaction; child difficulty (age 2)—child difficulty (age 4); role satisfaction (age 3)—child difficulty (age 4); and child difficulty (age 2)—mother–child interaction (age 3); the tested model included, too, the indirect path of role satisfaction (age 3)—child difficulty (age 4). Consistent with the hypothesis, for the total sample, the direct paths were insignificant, but the indirect path of role satisfaction—mother–child interaction—child difficulty was significant. Figure 2 presents the models for the total sample, for the nonemployed mother sample, and for the employed mother sample with their respective path coefficients and significance levels. As seen in the figure, neither early child difficulty nor mother's role satisfaction was significantly related to later child difficulty; nor was early child difficulty related to role satisfaction or mother–child interaction. However, role satisfaction was significantly related to maternal rejection, and maternal rejection was significantly related to later child difficulty. When the nonemployed mother group and the employed mother groups were tested separately, the same trends emerged; however, in the nonemployed sample, only the path coefficient from role satisfaction to mother–child interaction reached significance, and in the employed sample only the path coefficient from mother–child interaction to child difficulty (age 4) reached significance. In each case, however, the coefficients for the indirect path were greater than any of the coefficients

TOTAL SAMPLE (N = 89)

CHILD DIFFICULTY (Age 2) —-.08→ ROLE SATISFACTION (Age 3) —-.31**→ MATERNAL REJECTION (Age 3)

.12 (curved top arrow from Child Difficulty Age 2 to Maternal Rejection Age 3)

.17 → CHILD DIFFICULTY (Age 4); -.09 from Role Satisfaction to Child Difficulty (Age 4); .25* from Maternal Rejection to Child Difficulty (Age 4)

EMPLOYED MOTHER SAMPLE (N = 38)

CHILD DIFFICULTY (Age 2) —-.04→ ROLE SATISFACTION (Age 3) —-.23→ MATERNAL REJECTION (Age 3)

.14 (curved top arrow)

.19 → CHILD DIFFICULTY (Age 4); -.04 from Role Satisfaction; .31* from Maternal Rejection

NONEMPLOYED MOTHER SAMPLE (N = 51)

CHILD DIFFICULTY (Age 2) —.00→ ROLE SATISFACTION (Age 3) —-.41**→ MATERNAL REJECTION (Age 3)

.16 (curved top arrow)

.13 → CHILD DIFFICULTY (Age 4); -.15 from Role Satisfaction; .17 from Maternal Rejection

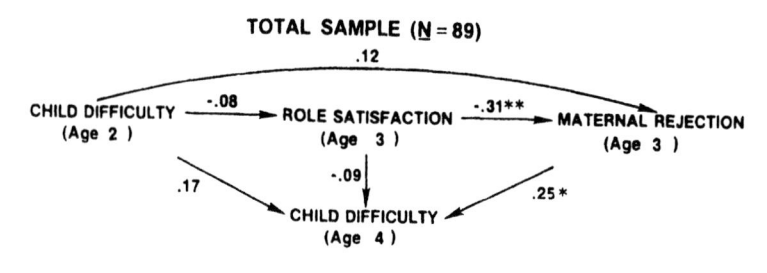

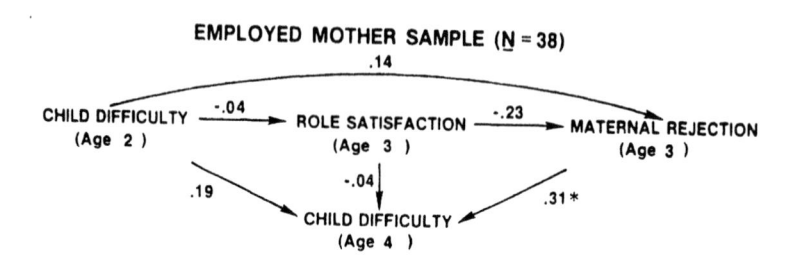

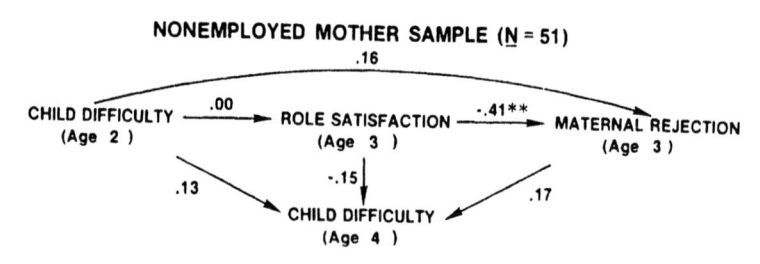

Figure 2. Direct and indirect relationships between maternal role satisfaction, mother–child interaction, and child difficulty.

for the direct paths, indicating that the smaller sample sizes may have caused these coefficients to be insignificant.

These results support the notion that the relationship between maternal role satisfaction and child outcomes may be mediated by a third factor—that of mother–child interaction. Recently researchers (Hock, 1980; Hoffman, 1980; Zaslow, Rabinovich, & Suwalsky, 1983) have speculated that the reason satisfied mothers have children with higher adjustment scores may be because role satisfaction leads to more positive parent–child interaction that, in turn, enhances child development. Our analyses of the NYLS data demonstrate that neither early child difficulty

Table 5. Correlations between Mother's Work History and Adolescent and Early Adulthood Outcome Variables[a]

Variable	Work age 0–1	Work age 1.1–5	Work age 5.1–16
DIFADOL	−0.133 (85) NS	−0.05 (85) NS	−0.04 (85) NS
DIFADULT	0.01 (128) NS	−0.01 (128) NS	0.06 (128) NS
ADAPTADOL	0.08 (107) NS	0.07 (107) NS	0.02 (107) NS
ADAPTAD	0.06 (132) NS	0.07 (132) NS	−0.08 (132) NS
CLIN15	−0.03 (133) NS	−.11 (133) NS	−0.06 (133) NS
CLINADUL	−0.03 (132) NS	0.08 (132) NS	0.10 (132) NS

[a] Numbers in parentheses indicate number of subjects with both variables coded; NS = not statistically significant.

nor role satisfaction significantly relates to later difficulty; however, highly dissatisfied mothers have high levels of rejection and, in turn, more difficult children. At least for the present sample, then, a process of influence model that links maternal role satisfaction—parent–child interaction—development in early childhood finds some support.

D. Findings from Adolescence and Early Adulthood

During the adolescent and young adulthood years, data were not collected on maternal role satisfaction and mother–child interaction. Therefore, we were not able to test the process of influence model during these years. We were able, however, to assess the relationships between the mother's work history and adolescent and early adult outcome variables. Mother's employment status was categorized as 0 = *nonemployed*, 1 = *employed part-time*, 2 = *employed full-time*. Mother's work status at three points in time (when the child was 0–1 year, 1.1–5 years, and 5.1–16 years) were intercorrelated with six adolescent/early adult adjustment scores. These were (1) difficult temperament score in adolescence (DIFADOL), (2) difficult temperament score in adulthood (DIFADULT), (3) Global adaptation score in adolescence (ADAPTADOL), (4) Global adaptation score in early adulthood (ADAPTAD), (5) presence of a clinical psychiatric diagnosis by age 15 (CLIN15), and (6) presence of a clinical psychiatric diagnosis in early adult life (CLINADUL). Table 5 details these intercorrelations. As can be seen in Table 5, none of the correlations reached statistical significance. Due to the lack of data on other variables such as maternal role satisfaction, mother–child interaction, or other contextual variables during adolescence and young adulthood, all that can be said about these relationships is that, at least for this sample, maternal work status does not have an effect on child outcomes in adolescence and young adulthood.

V. SUMMARY, CONCLUSIONS, AND DIRECTIONS FOR FUTURE RESEARCH

The results of the NYLS show that for this group of children, maternal employment had no concurrent or long-term direct effects except for a main effect for temperament. These findings reaffirm the conclusions of recent reviews of the literature indicating that the children of employed mothers do not suffer. It is true that the families of the NYLS sample represent, on the whole, an economically advantaged group, so that the working mothers could provide high quality substitute child care during their working hours. They were also highly committed to their maternal roles in their time at home. And the great majority worked at professional or administrative occupations that brought them substantial personal satisfaction. In this sense, then, the findings of this study illustrate the effect of a mother's working on her children's psychological development when working and financial conditions are close to optimal. This reaffirms the issue emphasized in the recent literature on the need to distinguish between the fact of a mother's working as such and the effect of unsatisfactory working conditions or inadequate substitute child care arrangements.

When we look beyond the direct effects of being employed or not, several interesting findings emerge. For example, we found with the NYLS data that when the mother has regular help with housework, when her job is flexible, and when there are not many preschoolers in the family, she experiences less role strain than the mother who does not have household help, has an inflexible job, and has several young children. This is consistent with other research that has found that the number of young children in the family, the degree to which the mother's job accommodates the parenting role, and the availability of household help serve to ease or make more difficult the mother's role, thus potentially influencing the degree of maternal role strain (Bohen & Viveros-Long, 1981; Hofferth & Moore, 1979). We also found that role strain *per se* was not related to child outcomes. This may indicate that there is another link or mediator in the chain of influences from maternal and contextual variables to child outcomes. We have speculated that this mediator may be mother–child interaction and have tested it, using a "process of influence" model.

Our results also indicated that the mothers' and fathers' attitudes and feelings significantly influenced the interactions between the mothers and the children. Specifically, when fathers were not positive about their wives' roles (as perceived by the mothers) and when mothers were not satisfied with their roles, higher amounts of maternal rejection of the child were present for the total sample. With employed mothers only, high maternal role strain and negative feelings by the father with regard to the mother's role were associated with higher amounts of limit setting on the child. These findings show the importance of going beyond the direct influences of maternal employment status to investigating how other maternal and contextual variables influence the child.

An analysis of the NYLS data indicated that if we go beyond employment status to maternal role satisfaction, we find differences in child outcomes. Our results lend support to the notion that the relation between maternal role satisfaction and child outcomes may be mediated by a third factor—that of mother–child interaction. Researchers (Hock, 1980; Hoffman, 1963; Zaslow et al., 1983) have speculated that maternal role satisfaction leads to more positive mother–child interactions that, in turn, enhance child development. Our analyses of the NYLS data demonstrate that neither early child difficulty nor role satisfaction significantly relates to later difficulty; however, highly dissatisfied mothers have high levels of rejection and, in turn, more difficult children. At least for the present sample, then, a process of influence model that links maternal role satisfaction → mother–child interaction → child development is supported. In addition, mothers who were highly satisfied with their roles, whether they were working or not, displayed higher levels of warmth and acceptance than did dissatisfied mothers. Our results suggest that the mother's satisfaction with her role, whether she is employed or not, influences her relationship with her child. This relationship, in turn, may influence her child's subsequent development.

We should point out here that the NYLS is a very homogeneous sample; therefore our results may not be generalizable across race and socioeconomic class. In addition, the data were collected in an era when social attitudes toward employed women were generally quite different than they are today. We recognize that these attitudes could have influenced these mothers' feelings and their interactions with their children. Unfortunately, these influences were not directly measured, and we have no way of assessing their impact. In addition, the relations found in the present study could have been the result of other, unmeasured factors. However, we should emphasize that the opportunity to examine maternal employment influences in any longitudinal data set is rare. Thus, if the process model that we are forwarding can be supported in more current data sets—if it can be demonstrated that this model depicts the way in which maternal role satisfaction functions to influence child development—support will thereby be provided for the existence of the idea that a historically general process of human development describes the relation between maternal role satisfaction and child development in the early childhood years. In sum, our results suggest that research aimed at determining what factors influence child development, be it maternal employment research or otherwise, needs to focus on the parent-child relationships and the variables that affect that relationship.

ACKNOWLEDGMENTS

Jacqueline V. Lerner's work on this chapter was supported in part by a grant from the W. T. Grant Foundation and by NIMH Grant MF 39957.

REFERENCES

Berndt, T. J. (1983). Peer relationships in children of working parents: A theoretical analysis and some conclusions. In C. D. Hayes & S. B. Kamerman (Eds.), *Children of working parents: Experiences and outcomes* (pp. 13–43). Washington, DC: National Academy Press.

Bohen, H. H., & Viveros-Long, A. (1981). *Balancing jobs and family life: Do flexible work schedules help?* Philadelphia: Temple University Press.

Brookhart, J., & Hock, E. (1976). The effects of experimental context and experiential background on infants' behavior toward their mothers and a stranger. *Child Development, 47*, 333–340.

Cameron, J. R. (1977). Parental treatment, children's temperament, and the risk of childhood behavioral problems: I. Relationships between parental characteristics and changes in children's temperament over time. *American Journal of Orthopsychiatry, 47*, 568–576.

Davis, J. A. (1980). *General social surveys, 1972–1980 cumulative codebook.* Chicago: University of Chicago.

Eichorn, D. (1984, October). Comments made at the Radcliffe Conference, The Use of Archival Data to Study Women's Lives, Cambridge, MA.

Farel, A. N. (1980). Effects of preferred maternal roles, maternal employment, and sociographic status on school adjustment and competence. *Child Development, 50*, 1179–1186.

Farran, D., & Ramey, C. (1977). Infant day care and attachment behaviors toward mothers and teachers. *Child Development, 48*, 1112–1116.

Galambos, N. L., & Lerner, J. V. (1987). Child characteristics and the employment of mothers with young children: A longitudinal study. *Journal of Child Psychology and Psychiatry, 28*, 87–98.

Hayghe, H. (1986). Rise in mothers' labor force activity includes those with infants. *Monthly Labor Review*, February, pp. 43–45.

Hock, E. (1978). Working and nonworking mothers with infants: Perceptions of their careers, their infants' needs, and satisfaction with mothering. *Developmental Psychology, 14*, 37–43.

Hock, E. (1980). Working and nonworking mothers and their infants: A comparative study of maternal caregiving characteristics and infant social behavior. *Merrill-Palmer Quarterly, 26*, 79–101.

Hofferth, S. L., & Moore, K. A. (1979). Women's employment and marriage. In R. E. Smith (Ed.), *The subtle revolution: Women at work* (pp. 99–124). Washington, DC: The Urban Institute.

Hoffman, L. W. (1963). Mother's enjoyment of work and effects on the child. In F. I. Nye & L. W. Hoffman (Eds.), *The employed mother in America* (pp. 21–43). Chicago: Rand McNally.

Hoffman, L. W. (1980). The effects of maternal employment on the academic attitudes and performance of school-aged children. *School Psychology Review, 9*, 319–335.

Jessor, R. (1982, December). *Psychosocial development in adolescence: Continuities with young adulthood.* Paper presented at Social Science Research Council Subcommittee Child Development in Life-Span Perspective Conference, Pubertal and Psychosocial Change, Tucson, AZ.

Lerner, J. V., & Galambos, N. L. (1985). Maternal role satisfaction, mother–child interaction, and child temperament. *Developmental Psychology, 21*, 1157–1164.

Maccoby, E. E., & Feldman, S. S. (1972). Mother attachment and stranger reactions in the third year of life. *Monographs of the Society for Research in Child Development, 37*, Whole Number 146.

Rubenstein, J. L., Howes, C., & Boyle, P. (1981). A two-year follow-up of infants in community-based day care. *Journal of Child Psychology and Psychiatry, 22*, 209–218.

Schachter, F. F. (1981). Toddlers with employed mothers. *Child Development, 52*, 958–964.

Stuckey, M. F., McGhee, P. E., & Bell, N. J. (1982). Parent-child interaction: The influence of maternal employment. *Developmental Psychology, 18*, 635–644.

Thomas, A., & Chess, S. (1977). *Temperamental and development.* New York: Brunner/Mazel.

Thomas, A., & Chess, S. (1980). *The dynamics of psychological development.* New York: Brunner/Mazel.

Thomas, A., Chess, S., & Birch, H. G. (1968). *Temperament and behavior disorders in children.* New York: New York University Press.

Tryon, R., & Baily, D. (1966). The BC TRY computer system of cluster and factor analysis. *Multivariate Behavioral Research, 1*, 95–111.

Williamson, S. Z. (1970). The effects of maternal employment on the scholastic performance of children. *Journal of Home Economics, 62*, 609–613.

Woods, M. B. (1972). The unsupervised child of the working mother. *Developmental Psychology, 6*, 14–25.

Yarrow, M. R., Scott, P., DeLeeuw, L., & Heinig, C. (1962). Child-rearing in families of working and nonworking mothers. *Sociometry, 25*, 122–140.

Zaslow, M., Rabinovich, B., & Suwalsky, J. (1983). *The impact on the child of maternal employment: An examination of mediating variables.* Paper presented at the Lecture series, Developmental Plasticity "Social Context and Human Development," Boulder, CO.

4

Maternal Employment and the Transition to Parenthood

Margaret Tresch Owen and Martha J. Cox

Scientific interest in maternal employment has focused predominantly on its impact on children. Past reviews have emphasized, however, that few consistent differences in children have been directly attributable to maternal employment (Bronfenbrenner & Crouter, 1982; Hoffman, 1980; Lamb, 1982; Rutter, 1981). Although some might conclude that a mother's employment status has little relevance to the child's development, others call these views premature (see, in particular, Belsky & Isabella, 1987; Rutter, 1981) and point to the relative lack of study of maternal employment effects on infants and toddlers. At the same time, it is noted that it is mothers of infants and toddlers who as a group have shown the most dramatic increase in employment rates, a fact that has stimulated many new research efforts (Hoffman, 1984).

In addition to a growing body of research on the effects of maternal employment on very young children, there is an increased concern among researchers for illuminating the mediating links between maternal employment and the child's development (e.g., Bronfenbrenner & Crouter, 1982; Zaslow, Rabinowich, & Suwalsky, 1983). There is a general consensus that the impact of maternal employment on the development of children is complicated and may be mediated by several important factors such as the mother's feelings about working, the sex of

---

Margaret Tresch Owen and Martha J. Cox • Timberlawn Psychiatric Research Foundation, P.O. Box 270789, Dallas, Texas 75227.

the child, and characteristics of the job situation. In this chapter, data from a longitudinal study are used to examine the impact of maternal employment in 38 families going through the transition to parenthood. In this study, couples expecting their first child were interviewed, tested, and observed prenatally and at 3 months and 1 year after the birth of the child. The focus of this analysis is on the impact of maternal employment on the attitudes and functioning of the mothers as well as the types of interactions and relationships established between the mothers and their infants.

Current studies on the employment of mothers of young children are critically important because the employment scene is changing so dramatically. In the early 1970s, mothers typically waited until their children were in school to return to paid employment; in contrast, by 1980, nearly half of all mothers with preschoolers were in the work force (Waldman, 1983). In another decade, the employment rate of mothers with preschoolers is expected to reach 75% (Belsky, Steinberg, & Walker, 1982). Moreover, employment rates of mothers of infants under 1 year have increased from 32% in 1977 to 48% in 1985 (U.S. Bureau of the Census, 1986). Thus the employment of mothers with very young infants is no longer unusual in our society. Many young mothers today experience an almost continuous state of employment throughout their adult life, with only a few months or even a few weeks away from their jobs, following the birth of their babies. A past study found that 35.7% of the mothers had returned to work by the time their infants were 2 months of age (Myers-Walls, 1984).

Hoffman (1984) points out that the situation of today's homemaker represents a change from the past as well. Although Hoffman considers the differences between today's homemaker and homemakers of the past in terms of new household conveniences that change the allocation of a mother's time, we would point out differences of another type. In particular, among the mothers of infants, the nonemployed and employed mothers themselves may not differ as much as they did in the past or as much as their counterparts with school-aged children, for this reason: It is now likely that the nonemployed mother of an infant was employed before the birth of the infant and will become an employed mother of a preschooler. These are not, then, two distinct groups of women, permanently differentiated by their work status. Attitudes regarding the employment of women may differ less among employed and nonemployed mothers of infants because the majority of women are likely to return to employment at some point during their children's preschool years. Previously, mothers who were not employed had perhaps never been and did not expect to be employed.

Although the rapid increase in the employment of mothers is a recent phenomenon, interest in the effects of a mother's employment on her children is not new (for an historical overview of this research, see Bronfenbrenner & Crouter, 1982). The research stimulated by this question has primarily been "child-centered" (Bronfenbrenner & Crouter, 1982), that is, it has focused mainly on two factors: the mother's employment status and the child's development and behavior. Periodic critiques of this literature, however, have all tended to stress what Hoffman (1974) has stated so well: "The distance between an antecedent condition like maternal employment and a child characteristic is too great to be covered in a single leap" (1974, p. 128). Indeed, to make sense of the vast array of research on the effects of maternal employment, attention has had to be given to "mediating variables" such as the sex of the infant and maternal role satisfaction (Bronfenbrenner & Crouter, 1982; Etaugh, 1974; Hoffman, 1974, 1979; Zambrana, Hurst, & Hite, 1979; Zaslow et al., 1983). It has become clear that understanding the effects of maternal employment on the child is a complex matter.

Although research that addresses some of the processes by which maternal employment might affect the school-aged child has slowly accrued, there are few comparable studies with infants. With only a few notable exceptions (most prominently Hock, 1976), research into the effects of maternal employment during a child's infancy has been child-centered and most often focused on the infant–parent attachment as outcome.

There has seemed to be an implicit if not explicit assumption that the process by which maternal employment affects infants is by way of maternal absence (e.g., Vaughn, Gove, & Egeland, 1980). Although daily separation from the mother is a highly salient difference between the infants with employed and nonemployed mothers, other differences in the infants' developmental contexts may also be powerful contributors to infant development. When one considers research reporting that full-time maternal employment was associated with greater frequencies of insecure infant–father attachment for boys but not girls (Chase-Lansdale & Owen, 1987) and that full-time but not part-time employment was negatively related to the quality of infant–mother attachment (Schwartz, 1983), it must be concluded that the mother's absence is not the only employment-related influence on the child's outcome. We need to address such issues as the nature of the mother's employment, maternal attitudes regarding employment, how the mother's psychological state is related to employment, and how infant characteristics (e.g., gender) interact with maternal employment, parenting, and the child's development.

Reports of simple main effects of maternal employment on the child's functioning, without consideration of mediating processes, may reduce the complexity of the issue and lead to social policy decisions based on erroneous conclusions. Although some studies have found that infants with employed mothers are more likely to develop insecure attachments with their mothers than infants with nonemployed mothers (Barglow, Vaughn, & Molitor, 1987; Schwartz, 1983), concluding that a mother's employment will lead to an insecure attachment between infant and mother ignores the substantial percentage of infants of employed mothers in all of the studies who have *not* developed insecure attachments. If maternal employment is a "risk factor" in the development of attachments in the family, questions about the process by which this occurs become even more important. We need to be able to specify more clearly the mediating factors, that is, the conditions under which the development of insecure attachment is increasingly likely and the conditions under which maternal employment supports the development of secure attachment relationships.

I. RATIONALE FOR THE PRESENT STUDY

The findings to be reported in this chapter are derived from the Timberlawn Young Family Project, a longitudinal study of young families as they make the transition to parenthood. The study's focus on the developing family system has emphasized both individual adult functioning and developing relationships in the family, offering the opportunity to explore the impact of maternal employment on the mother's functioning and her developing relationship with her infant over this major transition.

A. Employment, Attitudes, and Psychological Functioning

One of the major theses since the earliest reviews of research on maternal employment (see Stoltz, 1960) is that a mother's satisfaction with her role, whether employed or not employed, is more important to her child's development than her employment status *per se*. Early studies (Hoffman, 1963; Yarrow, Scott, de Leeuw, & Heinig, 1962) and more recent studies (Baruch, 1972; Farel, 1980; Gold & Andres, 1978; Lerner & Galambos, 1985; Williamson, 1970; Woods, 1972) consistently have offered findings showing that congruence between the mother's attitude toward work and her actual employment status has positive effects on her child in such areas as school achievement, adjustment, and temperament.

Less clear, however, has been the process by which role satisfaction affects child outcome. Several researchers suggest that role satisfaction affects parenting. Lerner and Galambos (1986) report that role dissatisfaction is associated with maternal rejection, and Warr and Parry (1982) found a relationship between dissatisfaction and the mother's negative mood. Studies are still needed that address the meaning of the mother's role satisfaction for her functioning as mother of a young infant and for the child's development.

Guilt has been another response to employment that is often mentioned as an important mediator of the effects of maternal employment (Hoffman, 1974; Lamb, Chase-Lansdale, & Owen, 1979). Although it has figured strongly in some of the theorizing concerning the effects of maternal employment, guilt has not received much study. For example, Hock (1980) interviewed mothers extensively about their attitudes regarding employment and observed attachment behaviors of the mothers' 12-month-olds. She found that mothers of infants displaying more concerning behaviors (i.e., conflict in reunions) were more likely to be employed mothers who expressed the belief that infants deserved exclusive maternal care. Such mothers may have been experiencing feelings of guilt or conflict. For different reasons, Yarrow *et al.*'s (1962) finding of a negative relationship between role dissatisfaction and mothering among homemakers might also stem from feelings of guilt and an accompanying anxiety. A mother who feels she would rather be employed may feel guilt over what she feels this implies about her ability to enjoy motherhood and her baby.

Other feelings regarding employment may also mediate the effects of maternal employment on the infant's development. Brazelton (1985) has speculated that when mothers must return to work very soon after the birth of their babies, they defend against strong feelings of attachment that might make separation from their babies too difficult. The degree to which a mother has a strong work orientation might bring about a similar effect. Role strain is experienced with the degree to which one context of the mother's life intrudes into the other (Johnson & Johnson, 1980; Rollins & Galligan, 1978); because work and parenting may sometimes be experienced as competing roles for the mother, role strain is another process that may mediate the effects of maternal employment on infant development. Owen, Chase-Lansdale, and Lamb (1981) found that mothers of infants who valued work more highly valued parenthood less than mothers with lower work orientation. This may be a strategy that serves to lessen the stress of balancing the roles, or it may reflect an initial difference between mothers with differing orientations toward work and toward parenting.

Effects of maternal employment could be related to personality differences between the employed and nonemployed mothers. It is important to determine whether such differences exist and whether they predate the employed mother's return to work or develop as a consequence of combining employment with motherhood.

A consistent problem with attributing cause and effect in studies of mediators of employment's effects such as maternal role satisfaction is that (1) the purported cause and effect are usually measured at the same time, thus leaving open the possibility that, for example, dissatisfaction with her role may stem from observations of her child who may not be doing well, and (2) dissatisfaction with her employment status may actually be as much of a general personality characteristic of the mother as it is a product of dissatisfaction with her role *per se*. Such questions are partially addressed in the present study by testing the relations between role satisfaction and parenting at 3 months and child outcome at 12 months and the relation between work satisfaction and a number of measures of the women's psychological health. Of particular interest are prenatal and 3-month measures of anxiety, depression, and self-esteem. We expect that, in general, anxiety and depression should be greater and self-esteem lower for women who are dissatisfied with their employment during their child's infancy.

We also compare the employed and nonemployed mothers on these measures of psychological health. It can be argued that where maternal employment during infancy leads to role strain, the employment can be detrimental to the mother's psychological health and affect parent–child interactions (see, for example, Warr & Parry, 1982). Employment *per se* does not itself imply role strain. The number of hours worked per week may be a more sensitive designation (Burr, 1973), but, as Lerner and Galambos (1986) argue, role strain is more properly considered the dynamic outcome of job, family, and child negotiations.

B. Employment and Mother–Infant Interaction

As implied before and argued by others as well, we expect that, to the extent that maternal employment increases stress, anxiety, and/or depression and affects attitudes regarding parenthood and perceptions of the baby, maternal employment will be related to the quality of parent–infant interactions.

Of particular interest in the present study were the sensitivity, responsiveness, and warmth of parenting as these have been associated with the development of secure attachments in previous studies (e.g., Ainsworth, Bell, & Stayton, 1974; Belsky, Rovine, & Taylor, 1984; Egeland & Farber, 1984; Grossmann, Grossmann, Spangler, Suess, & Unzner, 1985).

C. Employment and Infant–Mother Attachment

While many studies of the effects of maternal employment on child development have found that the mother's satisfaction with her work status is a better predictor of the child behavior in question than is her actual work status, the impact of the mother's role satisfaction has generally not been addressed in relation to infant attachment. Hock (1980), who studied mothers' role congruence, did not address the patterning of attachment behaviors in terms of the security of attachment.

The present study tests the relationship of infant attachment to: (a) maternal employment status; (b) maternal role satisfaction; and (c) mother's anxiety and depression, perception of the infant, and investment in the parenting role.

D. Employment and the Sex of the Infant

There is some evidence suggesting that the effects of maternal employment differ according to the sex of the child, and differ for boys and girls depending on particular outcomes examined (Zaslow et al., 1983). Specifically, where sex differences occur, the pattern most often obtained is that detrimental effects of maternal employment occur for middle-class boys, whereas positive effects are seen for girls (see the reviews of Bronfenbrenner & Crouter, 1982; Hoffman, 1980; Zaslow et al., 1983). Bronfenbrenner and Crouter's (1982) conclusion that the male's vulnerability to negative effects of maternal employment appears increasingly probable with maternal employment during younger ages is of particular concern. However, there is inconsistency in finding sex differences, with many studies finding none at all. Therefore, child gender was examined in the present study.

The present study addresses the role of maternal employment through the end of the infant's first year of life. As in the majority of studies concerning the effects of maternal employment on infant development, our major child outcome variable of interest is the quality of infant–parent attachment. It is our thesis that maternal employment relates to infant development not merely as a result of maternal absence but by affecting the mother in her child-rearing role. Accordingly, in the present study, the relations between maternal employment and the mother's attitudes and functioning are described first. Second, maternal employment and its correlates are analyzed for their relation to infant attachments.

Several mediators of the effects of maternal employment on infant development are addressed in this study: (a) attitudes toward employment (role satisfaction, work orientation), (b) maternal personality characteristics and functioning (anxiety, depression, personal adjustment), (c) parent–child relations (qualities of interaction, attitudes toward parenthood and the infant), and (d) sex of the infant. In addition, in this longitudinal study, prenatal comparisons of the attitudinal and personality variables are made between the mothers who subsequently return and those who do not return to work. Such a design is particularly important to the delineation of developmental processes relevant to the relation between maternal employment and child development.

II. METHOD

A. Subjects

The subjects of the present investigation were selected from the Timberlawn Young Family Project. There are 38 couples in this ongoing longitudinal research project. The sample was recruited from the healthy patients of several obstetrical practices at a large medical center in Dallas, Texas. Only white couples in which neither husband nor wife had ever had a living child were included in the study. An attempt was made to contact all couples in the practices of these obstetricians who fitted the project's criteria. Of those contacted, 74% agreed to participate, giving an initial sample of 40 couples. There were 2 couples who dropped from the study following the initial interviews; 1 additional couple withdrew following the assessments when the infant was 1 year of age.

The mean length of marriage for the couples was 3.5 years. The average age of the wives was 27.3 years, with a range of 18–35. The average age of the husbands was 29.4 years, with a range of 21–42. The mean family income fell in the range of $35,000 to $39,999. The mean education for husbands was 15.8 years and for wives was 15.5 years. Using the Hollingshead four-factor index of social class (Hollingshead, 1975), couples' scores on social class ranged from 32 to 66 with a mean of 52.4. Descriptively, that meant that about 48% of the couples were in a major business and professional category, 42% in a medium business, minor professional, and technical category, and 10% in a skilled craftsman, clerical, and sales category.

All but one of the 38 infants born to these couples were healthy newborns. The 1 exception was a female infant born 6 weeks prematurely. The mother of this infant was not employed over the infant's first year. At 3 months, all infants were considered to be healthy and developing normally as viewed from physical and developmental examinations.

The criteria for inclusion in the present study of maternal employment were that the mothers must have either been homemakers for the entire first year of their infant's life or have returned to full- or part-time employment or schooling before their infants were 7 months old. A final criterion was that the mother's employment status must have been stable by the time the infant was 7 months; four families were thereby omitted from the analyses because periods of employment had been interspersed with a period of nonemployment ($n = 1$), or a change in employment status occurred after the infant was 7 months ($n = 3$).

B. Procedures

Data collection for the measures reported in the study took place in the family home and in the Timberlawn Research Foundation. Data were gathered using semistructured interviews, structured and semistructured observations of parent–child and marital interactions, standardized personality measures, questionnaires, and the standardized strange situation procedure with the child and each parent. All interviewers had extensive training and experience in interviewing; all raters were also experienced individuals with extensive training in rating.

Data for the present study came from the first three data collection periods of the Young Family Project. These occurred during the second trimester of the wife's first pregnancy, when the infants were 3 months and when they were 12 months of age.

The first prenatal visit with the couples occurred in the family home. The couple was visited by the director of the project who explained the purpose of the study, obtained informed consent and conducted semistructured, audiotaped interviews with each spouse individually. The interviews were from 2 to 3 hours in length. They explored each subject's marriage, work, friendships, social networks, families of origin, and perceptions of self in depth. The subjects were also asked to fill out a series of questionnaires at this visit regarding marital satisfaction, state/

trait anxiety, depression, personal adjustment, social network, and stress. The questionnaires used in the current analyses are described in detail later. At a second visit, approximately 1 week later in the laboratory, couples were interviewed together about how their relationship developed, feelings about pregnancy, expectations of parenthood, religious issues, and plans for the future. After this interview, the couples were left alone in the same room to undertake a series of videotaped marital interaction tasks. For example, they were asked to discuss their major source of disagreement and to attempt to make progress toward its resolution.

At 3 months after the birth of the child, three visits occurred with the couples over a 2-week period. In the first visit, a home visitor spent a morning with the mother and child during which the HOME observation interview for the assessment of the environment was completed (Caldwell & Bradley, 1987). This interview involves conversational questioning of the mother as well as unstructured observation of the home and the mother–child relationship. On the second visit, the parents were interviewed individually for approximately 2 hours in a comfortable setting in the laboratory. Areas of the interview were similar to those described here for the prenatal interview and also included feelings about the infant and the parenting role, feelings about the mother's employment status and child care arrangements (where appropriate), and the sharing of child care between husband and wife. After these interviews, the parents again engaged in a videotaped, structured marital interaction task much like the one described in the prenatal period. In a third visit in the home about a week later, each parent was videotaped in separate 15-minute semistructured interactions with their 3-month-old, followed by 15 minutes of interaction among all three family members. For these observations of interaction, the camera was fixed, and the family members were left alone in their own living room. Parents were instructed to stay in camera range and to "do whatever you would normally do with your infant at this time of day in your own home." After the parent–child interactions, the couple was interviewed together. The interview focused mainly on their adjustment to parenthood as a couple, their perception of the baby, and the way in which their family roles had been worked out.

When the baby was 12 months old, a series of four visits was begun. These were similar to the visits described for the 3-month visits, except that the interviews again took place in the home and there were two lab visits, separated by approximately 1½ to 2 months, in which the infant was videotaped once with each parent in the strange situation procedure (Ainsworth, Blehar, Waters, & Wall, 1978).

C. Measures

1. *Maternal Employment Status*

Employment status of the mothers was determined from the interviews conducted during the women's second trimester of pregnancy and when the infants were 3 and 12 months of age. Three indexes of employment status were used in the analyses reported: (1) the mother's actual work status at 3 months postpartum (greater than 30 hours weekly was designated full-time, 8 to 30 hours was designated part-time, and nonemployed); (2) employment status from 7 to 12 months postpartum (full-time, part-time, and nonemployed); and (3) the degree of employment from 7 to 12 months expressed as a ranking from 1 to 6 describing the number of hours employed (1 = none, 2 = less than 12 hours weekly, 3 = 12 to 20 hours weekly, 4 = 21 to 35 hours weekly, 5 = 36 to 40 hours weekly, and 6 = greater than 40 hours per week). A ranking was used with this last variable because, in many cases, it was impossible to specify an exact number of hours employed weekly, particularly for some of the part-time employed mothers and some of the mothers who typically worked over 40 hours per week.

The distribution of families according to maternal employment status and sex of infant is shown in Table 1 as determined during the women's second trimester of pregnancy and when the infants were 3 months and 12 months of age. All but nine mothers were employed at the time of their prenatal interview (during their pregnancy's second trimester); among these, six had either quit their jobs at some point earlier in pregnancy or just prior to pregnancy, and three had not been employed since their marriages. All but three of the mothers who re-

Table 1. Distribution of Maternal Work Status at 3 Months and at 12 Months by Sex of Infant

	Boys	Girls	Total
3 months			
Full-time	8	3	11
Part-time	3	2	5
Nonemployed	10	8	18
12 months			
Full-time	9	4	13
Part-time	3	3	6
Nonemployed	9	6	15

sumed employment following the baby's birth did so before their infants were 3 months.

Table 2 shows the means and standard deviations for the nonemployed, part-time employed, and full-time employed mothers on each of the measures described below.

2. Role Satisfaction

The mother's role satisfaction, that is, her satisfaction with employment status (whether employed or nonemployed), was rated from the interviews given at the 3-month and 12-month assessment periods. This variable was rated on a 5-point scale ranging from dissatisfaction and resentment to complete satisfaction. Some of the specific questions used to rate the responses of the employed mothers on this scale included: "How do you feel about working? How well is work going for you? How well is work fitting in with family life? Do you enjoy work?" The responses of the nonemployed mothers were rated from such questions as: "How do you feel about not being employed? Do you miss it? Do you enjoy being at home? Do you plan to resume work?"

The proportion of exact interrater agreement was .83 for the 3-month role satisfaction scale, as determined from the interviews that were scored independently by two raters (68% of the 3-month interviews). All of the 12-month interviews were scored independently by two raters; the proportion of exact agreement was .82 for the 12-month role satisfaction scale.

3. The Mother's Commitment to Employment

This variable, rated from transcripts of the prenatal and 3-month interviews, assessed the amount of interest the mother expressed in a career, job, or occupation for herself, whether for financial reasons or personal growth. The scale ranged from 1 (*lack of career orientation or motivation for employment*) to 6 (*a strong commitment to employment and a view of employment as a gratifying or necessary experience to life's goals*). Raters used the subjects' responses to probes regarding commitment to and "inner dreams" about work and career to assign scores on this scale. Again, different teams of raters scored the prenatal and 3-month interviews. When ratings within one point of each other were counted as agreements, interrater reliability was .90 prenatally and .85 at 3 months.

4. The Mother's Psychological Health and Functioning

During the prenatal and 3-month assessment periods, the mothers completed several standardized and validated measures of individual

Table 2. Means and Standard Deviations for All Variables by Maternal Employment Status

	3-month employment status			7-12-month employment status		
	Nonemployed	Part-time	Full-time	Nonemployed	Part-time	Full-time
Prenatal measures						
SES total score	56.0	56.0	47.7	55.0	55.7	50.3
	(5.5)	(5.4)	(8.3)	(5.4)	(4.0)	(9.9)
SES category	1.3	1.4	2.1	1.4	1.3	1.9
	(0.5)	(0.5)	(0.5)	(0.5)	(0.5)	(0.6)
Anxiety-state	30.1	28.6	33.1	30.1	30.2	32.0
	(7.4)	(4.6)	(7.6)	(7.5)	(6.5)	(7.4)
Anxiety-trait	33.9	29.8	36.1	32.7	34.1	35.5
	(5.5)	(4.1)	(8.4)	(4.8)	(6.6)	(8.3)
Depression	6.6	3.8	5.9	5.9	6.3	5.8
	(2.9)	(2.3)	(4.0)	(2.5)	(4.2)	(3.8)
Adjustment	69.5	77.0	67.2	70.9	72.5	70.9
	(9.2)	(9.8)	(14.8)	(9.1)	(10.7)	(14.4)
Work commitment	2.9	2.2	2.7	3.2	2.2	2.7
	(1.1)	(0.5)	(1.0)	(1.1)	(0.7)	(1.0)
3-month measures						
Role satisfaction	4.3	4.2	4.1	4.6	4.2	3.8
	(1.0)	(.45)	(1.6)	(.74)	(.75)	(1.7)
Work commitment	2.6	3.6	3.5	2.3	3.5	3.7
	(1.3)	(1.0)	(1.2)	(1.3)	(1.0)	(1.2)
Anxiety-state	31.4	28.2	34.2	29.2	30.1	32.0
	(9.7)	(4.9)	(8.9)	(8.5)	(6.5)	(7.4)
Anxiety-trait	33.4	31.2	35.9	32.2	34.2	35.5
	(6.9)	(6.1)	(5.5)	(6.6)	(6.6)	(8.3)
Depression	6.1	3.8	5.4	4.6	6.8	6.1
	(5.2)	(3.3)	(3.0)	(3.4)	(5.0)	(5.1)

(continued)

Table 2. (Continued)

	3-month employment status			7–12-month employment status		
	Nonemployed	Part-time	Full-time	Nonemployed	Part-time	Full-time
3-month measures (continued)						
Adjustment	69.5	81.0	67.2	71.9	78.5	67.2
	(16.5)	(13.1)	(13.4)	(13.4)	(13.3)	(17.7)
Mother–infant interaction						
Sensitivity	6.5	7.0	6.7	6.7	6.7	6.6
	(1.5)	(1.0)	(1.8)	(1.5)	(1.5)	(1.7)
Appropriateness of play	6.2	6.4	6.4	6.4	6.2	6.2
	(1.6)	(1.5)	(2.2)	(1.4)	(1.9)	(2.0)
Activity level	5.3	5.2	5.7	5.3	5.2	5.7
	(1.4)	(1.1)	(1.2)	(1.3)	(1.6)	(1.1)
Animation	3.9	4.0	4.1	4.1	3.7	4.0
	(1.1)	(.71)	(.83)	(.92)	(1.5)	(.76)
Reciprocal play	3.6	4.2	3.7	3.5	4.2	3.8
	(1.0)	(.8)	(1.3)	(1.0)	(1.0)	(1.2)
Interview measures						
Investment[a]	2.2	3.0	2.7	2.1	2.3	3.0
	(1.6)	(1.2)	(1.0)	(1.4)	(1.5)	(1.3)
Infant description	1.4	1.0	1.2	1.4	1.2	1.2
	(.7)	(0.0)	(.4)	(.7)	(.4)	(.4)
Fussiness	2.6	2.2	2.0	2.6	2.5	1.9
	(1.2)	(.8)	(.9)	(1.3)	(.5)	(.9)
Demandingness	2.3	2.0	2.0	2.5	2.2	1.9
	(1.5)	(1.0)	(1.0)	(1.6)	(1.0)	(1.0)
HOME measures						
Responsivity	8.6	8.0	8.4	8.8	8.7	7.9
	(2.1)	(2.0)	(2.8)	(2.1)	(1.6)	(2.8)

Restrictiveness	6.8	7.0	7.0	6.8	7.2	6.9
	(.9)	(.7)	(.9)	(.9)	(.7)	(.9)
Organization	5.5	5.6	5.5	5.5	5.3	5.5
	(.7)	(.9)	(.8)	(.6)	(1.0)	(.8)
Play materials	7.1	6.4	6.3	6.8	6.7	6.7
	(2.3)	(2.2)	(2.4)	(2.4)	(2.1)	(2.4)
Involvement	4.2	4.4	4.0	4.1	4.2	4.2
	(2.1)	(2.1)	(2.4)	(2.3)	(2.0)	(2.3)
Stimulation	3.6	4.0	3.5	3.6	3.7	3.5
	(1.1)	(.7)	(1.2)	(1.2)	(1.0)	(1.1)
Total score	35.8	35.4	34.7	35.7	35.7	34.9
	(7.0)	(5.7)	(8.8)	(7.0)	(5.7)	(8.8)
12-month measures						
Role satisfaction	4.3	4.4	2.2	4.4	4.0	2.6
	(1.0)	(.9)	(1.3)	(1.1)	(.9)	(1.6)
Attachment measures						
Resistance in first reunion	1.7	1.4	1.8	1.5	1.7	1.9
	(1.1)	(.9)	(1.2)	(1.1)	(1.0)	(1.2)
Resistance in second reunion	2.3	3.8	4.1	2.4	3.4	4.2
	(1.9)	(1.3)	(1.7)	(1.9)	(1.7)	(1.6)
Security of attachment[b]	2.5	2.2	2.0	2.6	2.5	1.8
	(1.2)	(.8)	(1.3)	(1.2)	(1.0)	(1.3)

[a] Reverse order variable.
[b] Rated continuum of security.

psychological health and functioning. These included the Spielberger State-Trait Anxiety Measure (Spielberger, Gorsuch, & Lushens, 1970), the Beck Depression Inventory (Beck, Ward, Mendelson, Mock, & Erbaugh, 1961), and the Personal Adjustment Scale of the Adjective Checklist (Gough & Heilbrun, 1965).

5. The Mother's Attitudes regarding Parenthood and Her Infant

Attitudes regarding parenthood and perceptions of the baby were rated from the 3-month interview. A major part of the interview dealt with the parent's perceptions of new parenthood and descriptions of the baby. For example, mothers were asked to describe their baby and to comment on the demands made by their infant. Rating scales defined (1) the positiveness of the parent's description of the baby (1 = *highly positive*, 5 = *highly negative*), (2) the amount of infant fussiness described (1 = *not at all fussy*, 5 = *extremely fussy*), (3) the perception of demandingness (1 = *not at all demanding*, 5 = *extremely demanding*), and (4) the parent's investment in parenthood and the child (1 = *highly invested*, 7 = *not invested*). Note that the investment scale was ordered in reverse of the other scales described. The scales describing perceptions of the infant were scored by a team of raters different from the raters of the investment scale. Counting ratings within 1 point of each other as agreements, interrater reliability ranged from .84 to 1.00.

6. Mother–Infant Interaction

Global observation ratings were adapted from Ainsworth *et al.* (1978) and Egeland and Farber (1984). At 3 months, mother–infant interactions were rated by two independent developmental psychologists who were blind to other information about the family. For the present study, particular interaction variables were chosen *a priori* from among the variables rated to represent parental sensitivity, competence, warmth, and enjoyment of interaction with the baby. The specific variables analyzed in the present study were measured with the following rating scales: (1) The 9-point Sensitivity scale dealt with the mother's ability to perceive and to interpret accurately the signals and communications implicit in her infant's behavior and to respond to them appropriately and promptly. (2) The mother's conveyance of warmth to her infant was rated on a scale called Animation. This 5-point scale described the degree of animation in terms of facial and vocal expressions of warmth to the infant. (3) Reciprocal interaction was rated on a 9-point scale ranging from none or a few brief unsuccessful attempts through increasing proportions of sustained reciprocal play. The interactions were scored independent of the interviews. Interrater reliabilities within 1 point ranged from .94 to 1.00.

7. *Home Observation for Measurement of the Environment (HOME) Inventory*

The HOME inventory was developed by Caldwell and Bradley (1987) for measuring a child's early developmental environment. The HOME is an interview/observation procedure made up of 45 items scored for the presence or absence of each characteristic in the child's home. The items are clustered in six subscales: (1) Emotional and Verbal Responsivity of the Mother, (2) Avoidance of Restriction and Punishment, (3) Organization of the Physical and Temporal Environment, (4) Provision of Appropriate Play Materials, (5) Maternal Involvement with the Child, and (6) Opportunity for Variety in Daily Stimulation. Extensive validity and reliability information is available on the HOME inventory (Caldwell & Bradley, 1987). The HOME measures are reported for observations made at 3 months.

8. *Infant–Mother Attachment*

The security of infant–mother attachment was assessed at 12 months of age using Ainsworth's strange situation procedure (Ainsworth *et al.*, 1978). This procedure was designed to index individual differences in the quality of infant–mother attachment and has been used to index differences in infant–father attachment as well (e.g., Main & Weston, 1981).

The procedure consists of a set series of 3-minute episodes, designed to gradually stress the infant. It begins with the infant and parent in an unfamiliar room equipped with attractive toys; this is followed in turn by the entrance of an unfamiliar woman, the departure of the parent, the parent's return (and the unfamiliar woman's departure), the parent's second departure, the unfamiliar woman's return, and finally the parent's return. Patterns of the infant's behavior, particularly within the periods of reunion with the parent following the brief separations, can be reliably classified into one of three major patterns of attachment denoting a secure attachment relationship (group B), an insecure avoidant (group A) attachment, or an insecure resistant (group C) attachment. Securely attached infants may or may not be distressed when separated from their parents but seek contact with their parents or greet them positively when the parent returns. If distressed, they are quickly comforted by their parent. Infants with an insecure-avoidant attachment tend not to show distress in the strange situation, and they avoid interaction with their parent when the parent returns to the room. Infants with an insecure-resistant attachment are highly distressed when separated from their parent and have difficulty being comforted when their parent returns; they show a mixture of behaviors combining contact seeking, resistance to contact, and resistance to interaction. Subgroupings of the three major patterns of attachment are also coded, yielding four subgroups of secure attachments, two subgroups of avoidant attachments, and two subgroups of resistant attachments. Among the subgroupings of the secure (B) classification, B_3s are considered optimally secure, B_1s, B_2s, and B_4s less so.

In addition, a fourth major pattern or dimension of attachment has been recently described in the literature. This pattern, described as representing an insecure-disorganized/disoriented attachment (the D group), is thought to represent a third type of insecure attachment relationship (Main & Solomon, 1986). Infants who meet the criteria for a D classification display a variety of disturbing and often contradictory patterns of behavior with their parents.

Three different types of scores were used in the analyses to represent the quality of attachment. First, a classification of attachment was made according to the standard classification scheme specified by Ainsworth et al. (1978): The quality of infant–parent attachment was coded for its major classification (secure, insecure avoidant, and insecure resistant) and for a subgrouping within these major classes. In addition, the videotapes were scored for the presence of the insecure-disorganized/disoriented ("D") pattern of attachment in accordance with the criteria described in Main and Solomon (1986). In the present analyses, the different insecure patterns of attachment were combined into one category of insecure attachment. Second, scores for the interactive scales of proximity seeking, contact maintaining, avoidance, resistance, and distance interaction were coded for the two periods of reunion between mother and infant. The scales are published in Ainsworth et al. (1978). Scores on the interactive scales reflect the intensity and persistence of these behaviors; the scores for resistance and avoidance, in particular, and considered to represent indexes of insecurity in the infant–parent attachment relationship and are typically used in determining classifications of resistant and avoidant relationships (Ainsworth et al., 1978). These interactive scales of avoidance and resistance were therefore used in the analyses of attachment. Third, a continuum representing the security of attachment was devised, and a score ranging from 1 (insecurely attached) to 4 (very securely attached) was given on the basis of the subclassification rating and review of written commentaries on each strange situation. A, C, and D codings were given a score of 1, B_4s displaying some qualities of insecurity were given a score of 2; B_1s and B_2s were scored 3; and B_3s were scored 4. This scale was similar to the one utilized by Main, Kaplan, and Cassidy (1985).

All strange situations were coded by two independent raters. Independent agreement on the classifications occurred 85% of the time. Any disagreements were resolved by reviewing the videotape and reaching consensus. The ratings on the security of attachment continuum were made by the first author.

III. RESULTS

Given the relatively small number of women who were employed part-time ($n = 6$), analyses that tested for effects of employment in ANOVAs were based only on the full-time and nonemployed mothers. The decision was made to exclude the part-time employed mothers from the ANOVAs rather than to combine them with the full-time employed because previous research has indicated that some effects of employment may differ between full-time and part-time employment situations (e.g., Barglow *et al.*, 1987; Schwartz, 1983). In addition, in the present study, the full-time employed mothers had a significantly lower socioeconomic status than either the part-time employed or the nonemployed, as determined from Duncan *post-hoc* analyses of the significant differences between the groups on both the Hollingshead total score and the SES category. The part-time and nonemployed mothers did not differ in SES. Because of this difference in socioeconomic status, analyses that detected a significant effect for maternal employment status were repeated, using the total SES score as a covariate in order to determine if significant effects of employment status remained significant after the partialling out of effects of SES.

In order to provide some consideration of potential associations with part-time employment, the part-time employed mothers were included in correlational analyses. For these analyses, it was assumed that the three categories of employment status (1 = nonemployed, 2 = part-time employed, 3 = full-time employed) had an underlying continuum representing the "degree of employment." In addition, the correlational analyses were performed, using the 6-point scale "number of hours employed."

We wished to consider the infant's gender in the analyses because several of the findings in the literature on maternal employment have suggested that the effects of maternal employment differ for boys and girls. We have therefore included infant gender as a factor in the ANOVAs, and we performed the correlations both for the sample as a whole and separately by infant gender. However, the findings by infant gender should be considered highly tentative due to the size of this longitudinal sample that was made particularly small after the cases with unusual employment histories were excluded. We were concerned, for example, that a significant correlation was more likely to be obtained for the mothers of boys than the mothers of girls, simply because the sample contained a greater number of boys than girls. Because such differences in correlations might be unreliable, the decision was made to report the correlations only for the sample as a whole, unless the separate Fisher r to z scores for the corresponding correlations for boys and girls differed significantly.

Most of the proposed relationships in the literature and in the present discussion have dealt with either the correlates of maternal employment during infancy or the correlates of maternal role satisfaction. Therefore, for purposes of comparison, both maternal work status and the satisfaction with work status (role satisfaction) are analyzed in relation to maternal attitudes, psychological health, parenting, and child outcome.

In the sections that follow, analyses of the relation between each of the proposed mediating factors and maternal employment are discussed in turn. This is followed by analyses of the relation between infant–mother attachment and the correlates of maternal employment that were found to be significant in the first set of analyses.

A. Maternal Attitudes regarding Employment

Role satisfaction measured at 3 months was unrelated to 3-month employment status unless considered by sex of infant: There was a significant interaction between work status and infant sex in the 2 (full-time vs. nonemployed) × 2 (infant gender) ANOVA ($F(1,28) = 5.41$, $p < .05$], indicating that full-time employed mothers of girls and nonemployed mothers of boys were both more satisfied than full-time mothers of boys and nonemployed mothers of girls. However, by 12 months, there was a strong effect of 7 to 12-month work status on the mother's role satisfaction [$F(1,28) = 12.28$, $p < .001$] but no sex of infant or interaction effects, suggesting that, at 12 months, full-time employed mothers were significantly more dissatisfied with their employment status than nonemployed mothers. When the total SES score from the Hollingshead was added as a covariate, the relationship between role satisfaction and employment status remained significant [($F(1,26) = 8.64$, $p < .01$]. These results were similarly reflected by a strong negative correlation between the mother's role satisfaction at 12 months and the rating for the number of hours employed at 7 to 12 months ($r = -.54$, $p < .001$). A three-way ANOVA indicated that role satisfaction among the part-time employed mothers did not differ from that of the nonemployed mothers.

All of the women who returned to full-time employment were employed throughout most of their pregnancy, whereas all but one of the women who quit work early in pregnancy (or just before the conception) did not return to work. Nonetheless, prenatal ratings of the mother's commitment to career/job were unrelated to her subsequent employment status, but postnatal (3-month) career/job commitment was related both to the 7- to 12-month employment status ($r = .46$, $n = 34$, $p < .01$) and the number of hours employed from 7 to 12 months ($r = .46$, $p < .01$). These correlations did not differ by sex of infant.

B. Maternal Psychological Health

Prenatal measures of psychological health were unrelated to the mothers' subsequent employment status. That is, there was no indication that mothers who resumed employment during their infant's first year differed from mothers who did not return to work in terms of the psychological health measures of anxiety, depression, or personal adjustment.

Postnatally, there were no significant correlations between these measures and employment status at 3 months, but the mother's anxiety state at 3 months was correlated with the number of hours employed from 7 to 12 months ($r = .34$, $p < .05$). The separate correlations for mothers of boys and mothers of girls did not differ significantly. The 2 × 2 analysis of variance that excluded the part-time employed mothers did not corroborate the correlation between 3-month anxiety and the number of hours employed from 7 to 12 months. The mother's anxiety state at 3 months was not significantly different between full-time and nonemployed mothers whether designated by 3-month status or 7- to 12-month status ($p = .11$).

The lack of significant effects in the preceding ANOVA in the face of the significant but modest correlation between anxiety and the hours of employment was puzzling but could indicate either that the mothers working extremely long hours (and distinguished in the "hours employed" variable) were important to the correlation between anxiety and the hours of employment. To test this *post-hoc* hypothesis, the ANOVA was repeated, replacing the independent variable of employment status with "hours of employment" collapsed into three groups: "nonemployed + employed 20 hours per week or less," "employed greater than 20 hours but less than or equal to 40 hours per week," and "employed more than 40 hours per week." As a result, there was a significant effect of employment status on the mother's anxiety state at 3 months [$F(2,27) = 6.80$, $p < .01$]. In Duncan *post-hoc* comparisons of the three employment groups, it was found that the mothers working more than 40 hours per week (mean anxiety state = 41.7) were significantly more anxious than the mothers working 40 hours or less ($M = 27.4$) or the mothers working a few hours weekly or not employed ($M = 30.5$), with the latter two groups not differing significantly.

There were three significant correlations between the measures of psychological health and the mother's role satisfaction. Prenatal anxiety state was negatively correlated with 12-month role satisfaction ($r = -.37$, $p < .05$), and 3-month role satisfaction was negatively correlated with 3-month depression ($r = -.45$, $p < .01$) and positively correlated with personal adjustment ($r = .44$, $p < .01$). These correlations were consistent in their indication that mothers who were more satisfied with their employment status were psychologically healthier, with less prenatal anxiety associated with greater role satisfaction at 12 months and role satisfaction measured at 3 months associated with less depression and greater personal adjustment. The separate correlations for mothers of boys and mothers of girls differed in one respect: The negative correlation between 3-month depression and 3-month role satisfaction was significantly greater for mothers of girls ($r = -.66$) than mothers of boys ($r = .13$) ($z = 2.35$, $p < .01$). This may be due in part to the fact that, in the present sample, mothers of girls were generally more depressed at 3 months than mothers of boys.

C. Maternal Investment in Parenthood

The mother's investment in parenthood at 3 months was significantly correlated with the scale representing the number of hours employed from 7 to 12 months ($r = .34$, $p < .05$) but not with the three levels representing employment status for either 3 months or 7 to 12 months. Because a low score on the variable investment represented a high degree of investment, the significant correlation indicated that mothers who were employed a greater number of hours or who would subsequently be employed more hours (three additional women who were not yet employed at 3 months) were rated with a lower degree of investment in parenthood at 3 months.

Significant effects for both 7- to 12-month employment status ($F(1,24) = 4.51, p < .05$] and sex of infant [$F(1,24) = 5.51, p < .05$] were obtained in the 2 (full-time vs. nonemployed) × 2 (sex of infant) analysis of variance, with nonemployed mothers expressing a greater investment in parenthood than full-time employed mothers as well as mothers of boys expressing a greater investment than mothers of girls regardless of employment status. There was no interaction between the factors. When the total SES score was added as a covariate, the relationship between employment status and investment in parenthood remained significant [$F(1,23) = 5.43, p < .05$]. The ANOVA with 3-month employment status found only a significant effect for infant sex [$F(1,24) = 4.10, p < .05$]. These analyses suggest that investment in parenthood at 3 months is related to maternal employment only when the mothers who will shortly return to work are grouped with the mothers who are concurrently employed.

Investment in parenthood at 3 months was unrelated to maternal role satisfaction. This was the case for both the concurrent 3-month employment status and the 7- to 12-month employment status.

General perceptions of the infant and specific perceptions of the demandingness and fussiness of the infant at 3 months were unrelated to any measure of employment status or role satisfaction.

D. Mother–Infant Interaction and Ratings of the Home Environment

In both the correlational analyses and the ANOVAs, there were no direct relationships between maternal employment status and the qualities of mother–infant interaction rated from observations when the infants were 3 months. There were also no significant relationships with maternal role satisfaction.

There were some significant relations between the HOME ratings and maternal employment status, but these were due to the low ratings obtained from the full-time employed mothers of girls. For just the mothers of girls, employment status at 3 months was negatively related to the 3-month HOME measures of maternal involvement ($r = -.56, p < .05$), provision of play materials ($r = -.76, p < .01$), and the total score from the HOME ($r = -.64, p < .01$). These correlations were significantly greater for mothers of girls than for mothers of boys (z differences ranged from 2.14, $p < .05$, to 2.91, $p < .01$). Although the correlations for the mothers of girls between the HOME variables and 7- to 12-month employment status were less strong than those obtained with 3-month employment status, the ANOVAs indicated a similar pattern of results whether the groupings were by 3-month or 7- to 12-month employment status: There were significant Infant Gender × Employment Status interactions for the HOME measure of maternal responsiveness [at 3 months: $F(1,24) = 7.56$, $p < .01$; at 7–12 months; $F(1,24) = 5.47$, $p < .05$) and the HOME total score (at 3 months: $F(1,24) = 7.58$, $p < .01$; at 7–12 months: $F(1,24) = 4.19$, $p < .05$]. In addition, each of the interactions remained significant in the analyses of covariance with the total SES score as covariant. Each of these interactions indicated that the home environments of the full-time employed mothers of girls were less good than those of the full-time employed mothers of boys or the nonemployed mothers of either sex of infant; however, given that the full-time employed mothers of girls was the smallest cell when the sample was divided by infant sex, these findings should be considered as highly tentative.

E. Maternal Employment and the Quality of Infant–Mother Attachment

The distribution of the classifications of infant–mother attachment by maternal employment status is shown in Table 3. If the insecure-avoidant (A) and insecure-resistant (C) attachments are combined into one group of insecure attachments, it can be seen that twice as many infants were securely attached as insecurely attached when their mothers were not employed (i.e., 67% were securely attached), whereas twice as many infants were insecurely attached as securely attached when their mothers were employed full-time (i.e., 33% securely attached). These differences, however were not statistically significant in a 2 × 2 chi-square analysis of full-time versus nonemployed ($\chi^2 = 2.97$, $p < .09$; Fisher's Exact Test, $p < .10$). Similarly, the chi-square analysis testing the distribution of the A, B, and C qualities of attachment for nonemployed versus full-time employed mothers (shown in Table 3) was not statistically significant ($\chi^2 = 5.11$, $p < .08$). Thus, there was only a trend

Table 3. Qualities of Attachment by Maternal Employment Status[a]

Maternal employment status	A: Insecure-avoidant	B: Secure	C: Insecure-resistant
Full-time	3	4	5
Nonemployed	4	10	1

[a] $\chi^2(2) = 5.11$, $p < .08$.

for infants of full-time employed mothers to be insecurely attached more frequently than infants of nonemployed mothers. In the six cases where mothers were employed part-time, 83% of the infants were securely attached.

To further test for the relation between employment status and infant–mother attachment and include the infants of part-time employed mothers, the employment measures were correlated with the security of attachment continuum and the scores for resistance and avoidance in the strange situation. The correlations between employment and the security of attachment continuum was not significant; however, infant resistance in the second reunion episode was significantly correlated with all of the measures of employment status: 3-month employment status ($r = .37$, $p < .05$), 7- to 12-month employment status ($r = .44$, $p < .01$), and the 7- to 12-month rating of the number of hours employed ($r = .45$, $p < .01$), with greater degrees of resistance associated with more hours employed. Behaviors such as throwing toys, refusing to interact, a failure to comfort, or temper tantrums after the mother returns are considered resistant behaviors and indicative of a less secure attachment relationship (particularly of the insecure-resistant type). The ANOVA for resistance also found a significant effect of 7- to 12-month employment status, [$F(1,23) = 6.83$, $p < .01$], indicating that infants of full-time employed mothers displayed significantly more resistance in the second reunion than infants of nonemployed mothers. When the total SES score from the Hollingshead was added as a covariate, the relation between employment status and the infant's resistance in the second reunion remained significant [$F(1,24) = 5.58$, $p < .05$].

Overall, these results do not offer an unequivocal conclusion regarding the relation between maternal employment and the quality of infant–mother attachment. Although employment was not significantly related to the security of attachment for boy and girl infants, there is a nonsignificant tendency toward an association between employment and insecure attachments within this small sample, and significant relations between employment and resistance in the strange situation suggest the importance of further exploration of these relationships.

F. Relations between Attachment and Correlates of Maternal Employment

To investigate the processes by which maternal employment could affect the quality of infant–mother attachment, the variables that were significantly related to employment status were tested for their relation to the infant's attachment. These variables were identified as the mother's anxiety state at 3 months, her investment in parenthood at 3 months, and satisfaction with her employment status. The relation between the quality of attachment and these variables was examined in both correlational analyses and ANOVAs.

There was no relation between maternal role satisfaction and the classifications of attachment or the continuum of attachment security. However, among the ratings of interactive behavior in the strange situation, resistance in the second reunion was related to role satisfaction at 3 months ($r = -.33$, $p < .05$) and at 12 months ($r = -.43$, $p < .01$), indicating that the mothers who were more satisfied with their roles had infants who were less resistant with them following reunions in the strange situation.

The mother's anxiety state at 3 months was correlated with the attachment continuum ($r = -.44$, $p < .01$) and with the infant's resistance in the second reunion ($r = .48$, $p < .01$). In a 2 (secure vs. insecure attachment) × 2 (infant gender) ANOVA, there was a significant effect of attachment for the mother's anxiety [$F(1,23) = 5.08$, $p < .05$]. This set of analyses indicated that mothers who were more anxious at 3 months had infants who were more likely to be insecurely attached and specifically more resistant at 12 months than mothers who were less anxious.

The mother's investment in parenthood (a reversed variable) was significantly correlated with the infant's resistance to mother ($r = .37$, $p < .05$) but not to the attachment continuum. Investment in parenthood was not related to the security of attachment in the ANOVA.

The negative relations found between the anxiety state of the mothers and their employment status and between anxiety and the security of attachment suggested the hypothesis that maternal employment may affect the infant's attachment to the mother if it heightens anxiety in the mother. Based on our findings, we would also offer the hypothesis, albeit more tentatively, that investment in parenthood may also mediate effects of maternal employment on the quality of infant attachment. To explore how anxiety and investment may relate to infant–mother attachment, correlational analyses were performed between both 3-month anxiety and investment in parenthood and the measures of 3-month mother–infant interaction as well as between 3-month parenting and attachment. These analyses were run for the sample as a whole. For mothers of boys and mothers of girls, a heightened state of anxiety at 3 months was negatively related to most of the parenting variables rated at 3 months, and in particular to the three variables chosen *a priori* to represent broadly important characteristics of parent–child interaction: sensitivity ($r = -.42$, $p < .01$), animation ($r = -.41$, $p < .01$), and reciprocal interaction ($r = -.48, p < .01$). The mother's investment in parenthood (a low score represented high investment) was correlated with the mother's sensitivity ($r = -.40, p < .01$) and her animation with her infant ($r = -.35, p < .05$) but not with reciprocal play. In turn, a summed composite of these parenting variables was significantly correlated with the amount of resistance to the mother shown by the infant in the strange situation ($r = -.46, p < .01$). For boys only, the composite score for 3-month parenting was also correlated with the security of attachment continuum ($r = .51, n = 21, p < .05$). Thus, although direct effects of maternal employment on mother–infant interaction were not found, there were significant correlations between the 3-month parenting variables and qualities of maternal functioning at 3 months that had been found to be related to maternal employment status. These variables representing 3-month mother–infant interaction were also significantly related to the infant's resistance in the strange situation.

IV. DISCUSSION

A. Processes of Maternal Employment's Influence in Infancy

In general, there was support for the notion that the process by which maternal employment is related to child outcome is through maternal attitudes that are related to parenting and the development of the infant's attachment to the mother.

We believe that a particularly important finding was the mothers were more anxious when they were working at their jobs more than 40 hours per week than when they worked less. Among the variables that were found to be related to maternal employment, anxiety was the most strongly related to the security of infant–mother attachments. In addition, analyses that explored the relation between anxiety, parenting, and attachment found that anxiety was strongly related to various qualities of parenting that were also related to attachment. Thus maternal employment was related to the mother's anxiety, which, in turn, was related negatively to qualities of parenting and to the security of attachment.

It is important to note here that the mothers' prenatal state of anxiety was not related to the mothers' subsequent employment status. In fact, as measured prenatally, none of the measures of the mother's psychological health were related to the mother's subsequent employment situation. In addition, it was a state of anxiety rather than anxiety as a trait of the mother that was associated with employment. It was also the case that anxiety state at 3 months was not significantly different between the nonemployed and the full-time employed groups, but it did differ between the mothers who were employed more than 40 hours per week and those who were employed less or not at all. Thus employed mothers as a whole were not an inherently more anxious group of women than nonemployed mothers, but simultaneously working long hours in a job while maintaining the new role of mother apparently led to a more anxious state in these women.

Anxiety is a state that is associated with a preoccupation with oneself. That it was found to be related to qualities of parenting such as sensitivity, animation, and reciprocal interaction makes theoretical sense if sensitivity to an infant involves an ability to observe, correctly interpret, and respond appropriately to an infant's signals. To be sensitive requires an appreciation of the infant's point of view, an ability that would be undermined with anxious preoccupation with one's own state. Feelings of anxiety could similarly preclude an ability to be warmly animated in interaction with the infant. However, when employment is not associated with anxiety, it would appear less likely that child rearing is compromised as a consequence.

Anxiety, then, appears to be an important correlate of a young mother's employment situation. In relation to mother–infant interaction, we found that when the mother's anxiety was greater, the mother was less animated in interaction with her infant, less sensitive with her infant, both parent and infant engaged in less reciprocal interaction, and the attachment relationship was less often secure. Thus we suggest that anxiety is related to parenting, and, to the extent that maternal employment raises anxiety, there may be an indirect relation to child outcome.

The mother's investment in parenthood at 3 months was not related to her concurrent employment status but was related to eventual (7- to 12-month) employment status. Thus, mothers who were employed full-time from 7 to 12 months had expressed less investment in parenthood at 3 months than mothers who were not employed. In effect, this meant that the women who had not yet returned to work at 3 months but expected to return soon expressed views of parenthood that were more representative of women who were actually employed than women who would not be employed in their infants' first year. Specific descriptions of their infants, however, in terms of fussiness and demandingness, did not differ by either current or eventual employment status.

Although investment was not related to attachment in some of the analyses, it was found to be related to a number of qualities of mother–infant interaction rated at 3 months that were in turn related to the quality of attachment at 12 months. Another indirect relationship between maternal employment and infant development was therefore suggested for the sample, with an early resumption of employment associated with less investment in parenthood that was related to a lower quality of mother–infant interaction at 3 months that was in turn related to less secure infant–mother attachment at 12 months.

There were some attitudes and interrelations with maternal employment that differed between mothers of boys and mothers of girls. For mothers of boys but not mothers of girls, a greater commitment to career at 3 months was associated with a greater likelihood of employment at 3 months. In addition, consistent with social stereotypes about the value of male infants, mothers of boys were more invested in parenthood and their infants than mothers of girls. The mother's investment when she had a son and was employed full-time was in fact equal to the mother's investment when she had a daughter but was not employed. Thus, regardless of the effects of employment, investment was greater for boys than for girls. Although the mothers of girls were not employed more than mothers of boys, these findings with investment may mean that there are greater disincentives to employment when one has a son and that an early return to work requires a high commitment to work when a son is born.

There was also evidence to suggest that employment had a negative effect on the home environment for girls but not for boys. We are hesitant to attempt an explanation for these findings, given the small number of full-time employed mothers of girls in this sample. For this reason, we are reluctant to introduce any notion such as a differential vulnerability to effects of maternal employment between the sexes based on these data, particularly because the independent ratings of mother–infant interaction did not differ by maternal employment status for either the boy or girl infants.

B. Role Satisfaction and Maternal Employment during the Infancy Period

Somewhat surprisingly, full-time employed mothers were less satisfied with their employment status than nonemployed mothers. Many employed mothers expressed their conflict and sadness over working during their child's infancy. Although the mothers' jobs were of various types (e.g., lab technicians, nurses, managers, lawyers), our impression, based on the interviews with these middle-class women, was that most of the women who returned to full-time employment did so because of finances. To maintain the standard of living that they had achieved based on two salaries prenatally, the mothers generally felt compelled to return to their jobs soon after their babies' births. Mothers who decided not to return to work voiced that they did so with some financial sacrifice. Yet the nonemployed mothers were mostly quite satisfied with their roles. Only 2 (of 15) could be rated as dissatisfied, and approximately one-third of the nonemployed mothers were given the highest ratings in role satisfaction. This distribution, unfortunately, made it impossible to test the effects of maternal role satisfaction relative to maternal employment status because the dissatisfied mothers were predominantly the employed mothers and the satisfied mothers the nonemployed (and largely the part-time employed as well).

To find so little satisfaction among the employed mothers of young infants suggests that this may be a period of childhood when the balance of costs to benefits of working falls on the cost side for most mothers. Thus the positive effects of working that have been found for mothers of older children may not have as potent an effect on the functioning and parenting of mothers of infants.

We did find evidence for a relation between the mother's satisfaction with her role and her psychological functioning. More satisfied mothers were better adjusted, and the satisfied mothers of girls were less depressed. There was also an indication that mothers who were more anxious prenatally were less satisfied with their role when their infants were 1 year of age. This suggests that the mother's satisfaction with her employment status may not be just a condition of employment status and role preference but may be influenced as well by personality characteristics. This relation should be examined further in other samples.

C. Conclusions

The relation between maternal employment and the quality of infant–mother attachments has been a controversial one. The present study should not simply be added to the other studies in an attempt to "tally" the child outcomes for maternal employment. First, the size of its sample was smaller than is generally felt to be necessary for research on attachment differences between groups (Vaughn et al., 1985). Second, we see the study's value more with regard to an exploration of the relation between maternal employment and other variables that could serve to describe the family environment when a mother is employed during her child's infancy.

The importance of these findings is in the suggestion that family situations can be identified that support the development of healthy family relations. Obviously, the specific processes suggested by the findings in this study by which maternal employment might disrupt the development of secure infant–mother attachments are likely not the only ones. Efforts are still needed to investigate the role played by marriage and other support systems in the integration of employment and new parenthood. We would expect that the support of the mother's husband and friends plays an important role in alleviating stress, anxieties, and dissatisfaction that appear part of juggling new parenthood with full-time employment.

It should be pointed out that the processes identified here may be particularly relevant to this developmental stage. Lamb (1982), for example, suggests that when employment enhances self-esteem, it may have positive effects on mothers despite the role strain. Kappel and Lambert (1972) argue that when full-time employment is associated with little pressure, it may have a positive effect on the children. Although we would agree with both positions, our findings suggest that full-time employment with a child under 1 year of age may heighten anxiety for many women. Crouter (1984) has noted that the spillover from family to work is greatest when children are infants. It is likely that infancy is the period when the demands of work and the demands of child rearing are the most incompatible. Thus it appears that it is the time when stress, anxiety, and perhaps defensive withdrawal from the child are most likely to occur.

The findings have implications for social policy regarding the employment of young mothers and care for their infants. First, because anxiety seems to figure so prominently in the disruption of parenting, any policies that serve to alleviate stress and anxiety may be particularly important. For example, availability of quality day care and support in locating child care options for infants would help to ease a major source of difficulty with mothers' employment in the infancy period. We also need to investigate what job characteristics produce anxiety, and whether these characteristics interact with the age of the mother's children. There is some support, both in the present study and in others (e.g., Parry & Warr, 1980; Schwartz, 1983; Vaughn et al., 1987), that part-time employment is not associated with the negative outcomes found for full-time employment during infancy. This would suggest that the disincentives to part-time employment, such as loss of benefits, should be removed. Policies that would allow flexible work hours and assure job security after several months of maternity leave could serve to lessen the stress in the transition back to employment in the first year after childbirth.

V. SUMMARY

In this longitudinal study spanning the transition to parenthood, we investigated the impact of mediating factors of maternal employment that seemed likely to affect the mother's child-rearing functions (the mother's attitudes, satisfactions, psychological health and functioning, and interactions with her infant) as well as the nature of the infant's attachment relationship with her.

There were no significant relations between prenatal measures of maternal functioning (state/trait anxiety, depression, personal adjustment) and the number of hours employed postnatally. Similarly, when the infants were 3 months old, there were no differences in personal adjustment or depression according to employment status. Qualities of parent–infant interaction, the mother's perception of infant qualities and measurements of the home environment also did not differ between employed and nonemployed mothers. There were, however, two differences noted at 3 months: Mothers employed full-time, or soon to become employed full-time, were significantly less invested in parenthood, and maternal anxiety was higher when mothers were working more than 40 hours per week.

At 12 months, a comparison of the proportion of secure infant–mother attachments between indicated only a trend for more insecure attachments among full-time employed mothers, but the amount of the infant's resistance to the mother was significantly greater when the mother was employed full-time. Although there were no direct effects of maternal employment on the measures of mother–infant interaction at 3 months, indirect relations were suggested in that mothers were more sensitive, responsive, and animated when their anxiety was lower and their investment greater. In addition, these measures of interaction were related to less resistance in the infant–mother attachment relationship. Thus, to the extent that an early resumption of full-time, or greater than full-time, employment may be related to heightened anxiety or decreased investment in parenthood, the findings suggested that mother–infant interaction may be less positive and the quality of attachment less secure.

Mothers who were more satisfied with their employment status were psychologically healthier and less anxious prenatally, but the mother's satisfaction with her role was unrelated to child outcome. In this sample, mothers who were not employed during their infant's first year were more likely to be satisfied with their role than mothers who were employed.

REFERENCES

Ainsworth, M. D. S., Bell, S. M., & Stayton, D. F. (1974). Infant-mother attachment and social development: "Socialization" as a product of reciprocal responsiveness to signals. In M. P. M. Richards (Ed.), *The integration of a child into a social world* (pp. 99–136). London: Cambridge University Press.

Ainsworth, M., Blehar, M., Waters, E., & Wall, S. (1978). *Patterns of attachment*. Hillsdale, NJ: Erlbaum.

Barglow, P., Vaughn, B. E., & Molitor, N. (1987). Effects of maternal absence due to employment on the quality of infant-mother attachment on a low risk sample. *Child Development, 58*, 945–954.

Beck, A. T., Ward, C. H., Mendelson, M., Mock, J., & Erbaugh, J. (1961). An inventory for measuring depression. *Archives of General Psychiatry, 4*, 53–63.

Belsky, J., & Isabella, R. (1987). The "effects" of infant day care on social and emotional development. In M. Wolraich & D. Routh (Eds.), *Advances in developmental and behavioral pediatrics, Vol. 9* (pp. 41–94). Greenwich, CT: JAI Press.

Belsky, J., Steinberg, L., & Walker, A. E. (1982). The ecology of day care. In M. Lamb (Ed.), *Nontraditional families: Parenting and child development* (pp. 71–116). Hillsdale, NJ: Erlbaum.

Belsky, J., Rovine, M., & Taylor, D. G. (1984). The Pennsylvania Infant and Family Development Project, III: The origins of individual differences in infant-mother attachment: Maternal and infant contributions. *Child Development, 55*, 718–728.

Brazelton, T. B. (1985). Issues for working parents. *American Journal of Orthopsychiatry, 56*, 14–25.

Bronfenbrenner, U., & Crouter, A. C. (1982). Work and family through time and space. In S. G. Kamerman & C. D. Hayes (Eds.), *Families that work: Children in a changing world* (pp. 39–84). Washington, DC: National Academy Press.

Burr, W. R. (1973). *Theory construction and the sociology of the family*. New York: Wiley.

Caldwell, B. M., & Bradley, R. H. (1987). *Home observation for measurement of the environment*. Homewood, IL: Dorsey Press.

Chase-Lansdale, P. L., & Owen, M. T. (1988). Maternal employment in a family context: Effects on infant-mother and infant-father attachments. *Child Development, 58*, 1505–1512.

Crouter, A. C. (1984). Spillover from family to work: The neglected side of the work-family interface. *Human Relations, 37*, 425–442.

Egeland, B., & Farber, E. (1984). Infant-mother attachment: Factors related to its development and changes over time. *Child Development, 55*, 753–771.

Etaugh, C. (1974). Effects of maternal employment on children: A review of recent research. *Merrill-Palmer Quarterly, 20*, 71–98.

Farel, A. N. (1980). Effects of preferred maternal roles, maternal employment, and sociographic status on school adjustment and competence. *Child Development, 50*, 1179–1186.

Gold, D., & Andres, D. (1978). Developmental comparisons between ten year old children with employed and nonemployed mothers. *Child Development, 49*, 75–84.

Gough, H. G., & Heilbrun, A. B. (1965). *The adjective Checklist*. Palo Alto, CA: Consulting Psychologists Press.

Grossman, K., Grossman, K. E., Spangler, G., Suess, G., & Unzner, L. (1985). Maternal sensitivity and newborn orientation responses as related to quality of attachment in Northern Germany. In I. Bretherton & E. Waters (Eds.), *Growing points of attachment*

theory and research. *Monographs of the Society for Research in Child Development, 50* (1-2, Serial No. 209), 233-256.
Hock, E. (1976). *Alternate approaches to child-rearing and their effects on the mother-infant relationship.* Final report to the Office of Child Development, U.S. Department of Health, Education, and Welfare.
Hock, E. (1980). Working and nonworking mothers and their infants: A comparative study of maternal caregiving characteristics and infant social behavior. *Merrill-Palmer Quarterly, 26,* 79-101.
Hoffman, L. W. (1963). Mother's enjoyment of work and effects on the child. In F. I. Nye & L. W. Hoffman (Eds.), *The employed mother in America* (pp. 95-105). Chicago: Rand McNally.
Hoffman, L. W. (1974). Effects on child. In L. W. Hoffman & F. I. Nye (Eds.), *Working mothers.* San Francisco: Jossey-Bass.
Hoffman, L. W. (1979). Maternal employment: 1979. *American Psychologist, 34,* 859-865.
Hoffman, L. W. (1980). The effects of maternal employment on the academic attitudes and performance of school-aged children. *School Psychology Review, 9,* 319-335.
Hoffman, L. W. (1984). Maternal employment and the young child. In M. Perlmutter (Ed.), *Minnesota Symposium in Child Psychology, Vol 17* (pp. 101-127). Hillsdale, NJ: Erlbaum.
Hollingshead, A. B. (1975). *Four-factor Index of Social Status.* Available from author: P. O. Box 1965 Yale Station, New Haven, Connecticut 06520)
Johnson, C. L., & Johnson, F. A. (1980). Parenthood, marriage, and careers: Situational constraints and role strain. In F. Pepiton-Rockwell (Ed.), *Dual-career couples* (pp. 143-161). Beverly Hills, CA: Sage.
Kappel, B. E., & Lambert, R. D. (1972). *Self worth among the children of working mothers.* Unpublished manuscript, University of Waterloo, Waterloo, Ontario, Canada.
Lamb, M. E. (1982). Maternal employment and child development: A review. In M. E. Lamb (Ed.), *Nontraditional families: Parenting and child development* (pp. 45-69). Hillsdale, NJ: Lawrence Erlbaum Associates.
Lamb, M. E., Chase-Lansdale, L., & Owen, M. T. (1979). The changing American family and its implications for infant social development: The sample case of maternal employment. In M. Lewis & L. A. Rosenblum (Eds.), *The child and its family* (pp. 267-291). New York: Plenum Press.
Lerner, J. V., & Galambos, N. L. (1985). Maternal role satisfaction, mother-child interaction, and child temperament: A process model. *Developmental Psychology, 21,* 1157-1164.
Lerner, J. V., & Galambos, N. L. (1986). Child development and family change: The influences of maternal employment on infants and toddlers. In L. P. Lipsitt & C. Rovee-Collier (Eds.), *Advances in infancy research, Vol. 4* (pp. 39-86). Norwood, NJ: Ablex.
Main, M., & Solomon, J. (1986). Discovery of an insecure-disorganized/disoriented attachment pattern. In T. B. Brazelton & M. W. Yogman (Eds.), *Affective development in infancy* (pp. 95-125). Norwood, NJ: Ablex.
Main, M., & Weston, D. R. (1981). The quality of the toddler's relationship to mother and to father: Related to conflict behavior and the readiness to establish new relationships. *Child Development, 52,* 923-940.
Main, M., Kaplan, N., & Cassidy, J. (1985). Security in infancy, childhood and adulthood: A move to the level of representation. In I. Bretherton & E. Waters (Eds.), *Growing points of attachment theory and research. Monographs of the Society for Research in Child Development, 50* (1-2, Serial No. 209), 66-104.
Myers-Walls, J. A. (1984). Balancing multiple role responsibilities during the transition to parenthood. *Family Relations, 33,* 267-271.
Owen, M. T., Chase-Lansdale, L., & Lamb, M. E. (1981). *Mothers' and fathers' attitudes,*

maternal employment, and the security of infant-parent attachment. Unpublished manuscript, University of Michigan, Ann Arbor.

Parry, G., & Warr, P. (1980). The measurement of mothers' work attitudes. *Journal of Occupational Psychology, 53,* 245–252.

Rollins, B. C., & Galligan, R. (1978). The developing child and marital satisfaction of parents. In R. M. Lerner & G. B. Spanier (Eds.), *Child influences on marital and family interaction* (pp. 71–105). New York: Academic Press.

Rutter, M. (1981). Social-emotional consequences of day care for preschool children. *American Journal of Orthopsychiatry, 51,* 4–29.

Schwartz, P. (1983). Length of day-care attendance and attachment behavior in eighteen-month-old infants. *Child Development, 54,* 1073–1078.

Speilberger, C. D., Gorsuch, R. L., & Lushens, R. (1970). *State-trait anxiety inventory.* Palo Alto, CA: Consulting Psychologists Press.

Stolz, L. M. (1960). Effects of maternal employment research: Evidence from research. *Child Development, 31,* 749–783.

U.S. Bureau of the Census. (1986). *Fertility of American women* (Current Population Reports, Series P-20, No. 406). Washington, DC: U.S. Government Printing Office.

Vaughn, B. E., Gove, F. L., & Egeland, B. (1980). The relationship between out-of-home care and the quality of infant-mother attachment in an economically disadvantaged population. *Child Development, 51,* 1203–1214.

Waldman, E. (1983, December). Labor force statistics from a family perspective. *Monthly Labor Review, 106,* 16–19.

Warr, P., & Parry, G. (1982). Paid employment and women's psychological well-being. *Psychological Bulletin, 91,* 498–516.

Williamson, S. Z. (1970). The effects of maternal employment on the scholastic performance of children. *Journal of Home Economics, 62,* 609–613.

Woods, M. B. (1972). The unsupervised child of the working mother. *Developmental Psychology, 6,* 14–25.

Yarrow, M. R., Scott, P., deLeeuw, L., & Heinig, C. (1962). Child-rearing in families of working and nonworking mothers. *Sociometry, 25,* 122–140.

Zambrana, R. E., Hurst, M., & Hite, R. L. (1979). The working mother in contemporary perspective: A review of the literature. *Pediatrics, 64,* 862–870.

Zaslow, M., Rabinovich, B., & Suwalsky, J. (1983). *The impact on the child of maternal employment: An examination of mediating variables.* Paper presented at the Lecture Series on Development Plasticity, "Social Context and Human Development," Boulder, CO.

5

Maternal Employment When Children Are Toddlers and Kindergartners

Wendy A. Goldberg and M. Ann Easterbrooks

I. INTRODUCTION: MATERNAL EMPLOYMENT WHEN CHILDREN ARE YOUNG

Mothers of young children are in the labor force in record numbers: Over half (66%) of mothers with children under 18 years of age work outside the home or are seeking employment (Hayghe, 1986). In recent years, the fastest growing segment of the work force has been among mothers of very young children: In 1985, 51% of married women with children under 3 were entering or reentering the work force soon after giving birth (Hayghe, 1986). When employed, many of these women (65%) with young children are likely to work full-time.

The large, and increasing, number of mothers of young children in the labor force has sparked debate among child development experts (Brazelton, 1986; Bronfenbrenner & Crouter, 1982; Gamble & Zigler, 1986). One set of issues concerns whether nonmaternal care during infancy is damaging for the child's development. Other concerns reflect the lack of affordable infant day care and the absence of a statutory

---

Wendy A. Goldberg • Program in Social Ecology, University of California, Irvine, Irvine, California 92717.   M. Ann Easterbrooks • Department of Child Study, Tufts University, Medford, Massachusetts 02155.

maternity-leave policy (Zigler & Muenchow, 1983). The historical basis for the worry about the effects of nonmaternal care during infancy can be attributed to research documenting the adverse effects of early maternal deprivation on child development (Bowlby, 1951; Spitz, 1946). These studies demonstrated that the lack of a consistent parental caregiver resulted in socioemotional and cognitive deficits among young, institutionalized children. As a result of this research, the public became sensitized to the primacy of the bond between infant and mother, which resulted in arguments against maternal employment and day care and in favor of traditional motherhood roles.

Albeit against a backdrop of negative public opinion, mothers of young children did work outside the home during the 1960s and 1970s. Some mothers worked by virtue of economic necessity; others for personal reasons (Hoffman, 1974). The findings of the maternal deprivation research, coupled with the presence of significant numbers of mothers in the labor force, inspired a large number of empirical investigations of the consequences of maternal employment for children. From this research, questions emerged about the negative effects of maternal employment on both cognitive development (e.g., IQ, school achievement) and socioemotional development (e.g., attachment to mother). The results from these studies are not conclusive. Both beneficial effects (e.g., on children's conceptions of sex roles, see Gold & Andres, 1978) and adverse effects (e.g., on boys' cognitive development, see Hoffman, 1984) of maternal employment for children have been documented. Even within a particular domain of child development (for example, infant-parent attachment), findings have varied across studies: Some find adverse effects (e.g., Barglow, Vaughn, & Molitor, 1987), whereas others report no significant effects (e.g., Easterbrooks & Goldberg, 1985).

Research on the consequences of maternal employment for children is based largely upon correlational data using single time measurement designs. In this type of study, groups of infants, whose mothers vary in current employment status, are compared on some outcome measure, such as developmental quotient. These data inform us only about contemporaneous associations, and leave many unanswered questions regarding long-term effects and processes of influence. Clearly, longitudinal data, such as those presented in this volume, are needed in order to examine the "effects" of maternal employment on children's development. Longitudinal designs also permit examination of "sleeper effects" that can emerge at later points in development. For example, social interactional styles of 5-year-olds may vary, depending on their mothers' employment status during infancy, even though no differences among the children were discerned at that time.

In addition to the dearth of longitudinal designs, other methodological factors that attenuate the conclusions from the current data base include the absence of multivariate models and elaborated conceptualizations of maternal employment. Many studies have examined only maternal employment status and have neglected other potential contributors to child development such as mothers' attitudes about work and family arrangements. Furthermore, maternal employment typically has been "treated as an empty set, bereft of any structure or content" (Bronfenbrenner & Crouter, 1982, p. 41). Although simple main effects models using a dichotomous employed-nonemployed variable are informative, they are insufficient. Mediators of maternal employment effects, such as stability of the family environment, type and quality of alternate child care, reasons for maternal employment, maternal job satisfaction, and spousal support for maternal work status must be incorporated into research designs in order to represent accurately the ecology of maternal employment.

A recent strategy for the investigation of the ecology of maternal employment is the study of maternal employment in the family context. Much of this research concentrates on the consequences of maternal employment for the well-being of other family members. Several studies have analyzed the impact of wives' work on husbands' well-being: wives' labor force participation tends to be associated with increased rates of depression among husbands when these men are compared to men in traditional marital relationships (Cleary & Mechanic, 1983; Kessler & MacRae, 1982; Rosenfield, 1980, 1984). Other studies have focused on the consequences of mothers' employment for father–child relationships (Chase-Lansdale & Owen, 1987; Easterbrooks & Goldberg, 1985; Pedersen, Cain, Zaslow, & Anderson, 1982). The results of this research have been equivocal, as was the case for studies of mother–child outcomes. There is some evidence that full-time maternal employment may be associated with less father–infant interaction and more insecure infant–father attachments; however, it is notable that these findings hold only for certain interactive behaviors (e.g., types of tactile contact, Pedersen et al., 1982) and are gender-specific (e.g., infant boys' attachment to fathers, Chase-Lansdale & Owen, 1987). Other studies of child–father attachment in infancy and toddlerhood reveal no differences related to mothers' employment status (Easterbrooks & Goldberg, 1985; Lamb, Frodi, Hwang, & Frodi, 1982) but do find associations between other aspects of maternal employment (e.g., time of return; stability of alternate care) and security of family attachment patterns (Easterbrooks & Goldberg, 1985).

The use of longitudinal designs affords the opportunity to examine the effects of stability and change in familiy environments on young children's development. In this respect, an important aspect of family life concerns continuity in patterns of maternal employment and alternate (nonmaternal) child care. A study by Vaughn and his colleagues (Vaughn, Gove, & Egeland, 1980) found that, in a poverty sample, poorer adaptation of infants of employed mothers reflected instability in life circumstances that was unrelated to maternal employment *per se* but that was related to changes in caregiving. Change in maternal employment status is a proxy for change in caregiving practices. Maternal availability (i.e., in absolute amount of time with child or in scheduling of time) is affected by the mothers' employment status, as is the type or number of nonparental caregiving arrangements (i.e., introduction of new caregivers; change in time spent in alternate-care settings).

This issue of stability and change in family life has profound implications for the prediction of continuity in children's development. One aspect of continuity concerns whether early life events affect later development. Rutter (1984) concludes that the long-term outcomes of early life experiences vary according to the domains of development being considered and as to whether the experiences were of a favorable or adverse nature. In the socioemotional domain, some research suggests that early negative experiences may be especially potent, placing the individual at risk for subsequent developmental problems: for example, studies of the effects of maternal deprivation on young primates point to lasting detrimental effects in the absence of intervention (Suomi & Harlow, 1978). Similar evidence arises from studies of young children reared in institutions (Bowlby, 1969; Rutter, Quinton, & Liddle, 1983). Furthermore, an unstable family environment during the early years (e.g., multiple hospitalizations of child; parental divorce) appears to be associated with the risk for behavioral problems later on in childhood (Rutter, 1984). Rutter and colleagues (1983) have documented long-lasting adverse effects of certain experiences even when the environmental contingencies change. Favorable early experiences are likely to set a positive tone for future adaptation, but there also is evidence to suggest that such experiences may not be sufficient to buffer the child from later adversity (Kagan, Kearsley, & Zelazo, 1978).

Another dimension of the continuity issue that is more germane to the issue of effects of maternal employment on children concerns the significance of change or stability in the child-rearing environment (as distinguished from the effects of a particular event) for children's development. Sroufe (1983) describes a central role for the caregiving environment in his delineation of three conditions under which coherence in behavior patterns over time would be expected: (1) continuity in the caregiving environment (both in caregivers and quality of care); (2) cyclical transactions between the child and the caregiving environment; and (3) assumptions of a hierarchical model of development in which the resolution of earlier developmental tasks sets the stage for adaptation later in development.

In this light, we believe that, regardless of maternal employment status, continuity in quality of adaptation is maximized under conditions of environmental stability. There is evidence that changes in the caregiving environment, either for better or worse, result in reduced continuity in adaptation (or maladaptation) in early childhood (Easterbrooks & Goldberg, in press; Erickson, Sroufe, & Egeland, 1985; Vaughn, Egeland, Sroufe, & Waters, 1979). In another paper (Easterbrooks & Goldberg, in press), we report that the strength of prediction from security of child–parent attachment during toddlerhood to children's capacity to adapt to new demands at ages 5 to 6 in kindergarten (i.e., their ego resiliency, Block & Block, 1980) is influenced by stability in the mothers' employment history during the intervening years. Similarly, Vaughn and colleagues (1979) note little continuity over time in quality of child–mother attachment in an economically deprived sample characterized by single parent families, changes in employment, and unstable family relationships. Because quality of attachment is based on interactive quality between the child and the attachment figure, when environmental supports for sensitive (or insensitive) interaction are stable, continuity is maximized. In another study, the ability to predict from attachment to mother in infancy to preschool behavior problems was explained in part by knowledge of the continuing presence of the same male in the household during the intervening period (Erickson et al., 1985). These data highlight the importance of considering environmental stability (including maternal employment and alternate care giving) in longitudinal studies of children's development.

II. OUR RESEARCH

In our work, which studies the family ecology of child development, we have examined the links between characteristics of maternal employment and adaptation in families with young children. Our findings are based on data gathered from families when children were in the toddlerhood and kindergarten periods. In the present chapter, we present new data and a synthesis of data that have been previously reported in Easterbrooks and Goldberg (1985, in press) and Owen, Easterbrooks, Chase-Lansdale, and Goldberg (1984). The integration of contemporaneous and longitudinal data affords the opportunity to examine in a comprehensive manner the influence of maternal employment on young children and their parents. Correlational data at toddlerhood and kindergarten speak to the contemporaneous associations between various facets of maternal employment and child–parent outcomes. The longitudinal data permit examination of the issues of stability and change in maternal employment and allow for the investigation of "sleeper effects" of maternal employment.

A. Sample

1. Toddlerhood

The first phase of the project occurred when children were 19 to 21 months of age. There were 40 boys and 35 girls in this phase; all children were firstborn and only children at the time of the study. The 75 families resided within a 40-mile radius of Ann Arbor, Michigan.

Fifty-nine of the families had participated in an earlier study when the children were 12 months old (Chase-Lansdale & Owen, 1987; Owen et al., 1984). Families were recruited from newspaper birth announcements, La Maze classes, and pediatricians. Mothers' age averaged 30 years; fathers' age, 31 years. Families were primarily Caucasian and middle class: Scores ranged from 27 to 66, with a mean of 52, on the Hollingshead Four-Factor Index (1975) (the vast majority of scores were over 40, placing the families in the upper two categories of Hollingshead's index). The average family income was between $20,000 and $30,000 (1980 dollars). Parents were well-educated: 74% of the mothers and fathers were college graduates; 33% and 48%, respectively, held advanced degrees. The distributions of parental age, family income, and parental education for the kindergarten sample were virtually identical to those of the original sample.

Maternal employment status at the toddlerhood assessment was divided fairly equally among full-time (n = 26, 36%), part-time (n = 24, 32%) and nonemployed (n = 25, 33%) groups. The range of hours for full-time workers was 32 to 50 hours/week, with a mean of 41 hours. Hours for part-time work ranged from 8 to 25 hours/week, with a mean of 18 hours/week. These employment arrangements had remained constant for at least 8 months prior to the study. Fifty-eight percent (n = 29) of the employed mothers had returned to work by the time their infants were 6 months old; eighty-four percent (n = 42) had been continuously employed for at least 1 year prior to the study. Mothers' occupational status varied from professional to skilled workers (Hollingshead, 1975): 10% professional, 43% lesser professional, 36% clerical/ sales, and 11% skilled workers. Virtually all fathers (n = 71 of 73) were employed full-time in occupations ranging from professional to skilled worker. Types of nonmaternal care were largely individual: either babysitters or fathers. Infant day care centers rarely were used by these families.

2. Kindergarten

Families were contacted for a follow-up study when the children were in kindergarten. We were able to locate 62 of the original sample of 75 families. Fifty-eight families who had participated in the toddlerhood phase agreed to take part in the follow-up study (94% agreement rate). Due to geographical moves, not all families were able to participate in all phases (home visit, teacher ratings, parent questionnaires) of the follow-up study. In the kindergarten phase (Phase II), there were 30 boys and 28 girls; children were 5 to 6 years of age (M = 6.0) at the time parents returned questionnaires. Completed questionnaires were returned by 49 mothers and 44 fathers. Ratings for 53 children were obtained from teachers. Children's ages spanned only 4 months during the time that teacher ratings were made. Home visits were conducted with 47 families. Thirty-three families had a younger child by the Phase II assessment; only 4 families had born two more children.

The demographic and psychological profiles of the families in the longitudinal study were similar to the original sample in the distribution of SES, education, maternal employment status (see Table 1), and child–parent attachment classification. Mothers who were employed at the kindergarten phase were no more likely than nonemployed mothers to be older ($F_{1,47}$ = .52, n.s.); have more education ($F_{1,47}$ = .59, n.s.); have a higher family income ($F_{1,47}$ = .37, n.s.), or have more children ($\chi^2_{(1)}$ = .25, n.s.). At Phase II, slightly more than one-third (n = 21, 36%) of the mothers were employed full-time (M hours/week = 41.2, range = 32–85); about one-third (n = 19, 33%) were employed part-time (M hours/week = 16.4, range = 4–27); and slightly less than a third (n = 18, 31%) were not employed outside the home. Thirty-nine percent of these mothers had been continuously employed or not employed since the toddlerhood assessment (i.e., stable employment status); the majority (61%) experienced some change in their employment status during the intervening years, such as reentering or increasing hours of employment (n = 10), or decreasing hours (n = 7). A number of mothers also experienced multiple changes in employment during the 4 intervening years between assessments, first decreasing and then increasing

Table 1. Sample Demographics

	Phase 1: Toddlerhood		Phase 2: Kindergarten	
	Mothers	Fathers	Mothers	Fathers
Number of subjects	75	73	58	53
SES (mean and range)				
Hollingshead 4-Factor Index	52 [27–66]		53 [32–66]	
Education				
Four-year college degree	74%	74%	48%	31%
Postgraduate degree	33%	48%	33%	45%
Age (mean)	30	31	33	35
Child gender				
Boys	40 (53%)	—	30 (52%)	—
Girls	35 (47%)	—	28 (48%)	—
Maternal employment status				
Full-time (≥35 hrs/wk)	26 (36%)	—	21 (36%)	—
Part-time	24 (32%)	—	19 (33%)	—
Not employed	25 (33%)	—	18 (31%)	—

hours ($n = 9$) or vice versa ($n = 2$). However, for most mothers who experienced changes in labor force participation, the net effect was an increase in the number of work hours ($n = 19$ out of 28).

B. Procedures

1. Toddlerhood

During the toddlerhood phase, assessments were conducted over the course of two visits to a laboratory playroom. One visit involved observations of the child–mother dyad; the other, the child–father dyad, and family triad. The order of visits was counterbalanced, and the visits were separated by 3 to 4 weeks. (Analyses revealed no order effects.) Videotaped observations were conducted during the two sessions. Also, mothers and fathers completed questionnaires, independently, in adjoining offices.

2. Kindergarten

At the kindergarten assessment, data were gathered from the home and school settings. Kindergarten teachers were contacted and met with

Table 2. Table of Measures

	Toddlerhood
Child	Security of child–mother, child–father attachment; task affect; task orientation
Parent	Attitudes toward child rearing; behavioral sensitivity
Maternal employment	Maternal employment status (FT, PT, NE); number of hours of employment; stability of alternate caregiving arrangements; timing of return to work following childbirth
	Kindergarten
Child	Conceptions of attachment relationships; ego resiliency, ego control; emotional expression; language ability
Parent	Attitudes toward child rearing; emotional expression
Maternal employment	Maternal employment status (FT, PT, NE); number of hours of employment; stability and change in maternal employment since toddlerhood; reasons for employment decisions

on an individual basis for a 1-hour session. These sessions occurred in the winter and spring so that children had time to become acclimated to school and teachers had ample opportunity to become familiar with the children. Home visits were conducted. A researcher met individually with the child while parents completed some questionnaires. Most parental questionnaires were sent and returned by mail; separate envelopes were sent to mothers and fathers to encourage independent work on the measures.

C. Measures

A listing of measures used during the toddlerhood and kindergarten assessments is provided in Table 2. We next describe the specific measures and scoring procedures.

1. *Toddlerhood*[1]

In the toddlerhood phase, security of child–mother and child–father attachment was assessed in the "strange situation" (Ainsworth & Wittig, 1969). Qualitative differences in security of attachment were coded ac-

---

[1] For all observational measures, care was taken to ensure that raters were naive to the mothers' employment status. Furthermore, ratings of the Strange Situation and problem-solving behavior were made independently. Inter-rater agreement exceeded 91%.

cording to the standardized classification scheme of secure, insecure-avoidant, and insecure-resistant patterns described by Ainsworth and her colleagues (Ainsworth, Blehar, Waters, & Wall, 1978). (Note that this research was conducted prior to the designation of a new insecure category, disorganized/disoriented by Main and her colleagues, Main & Solomon, 1987). Using this classification scheme, 86% of the toddlers were securely attached to their mothers, whereas 14% were insecurely attached. With their fathers, 66% had secure attachment relationships, whereas 34% were insecurely attached.

Following the strange situation, toddlers and their mothers (or fathers) were observed in a 5-minute problem-solving task. The task consisted of work on a jigsaw puzzle that was too difficult for toddlers to complete unaided. Different puzzles were used in the child–mother and child–father observations, and the order of presentation was varied. From the videotapes, children's styles of approaching a difficult task and parents' styles of offering assistance and support were coded. Rating scales (5 points; 1 = low, 5 = high) were adapted from Matas, Arend, and Sroufe (1978) to measure (1) toddler affect, (2) toddler task orientation, and (3) parental behavioral sensitivity. Toddler affect in the problem-solving situation reflected the child's degree or quality of emotional expressiveness. Behaviors entered into the rating included facial expression (e.g., smile, frown), vocalizations (e.g., laughter, whining), body movements (e.g., bouncing, listlessness) and negative behavior (e.g., throwing toys, pushing away from parent). Task orientation measured the child's involvement with the task with minimal parental assistance and his or her persistence in working on the puzzle. Behaviors included the degree of the child's self-directedness and autonomous effort and the frequency and duration of off-task behavior. The measure of parental behavioral sensitivity captured the extent of parents' emotional supportiveness and the quality of assistance offered to the child. Parental behaviors included the extent of spontaneous encouragement, intrusiveness, and affective tone while the child worked at the puzzle task.

Among the questionnaires that parents completed were measures of (a) attitudes about maternal employment and (b) attitudes toward child rearing. The maternal employment questionnaire included open-ended questions and close-ended rating scales. Mothers were asked to rate the importance of five reasons for working or not working (e.g., finances, personal fulfillment) on a 6 point scale where 6 signified "very important." Two open-ended questions addressed perceptions of the impact of maternal employment on mother–child and father–child relationships. Responses were coded into one of four categories: positive effects, negative effects, mixed effects (both positive and negative), and no effects. Information also was gathered about the number of hours of employment, time of return to work, and the stability of alternate caregiving arrangements from the time of mothers' return to work to the toddlerhood assessment (coded stable, or coded unstable if any change occurred). Attitudes toward child rearing were indexed with the Parental Attitudes toward Child Rearing questionnaire (PACR), a composite of author-generated items and selected items from the Child Rearing Practices Report (Block, 1965) and the Maternal Attitude Scale (Cohler, Weiss & Grunebaum, 1966). Cluster analysis was used to confirm empirically four theoretically derived subscales: warmth (alpha = .58 mothers, .78 fathers); strictness (alpha = .67 mothers, .73 fathers); independence (i.e., the extent to which parents' encouraged children's autonomous behavior; alpha = .69 mothers, .69 fathers); and aggravation (i.e., the extent of feeling bothered or worried about the child; alpha = .69 mothers, .69 fathers).

2. *Kindergarten*

We, along with others (Bretherton, 1985; Main, Kaplan, & Cassidy, 1985) believe that issues of attachment are crucial for the infant and toddler and that they remain salient throughout various developmental periods, although the expression of attachment behavior takes different forms (Sroufe, 1983). We evaluated continuity in attachment across two developmental periods (toddlerhood and age 5–6) using the laboratory-based strange situation at the toddlerhood period and the Separation Anxiety Test (SAT) in a home visit when the children were kindergarten-aged. Whereas the quality of attachment in the first years of life is assessed using the strange situation (Ainsworth *et al.*, 1978; Ainsworth & Wittig, 1969), assessment of security of attachment relationships requires different methods as children develop more sophisticated competencies of verbal communication, cognition, and social cognition. A recent trend in the assessment of attachment relationships in early childhood is the use of the Separation Anxiety Test, a projective measure (SAT; Hansburg, 1980; Klagsbrun & Bowlby, 1976; Main *et al.*, 1985). The SAT was used in this study to assess children's conceptions of the security of their attachment relationships.

During the SAT procedure, individual children are presented with a series of pictures of a same-sex child in hypothetical separation situations that differ in stress level (e.g., parents go out for the evening; parents go away for the weekend; mother leaves child at school on the first day; parents go on vacation for 2 weeks, leaving child with a babysitter). The child is asked, "How does this child feel?" and "What is this child going to do?" Using rating scales developed by Mary Main and her colleagues (Main, Kaplan, & Cassidy, 1985), we coded answers to each situation on two 9-point scales: one evaluating the quality of solutions (the child's answers to "What would this child do?"), the other summarizing the overall security of the child's responses. The quality of solution scale ranged from a high of 9 for active solutions that may bring the attachment figure closer (e.g., ask parents not to go), to low scores of 1 for solutions that are harmful to self or attachment figure or which increase child–parent distance (e.g., kill parent; run away and never be found). The second rating scale measured the overall security of the child's responses to the task, taking into account both the answers and the child's style of response (for example, long pauses, refusal to answer, or nonsense answers). In this paper, two summary scores are used in the analyses: one reflecting the average solution to the individual situations; the other, a 3-level variable summarizing overall security.

The California Child Q-sort (CCQ) (Block & Block, 1980) was used to obtain personality descriptions of each child from their kindergarten teachers, yielding a score for two constructs—ego resiliency and ego control, which are fundamental aspects of developmental adaptation. With this Q-sort measure, teachers described the child's personality according to 100 attributes using a forced-choice distribution among nine categories. The scores (1–9) assigned to each of the 100 items per child then were correlated with criterion definitions of ego resiliency and ego control established by clinical psychologists (Block & Block, 1980). Two correlation coefficients were yielded for each child, one for ego resiliency and one for ego control. The resulting correlation coefficients (two per child) simply are used as scores rather than as true measures of association (Block & Block, 1980). Ego resiliency represents the flexibility or adaptability of the child, essentially the elasticity of "personality boundaries" according to situational demand characteristics. This ability to respond flexibly, persistently, and resourcefully in problem-solving situations has been considered to be an index of competence (Arend, Gove, & Sroufe, 1979). Low ego resiliency, thus, would imply being rigid or brittle in new situations and becoming disorganized when confronted with new or stressful events. The construct of ego control encompasses the child's ability to modulate impulses, delay gratification, and express affect in situationally appropriate ways. Ego undercontrollers (indicated by a negative score) tend toward impulsivity and an inability to delay gratification. On the other hand, overly controlling one's impulses and unduly delaying gratification are characteristics of ego overcontrollers (indicated by a positive score).

Our interest in socioemotional development led us to utilize the

Differential Emotions Scale (Izard, 1972; Izard, Dougherty, Bloxom, & Kotsch, 1974) as an index of parents' and children's emotional experience at the kindergarten-age assessment period. Parents independently described both their own and their child's emotional experience during the past week using 5-point Likert scales. Ten fundamental emotions were evaluated: joy, interest, surprise (which formed a positive emotion composite); anger, fear, disgust, contempt, shyness, guilt, and distress (which formed a negative emotion composite). The Cronbach's alphas for these composite emotion scores ranged from .53 to .78. The use of this instrument was prompted by our interest in the emotional climate and experience of families differing in maternal employment status.

Parents also completed questionnaires about their child-rearing attitudes at the kindergarten assessment. The Block (1965) Child Rearing Practices Report was adapted for use with parents of 5- to 6-year-olds. The 65 items were arranged in a 6-point Likert format, (strongly agree to strongly disagree). Items were organized into types of child-rearing styles in an iterative fashion, moving between a theoretically derived clustering and a factor structure based on a varimax factor analysis. For this report, we discuss three major subscales, two of which are described in terms of Baumrind's (1971) scheme for the classification of parenting styles. Our first subscale (n = 23 items; alpha = .89) constituted an index of "authoritative" attitudes, which reflected expressions of warmth, pleasure, and respect toward the child, as well as attitudes supportive of the child's strivings for autonomy. The second factor (n = 16 items; alpha = .73) fit Baumrind's description of an authoritarian parenting style; for example, variables assessing strict disciplinary practices and overprotective behavior loaded highly on this factor. The third factor (n = 10 items; alpha = .69) reflected conflict and anger in the parent–child relationship.

Extensive information was gathered about maternal employment, including the number of weekly hours of work; reasons for working or not working as rated on a 5-point scale (e.g., finances, self-esteem); change in labor force activity since the toddlerhood assessment (e.g., change from part-time to full-time); the number and type of alternate child care arrangements currently used; and plans for employment in the future. Parents also were asked about their perceptions of the impact, or anticipated impact, of maternal employment on their children: for example, "child does not have enough time with mother"; "child benefits from exposure to other adults and children." Both employed and nonemployed women and their husbands responded to these questions about maternal employment.

In the next section, we present the findings of our longitudinal research on the effects of maternal employment on toddlers, kindergarteners, and the parents themselves.[2] The reasons that mothers sought employment are described first to provide a context for understanding the results. Next, we examine contemporaneous associations between maternal employment and several domains of development (e.g., socioemotional; social cognitive) at both the toddlerhood and kindergarten periods. (As noted earlier, the toddlerhood data are synthesized from previously published articles.) Finally, we present the results of longitudinal analyses focusing on "sleeper" effects of maternal employment and issues of stability and change in maternal employment status. Gender of child differences were examined in all analyses and, when found, are reported (we caution, however, that when gender of child by parent gender analyses were conducted within employment groups, the n of cases was small).

III. RESULTS

A. Mothers' Reasons for Working or Not Working outside the Home

Employed and nonemployed women were queried about their reasons for working outside the home or for seeking employment in the future (80% of nonemployed women at Phase I planned to seek future employment). At the toddlerhood assessment, over 84% of the women stated that they would work outside the home (now or in the future) even if they did not need the money.

At the kindergarten assessment, reasons of personal self-esteem, finances, and the opportunity to be with other adults were ranked the highest reasons for employment among employed women. Seventy-two percent of full-time workers rated personal self-esteem and finances as very important (5 or 6 on a 6-point scale) reasons for working. The opportunity for being with other adults also was very important (55.5%); getting out of the house was somewhat less important (38.9% rated this a 5 or 6). Among part-time employed women, self-esteem also was a very important reason for the majority (77.8%) of the women; however, the opportunity to be with other adults was ranked most frequently as very important (83.3%). Finances (61.1% rated 5 or 6) and the opportunity to be out of the home (55.6%) followed in importance for part-time employed women.

---

[2] The homogeneity of our sample with respect to SES and number of other children in the home did not suggest a need to control for these factors in most analyses.

Satisfaction with other realms of daily life may contribute to mothers' decisions to work outside the home. At the kindergarten assessment, we asked mothers about the extent of their satisfaction with their other "major life roles." When compared to employed mothers (E), nonemployed mothers (NE) were more satisfied with their roles as parents [one-way ANOVA; $M_E = 5.03$, $M_{NE} = 5.69$, $F(1,47) = 11.17$, $p < .01$], and were more satisfied with work around the house [one-way ANOVA; $M_E = 3.56$, $M_{NE} = 4.69$, $F(1,47) = 7.10$, $p < .01$].

Interestingly, the number of child care arrangements at the kindergarten assessment was related to employed mothers' satisfactions with their various life roles. The fewer types of child care arrangements, the more satisfied these mothers were with their work ($N = 36$, $r = -.70$, $p < .001$), their spouse ($r = -.37$, $p < .01$), and being a parent ($r = -.23$, $p < .05$). These findings may be understood best if the number of child care arrangements is conceptualized as a potential "hassle" (cf. Lazarus & Folkman, 1984); the less this hassle is experienced, the greater the satisfaction with the roles and patterns of daily living.

B. Relation of Maternal Employment to Children's Socioemotional and Socio-Personality Development

1. Toddlerhood Phase

One of the goals of the toddlerhood study was to investigate the relation between maternal employment status and the quality of toddlers' attachments to their mothers and fathers because forming secure attachment relationships is considered one of the principal developmental tasks of the early years. Although there is not an extensive body of research, most studies in this area have indicated that mothers' employment is not related to infant–mother attachment quality and is related to infant–father attachment only for boys (Chase-Lansdale & Owen, 1987; Hock, 1980). We expected that among the families in our sample in which mothers had been employed for at least 1 year, maternal employment status *per se* would not differentiate patterns of toddler–parent attachment.

At toddlerhood, maternal employment status (both the 2-level employed, not employed, and the 3-level full-time, part-time, and not-employed variables) was not significantly associated with quality of toddler–mother or toddler–father attachment (2-level variable: secure, insecure), based on 2 × 2 and 3 × 2 chi-square analyses. This pattern of results was obtained whether part- and full-time maternal employment groups were considered separately or together and was consistent for boys and for girls.

Thus our toddlerhood data were consonant with other studies that found no significant associations between maternal employment and infant–mother attachment or daughter–father attachment; we also found no significant associations with son–father attachment, which supports some, but not all, other studies in this area. However, it could be the case that insecure attachment associated with maternal employment status is not specific to a particular child–parent relationship but might be manifested when the child's relationships with both parents are considered together. When we combined patterns of attachment to mother and father to form a family attachment variable and tested for associations between maternal employment and family attachment patterns (e.g., between children with two secure attachment relationships and those with only one secure attachment or no secure attachments), we found no evidence of employment-attachment connections (again, 2×2 and 3×2 chi-square analyses were used). Thus we concluded that maternal employment status *per se* did not affect toddler–parent attachment relationships.

An additional aim of this study was to examine the role of two potentially important mediators of maternal employment effects on child–parent attachment: the baby's age when mother returned to work and the stability of alternate caregiving environments. The time of mother's return to work was coded into two categories, early return (when the infant was between 6 weeks and 5 months) and later return (when the infant was 6 months of age or older). In our sample, all employed mothers had returned to work at least 8 months prior to the attachment observations. No significant differences were found in toddler–father or toddler–mother attachment on the basis of the timing of mothers return to work (2×2 chi-square analyses). However, a significant difference was revealed for family attachment (comparing toddlers with two secure attachments versus those with only one or no secure attachments). Toddlers whose *mothers had resumed their employment before they were 6 months old* had fewer secure attachments to both parents than did toddlers whose mothers returned to work later in the first year (2×2 chi-square analyses).

The second mediating variable, stability of alternate caregiving from the time that mothers returned to work to the toddlerhood assessment, revealed similar associations with security of attachment. Toddlers who received stable caregiving were those who had not experienced changes in alternate caregivers or mother's employment hours since their mothers had resumed their employment; unstable care reflected changes in alternate caregivers (e.g., changing baby-sitters or from baby-sitter to family day care) or major changes in maternal employment hours (e.g., changing from part-time to full-time employment). Stability of alternate caregiving was not related to toddler–mother or toddler–father attachments alone; however, *stability in alternative caregiving* (i.e., in hours or in caregivers) was related to quality of family attachments (2 × 2 chi-square analyses). Toddlers of employed mothers who had received stable alternate care were more likely to have two secure attachments than were toddlers of employed mothers who had experienced caregiving changes.

To summarize, then, we found no main effects of maternal employment status on toddler–mother or toddler–father attachment relationships when the child–parent relationships were considered separately. We did find preliminary evidence that the timing of mother's return to work and the stability of alternate caregiving influenced security of attachment. Early maternal return to work (before 6 months) was associated with a greater likelihood of at least one insecure *family* attachment when compared to toddlers of employed women who delayed their return beyond their infants' sixth month. Stability in alternate caregiving (number of hours or caregivers) also was related only to security of family attachments such that instability in caregiving arrangements since the time of mothers' return to work was associated with greater likelihood of at least one insecure attachment.

2. Kindergarten Phase

The issue of the quality of child–parent attachment persists past the infancy period, although methods are scarce for operationalizing the construct later in childhood. In this study, we used the Separation Anxiety Test (Main et al., 1985) to measure kindergarten-aged children's "working models" (Bretherton, 1986) of the attachment relationship. The quality of children's solutions to the various separation situations was examined in relation to maternal employment status and child gender. At the kindergarten phase, maternal employment status (employed, not employed) was not related to the quality of children's solutions [2 (work status) × 2 (child gender) ANOVAs; F's$(2,37) < 1.43$, n.s.]. Furthermore, no differences were found when the 3-level employment status variable was used (not employed, part-time, full-time, $F(2,35) < 1.63$, n.s.), or when the employment variable was the number of weekly hours of work (Pearson correlations, r's $\leq .19$, n.s.).

Children's socioemotional development also was studied through parental reports of their children's emotional expressiveness (the Differential Emotions Scale). The children's frequency of experience of positive (e.g., joy, interest) and negative (e.g., anger, fear) emotions was examined in relation to maternal employment status at the kindergarten period. Our objective was to see whether parents in employed and nonemployed mother families differed in their perceptions of the emotional climate of their children's lives. Mothers' employment status *per se* was not associated with childrens' expression of positive or negative emotions [2 (work status) × (child gender) ANOVAs] as reported by mothers [F's(2,45) < 1.45, n.s.] or fathers [F's(2,40) < 1.19, n.s.]. However, associations were obtained between mothers' *number of hours of work per week* and *fathers'* reports of their children's emotional expressiveness. Fathers rated their sons as expressing more negative emotions as mothers' weekly hours of employment increased ($r = .56$, $p < .05$, $n = 15$). In contrast, fathers' ratings of their daughters' emotions, although not significantly related to mothers' work hours, tended in the opposite direction (increasing work hours associated with less negative and less positive emotional expressiveness, r's = $-.32$, $-.35$, n.s., $n = 18$). Fathers' ratings of sons' positive emotions were not related to mothers' work hours; additionally, mothers' descriptions of their children's emotions were not associated with the number of hours that mothers worked.

Perhaps the indexes in this study that are most central to children's "adaptation to kindergarten" are our measures of children's ego resiliency and ego control. Children's flexibility, resourcefulness, and impulse control are important elements of "competence" (Arend et al., 1979). Using these measures, we examined children's adaptive functioning in the context of conceptualizing mothers' work as a catalyst for change and adjustment in the family system (Easterbrooks & Goldberg, 1985). Children in families with employed mothers may experience extra demands and expectations for autonomous or mature behavior; these expectations may translate into more independence and flexibility and a greater capacity to modulate impulses. Whereas the main effect of maternal employment was not significant for children's ego resiliency [$F(1,47) = .92$, n.s.], there was a significant interaction between *maternal employment status* and child gender [2 × 2 ANOVA; $F(1,40) = 7.17$, $p < .01$]. Inspection of the means indicated that the most ego-resilient children were boys whose mothers were employed ($M_E = .67$, $M_{NE} = .40$) and girls whose mothers were not employed ($M_E = .43$, $M_{NE} = .61$). The extent of ego control displayed by children was not associated with the 2-level [2 × 2 ANOVA; $F(2,40) < 1.11$, n.s.] or 3-level variable for maternal employment status [3 × 2 ANOVA; $F(3,38) = 1.31$, n.s.].

3. Summary

Thus, as in toddlerhood, we found no support for a contemporaneous main effect of maternal employment status (or hours) on the 5-

to 6-year-old child's conceptualization of attachment relationships. The number of hours that employed mothers worked outside the home was related to fathers' perceptions of children's emotional expression: Sons were seen by their fathers as expressing more negative emotions when mothers worked more hours outside the home. A different pattern for boys and girls was revealed for the dependent measure of ego resiliency. The most ego-resilient children were boys with employed mothers and girls with nonemployed mothers.

C. Relation of Maternal Employment to Children's Social-Cognitive Development

1. Toddlerhood Phase

Children's performance on a cognitive problem-solving task in a social context (parent present) was observed during toddlerhood. Children worked on a difficult puzzle with each parent; their affective expression and perseverance in the face of frustration were coded. Mothers' employment status, timing of return to work, and the stability of alternate caregiving were examined in relation to toddler problem-solving behavior using ANOVA. Maternal employment status during toddlerhood was not related significantly to toddlers' affect during the task or orientation to the task with mother or with father present. The time of mothers' return to work did not mediate the relationship between maternal employment and toddlers' problem-solving behavior. In other words, children whose mothers returned to work when they were young infants (6 weeks to 5 months) did not differ from children whose mothers resumed employment later on in the children's infancy. Additionally, the stability of alternate caregiving since mothers' returned to work was not related significantly to child task affect or task orientation.

Analysis by gender of child [3 (work status) × 2 (child gender) ANOVA] revealed one significant difference. Daughters of mothers employed full-time outside the home were less task-oriented than daughters of part-time or nonemployed women. However, this difference was not observed for girls with their fathers or for boys with either mothers or fathers.

2. Kindergarten Phase

During the home visits, the Peabody Picture Vocabulary Test (PPVT), a measure of estimated verbal intelligence, was administered as a control for the degree of children's verbal fluency on the Separation Anxiety Test. The administration of the PPVT also offered the opportunity for a *post-hoc* examination of the relationship between maternal employment and this dimension of children's language development. It should be noted that all the children in our sample fell into one of the top three (out of five) categories on the PPVT: average learner ($n = 7$), rapid learner ($n = 21$), and very rapid learner ($n = 20$). Using the raw PPVT scores, associations between maternal employment status (employed, not employed) and verbal ability were tested using a two-way ANOVA (second factor was child gender); results were nonsignificant [$F(2,39) = 2.24$, n.s.].

3. Summary

In the domain of social-cognitive development, there was one indication that full-time maternal employment might be related adversely to toddler girls' persistence and concentration in a problem-solving situation; all other analyses (seven of eight tests) were not significant. At kindergarten, when language ability was examined, no support was found for a significant main effect of maternal employment.

D. Relation of Maternal Employment to Parental Attitudes, Behavior, and Emotions

1. Toddlerhood Phase

In theory and research, there have been questions as to whether mothers who are employed outside the home hold different parenting attitudes than do nonemployed mothers and whether they have disparate styles of interaction with their children. In order to test these ideas at the toddlerhood phase, we examined the four parental attitude subscales from the Parental Attitudes toward Child Rearing instrument (warmth, encouragement of independence, strictness, and aggravation) and the measure of parental behavioral sensitivity in the problem-solving task for maternal employment effects. Using analysis of variance procedures, we found several differences among mothers and fathers related to maternal employment status. Considering mothers first, *maternal employment status* was associated with warm and strict child-rearing attitudes but not with feelings of aggravation, attitudes about child independence, or observations of sensitivity in mother–child interaction. Nonemployed mothers held warmer attitudes than mothers employed full-time [means were 5.71 (NE) and 5.46 (FT) on a 6-point scale], and nonemployed women were stricter than were mothers employed part-time [means were 2.62 (NE) and 2.16 (PT)]; although significant statistically, these differences in means were not great. There were no differences between the part-time and full-time groups on these measures of maternal attitudes.

The influence of maternal employment was not restricted to maternal attitudes. *Fathers'* aggravation and behavioral sensitivity in the problem-solving task also were related to their *wives' employment status* (one-way ANOVAs were used). Perhaps due to having more responsibility for childcare when their wives worked outside the home, men whose wives were employed part- or full-time felt more aggravated about their toddlers than men whose wives were not employed. Men whose wives were employed full-time displayed less sensitive behavior in the problem-solving task than were men whose wives were not employed or men whose wives were employed part-time. There were no significant patterns related to child gender in any of the analyses investigating links between maternal employment and parental attitudes and behavior.

2. Kindergarten Phase

Based on toddlerhood data, we expected parental attitudes at the kindergarten assessment to be significantly related to maternal employment status. However, parents' scores for the three child-rearing attitude factors used in this report did not vary significantly by maternal employment status [one-way ANOVA, F's(1,47), mothers; F's(1,41), fathers < 3.35, n.s.], and no significant interaction was found between maternal employment status and the presence or absence of other children in the home on any of the three parental attitudes [2 (work status) × 2 (number of children) ANOVA; F's(2,46), mothers; F's(2,40), fathers $< .81$, n.s.].

The emotional climate of employed and nonemployed mother families was studied in relation to parents' reports of their own emotional experiences during the preceding week. When parents' emotional experience was examined in relation to the 3-level variable for maternal employment status, no significant differences were found for mothers [one-way ANOVA, F's(2,46) < 2.32, n.s.] or fathers [F's(2,40) $< .57$, n.s.].

3. Summary

When mothers worked outside the home during toddlerhood, they were less likely than nonemployed mothers to hold child-rearing attitudes that emphasized warmth and firm control, characteristic of Baumrind's (1971) authoritative parenting style. Husbands with employed wives were more likely to feel annoyed and concerned about their children and displayed less behavioral sensitivity in a problem-solving situation. There were no significant differences in relation to maternal employment status or mothers' attitudes toward child independence, her feelings of aggravation, and her behavioral sensitivity in a problem-solving situation. Maternal employment status also was not associated with fathers' attitudes about warmth, strictness, and child independence. At the kindergarten period, no significant associations were found between maternal employment status and parents' attitudes toward child rearing and reports of their own emotional expressiveness.

E. Sleeper Effects of Maternal Employment on Children's Development

Although we did not find a substantial number of contemporaneous effects of maternal employment on children's development at the toddlerhood assessment, the possibility remained that children were, in fact, being affected in ways that would not become manifest until a later developmental period. The toddlerhood-phase findings of more significant associations between maternal employment and parenting characteristics than between maternal employment and child development prompted us to investigate whether these "parenting effects" might translate into "child effects" later on. Therefore, with our longitudinal data set, we examined whether "sleeper effects" of maternal employment were apparent. Maternal work status during toddlerhood was tested with our major indexes of children's functioning at age 5–6: teacher's ratings of ego resiliency and ego control; children's emotional expression as perceived by parents; and children's interview responses to the Separation Anxiety Test.

In the domain of children's socioemotional development, children's affective expression was predicted by toddlerhood maternal employment status. Five- to 6-year-old children whose *mothers worked during toddlerhood* were described by their *fathers* as displaying more negative emotions than children whose mothers did not work outside the home [2 (work status) × 2 (child gender) ANOVA; $M_E = 1.87$, $M_{NE} = 1.57$, $F(1,40) = 5.50$, $p < .05$]. Although the means were in the same direction for mothers' rating of children's negative emotions, the differences were not significant. Children's expression of positive emotions was not predicted by toddlerhood maternal employment status. When the sample was confined to mothers employed at the toddlerhood phase, the *number of hours of employment during toddlerhood* was predictive of fathers' ratings of their sons' expression of negative emotions. Increasing work hours were associated with higher negative emotion scores ($r = .72$, $p < .01$, $n = 12$). (Recall that the same pattern emerged when contemporaneous associations were examined between mothers' work hours and fathers' descriptions of their sons' emotional expressiveness.) The number of hours that mothers were employed during toddlerhood was not associated with fathers' perceptions of positive emotions of sons, the positive and negative emotions of daughters, or with mothers' reports of children's emotional expressiveness.

A significant interaction was found between *toddlerhood maternal employment status and child gender* for the social-personality measure, ego control [2 × 2 ANOVA; $F(1,49) = 7.82$, $p < .01$]. From an examination of the means, kindergarten-aged boys were more undercontrolled ($M = -.16$) if their mothers were *not* employed when they were toddlers; kindergarten-aged girls were more overcontrolled ($M = .15$) under these circumstances. Scores for boys and girls whose mothers were employed when they were toddlers did not vary greatly ($M = .05$, $M = .01$, respectively). Thus the consequences of having a mother at home during toddlerhood appears to vary by gender of child. Ego-resiliency scores were not predicted by toddlerhood maternal employment status [$F(2,49) = 2.22$, n.s.].

Solutions to the Separation Anxiety Test also were not predicted by toddlerhood maternal employment status *per se* [2 × 2 ANOVAs; $F's(2,42) < 1.05$, n.s.]. However, correlations between the number of hours of employment during toddlerhood and the security of children's SAT solutions conducted separately by child gender again proved informative: Increasing *hours of maternal employment* during toddlerhood were associated with *less* overall security for *boys* ($r = -.49$, $p < .05$, $n = 15$) and with a near significant trend for *more* overall security for kindergarten-aged *girls* ($r = .41$, $p < .056$, $n = 18$). Last, children's linguistic ability, as measured by the PPVT at age 5–6, was not related to mothers' employment status during toddlerhood [2 (work status) × 2 (child gender) ANOVA $F(2,44) = 1.44$, n.s.].

1. Summary

Limited support was found for "sleeper effects" of toddlerhood maternal employment. As was found in the contemporaneous kindergarten analyses, we obtained some evidence for indirect effects between mothers' employment at toddlerhood and fathers' perceptions of children's emotions. Children's expression of negative emotions at the kindergarten phase, as reported by fathers, was predicted by mothers' employment status and number of weekly work hours during toddlerhood. Children's personality development, as indicated by their ego-control scores, was related to maternal employment status. Gender differences in ego control were found between the children whose mothers were not employed at the toddlerhood period, but no differences were found for children of employed mothers.

A "sleeper effect" (but not a contemporaneous association) was found for the measure of attachment relationships at age 5–6. In the employed group, the more hours that mothers were employed at the toddlerhood phase, the less secure boys' overall solutions to the Separation Anxiety Test, but the more secure girls' solutions. However, mothers' employment status *per se* at toddlerhood did not predict children's responses to this measure. Finally, neither ego resiliency nor language ability as measured by the PPVT was predicted by toddlerhood maternal employment status.

F. Stability and Change in Maternal Employment from Toddlerhood to Kindergarten

We expected the relative stability or instability of family life during the years between assessments to be predictive of children's development. Changes in family life that affect the caregiving environment, that is who cares for the child, for how long, and in what setting, were hypothesized to be salient for children's functioning. In this context, maternal employment figures prominently as a catalyst for change in family life.

For our sample, change in maternal employment typically entailed either an increase or decrease in work hours; some mothers ($n = 11$) experienced multiple changes in their work hours over the course of the 4 intervening years. In the following analyses, a 2-level (change, no change) variable for work change is used. "No change" means either mothers were not employed at toddlerhood and were not employed at kindergarten, or mothers' part-time or full-time employment status remained the same at both assessments.

In a 2 × 2 ANOVA with work change and child gender as independent variables, a significant main effect emerged for work change on children's ego-resiliency scores. Children's ego resiliency was *higher* if mothers' did not change (NC) their labor force activity during the intervening years between assessments [$M_C = .49$, $M_{NC} = .61$, $F(1,40) = 4.42$, $p < .05$]; no interaction with child gender was found, but on the whole, boys in the sample were more ego resilient than girls [$F(1,40)$

= 6.03, $p < .05$]. Significant effects of work change were not found for ego control nor for the two summary variables that measure the security of children's SAT solutions [F's(1,37) $< .36$, n.s.]; as well, work change was not associated with children's emotional expressiveness as reported by mothers or fathers [F's(1,40) < 1.78, n.s.].

IV. SUMMARY

Our objective in this chapter was to bring together findings about the contemporaneous and longitudinal influences of maternal employment on firstborn, young children's social development and on parents' attitudes and behavior. Maternal employment was conceptualized as a characteristic of *family* life; thus data were reported for mothers, fathers, daughters, and sons. Maternal employment also was viewed as a complex social phenomenon—more than a "social address" (cf. Bronfenbrenner & Crouter, 1982). Several of the subtle issues raised by mothers' participation in the labor force were addressed in this study: the number of hours per week that mothers were employed; the timing of mothers' return to work following childbirth; and, once back in the labor force, the continuity or discontinuity in mothers' patterns of employment. Data on child outcomes were obtained through direct observation of children in the lab, home visits, parental reports, and teacher ratings.

Direct associations between maternal employment status *per se* at the toddlerhood phase and toddler outcomes were limited to the sociocognitive domain: Daughters of full-time employed mothers showed less task orientation than daughters whose mothers worked part-time or were not employed. However, we do not give much weight to this finding because it was the only one of eight related analyses that reached significance and it was not theoretically predicted. Maternal employment status itself was not associated with the security of child–parent attachment (the toddlerhood measure of socioemotional development). Instead, specific aspects of maternal employment and the family environment (timing of return to work; stability in alternate care) proved informative. Return to work before infants were 6 months and many changes in alternate care during infancy were associated with a greater likelihood of toddlers having at least one insecure attachment.

At the kindergarten phase, we had several measures of children's socioemotional development. Differences were not found among children whose mothers were employed and not employed for the measures of children's conceptions of the security of their attachment relationships (using the SAT). No differences between these groups emerged on the dependent measure of children's emotional expressiveness. However, when analysis was confined to the subsample of children whose mothers were employed at the kindergarten phase, increasing hours of maternal employment were associated with fathers' reports of more negative emotional expression by their sons. Additionally, one of our measures of socio-personality development, ego resiliency, was associated with maternal employment status but only in interaction with child gender. Boys were found to be more ego resilient when their mothers were employed; girls were more resilient when their mothers were not employed. Maternal employment at the kindergarten phase was not related to children's linguistic ability as measured by the PPVT.

At toddlerhood, several maternal and paternal child-rearing attitudes varied according to maternal employment status. Employed women held less strict and less warm attitudes and husbands of employed wives expressed more aggravation than parents in nonemployed mother families. However, by the time of the kindergarten assessment, there were no significant associations between maternal employment and parents' child-rearing attitudes or self-reported emotional expressiveness.

When we used our longitudinal data to address sleeper effects of maternal employment and issues of stability and change, several interesting findings were noted. Among the sample of children whose mothers were employed during toddlerhood, increasing hours of employment predicted several socioemotional outcomes: more negative emotional expressiveness by sons at kindergarten as perceived by fathers but not by mothers; a trend ($p < .056$) toward more secure representations of the attachment relationship by daughters; and more insecure representations of the attachment relationship by sons. Ego resiliency and linguistic ability were not predicted by toddlerhood maternal employment. A significant interaction term revealed an unexpected finding: Maternal presence at home during toddlerhood predicted boys being undercontrolled at age 5–6 and girls being overcontrolled, whereas no significant differences were attributable to mothers' being employed.

Issues around stability and change in maternal employment, which lead to changes in alternate care and family environments, were important in the infancy–toddlerhood analyses and also in the toddlerhood–kindergarten analyses. Five- to 6-year-old children were less ego resilient when their mothers changed employment status between toddlerhood and kindergarten (i.e., when mothers went from full-time to part-time, nonemployed to employed, employed to nonemployed). Other child outcomes (ego control, security of SAT solutions, emotional expressiveness) were not affected by stability and change in maternal employment.

V. DISCUSSION

As indicated by the preceding summary, when "effects" of maternal employment status or employment hours emerged in our study, the outcomes were at times favorable for families with employed mothers (e.g., more adaptive ego resiliency among sons; more secure SAT solutions among daughters) and at times, less desirable (e.g., higher levels of fathers' aggravation; more negative child emotions as perceived by fathers). We found far more nonsignificant results than significant ones; when significant, we found more negative correlates and consequences of maternal employment than positive ones. Both favorable and adverse outcomes need to be understood in the context of the numerous nonsignificant findings and with the caveat that the significant findings varied nonsystematically by gender of child, gender of parent, domain of development, and the aspect of maternal employment under study.

The relatively small number of main effects of maternal employment status *per se* is, in some respects, not surprising. In our sample, mothers' preference to be employed or not was congruent with their perceptions of the impact of maternal employment on parent–child relations (Easterbrooks & Goldberg, 1985). In other words, mothers who believed that maternal employment led to greater mutual appreciation, for example, were those who were working outside the home. Mothers who expected less quality time to result from their employment were not in the labor force. Husbands' preferences for their wives' employment status generally concurred with their wives' actual employment status. Thus, in this sample, potentially adverse effects of maternal employment on children could have been buffered by mothers' satisfaction with their employment status.

We suggest that the less optimal patterns of ego control displayed by 5- to 6-year-old children whose mothers were not employed when the children were toddlers reflect the impact of alternate care experiences on the children whose mothers were employed. Much of the construct of ego control revolves around the issue of impulse control or the ability to delay gratification. Most of the children in employed-mother families had been in group care settings for several years, where demands exist for impulse control. Certainly the peer group experience entails learning to wait one's turn, wait for the group, and share with others; furthermore, children typically are rewarded for displaying these socially appropriate behaviors. Opportunities for appropriate self-expression and assertiveness also are present in these peer group experiences, thus explaining why daughters of employed mothers did not exhibit the overcontrol that characterized daughters of nonemployed mothers.

That sons displayed more ego resiliency when mothers were employed speaks to a favorable correlate of early maternal employment for son's development. The finding that 5- to 6-year-old girls were more flexible and adaptive in the face of situational challenges and demands (i.e., more ego resilient) when their mothers did *not* work outside the home during kindergarten was surprising, given Hoffman's (1974) conclusion that maternal employment seems to further the related constructs of independence and achievement motivation. Douvan's (1963) research with adolescent girls may be helpful here. She found that maternal employment had greater effects on parent–child relationships for girls than for boys and that employed mothers of girls were lenient in disciplinary style and unconcerned with supervising their daughter's behavior. In our sample, we found that employed mothers were less warm and less strict in their attitudes toward rearing their toddlers. Thus, to the extent that the effects of parenting styles noted by Douvan apply to daughters of employed mothers in our sample and to the extent that parental involvement, concern, and well-being foster the development of ego resiliency, our results become less paradoxical. Five- to 6-year-old girls' ego resiliency was associated only with kindergarten maternal employment status; it was not predicted by maternal employment during toddlerhood. Perhaps at the kindergarten assessment, a time when many mothers also had another child, there were enough other stressors that affected family interactions and parent–child relationships to render maternal employment *per se* more problematic.

When we examined effects due to the extent of maternal employment (part-time, full-time status, and number of hours employed), some support was found for less advantageous outcomes associated with more intense labor force activity. At toddlerhood, daughters of mothers employed full-time displayed less task orientation than daughters of mothers employed part-time or not employed. Also, the more hours worked by mothers, the more negative were boys' emotional expressions as rated by fathers. The more hours that mothers worked during toddlerhood, the less secure their 5- to 6-year-old sons' solutions to a separation anxiety situation but the more secure their daughters' solutions (trend). We caution that the part- versus full-time differences in our study are not pervasive; yet, it is noteworthy that when they exist, the correlates and consequences of mothers' intensive labor force activity largely are less than favorable. Boys in particular may be vulnerable to adverse effects of full-time maternal employment but may benefit from part-time maternal employment (cf. Bronfenbrenner, Henderson, Alvarez, & Cochran, 1982). One explanation for more favorable correlates of part-time employment may be that it is easier for middle-class mothers to combine part-time employment with child rearing (Rapoport & Rapoport, 1976). However, reasons for part-time employment are diverse; because we cannot randomly assign mothers to part- or full-time groups, the effects of employment hours may be confounded with other factors (Berndt, 1983); for example, economic well-being, work commitment, physical health, or psychological well-being.

Although associations between maternal employment and maternal attitudes and behaviors were not numerous, there was some evidence for indirect, cross-parent influences. Evidence was found for contemporaraneous and longitudinal outcomes of maternal employment at toddlerhood on some aspects of fathering and the father–child relationship. Fathers seemed to be more negatively affected by their wives' employment during toddlerhood: Men whose wives were employed expressed more aggravation about their children and displayed less sensitive behavior in interaction with their children (contemporaneous findings at toddlerhood) and reported more negative emotional expressiveness by their children, particularly their sons (a longitudinal finding). It is interesting that, by the time of the kindergarten assessment, maternal employment no longer yielded any contemporaneous effects on fathers. Thus our findings seem to converge with other reports of negative father–child relations under circumstances of early maternal employment (Chase-Lansdale & Owen, 1987; Pederson et al., 1982). However, in these studies the sample sizes are small and the number of significant results are few relative to the number of analyses conducted. We understand our findings as support for a family systems orientation, in which maternal employment affects, and is affected by, other family members besides the mothers themselves.

Stability in children's lives proved to be a concomitant of children's adaptive functioning. In our study, two dimensions of stability were examined: stability in alternate care arrangements and stability in maternal employment. Results in both instances indicated that children fared better under conditions of stability. When mothers returned to work before children were 6 months old, joint secure attachments (to mother and father during toddlerhood) were more likely if the child experienced stability in alternate care (either the number of hours or caregivers). Our longitudinal analyses indicated that stability in maternal employment status (e.g., not working at both assessments or working the same number of hours at both assessments) enhanced children's ego resiliency. One explanation that has been offered for the oft-noted lack of consistent direct effects of maternal employment on children's development across studies (Hayes & Kamerman, 1983) is that maternal employment *per se* is a situation to which families can, and often do, adjust (Easterbrooks & Goldberg, 1985). However, once an arrangement is in place and adjustments are made, further change does not appear beneficial. Indeed, a certain amount of change can be a positive challenge for a family. However, too much instability seems to interfere with children's capacity to respond in a flexible and resourceful way.

Several theoretical traditions (e.g., psychoanalytic, cognitive developmental) concur that milestones in the years from 2 to 5 include the development of autonomy and gender identity. These psychological processes are experienced differently by boys and girls, due in large measure to variations in socialization practices. Therefore, father–son, father–daughter, mother–son, and mother–daughter relationships can be expected to differ in important ways. In our study, we found some support for gender of child by gender of parent differences. Examination of these relationships in larger samples is needed to replicate our Parent × Child associations.

The findings from our longitudinal study underscore the utility of including specific measures of various aspects of maternal employment, notably indexes of the timing of return to work following childbirth, the stability of nonmaternal care arrangements, the stability of maternal labor force activity, and the number of hours per week worked by mothers. Our study also treated maternal employment as a structural characteristic of family life that has implications for the quantity of family interaction, but what is more important, for the quality of individual development and dyadic relationships. The results that were specific to gender of child or parent and the cross-parent influences indicate that a family context approach continues to be promising for illuminating which individuals and relationships in the family are influenced by maternal employment and how that influence becomes manifest.

Our findings regarding the importance of stability in nonmaternal care arrangements and maternal labor activity bear on policy issues concerning alternate care and family supportive benefits. Our data can be interpreted as providing support for the advantages of stability in middle-class children's environments. Thus we concur with others who see a major criterion of quality child care being the need for adequate salaries to minimize staff turnover and promote continuity in caregiving (Zigler, 1987). Our findings of better child outcomes when mothers are able to maintain their work status over time, be it being employed or not, are in accord with efforts to make work environments, benefits, and policies flexible enough to accommodate the needs of today's parents.

Acknowledgments

This study was supported by a grant to the authors from the Foundation for Child Development. We gratefully acknowledge the able research assistance provided by Dorothy Feeman, Lisa Canin, Connie Keenan, and Lydia DiBella. We thank Jill Vidas for typing the drafts of this manuscript.

REFERENCES

Ainsworth, M. D. S., & Wittig, B. A. (1969). Attachment and exploratory behavior of one-year-olds in a strange situation. In B. M. Foss (Ed.), *Determinants of infant behavior* (Vol. 4, pp. 111–136). London: Methuen.

Ainsworth, M. D. S., Blehar, M. C., Waters, E., & Wall, S. N. (1978). *Patterns of attachment: A psychological study of the strange situation.* Hillsdale, NJ: Erlbaum.

Arend, R., Gove, F., & Sroufe, L. A. (1979). Continuity of individual adaptation from infancy to kindergarten: A predictive study of ego-resiliency and curiosity in preschoolers. *Child Development, 50,* 950–959.

Barglow, P., Vaughn, B., & Molitor, N. (1987). Effects of maternal absence due to employment on the quality of infant-mother attachment in a low-risk sample. *Child Development, 58,* 945–954.

Baumrind, D. (1971). Current patterns of parental authority. *Developmental Psychology Monograph, 4*(1).

Berndt, T. (1983). Peer relationships in children of working parents: A theoretical analysis and some conclusions. In C. D. Hayes & S. B. Kamerman (Eds.), *Children of working parents* (pp. 1–12). Washington, DC: National Academy Press.

Block, J. H. (1965). *The Child Rearing Practices Report: A set of Q-items for the description of parental socialization attitudes and values.* Berkeley, CA: Institute of Human Development, University of California.

Block, J. H., & Block, J. (1980). The role of ego-control and ego-resiliency in the organization of behavior. In A. Collins (Ed.), *Minnesota Symposium of Child Psychology, 13,* 39–101. Hillsdale, NJ: Erlbaum Associates.

Bowlby, J. (1951). *Maternal care and mental health.* Geneva: WHO; London: HMSO; New York: Columbia University Press.

Bowlby, J. (1969). *Attachment.* New York: Basic Books.

Brazelton, T. B. (1986). Issues for working parents. *American Journal of Orthopsychiatry, 56*(1), 14–25.

Bretherton, I. (1985). Attachment theory: Retrospect and Prospect. In I. Bretherton & E. Waters (Eds.), *Growing points of attachment theory and research. Monographs of the Society for Research in Child Development, 50,* 3–35.

Bronfenbrenner, U., & Crouter, A. (1982). Work and family through time and space. In S. Kamerman & C. Hayes (Eds.), *Families that work: Children in a changing world.* Washington, DC: National Academy Press.

Bronfenbrenner, U., Henderson, C., Alvarez, W., & Cochran, M. (1982). *The relation of the mother's work status to parents' spontaneous descriptions of their children*. Ithaca, New York: Dept. of Human Development and Family Studies, Cornell University.

Chase-Lansdale, P. L., & Owen, M. T. (1987). Maternal employment in a family context: Effects on infant-mother and infant-father attachments. *Child Development, 58*, 1505–1512.

Cleary, P. D., & Mechanic, D. (1983). Sex differences in psychological distress among married people. *Journal of Health and Social Behavior, 24*, 111–121.

Cohler, B. J., Weiss, J. L., & Grunebaum, H. U. (1966). *The Maternal-Attitude Scale: A questionnaire for studying child rearing attitudes in mothers of young children*. Unpublished manuscript, Harvard University, Cambridge.

Douvan, E. (1963). Employment and the adolescent. In F. I. Nye & L. W. Hoffman (Eds.), *The employed mother in America* (pp. 142–164). Chicago: Rand McNally.

Easterbrooks, M. A., & Goldberg, W. A. (1985). Effects of early maternal employment on toddlers, mothers, and fathers. *Developmental Psychology, 21*(5), 774–783.

Easterbrooks, M. A., & Goldberg, W. A. (in press). Security of toddler-parent attachment: Relation to children's socio-personality functioning during kindergarten. In M. Greenberg, D. Cicchetti, & M. Cummings (Eds.), *Attachment in the preschool years: Theory, research and intervention*. Chicago: University of Chicago Press.

Erickson, M. F., Sroufe, L. A., & Egeland, B. (1985). The relationship between quality of attachment and behavior problems in preschool in a high-risk sample. In I. Bretherton & E. Waters (Eds.), *Growing points of attachment theory and research. Monographs of the Society for Research in Child Development, 50*, 147–166.

Gamble, T., & Zigler, E. (1986). Effects of infant day care: Further look at the evidence. *American Journal of Orthopsychiatry, 56*(1), 26–42.

Gold, D., & Andres, P. (1978). Developmental comparisons between 10-year-old children with employed and non-employed mothers. *Child Development, 49*, 75–84.

Hansburg, H. G. (1980). *Adolescent separation anxiety: A method for the study of adolescent separation problems*. New York: Krieger.

Hayes, C. D., & Kamerman, S. B. (1983). Conclusions and recommendations. In C. D. Hayes & S. B. Kamernon (Eds.), *Children of working parents* (pp. 220–247). Washington, DC: National Academy Press.

Hayghe, H. (1986). Rise in mothers' labor force activity includes those with infants. *Monthly Labor Review, 109*(2), 43–45.

Hock, E. (1980). Working and non-working mothers and their infants: A comparative study of maternal caregiving characteristics and infant social behavior. *Merrill-Palmer Quarterly, 26*(2), 79–101.

Hoffman, L. W. (1974). Effects of maternal employment in the child—A review of the research. *Developmental Psychology, 10*, 204–229.

Hoffman, L. W. (1984). Maternal employment and the young child. In M. Perlmutter (Ed.), *Parent-child interaction and parent-child relations in child development. The Minnesota Symposia on Child Psychology* (Vol. 197 pp. 101–127). Hillsdale, NJ: Erlbaum.

Hollingshead, A. B. (1975). *Four factor index of social status*. Unpublished manuscript, Yale University.

Izard, C. (1972). *Patterns of emotion*. New York: Academic Press.

Izard, C., Dougherty, F., Bloxom, B., & Kotsch, W. E. (1974). *The Differential Emotions Scale: A method of measuring the subjective experience of discrete emotions*. Unpublished manuscript, Department of Psychology, Vanderbilt University.

Kagan, J., Kearsley, R., & Zelazo, P. (1978). *Infancy: Its place in human development*. Cambridge, MA: Harvard University Press.

Kessler, R. C., & McRae, J. A., Jr. (1982). The effect of wives' employment on the mental health of married men and women. *American Sociological Review, 47,* 216–227.

Klagsbrun, M., & Bowlby, J. (1976). Responses to separation from parents: A clinical test for young children. *British Journal of Projective Psychology, 21,* 7–21.

Lamb, M. E., Frodi, A., Hwang, P., & Frodi, M. (1982). Mother- and father-infant interaction involving play and holding in traditional and non-traditional Swedish families. *Developmental Psychology, 18,* 215–221.

Lazarus, I., & Folkman, S. (1984). *Stress, appraisal, and coping.* New York: Springer.

Main, M., & Solomon, J. (1987). Discovery of an insecure disorganized/disoriented attachment pattern: Procedures, findings, and implications for the classification of behavior. In M. Yogman & T. B. Brazelton (Eds.), *Affective development in infancy.* Norwood, NJ: Ablex.

Main, M., Kaplan, N., & Cassidy, J. (1985). Security in infancy, childhood, and adulthood: A move to the level of representation. In I. Bretherton & E. Waters (Eds.), *Growing points of attachment theory and research. Monographs of the Society for Research in Child Development, 50,* 66–104.

Matas, L., Arend, R. A., & Sroufe, L. A. (1978). Continuity of adaptation in the second year: The relationship between quality of attachment and later competence. *Child Development, 49,* 547–556.

Owen, M. T., Easterbrooks, M. A., Chase-Lansdale, P. L., & Goldberg, W. A. (1984). The relation between maternal employment status and the stability of attachments to mother and to father. *Child Development, 55,* 1894–1901.

Pedersen, F. A., Cain, R. L., Zaslow, M., & Anderson, B. J. (1982). Variation in infant experience associated with alternative family roles. In L. Laosa & I. Sigel (Eds.), *Families as learning environments for children* (pp. 203–221). New York: Plenum Press.

Rapoport, R., & Rapoport, R. (1976). *Dual-career families re-examined.* New York: Harper & Row.

Rosenfield, S. (1980). Sex differences in depression: Do women always have higher rates? *Journal of Health and Social Behavior, 21,* 33–42.

Rosenfield, S. (1984). *Sex differences in mental health: Explanations for relative risk.* Paper presented at the annual meeting of the American Sociological Association, San Antonio, TX.

Rutter, M. (1984). Continuities and discontinuities in socio-emotional development. In R. N. Emde & R. J. Harmon (Eds.), *Continuities and discontinuities in development* (pp. 41–68). New York: Plenum Press.

Rutter, M., Quinton, D., & Liddle, C. (1983). Parenting in two generations: Looking backwards and looking forwards. In N. Madge (Ed.), *Families at risk* (pp. 60–98). London: Heinemann.

Spitz, R. (1946). Anaclitic depression. *Psychoanalytic study of the child, 2,* 313–42.

Suomi, S., & Harlow, H. (1978). Early experience and social development in rhesus monkeys. In M. E. Lamb (Ed.), *Social and personality development* (pp. 252–271). New York: Holt, Rinehart & Winston.

Sroufe, L. A. (1983). Infant-caregiver attachment and patterns of adaptation in preschool: The roots of maladaptation and competence. In M. Perlmutter (Ed.), *Minnesota symposium in child psychology, 16* (pp. 41–81). Hillsdale, NJ: Erlbaum.

Vaughn, B., Egeland, B., Sroufe, L. A., & Waters, E. (1979). Individual differences in infant-mother attachment at twelve and eighteen months: Stability and change in families under stress. *Child Development, 50,* 971–975.

Vaughn, B., Gove, F., & Egeland, B. (1980). The relationship between out-of-home care and the quality of infant-mother attachment in an economically disadvantaged population. *Child Development, 51,* 1203–1214.

Zigler, E. (1987). *Childcare for parents who work outside the home: Problems and solutions.* Invited address to the meetings of the Society for Research in Child Development, Baltimore.

Zigler, E., & Muenchow, S. (1983). Infant day care and infant-care leaves. *American Psychologist, 38,* 91–94.

6

Maternal Employment and Sex Typing in Early Adolescence
Contemporaneous and Longitudinal Relations

Nancy L. Galambos, Anne C. Petersen, and Kathleen Lenerz

One of the most remarkable sociocultural changes since World War II is the steady and substantial rise of women joining the labor force. With nearly 68% of married mothers with school-age children working outside of the home (Hayghe, 1986), maternal employment has clearly become a modal aspect of life in American families. The movement of mothers into the labor market constituted a departure from those behaviors that have been long considered to be inherent in the feminine sex role (Smith, 1979). As such, employed mothers crossed the boundaries drawn by shared societal expectations for appropriate behavior in women. It is this tension between cultural expectations for mothers and their actual choices over the last several decades that has stimulated much speculation and research about the lives of children whose mothers are employed.

In the present chapter, we address a core area of research within the maternal employment literature, namely the relationship between

---

Nancy L. Galambos • Department of Psychology, University of Victoria, Victoria, British Columbia, Canada V8W 2Y2.   Anne C. Petersen • Department of Human Development and Family Studies, Pennsylvania State University, University Park, Pennsylvania 16802.   Kathleen Lenerz • Department of Education, University of California, Los Angeles, Los Angeles, California 90024.

the employment status of mothers and the sex-typed characteristics of their adolescent children. Sex typing is the process by which individuals develop the attributes that are consistent with their sex role or with general societal expectations for their gender. The products of this process are seen in sex-typed attributes, for example, sex-typed behaviors, personality characteristics, beliefs, preferences, and attitudes (Huston, 1983; Mussen, 1969). The sex typing of children and adolescents has been of special concern to researchers of maternal employment because the employed mother has gone beyond what was once the typical role for a women—that of homemaker. The key issue of interest for researchers has been in discerning whether and to what extent the mother's choice of life-style has led to differences in the sex role socialization of her children (Hoffman, 1977). With evidence that a mother's employment is among the most consistent and best predictors of a lower level of sex-typed characteristics among children, adolescents, and young adults, particularly females (Hoffman, 1974; Huston-Stein & Higgins-Trenk, 1978), a second issue has attained significance. That is, by what process does a mother's employment status influence the sex-typed characteristics of her children?

One goal of this chapter is to review the literature on maternal employment and sex typing in adolescence. First, research will be reviewed that has examined differences in sex typing in the children of employed and nonemployed mothers. This will allow us to make conclusions about the general nature of the relationship between maternal employment and sex-typed attributes. Second, we discuss empirical studies that have looked beyond differences in the children of employed and nonemployed mothers in attempts to explain the process by which maternal employment shapes sex-typed attributes. We argue that the mother's satisfaction with her role and the nature of the mother–adolescent relationship are important components of this process. Furthermore, we propose that maternal role satisfaction influences mother–adolescent relations, which in turn, influence adolescent sex typing. Following our explication of this process, we describe results from our study of maternal employment and adolescent sex typing.

Before proceeding to the review of the literature, we will briefly discuss our theoretical approach to research on maternal employment and adolescent sex-typed attributes. This approach, known as the life-span perspective on individual development, has guided our view of the issues that need to be addressed.

I. THE LIFE-SPAN DEVELOPMENTAL PERSPECTIVE

The investigation of the process through which maternal employment influences sex-typed attributes in adolescence may be addressed usefully by concepts found within the life-span approach to human development (Baltes, Reese, & Lipsitt, 1980; Huston-Stein & Higgins-Trenk, 1978; R. Lerner & Busch-Rossnagel, 1981). This perspective assumes that reciprocal relationships exist among the adolescent, the adolescent's contexts, and the significant others in those contexts, all of which may continually change and interact to influence development. Because earlier development and experiences may be interconnected with later ones, individual development is necessarily a life-span phenomenon, one in which the individual takes an active role (Baltes et al., 1980; Elder, 1974; R. Lerner & Busch-Rossnagel, 1981).

Two important assumptions of the life-span perspective are that (a) development is assumed to have multiple determinants, including those deriving from the historical and social contexts, the family, and the individual, and (b) development is believed to be potentially multidirectional, that is, following one of many different paths (Baltes et al., 1980). Because of these assumptions, there is a focus on the potential for plasticity in the organism and on the processes underlying development. The potential for plasticity refers to "systematic changes within the person in his or her structure and/or function" (R. Lerner, 1984, p. xi). Plasticity may lead ultimately to behavioral flexibility, which is defined as the capability of changing behavior to meet contextual demands (Kendall, R. Lerner, & Craighead, 1984; R. Lerner, 1984). As such, the potential for plasticity and the behavioral flexibility associated with it are directly linked to a key concept in sex role research, namely, sex role flexibility.

Sex role flexibility has been discussed as the capability of changing one's behavior, regardless of gender, to meet the demands of the context (Bem, 1975; Hefner, Rebecca, & Oleshansky, 1975; Worell, 1981). The adoption of behaviors consistent with one's sex role may restrict the individual's life choices, but sex role flexibility opens more avenues to behaviors and choices, and hence, is thought to be associated with more optimal psychological health (Bem, 1974; Block, 1973; Hefner et al., 1975; Huston, 1983; Robinson & Green, 1981; Worell, 1978). How do we measure sex role flexibility? Although there is no single measure, it is assumed that a lower level of sex typing on indexes of sex-typed attributes means that the individual *may* be more behaviorally flexible (Bem, 1974; Pleck, 1975; Robinson & Green, 1981; Worell, 1981). Thus, those individuals who see a wide variety of behaviors and personality traits as open to males and females, who feel comfortable in pursuing interests and careers that may not be a part of their prescribed sex role, and who describe themselves as both masculine and feminine may be most likely to be among the people who show behavioral flexibility (Bem, 1975).

The life-span perspective aids us in conducting research on sex role flexibility and maternal employment by emphasizing the necessity for studying multiple dimensions of sex typing (Huston, 1983; Worell, 1981), by focusing on the need for process-oriented, multivariate, longitudinal research, and by stressing the need to consider the interrelations between the many contexts of which the individual is a part and individual development (J. Lerner & Galambos, 1986).

II. THE INFLUENCES OF MATERNAL EMPLOYMENT ON SEX TYPING IN ADOLESCENTS: A REVIEW

Several reviews of the influences of maternal employment on aspects of child and adolescent development have concluded in the past decade that there is evidence for a direct link between maternal employment and children's sex-typed attributes. More specifically, across the range of preschool- to college-age samples, daughters with employed mothers are more likely than those with nonemployed mothers to have less stereotyped views of the feminine role, higher career aspirations, more favorable attitudes toward careers for women, more masculine self-descriptions, and more masculine occupational choices (Hoffman, 1974, 1979, 1980; Huston-Stein & Higgins-Trenk, 1978; Montemayor & Clayton, 1983). There is evidence, too, that preschool, young adolescent, and adolescent boys show less stereotyped beliefs about masculine and feminine sex roles when their mothers are employed (Gold & Andres, 1978a,b,c; Gold, Andres, & Glorieux, 1979).

In part, these conclusions are based on simple comparisons of children with employed and nonemployed mothers—studies that look only at the direct link between maternal employment and aspects of child development (Banducci, 1967; Chandler, Sawicki, & Stryffeler, 1981; Rosenthal & Hansen, 1981). Given that this was the predominant method of research until recently (Bronfenbrenner & Crouter, 1982; J. Lerner & Galambos, 1986), the empirical data base is quite extensive. On the other hand, some studies have examined indirect paths from maternal employment to the child's development, attempting to elucidate the processes by which maternal employment influences children's lives. We review first those studies or parts of studies dealing with the direct relationship between maternal employment and sex-typed outcomes. Then we review studies that have addressed maternal role satisfaction and mother–adolescent relations as important variables that may link maternal employment to sex-typed attributes.

A. Direct Links

The adolescent's aspirations for educational and occupational attainments belong to the class of sex-typed attributes known as *sex role preferences* (Huston, 1983). These aspirations have been examined by researchers interested in the influences of maternal employment on the adolescent. Banducci (1967), for example, studied high-school seniors in three SES categories based on the father's occupation: professional, skilled worker, and laborer. Results indicated that, with the exception of boys in professional families, maternal employment was associated with higher aspirations and expectations to attain a college education. Roy (1963) also found maternal employment to be related to rural high-school students' plans to attend college; those students with employed mothers were more likely to plan on attending college than were students with nonemployed mothers. There were no such differences, however, in high-school students living in an urban area. Stein (1973) reported that college females with employed mothers had higher educational aspirations than those whose mothers were not working outside of the home. In another study, maternal employment was not associated with any differences in the educational or vocational aspirations of adolescent boys and girls from middle- or working-class families (Gold & Andres, 1978a). The evidence suggests a tendency for adolescents with employed mothers to have higher educational goals, although the extent to which these findings can be generalized is not clear.

Daughters of employed mothers tend to have higher *occupational* aspirations. In fact, Huston-Stein and Higgins-Trenk (1978) claimed that maternal employment is the most well-documented and consistent correlate of a female's departure from the feminine role, as evidenced in her career orientation (i.e., desire to pursue a career). This was seen in Banducci's (1967) study in which high-school girls with employed mothers were more likely than those with homemaker mothers to expect to pursue lifetime careers, regardless of SES. Similarly, Stephan and Corder (1985) reported that significantly more female adolescents from dual-career families (i.e., those in which mothers and fathers were in high-status occupations) wished to work outside of the home relative to females in traditional families (i.e., father only employed in a high-prestige occupation, mother not employed). The comparison of male adolescents from dual-career and traditional families showed that a greater number of males in dual-career homes desired their future wives to combine work and motherhood. Studies of college women have also found that the daughters of mothers with a history of employment were more career-oriented than the daughters of nonemployed mothers (Almquist &

Angrist, 1971; Altman & Grossman, 1977; Stein, 1973). Moreover, college women and adolescent girls who were preparing for male-dominated occupations were more likely to be the daughters of employed mothers than were those who preferred typically feminine occupations (Almquist, 1974; Douvan, 1963; Tangri, 1972).

It should be noted, however, that a few studies have indicated no differences in occupational aspirations according to maternal employment status. Rosenthal and Hansen (1981) found that young adolescents with employed mothers were no more likely than those with nonemployed mothers to aspire to prestigious occupations or to have a greater degree of vocational planfulness. The absence of a relationship between maternal employment and vocational aspirations and planfulness remained when the mother's education and marital status were taken into account. In another study, the occupational aspirations of a sample of black and white girls in their senior year in an urban high school were not related to maternal work status alone. Rather, the influences of maternal employment were dependent on the mother's sex role attitudes and the nature of the mother–adolescent relationship (Macke & Morgan, 1978). A study of college women found no differences in occupational aspirations related to maternal employment status. Still, in this study, the daughters of employed women felt more favorable toward women who pursue careers (Lipman-Blumen, 1972). The studies finding a significant relationship between maternal employment status and adolescent and young-adult occupational aspirations are not obviously different from those reporting no relationship. In the absence of a clear explanation, it may be best simply to acknowledge that there is not unanimous support for the finding that daughters with employed mothers have higher occupational aspirations.

Another sex-typed attribute that has been investigated in maternal employment research is *sex stereotypes*. A sex stereotype is the belief that particular behaviors or attributes are characteristic of one sex group as opposed to another (R. Lerner & Hultsch, 1983; Worell, 1981). Comparisons of sons and daughters with employed and nonemployed mothers demonstrate that maternal employment is associated with a lower level of sex stereotyping. Chandler et al. (1981) reported that in a midwestern community eighth-grade sons and daughters of employed mothers were less likely than the adolescents of nonemployed mothers to agree with sex stereotyped statements concerning the role of women. Moreover, girls with employed mothers were more likely to consider conventionally masculine and feminine occupations (e.g., hairdresser, nurse, doctor) as appropriate for both sexes (Chandler et al., 1981). Bacon and R. Lerner (1975) found that in a working-class sample, second-, fourth-, and sixth-grade girls with employed mothers saw more male-dominated occupations as being available to both boys and girls, although their own vocational aspirations were for female-dominated occupations. In addition, Gold and Andres (1978a) discovered that, in working- and middle-class families, adolescent boys and girls with employed mothers differentiated less between the sexes with respect to the attribution of personality traits than did the adolescents with nonemployed mothers. Similar results have been found with college students (Vogel, Broverman, Broverman, Clarkson, & Rosenkrantz, 1970).

A few studies suggest that maternal employment may be related to the adolescent's greater *psychological androgyny*, which is the endorsement of both masculine and feminine personality characteristics. Psychological androgyny is believed to be associated with psychological health and sex role flexibility (Bem, 1975). In one study, middle-class high-school girls with employed mothers were more likely to be androgynous, according to the Bem Sex Role Inventory, and to show a lower fear of success than were their peers with nonemployed mothers (Gilroy, Talierco, & Steinbacher, 1981). In another study, undergraduate females who were androgynous were more likely to have employed mothers (Hansson, Chernovetz, & Jones, 1977).

Some studies suggest that daughters with employed mothers are more likely to have *masculine personality* attributes such as independence, achievement motivation, and dominance (Huston-Stein & Higgins-Trenk, 1978). In a past analysis of archival data from the Oakland Growth Study, Elder and MacInnis (1983), for example, discovered that in the late 1930s, career-oriented adolescent girls who had strong achievement orientations, as measured by projective tests, were likely to be the daughters of mothers who had been employed in the mid-1930s. Although the historical time period of the 1930s is quite different from that of the past two decades, more recently gathered data show that adolescent and college-age children of employed mothers tend to be more achievement-oriented that do children of homemaker mothers (Powell, 1963; Stein, 1973).

The *sex role attitudes* of children with employed mothers when compared to children with homemaker mothers may be more egalitarian; children with employed mothers approve more of equality between men and women with respect to roles. For instance, Stephan and Corder (1985) noted that adolescents from high-prestige dual-career families had more egalitarian sex role attitudes than adolescents from single-earner families in which the father was employed in a high-status position. Dellas, Gaier, and Emihovich (1979) found that preadolescent boys and girls with employed mothers were more likely than preadolescents with nonemployed mothers to believe that women with children should work outside of the home. Furthermore, King, McIntyre, and Axelson (1968) observed that, irrespective of parental educational levels, ninth-grade boys and girls saw maternal employment as less of a threat to the marital relationship than did the adolescents whose mothers stayed home. On the other hand, Weeks, Wise, and Duncan (1984) found no evidence of a relationship between maternal work status and sex role attitudes in high-school girls. The sample in this study was quite small, however, and the analyses did not control for background variables such as mother's education and marital status. Baruch (1972) also found no relationship between maternal work status and attitudes about career women in a sample of college women from upper-middle-class backgrounds. Two studies controlling for SES and other background variables have shown that maternal employment *is* related to more egalitarian sex role attitudes in college women and men (Meier, 1972; Vanfossen, 1977).

1. Summary

Generally, the bulk of the previously mentioned investigations has provided support for the notion that adolescents and college students with employed mothers are less likely to be traditionally sex typed on a variety of indexes such as occupational aspirations, sex stereotypes, and sex role attitudes. This relationship appears, however, to be strongest and more pervasive for daughters than for sons (Hoffman, 1974, 1980). More specifically, the null hypothesis is more often rejected for daughters than for sons, and the size of the effect is often greater for daughters (Chandler et al., 1981; Dellas et al., 1979; Vogel et al., 1970). One problem associated with making generalizations of this type, however, is that numerous studies have *not* included males in their samples (Almquist & Angrist, 1971; Altman & Grossman, 1977; Elder & MacInnis, 1983; Gilroy et al., 1981; Stein, 1973; Tangri, 1972; Vanfossen, 1977). Thus, limited knowledge about the development of sex-typed attributes in males makes it difficult to discern the possible processes by which sex typing in males and females may differ within the context of maternal employment. In fact, Powell and Steelman (1982) found that adult men's attitudes about women in the labor force were more influenced by their mother's work history than were the attitudes of adult women in the sample. One aim of the present investigation is to examine the processes that influence the sex-typed attributes of both adolescent girls *and* boys.

Another criticism that can be leveled at this literature is that sex typing has not been assessed as multidimensional. That is, typically, any single investigation discussed here included just one or two, rather than multiple, dimensions of sex typing (e.g., vocational aspirations or sex role attitudes or sex stereotypes). In limiting the number of dimensions studied, the *pattern* of dimensions of sex typing as influenced by maternal employment is entirely unknown. A strategy directed to illustrating the interrelationships among multiple sex-typed attributes within a single study is more congruent with the current focus of sex role research (Huston, 1983; Spence & Helmreich, 1978) and with a life-span perspective on individual development (Baltes et al., 1980). In addition, if the pattern of interrelationships among various sex-typed dimensions is better understood, then life-span-oriented research can be conducted in order to determine how these patterns shift over time in response to changes in the context, such as maternal employment. Another goal of the present study, then, is to examine multiple indexes of sex typing in adolescent boys and girls and to determine how they are influenced by maternal employment.

One other concern related to the previously mentioned studies is the historical time period during which they were conducted. Most of the research cited before was conducted on working- or middle-class samples in the 1960s or 1970s, with a few studies from the early 1980s. It is doubtful, however, that the experience of maternal employment was the same for mothers and children in those two decades as it is in the 1980s (Bronfenbrenner & Crouter, 1982). Mothers who were employed in the 1960s may have been those with the most egalitarian sex role attitudes, perhaps somewhat ahead of their time relative to mothers who chose to stay home. We know that women's acceptance and endorsement of maternal employment grew significantly from the early 1960s to the late 1970s (Thornton, Alwin, & Camburn, 1983). This was coupled with the steady increase in married mothers' labor force participation, rising from 28% in 1960 to 61% in 1985 (Hayghe, 1986; Waldman, 1983). Thus it may be that the distinction (e.g., in sex role ideology) between the employed and nonemployed mothers and their families was greater in the 1960s than it is currently. The fact that it is normative for a mother in the 1980s to be employed may lessen the potential effect of maternal employment on sex typing in adolescents.

B. Processes of Influence

1. Role Modeling and Identification

What process accounts for the significant relationship that has been observed for sex typing and maternal employment? Most writers have discussed the mother's effect as a competent feminine role model. The argument is that the employed mother is perceived by her child as possessing some of the qualities belonging more typically to the masculine cluster of traits indicative of competence (i.e., earning wages, going to work). In contrast, the nonemployed mother is seen largely in a restricted setting, modeling behaviors that are considered to be typically feminine (i.e., being nurturant, keeping house) and that are not monetarily or socially rewarded. The mechanism by which daughters of employed mothers come to evidence fewer sex-typed attributes and which explains why sons of employed mothers may not be so strongly influenced is believed to be identification with the "competent" mother (Baruch, 1972, 1974; Hoffman, 1974).

Identification is defined by Kagan (1958) as a belief that some of the attributes of the model (e.g., mother) belong to the self. In Kagan's (1958) explication of the concept, it is argued that three conditions must be met if an optimally strong identification is to occur: (a) the model must be perceived by the child as being warm and nurturant, (b) the model must be in control of the goals, power, or competence that the child desires, and (c) the child must already perceive some objective basis of similarity with the model (e.g., gender, in the case of the same-sex parent). Thus a warm mother–daughter relationship (which may satisfy the first condition) and the mother's satisfaction with her role (which may satisfy the second condition) will enhance identification. It follows, then, that daughters who have a warm relationship with their satisfied nonemployed mothers will identify with them and be more likely to approve of and adhere to the feminine sex role. On the other hand, daughters having a warm relationship with their satisfied employed mothers are likely to subscribe to a less typically feminine sex role.

There is, in fact, some evidence to suggest that daughters of employed mothers identify with their mothers and are likely to view women as competent. Baruch (1974), for example, reported that college-age daughters with employed mothers were more likely to prefer their mothers' life-style pattern and to perceive themselves as more similar to their mothers than did the daughters of nonemployed mothers. Furthermore, in another study, Baruch (1972) found that daughters of employed mothers were less likely to devalue articles apparently written by women than were the daughters of nonemployed mothers. This was interpreted by Baruch (1972) as evidence that daughters with employed mothers had learned that women are competent. More recently, Stephan and Corder (1985) found that adolescent daughters from dual-career families were more likely than those from traditional single-earner families to select their mothers as an accessible model for the role of worker.

Overall, the hypothesis of the employed mother as a competent role model and the daughter's identification with her appears to be a viable one. As mentioned previously, however, the development of sex-typed attributes among sons has been relatively neglected in studies of maternal employment. Sons also seem to be influenced by the mother's role modeling, but may be less so, given their presumably lower identification with her. The potential salience of the nature of mother–adolescent relations and the mother's role satisfaction, as components of a process in which sex-typed attributes in both sexes are shaped, bears more discussion.

2. Role Satisfaction and Mother–Adolescent Relations

The satisfaction of the mother with her role, that is, how happy she is with being employed or being a homemaker, was raised as a key variable in maternal employment research conducted over two decades ago (Hoffman, 1963; Yarrow, Scott, de Leeuw, & Heinig, 1962). More recently, several studies have examined maternal role satisfaction in mothers of infants and toddlers (Farel, 1980; Hock, 1980; J. Lerner & Galambos, 1985; Stuckey, McGhee, & Bell, 1982). Reviews of the literature on maternal role satisfaction (Hoffman, 1974; J. Lerner & Galambos, 1986) suggest that higher satisfaction is related to the quality of mother–child relations. Greater maternal role satisfaction is believed to lead to higher quality interactions. In turn, these interactions may be related to positive outcomes for the adolescent, including greater behavioral flexibility and a higher level of adjustment (Bronfenbrenner & Crouter, 1982; Hoffman, 1974, 1979; J. Lerner & Galambos, 1985, 1986). A two-part process model is thus identified; (a) maternal role satisfaction leads to a more optimal mother–child relationship and (b) a more optimal mother–child relationship leads to the child's greater behavioral flexibility and competence.

This process was tested by J. Lerner and Galambos (1985) with a sample of preschoolers who were followed longitudinally. In this study, the mother's acceptance of the child (as reported by the mother when the child was 3) was found to mediate the relationship between maternal role satisfaction (age 3) and the child's easier temperamental style (age 4). That is, maternal role satisfaction affected the child only through the nature of the mother–child relationship. Furthermore, the indirect effect of maternal role satisfaction on the child's temperament at age 4 was greater than the effect of earlier temperamental style measured at age 2 (J. Lerner & Galambos, 1985). The authors interpreted the results as support for the two-part process model.

There is some evidence to suggest that a similar process may be evident in adolescence as well, although this process has not been tested within a single study of adolescents. Instead, support for components of this model is derived from studies that link maternal role satisfaction to sex-typed attributes or to aspects of the mother–daughter relationship. For example, maternal role satisfaction in employed mothers was related to fewer sex-stereotyped attitudes in 10-year-old boys and girls (Gold & Andres, 1978b), to a higher career orientation in adolescent daughters (Pearlman, 1981), and to young adult women's future plans for employment (D'Amico, Haurin, & Mott, 1983). Dissatisfaction among nonemployed mothers was related to college daughters' higher aspirations to pursue a career, whereas the reverse was true for the daughters of satisfied nonemployed mothers (Altman & Grossman, 1977). Lipman-Blumen (1972) found that adult daughters who perceived their homemaker mothers to be dissatisfied had more egalitarian sex role attitudes than did the daughters of satisfied homemakers.

These findings suggest, then, that satisfied employed mothers and dissatisfied nonemployed mothers tend to have daughters who have fewer sex-typed characteristics. Assuming that these findings are generalizable, we must argue that maternal role satisfaction may not inevitably lead to greater behavioral flexibility, as suggested by the two-part process model discussed here. Rather, in families where the mother is *not* employed, maternal role *dissatisfaction* may lead to greater (sex role) flexibility. The mother's employment status, then, may qualify the two-part process model forwarded by J. Lerner and Galambos (1985, 1986).

The evidence for the salience of the mother–adolescent relationship in linking maternal role satisfaction to sex-typed attributes is limited. Altman and Grossman (1977) found that daughters who perceived their mothers as satisfied also perceived them to be good parents. The *mediating* role of the mother–adolescent relationship was not, however, examined. Moreover, because the daughter's perceptions were used as the source for the indexes of maternal role satisfaction and parenting style, the intercorrelation between maternal role satisfaction and parenting could be due to common method variance.

3. Summary

What does it mean for a mother to be satisfied with her role? According to available research and hypotheses advanced by writers in the maternal employment field, the mother who is satisfied with her role is content with her daily activities whether or not she is gainfully employed. It is likely that the satisfied mother has high self-esteem and feels personally fulfilled (Baruch & Barnett, 1980; Lamb, 1982; Lamb, Chase-Lansdale, & Owen, 1979). As such, her mood will probably be positive, and she will be a more sensitive and warm parent (Lamb, 1982; Lamb et al., 1979; Stuckey et al., 1982).

Research and theory tell us that maternal role satisfaction and warm interactions with one's children set the stage for identification with the mother. At least for female children, this means that (a) when the mother is employed, the daughter will tend to follow in her mother's footsteps and may have fewer sex-typed characteristics and (b) when the mother is not employed, the daughter will be more likely to follow her mother's example and to have more sex-typed characteristics, relative to the daughters of employed mothers. The mother's role dissatisfaction, on the other hand, may be expected to result in the daughter's decreased enthusiasm for and lower adherence to her mother's choice of life-style. Empirical work in this area conducted with male children is so limited that it is difficult to make generalizations about their sex-typed attributes. With respect to choice of life-style, the mother's employment status is unlikely to influence the son's choice; virtually all men will seek employment. Maternal work status could influence, however, the son's attitudes regarding his wife's life-style preference (Stephan & Corder, 1985).

III. THE EARLY ADOLESCENCE STUDY

A. Plan of the Study

In order to examine maternal employment and sex typing in adolescence, we employ data from the Early Adolescence Study (Petersen, 1984), which followed sixth-grade girls and boys through the eighth grade. The plan of our study is as follows. First, we examine the sixth- and eighth-grade data cross-sectionally. One goal is to consider at two points in time the relationship between the mother's work status and four indexes of adolescent sex typing: sex role attitudes, masculinity, femininity, and vocational-educational goals. These analyses are comparable to studies that have investigated the direct link between maternal employment and sex-typed attributes. In another set of analyses using sixth-grade data, we test the two-part process model, which hypothesizes mother–child relations to mediate between maternal role satisfaction and adolescent sex-typed attributes.

Our next set of analyses involves an examination of the longitudinal data. First we ask about the relationship between maternal work status in the sixth grade and the adolescent's sex-typed characteristics 1 and 2 years later. Then we examine *changes* in the mother's work status between the sixth and eighth grades and determine whether these changes are related to the adolescent's eighth-grade sex-typing measures. In line with the life-span perspective on human development, we use multivariate statistical procedures to evaluate these relationships. Due to limitations of the data set, however, we are not able to investigate the two-part process model longitudinally.

B. Features of the Sample and the Data

1. Design and Sample

The subjects were drawn from a longitudinal study of early adolescent development—the Early Adolescence Study (EAS). The EAS has been described in several publications (see Crockett, Losoff, & Petersen, 1984; Petersen, 1984; Richardson, Galambos, Schulenberg, & Petersen, 1984; Schulenberg, Asp, & Petersen, 1984). The sample consists of two successive cohorts of subjects ($N = 335$) who were randomly drawn from the sixth-grade classes of two middle- to upper-middle-class midwestern suburban school districts. Cohort I (birth year 1967) was in the sixth grade during the 1978–1979 academic year, and Cohort II (birth year 1968) was in the sixth grade during 1979–1980. The total Cohort I sample consists of 188 adolescents (103 girls and 85 boys); the total Cohort II sample consists of 147 young adolescents (79 girls and 68 boys).

Analyses of variance with cohort as the single factor showed that the cohorts were equivalent with respect to such background variables as mother's education and age, father's education and age, and prestige of the father's occupation. Cohort I adolescents, however, came from families with a slightly larger number of children (Cohort I, $M = 2.87$; Cohort II, $M = 2.58$, $p < .05$) and thus were more likely to have a higher birth order (Cohort I, $M = 2.20$; Cohort II, $M = 1.90$, $p < .05$). A chi-square analysis showed that the proportion of employed mothers was equivalent in the cohorts. With respect to analyses of variance performed on the dependent variables, there were no systematic cohort differences across the sixth, seventh, and eighth grades that were likely to influence our results. Therefore, in the interest of increasing sample size and power, we combined Cohorts I and II in our analyses.

The mean age of the adolescents as of January 1 of the sixth-grade schoolyear was 11.6 years for the boys and girls in both cohorts. The mean age of their fathers was 42.4 years, and the mothers averaged 39.6 years. Eighty percent of the adolescents came from families with two or

Table 1. Demographic Characteristics of the Family in Grade 6 in the Total Sample by Mother's Work Status[a]

Demographic characteristic	Mother employed M	Mother employed SD	Mother not employed M	Mother not employed SD	Significance[c]
Mother's education[b]	4.65	1.03	4.46	.99	NS
Age of mother	39.63	4.35	39.44	4.26	NS
Father's education	5.04	1.24	5.19	1.09	NS
Age of father	42.39	5.52	42.28	4.91	NS
Father's job prestige	58.43	14.22	61.36	13.10	NS
Number of children living at home	2.71	1.00	2.86	1.02	NS
Birth order of adolescent	2.14	1.12	2.01	.93	NS

[a] The n for the mother variables, number of children, and birth order was 112 (not employed) and 191 (employed). The n for father's education, age, and job prestige was 109 (not employed) and 168 (employed).
[b] 1 = less than high school; 2 = some high school; 3 = high-school graduate; 4 = some college, technical, or semiprofessional; 5 = college graduate; 6 = some graduate or professional school or degree.
[c] Analysis of variance, with maternal work status (employed/not employed) as a single factor.

three children. One-third were firstborns or singletons; one-fifth were middleborns; and the remaining half were lastborns. In the sixth grade, 10% of the adolescents were from single-parent homes due to divorce (9%) or death of a parent (1%), whereas 84% were from intact families, and 6% were living in stepfamilies.

The fathers in this sample were highly educated; half had acquired professional or graduate training, and an additional one-fourth had attained college degrees. Their occupational standing averaged 60 (SD = 14), as indicated by National Opinion Research Center (NORC) prestige scores; these scores are continuous, ranging from 9 to 82, with a high score indicating a high-status position (Hodge, Siegel, & Rossi, 1965). Thus the typical father in this sample was a professional. The mothers in this sample also had a high level of education. Approximately 55% had attained college degrees, and an additional 25% to 30% had acquired some college education. Only 10% to 15% had no more than a high-school education. When their children were in the sixth grade, 64% of the mothers were employed. The mean occupational prestige score for the employed mothers was 48 (SD = 12).

Table 1 provides descriptive information about demographic features of the families with employed and nonemployed mothers when the adolescents were in the sixth grade. Analyses of variance with employment status of the mother (employed, not employed) as the inde-

Table 2. Occupational Classification of Employed Mothers, Grade 6, in Percentages by Cohort

Occupational classification	Total sample ($n = 201$)	Cohort I ($n = 121$)	Cohort II ($n = 80$)
Professional, technical, and kindred	41%	38%	45%
Managers and administrators	13%	16%	10%
Sales workers	17%	18%	16%
Clerical and kindred workers	21%	20%	24%
Craftsmen and kindred workers	1%	1%	1%
Laborers	1%	1%	1%
Service workers	5%	7%	3%

pendent variable indicated no significant differences on any of the demographic variables. The employed and nonemployed groups did not differ on mother's and father's education and age, father's job prestige, number of children living at home, and the adolescent's birth order. It should be noted, however, that 4% and 13% of the nonemployed and employed mothers, respectively, were single parents. This difference was statistically significant, $\chi^2(1,123) = 5.51, p < .05$.

For those mothers who held paying jobs, Table 2 presents the major occupational category to which the mothers belonged, according to the 1970 U.S. occupational codes. Clearly, the mothers in this sample tend to have higher status jobs, as just over half are employed as professionals or managers. Still, the range of traditional female-dominated jobs (e.g., clerical workers) is represented.

During the parental interview given when the adolescents were in the sixth grade, mothers were asked to describe their occupations and whether they were employed part- (5 to 29 hours) or full-time (30 hours or more). Table 3 presents the means and standard deviations for part- and full-time groups on a number of demographic characteristics: mother's and father's educational level, age, occupational prestige, number of children living at home, and the adolescent's birth order. Analyses of variance with full- or part-time status as the single factor revealed that there were two significant differences between the part- and full-time workers; part-time employed mothers had lower occupational prestige and had more children living in the home.

2. Data Collection

Through interviews and group assessments, data were gathered from subjects twice annually (during the fall and spring semesters) in

Table 3. Demographic Characteristics of Employed-Mother Families in the Total Sample by Part- and Full-time Status, Grade 6[a]

Characteristic	Part-time M	Part-time SD	Full-time M	Full-time SD	Significance
Mother					
Education[b]	4.66	.93	4.68	1.16	NS
Age	39.41	4.23	40.00	4.51	NS
Job prestige	45.76	11.86	50.31	12.00	$p < .05$
Father					
Education[b]	5.04	1.23	5.05	1.26	NS
Age	42.08	5.56	42.92	5.45	NS
Job prestige	58.79	13.46	57.82	15.53	NS
Number of children at home	2.83	1.06	2.53	.91	$p < .05$
Adolescent's birth order	2.10	1.23	2.23	.94	NS

[a] The n for the mother variables, number of children, and birth order was 114 (part-time) and 74 (full-time). The n for father's education, father's age, and father's job prestige was 106 (part-time) and 62 (full-time).
[b] 1 = less than high school; 2 = some high school; 3 = high-school graduate; 4 = some college, technical, or semiprofessional; 5 = college graduate; 6 = some graduate or professional school or degree.
[c] Analysis of variance with part- versus full-time status as the single factor.

the sixth, seventh, and eighth grades. Each interviewer conducted interviews with the same adolescents at all points of measurement. Because the study was longitudinal and every adolescent was not present at every point of data collection, the sample sizes are not constant across grade levels. However, the proportion of those *not* participating is sufficiently small (about 10% at each interview session) to allow for cross-time comparisons (Schulenberg et al., 1984). The interviews focused on family, school, peer, and pubertal issues and were semistructured with precoded responses for most open-ended questions and with some close-ended questions. The group assessments also were conducted twice annually and included several objective instruments and questionnaires. Among these instruments were the Attitudes toward Women Scale for Adolescents (AWSA) (Galambos, Petersen, Richards, & Gitelson, 1985), the Bem Sex Role Inventory (BSRI) (Bem, 1974), and the Self-Image Questionnaire for Young Adolescents (SIQYA) (Petersen, Schulenberg, Abramowitz, Offer, & Jarcho, 1984), all of which were administered once a year during the sixth, seventh, and eighth grades. In the present study, we use data from these scales because these data were most pertinent to the study of maternal employment and adolescent sex typing.

Individual interviews with parents of the subjects were conducted twice: once when their children were in the sixth grade and once when their children were in the eighth grade. These semistructured interviews, with primarily precoded responses, took place in the parent's home and focused on marital relations, occupational status and history, problems experienced by the parent, and parental perceptions of the parent–child relationship and the adolescent's social and physical development. In addition, the parents completed several objective instruments, some of which were parallel to those completed by the adolescent. The present investigation uses interview data from the mothers.

3. Measures

Variables measured in the present study include the mother's report of maternal work status, her role satisfaction, and perceptions of warmth in the mother–adolescent relationship. Data from the adolescents were used to measure sex-typed attributes (sex role attitudes, masculinity, femininity, and goal orientation) and adolescent perceptions of the mother–adolescent relationship (specifically, mother–adolescent warmth).

(a) Mother's Work Status. As noted previously, maternal work status groups were formed on the basis of an interview with the mother. In the sixth- and eighth-grade interviews, mothers were asked whether they were currently employed, and if so, whether they worked part- (5 to 29 hours) or full-time (30 or more hours). Furthermore, mothers were asked to describe the type of occupation in which they were engaged. This information was used to classify the mothers into occupational categories (see Table 2) and to code NORC prestige scores (see Table 3). Given the nature of these data, it was possible to determine the mother's work status stability from the sixth to the eighth grades, that is, whether she began, discontinued, or remained working. Mothers were not interviewed when their children were in the seventh grade, and hence, employment data during this year are not available.

(b) Sex Role Attitudes. The AWSA (Galambos et al., 1985), administered to the adolescents once in the sixth, seventh, and eighth grades, was used to measure the adolescent's sex role attitudes or the extent to which he or she approves of the gender-based division of roles, responsibilities, and behaviors. The AWSA consists of 12 items, each representing an attitude to which the subject indicates his or her level of agreement (e.g., "Girls should have the same freedoms as boys"). The

mean score is used, with a higher score indicative of higher disapproval of gender differences in roles (range: 1 to 4). Internal consistency estimates across grades ranged from .62 to .85 for girls and from .71 to .86 for boys in the present sample.

(c) *Femininity/Masculinity.* Items on the short form of the BSRI (Bem, 1974) were used to measure the adolescent's view of himself or herself as masculine and feminine in the sixth, seventh, and eighth grades. The Femininity and Masculinity scales are each comprised of 10 personality characteristics that are considered to be socially desirable in females (femininity) and males (masculinity). For example, "self-reliant" is a characteristic on the Masculinity scale and "yielding" is an item on the Femininity scale. Subjects respond to the items, describing the extent to which the adjectives describe themselves. The mean of the item responses for each scale was used in the present study (range: 1 to 7). The alpha coefficients for each scale were consistently in the .70s and .80s for subjects in the EAS.

It is possible to combine the masculinity and femininity items into a psychological androgyny index. However, because recent research demonstrates that the androgyny score does not predict adjustment to any greater extent than do the separate Masculinity and Femininity scores (Deaux, 1984), we opted to use separate scores only in the present investigation. Analysis of our data (Galambos, 1985) indicated that the Masculinity and Femininity scales are positively related in boys ($r = .51$, $p < .001$) and in girls ($r = .28$, $p < .05$), thus indicating that adolescents who describe themselves as masculine also describe themselves as feminine. It may be that young adolescents at the turn of the 1980s felt comfortable in possessing a variety of desirable personality traits, whether they were masculine or feminine. Furthermore, femininity is positively associated with a more positive global self-image, as measured by the SIQYA (Petersen *et al.*, 1984) in boys ($r = .49$, $p < .001$) and in girls ($r = .36$, $p < .01$). Our interpretation of these data, then, is that greater masculinity and femininity in the boys and girls in our sample may indicate higher, rather than lower, behavioral flexibility. In addition, femininity seems to be particularly meaningful, as it is associated with greater personal adjustment.

(d) *Goal Orientation.* The Vocational-Educational Goals subscale of the SIQYA (Petersen *et al.*, 1984), administered once in the sixth, seventh, and eighth grades, is comprised of 10 items that are meant to measure how well the adolescent is doing in preparing for his or her vocational future (e.g., "I feel that working is too much responsibility for me"). Adolescents respond by indicating the extent to which the item is descriptive of themselves (range: 1 to 6). The internal consistency of this subscale, averaged across sixth- and seventh-grade assessments was .67 for boys and .66 for girls.

(e) Mother–Adolescent Warmth: Adolescent's Perceptions. The degree to which the adolescent experiences positive feelings and warmth within the mother–adolescent relationship was measured by the Family Relations subscale of the SIQYA (Petersen *et al.*, 1984). This measure was administered in the sixth, seventh, and eighth grades. The sixth-grade data are used in the present study in analyses examining perceptions of warmth as a mediator of maternal role satisfaction and sex-typed attributes. This subscale consists of 17 items, reflecting feelings of closeness between the adolescent and the parents (e.g., "Most of the time my parents are satisfied with me"). The mean of the items is used with a higher score indicating greater warmth (range: 1 to 6). The alpha coefficients averaged across the sixth and seventh grades were .77 for boys and .79 for girls.

(f) Mother–Adolescent Warmth: Mother's Perceptions. The degree to which the mother experiences positive feelings and warmth within the mother–adolescent relationship was measured by an index constructed from four items coded during the sixth-grade mother's interview. The items were: (a) "In general, then, how would you say things go between the two of you?", (b) "How happy or unhappy are you with the way his/her life is going?", (c) "Does your daughter/son come to you to discuss problems that are most important to him/her?", and (d) "Who does he/she talk to first?" Coefficient alpha for this index was .53. The average of the items was used, with a higher score reflecting greater warmth (range: 1.25 to 4.75). This index was correlated significantly but moderately with the adolescent's perceptions ($r = .29$, $p < .001$).

(g) Maternal Role Satisfaction. The mother's enjoyment of her role was measured with four items, which were rated from the mother's responses to sixth-grade interview questions. Three items asked directly: (a) "When you made a decision to work (or not work), what were the reasons (or in different words, why do you work/not work outside of the home)?", (b) "How do you feel about working/not working," and, (c) "What do you like least about working/not working?" The fourth item was the rater's global impression of the mother's role satisfaction. Interrater reliabilities for these items ranged from .74 to .94. The internal consistency of the four items together for the nonemployed and employed mothers was .82 and .73, respectively. The average of the preceding items was computed to form a scale score, with a higher score indicating greater role satisfaction (range: 1 to 5).

IV. ANALYSES

A. Cross-Sectional Results

1. Maternal Employment and Sex-Typed Attributes: Direct Links

In line with other research that has demonstrated maternal employment status to be related to sex-typed attributes among adolescents, the purpose of our first set of analyses was to investigate this relationship for 281 pairs of adolescents and mothers with all available data in our sample. Four sex-typed attributes were examined: sex role attitudes, masculinity, femininity, and vocational-educational goals. We conducted a multivariate analysis of covariance, controlling for marital status, with sixth-grade maternal work status (nonemployed and employed) and sex of adolescent as the independent variables. The dependent variables were the sixth-grade sex-typed attributes. Marital status of the parents was controlled in this analysis because, first, most single mothers were employed, and second, single mothers were less satisfied with their roles and had children who indicated lower parent–adolescent warmth (Galambos, 1985). We report the results of analyses using a 2-level factor for maternal work status (not employed, employed) rather than a 3-level factor (not employed, part-time, full-time) because of the relatively small cell sizes associated with the latter. Analyses with the 3-level factor indicated no appreciable differences in the results; this strategy accounted for no more than a 1% increase in the amount of variance explained beyond what was explained by the 2-level factor (Galambos, 1985).

The multivariate test showed no overall effect of maternal work status on the dependent variables. Nor was there a significant multivariate Maternal Work Status × Sex interaction effect. There was, however, a significant multivariate main effect of Sex, Hotelling-Lawley Trace $F(4,273) = 24.91$, $p < .0001$. Follow-up univariate tests revealed that girls had more egalitarian sex role attitudes than did boys, $F(1,276) = 63.44$, $p < .0001$, boys were more masculine, $F(1,276) = 8.05$, $p < .01$, and girls were more feminine, $F(1,276) = 26.7$, $p < .0001$. These are sex differences that are typically found in sex role research (Bem, 1974; Galambos et al., 1985).

It should be noted that the univariate test for the main effect of maternal work status on sex role attitudes was significant, $F(1,276) = 3.98$, $p < .05$. This finding indicated that adolescents with employed mothers had more egalitarian sex role attitudes ($M = 3.07$) than those with nonemployed mothers ($M = 2.97$). The effect size, however, is

Table 4. Means and Standard Deviations of Four Sex-Typed Attributes across Three Grades by Sex of Adolescent, Total Sample

	Attribute							
	Sex role attitudes		Masculinity		Femininity		Goal orientation	
Grade and sex	M	SD	M	SD	M	SD	M	SD
6[a]								
Boys	2.81	.49	5.08	.79	4.91	.87	5.01	.65
Girls	3.25	.35	4.77	.75	5.43	.75	5.00	.59
7[b]								
Boys	2.74	.52	5.11	.80	5.07	.84	5.02	.63
Girls	3.32	.33	4.78	.77	5.49	.79	4.99	.68
8[c]								
Boys	2.72	.54	5.51	.90	5.24	.93	4.99	.63
Girls	3.36	.32	4.93	.83	5.57	.89	5.07	.59

[a] Boys: $n = 140$; girls: $n = 165$.
[b] Boys: $n = 119$; girls: $n = 143$.
[c] Boys: $n = 100$; girls: $n = 117$.

quite small, relative to the main effect of sex. We must conclude from this analysis that the adolescent's gender is a far better predictor of sex-typed attributes in the sixth grade than is maternal employment status. Due to the insignificant multivariate and univariate effects of the covariate, marital status is not used as a covariate in further analyses.

We repeated the multivariate analysis of variance, this time with the eighth-grade maternal work status and sex-typing data. (No information regarding maternal work status was available for the seventh grade). Similar to the sixth-grade results, the eighth-grade analyses showed only a multivariate main effect of sex, Hotelling-Lawley Trace $F(4,165) = 23.37$, $p < .0001$. The univariate sex effects were again on sex role attitudes, masculinity, and femininity, in the same direction as in sixth grade. There was no univariate effect of eighth-grade maternal work status on eighth-grade sex role attitudes. Table 4 presents the means and standard deviations of the four measures of sex typing by sex of adolescent in the sixth, seventh, and eighth grades. The consistent sex differences on three of these four measures are apparent across grades.

2. Test of the Process of Influence Model

In the next set of analyses, we (Galambos, 1985; Galambos & Petersen, 1986) explored the process from maternal role satisfaction through mother–adolescent relations (in our case, perceptions of warmth) to sex-typed attributes. Path analyses were conducted separately by sex within the nonemployed and employed groups for the dependent variables of sex role attitudes and femininity. Because maternal role satisfaction scores in the sixth grade were available only for Cohort II, Cohort I subjects were not included in these analyses. In addition, single parents were excluded. This resulted in a total of 111 subjects. All data are from the sixth grade.

Adolescent sex role attitudes (AWSA) were particularly relevant because of the great deal of prior research investigating their relationship to maternal employment. Femininity (BSRI) was selected because of its significant correlations with a more positive image of the self in boys and girls (Galambos, 1985). These correlations imply that adolescents who described themselves as more feminine may be more at ease with themselves and with their contexts, perhaps showing more flexibility with regard to sex-typed behavior.

The aim of the path analyses was to test whether each of three possible paths was significantly different from zero: (a) maternal role satisfaction to mother–adolescent warmth, (b) mother–adolescent warmth to sex-typed attributes (sex role attitudes and femininity), and (c) maternal role satisfaction to sex-typed attributes. Based on the two-part process of influence model, it was expected that the first two paths only would reach significance; maternal role satisfaction and sex-typed attributes would be linked only through mother–adolescent warmth. Two sets of analyses were conducted, one using adolescent perceptions of warmth and the other using maternal perceptions of warmth. Table 5 presents the means and standard deviations of the variables used in the path analyses.

The results of the analyses using adolescent and maternal perceptions of warmth are presented in Table 6. The pattern of results for the path leading from maternal role satisfaction to warmth illustrates that there is no significant link between these two elements; this holds true regardless of the source for the warmth index. There is a significant association, however, between warmth and sex-typed attributes in boys with employed mothers. Boys who reported close relations with their employed mothers had more egalitarian sex role attitudes and described themselves as more feminine. This relationship was observed also when the mother's report of warmth was used. The only other case in which warmth predicted sex-typed attributes was for daughters of employed mothers. That is, employed mothers who reported warm relations with their daughters had daughters who had less egalitarian attitudes. In the

Table 5. Means and Standard Deviations of Maternal Role Satisfaction, Mother–Adolescent Warmth, and Sex-Typed Attributes by Maternal Employment Status and Sex of Adolescent, Grade 6

	Employed				Nonemployed			
	Girls (n = 33)		Boys (n = 41)		Girls (n = 29)		Boys (n = 20)	
Variable	M	SD	M	SD	M	SD	M	SD
Role satisfaction	4.00	.65	3.92	.64	3.79	.82	3.80	.88
Warmth: Mother report	4.05	.52	3.63	.78	3.88	.59	3.94	.62
Warmth: Adolescent report	5.06	.40	4.84	.75	4.97	.66	4.93	.82
Sex-typed attributes								
Sex role attitudes	3.35	.36	2.83	.54	3.16	.32	2.90	.50
Femininity	5.64	.84	5.05	1.04	5.62	.51	5.10	.80
Masculinity	4.72	.80	5.11	.83	4.67	.79	4.97	.65
Goal orientation	5.03	.67	5.12	.52	5.14	.65	5.09	.61

absence of a plausible explanation, we attribute this finding to a random occurrence.

Contrary to expectation, the maternal role satisfaction to sex role attitudes path was significantly different from zero in girls with employed mothers. Employed mothers who were happy with their roles had daughters with more egalitarian sex role attitudes. This relationship was observed regardless of whether mother or adolescent perceptions of warmth were included in the regressions. Overall, there were very few differences in the results according to the source for the warmth index.

Figure 1 depicts the results of the path analyses predicting sex role attitudes in the employed sample (adolescent perceptions of warmth are shown). The adolescent's report of warmth does not appear to be a link between maternal role satisfaction and sex role attitudes. Rather, warmth operates independently of maternal role satisfaction to influence the sex role attitudes of boys. The paths from warmth to sex role attitudes were significantly different for girls and boys, $z = 2.19$, $p < .05$ (Cohen & Cohen, 1983). Similarly, the sex difference in the maternal role satisfaction to attitudes path was significant, $z = 2.45$, $p < .01$. These results suggest that boys were sensitive to the nature of the mother–adolescent relationship and girls were particularly sensitive to the effects or modeling of their mother's satisfaction. In a *post hoc* analysis, maternal role satisfaction scores were correlated with the adolescent's assessment of the mother's happiness with her role ("How often does she [your

Table 6. Unstandardized and Standardized (in Parentheses) Regression Coefficients for Paths from Maternal Role Satisfaction to Warmth to Sex Role Attitudes and Femininity by Maternal Employment Status, Grade 6

Source for warmth index	Satisfaction to warmth	Warmth to attitudes[a]	Warmth to femininity[a]	Satisfaction to attitudes[b]	Satisfaction to femininity[b]
Employed					
Mothers of girls	.03 (.03)	−.26 (−.37)*	−.04 (−.02)	.28 (.42)*	.37 (.25)
Girls (n = 29)	.06 (.09)	−.07 (−.08)	−.12 (−.05)	.28 (.42)*	.38 (.26)
Mothers of boys	.31 (.22)	.25 (.39)*	.37 (.27)	−.14 (−.15)	.61 (.32)
Boys (n = 34)	.35 (.26)	.32 (.46)**	.92 (.63)****	−.17 (−.19)	.41 (.21)
Nonemployed					
Mothers of girls	.15 (.22)	.12 (.22)	−.30 (−.34)	−.10 (−.25)	.00 (.01)
Girls (n = 28)	.07 (.09)	.01 (.02)	.17 (.22)	−.08 (−.20)	−.05 (−.08)
Mothers of boys	.13 (.19)	.17 (.22)	.14 (.11)	−.09 (−.16)	.29 (.32)
Boys (n = 20)	−.10 (−.10)	.18 (.30)	.34 (.35)	−.05 (−.09)	.34 (.37)

Note: Path coefficients of similar magnitudes may not have the same significance levels across subgroups due to differences in n.
[a] Controlling for maternal role satisfaction.
[b] Controlling for warmth.
*p < .05.   **p < .01.   ***p < .001.   ****p < .0001.

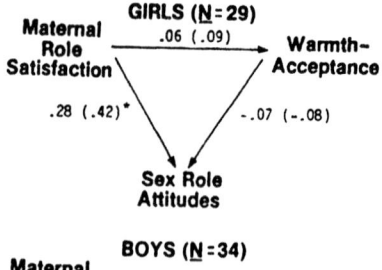

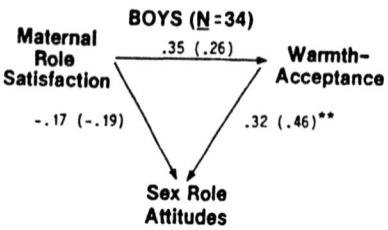

Figure 1. Path analyses testing the process from maternal role satisfaction to warmth (adolescent perceptions) to sex role attitudes in the employed sample. Unstandardized and standardized (in parentheses) path coefficients are presented, $*p < .05$, $**p < .01$.

mother] complain about what she is doing?"). The correlation between the mother's report and the adolescent's evaluation was significant only in girls with employed mothers, $r = .36$, $p < .05$, thereby suggesting that girls but not boys with employed mothers were aware of their mothers' feelings regarding her life situation. In general, we conclude that the two-part process model was not upheld in this sample.

B. Longitudinal Results

1. Sixth-Grade Work Status and Later Sex Typing

Although our initial set of analyses indicated no significant relationship between maternal employment status and the adolescent's sex-typed attributes in sixth grade, the purpose of the next set of analyses was to determine if there were perhaps delayed effects of maternal employment status. Therefore, we conducted a 2 × 2 (Sixth Grade Maternal Work Status × Sex) multivariate analysis of variance (MANOVA), using 252 subjects for whom the sex role measures in the seventh grade were available. The results were strikingly similar to the cross-sectional results. That is, there was only a multivariate main effect of Sex, Hotelling-Lawley Trace $F(4,245) = 35.90$, $p < .0001$. Univariate analyses showed again that girls had more egalitarian attitudes than did boys, $F(1,248) = 120.06$, $p < .0001$, girls were more feminine, $F(1,248) = 16.94$, $p < .001$, and boys were more masculine, $F(1,248) = 11.15$, $p < .001$. The univariate effect of maternal work status on sex role attitudes was not significant.

The next analysis examined the effects of sex and maternal work status in the sixth grade on eighth-grade sex-typed attributes. There was a multivariate main effect of sex, Hotelling-Lawley Trace $F(4,195) = 34.61$, $p < .0001$, with univariate effects comparable to those found with the seventh-grade data. The univariate test for the effect of maternal work status on sex role attitudes in the eighth grade was not significant, $F(1,198) = 2.35$, $p = .10$, although there was a tendency for adolescents with employed mothers to have more egalitarian attitudes.

2. Stability in Work Status and Sex-Typed Attributes

The next set of analyses to be reported examine stability and change in the mother's work status between the sixth and eighth grades and the four adolescent sex-typed attributes, measured in the eighth grade. Previous research with infants suggested that maternal employment stability was important to consider (Owen, Easterbrooks, Chase-Lansdale, & Goldberg, 1984). We were able to examine three groups, based on the mother's changing work status: (a) mothers who became employed between the sixth and eighth grades ($n = 25$), (b) mothers who remained nonemployed ($n = 37$), and (c) mothers who remained employed ($n = 97$). A fourth group—mothers who left paid employment—was too small ($n = 8$) to allow statistical comparisons. This group was omitted from the analyses.

A 3 × 2 (Work Stability × Sex) MANOVA was conducted on sex role attitudes, femininity, masculinity, and vocational-educational goals as measured in the eighth grade. In this analysis, there was no multivariate main effect of work stability, thus indicating that the mother's employment stability made no difference with respect to adolescent sex typing. There was also no significant multivariate Work Stability × Sex interaction. As in our previous analyses, there was a large multivariate effect of sex, Hotelling-Lawley Trace $F(4,150) = 21.41$, $p < .0001$, with univariate effects as before, except that the sex difference in femininity became nonsignificant ($p = .08$).

The univariate test for the effect of work stability on sex role attitudes proved to be significant, $F(1,153) = 3.85$, $p < .05$. Comparisons of the three means revealed that adolescents with mothers who entered employment between the sixth and eighth grades had significantly less egalitarian attitudes toward women ($M = 2.90$) than did adolescents with mothers who had been employed for at least 2 years ($M = 3.15$), $p < .01$. One interpretation of this finding is that mothers who joined the labor force may have had ambivalent feelings about employment or may have experienced some conflict upon entry into employment. It is also possible that these children resented the effects in their lives of a less available mother. The children of these mothers may then have questioned the value and competence of women who are employed, relative to children of mothers who remained active in the labor force.

V. SUMMARY

The results of the cross-sectional analyses, which tested for differences in adolescent sex-typed attributes as a function of maternal work status, suggest that relative to the sex of the adolescent, the effects of maternal work status are weak. The adolescent's gender was strongly related to three of the four sex-typed attributes. On the other hand, maternal work status was significantly related to sex role attitudes only in the sixth-grade analyses. Although this finding is consistent with other research that has clearly documented more egalitarian sex role attitudes among children with employed mothers (e.g., Stephen & Corder, 1985), we must question the extent to which adolescents in the 1980s may be influenced by maternal work status and whether the one difference found is *socially* significant.

Our use of multiple dimensions of sex-typing allows us to consider the possibility that the influences of maternal employment may be limited to some sex-typed attributes, for example, sex role attitudes. Even then, it may be necessary, given the powerful sex effects that were observed, to view maternal work status as just one of a number of shapers of attitudes toward the role of women. What we may be witnessing in the present data is evidence of the close of an historical period in which mothers' employment was nonnormative enough to strongly influence the attitudes of middle-class children. In effect, maternal employment may be regarded as a history-graded influence on sex typing (Baltes *et al.*, 1980), an influence that as a result of recent social change, may no longer be so powerful.

The results of the longitudinal analyses by and large support the interpretation suggested here. Sixth-grade maternal work status was not a significant predictor of seventh-grade sex-typed attributes and was only weakly related to sex role attitudes in the eighth grade. Our examination of stability in maternal work status from the sixth to the eighth grades determined that, of the sex-typed attributes, only sex role attitudes were related to stability. The largest difference in sex role attitudes was between adolescents with mothers who recently joined the labor force and those whose mothers had already been employed, calling attention to the potentially stressful situation created when the mother begins employment. Were these mothers in conflict about joining the labor force, and did they pass on their concerns to their children? Is early adolescence a critical period during which the mother's return to employment may most influence the adolescent's sex role attitudes? These are questions that are raised by the present research but that may be best answered in future studies that have a life-span oriented, multidimensional focus.

The preceding results suggest that studies that compare groups of adolescents according to maternal work status provide only a limited understanding of relationships and occurrences in different family types. As a first step toward describing general relationships, such comparisons are useful. The state of contemporary research, however, requires a more detailed and fine-grained analysis of family processes. Our path analyses were an initial attempt to consider the nature of the mother–adolescent relationship and the mother's role satisfaction as important variables. We turn now to an interpretation of the results of these analyses.

By introducing the constructs of maternal role satisfaction and mother–adolescent warmth, steps were taken to explore a possible process of influence. The lack of a significant relationship between mother–adolescent warmth, as reported by the mother or adolescent, and maternal role satisfaction may reflect the greater amount of time spent with peers relative to time spent with the family in early adolescence (Douvan & Adelson, 1966). That is, the mother's role satisfaction might influence the nature of the mother–child relationship when the child is young and there is extensive contact between them (J. Lerner & Galambos, 1985), but the nature and quantity of time spent with the mother in early adolescence may decrease the likelihood of such a relationship. One previous study documenting such a link in college women and their mothers used the daughter as the source for both role satisfaction and parenting measures (Altman & Grossman, 1977). Our use of both adolescent and mother perceptions to examine the relationship between warmth and maternal role satisfaction allows us to conclude that, at least in this sample, maternal role satisfaction and mother–adolescent warmth are not related.

As expected, warmth in the mother–adolescent relationship was related to more egalitarian sex role attitudes and higher femininity but only in boys with employed mothers. Boys may be especially vulnerable to the mother's absence due to employment and may receive less supervision than they need (Bronfenbrenner & Crouter, 1982). If mother–adolescent warmth implies that there is a greater degree of contact with and more supervision of the son, then higher warmth may be cast as a protective factor for sons with employed mothers. This may be important when we consider that, in the present sample, employed mothers reported warmer relations with their daughters than with their sons (Galambos, 1985), a finding that is consistent with other research demonstating that employed mothers have less positive perceptions of (Alvarez, 1985) and more arguments with their sons (Montemayor, 1984), relative to their daughters.

The significance of the relationship between maternal role satisfaction and more egalitarian sex role attitudes in girls with employed mothers is also consistent with past research (D'Amico et al., 1983; Gold & Andres, 1978b). This relationship was expected, however, to be mediated by mother–adolescent warmth. The fact that only girls with employed mothers seemed to have accurate perceptions of their mothers' role satisfaction, as shown by reports of the mother's complaints, suggests that the daughter's perceptions of the mother may play an important part in the sex-typing process. That is, the daughter who sees her mother making complaints is less likely to believe that women can handle work and family responsibilities.

Of course, our results are limited largely to adolescents in the middle class. Indeed, although most studies of maternal employment and sex typing have controlled for SES, or had relatively homogeneous samples, the range of socioeconomic backgrounds has been somewhat narrow. Because most research has used white working- and middle-class subjects, our knowledge about the influences of maternal employment and related processes affecting child development is restricted to these groups (see King et al., 1968, and Woods, 1972, for some notable counterexamples). The need to consider different ethnic groups and families with lower and higher SES backgrounds deserves further attention. For example, studies that sampled from the Hispanic or black populations might provide further support for results found with white samples, such as the observed relationship between sex typing and maternal work status, or they could illustrate how processes within the family are altered by the context to which the family belongs. Macke and Morgan (1978) noted that the history, attitudes, and work experiences of black women may be different from those of white women, thus potentially affecting the sex role socialization of the adolescent. More research on different subgroups is not only appropriate but should be a priority. For now, any conclusions about the processes linking adolescent sex-typed attributes to maternal employment must be limited to the populations from which the samples were drawn.

The results of the present investigation concur with the argument made nearly three decades ago by Maccoby (1958); that is, maternal employment is neither good nor bad. Rather, other features of the environment and of the parent–child relationship may be more crucial. A caring mother–adolescent relationship and mutual respect set the stage for greater behavioral flexibility in sons, and the mother's greater role satisfaction may enhance this flexibility in daughters. Of course, these are only two general features of the context that this study has addressed. It would be fruitful to examine other characteristics of the mother, for example, whether she experiences role strain or frequent negative moods. It is also important to consider characteristics of the father and the nature of the father–adolescent relationship. Different dimensions of the parent–adolescent bond could be measured in addition to warmth, for example, the nature of disciplinary practices, the degree of conflict, and the extent of parental monitoring and supervision. By addressing aspects of these diverse but interrelated influences, greater knowledge about adolescent development can be achieved.

Acknowledgment

This research was supported by a grant from the National Institute of Mental Health (MH 30252/38142) to A. Petersen.

REFERENCES

Almquist, E. M. (1974). Sex stereotypes in occupational choice: The case for college women. *Journal of Vocational Behavior, 5,* 13–21.

Almquist, E. M., & Angrist, S. S. (1971). Role model influences on college women's career aspirations. *Merrill-Palmer Quarterly, 17,* 263–279.

Altman, S. L., & Grossman, F. K. (1977). Women's career plans and maternal employment. *Psychology of Women Quarterly, 1,* 365–376.

Alvarez, W. F. (1985). The meaning of maternal employment for mothers and their perceptions of their three-year-old children. *Child Development, 56,* 350–360.

Bacon, C., & Lerner, R. M. (1975). Effects of maternal employment status on the development of vocational-role perception in females. *The Journal of Genetic Psychology, 126,* 187–193.

Baltes, P. B., Reese, H. W., & Lipsitt, L. P. (1980). Life-span developmental psychology. *Annual Review of Psychology, 31,* 65–110.

Banducci, R. (1967). The effect of mother's employment on the achievement, aspirations, and expectations of the child. *Personnel and Guidance Journal, 46,* 263–267.

Baruch, G. K. (1972). Maternal influences upon college women's attitudes toward women and work. *Developmental Psychology, 6,* 32–37.

Baruch, G. K. (1974). Maternal career-orientation as related to parental identification in college women. *Journal of Vocational Behavior, 4,* 173–180.

Baruch, G. K., & Barnett, R. C. (1980). On the well-being of adult women. In L. A. Bond

& J. C. Rosen (Eds.), *Competence and coping during adulthood* (pp. 240–257). Hanover, NH: University Press of New England.

Bem, S. L. (1974). The measurement of psychological androgyny. *Journal of Consulting and Clinical Psychology, 42,* 155–162.

Bem, S. L. (1975). Sex role adaptability: One consequence of psychological androgyny. *Journal of Personality and Social Psychology, 31,* 634–643.

Block, J. H. (1973). Conceptions of sex role: Some cross-cultural and longitudinal perspectives. *American Psychologist, 28,* 512–526.

Bronfenbrenner, U., & Crouter, A. C. (1982). Work and family. In S. B. Kamerman & C. D. Hayes (Eds.), *Families that work: Children in a changing world* (pp. 39–83). Washington, DC: National Academy of Sciences.

Chandler, T. A., Sawicki, R. F., & Stryffeler, J. M. (1981). Relationship between adolescent sexual stereotypes and working mothers. *Journal of Early Adolescence, 1,* 72–83.

Cohen, J., & Cohen, P. (1983). *Applied multiple regression/correlation analysis for the behavioral sciences* (2nd ed.). Hillsdale, NJ: Erlbaum.

Crockett, L., Losoff, M., & Petersen, A. C. (1984). Perceptions of the peer group and friendship in early adolescence. *Journal of Early Adolescence, 4,* 155–181.

D'Amico, R. J., Haurin, R. J., & Mott, F. L. (1983). The effects of mothers' employment on adolescent and early adult outcomes of young men and women. In C. D. Hayes & S. B. Kamerman (Eds.), *Children of working parents: Experiences and outcomes* (pp. 130–219). Washington, DC: National Academy Press.

Deaux, K. (1984). From individual differences to social categories: Analysis of a decade's research on gender. *American Psychologist, 39,* 105–116.

Dellas, M., Gaier, E. L., & Emihovich, C. A. (1979). Maternal employment and selected behaviors and attitudes of preadolescents and adolescents. *Adolescence, 14,* 579–589.

Douvan, E. (1963). Employment and the adolescent. In F. I. Nye & L. W. Hoffman (Eds.), *The employed mother in America* (pp. 142–164). Chicago: Rand McNally.

Douvan, E., & Adelson, J. (1966). *The adolescent experience.* New York: Wiley.

Elder, G. H., Jr. (1974). *Children of the great depression.* Chicago: University of Chicago Press.

Elder, G. H., Jr., & MacInnis, D. J. (1983). Achievement imagery in women's lives from adolescence to adulthood. *Journal of Personality and Social Psychology, 45,* 394–404.

Farel, A. M. (1980). Effects of preferred maternal roles, maternal employment, and sociodemographic status on school adjustment and competence. *Child Development, 51,* 1179–1186.

Galambos, N. L. (1985). *Maternal role satisfaction, mother-adolescent relations, and sex-typing in early adolescent girls and boys.* Unpublished doctoral dissertation, The Pennsylvania State University.

Galambos, N. L., & Petersen, A. C. (1986). *Maternal role satisfaction, mother-adolescent relations, and sex-typing in early adolescence.* Unpublished manuscript, The Pennsylvania State University.

Galambos, N. L., Petersen, A. C., Richards, M., & Gitelson, I. B. (1985). The Attitudes toward Women Scale for Adolescents (AWSA): A study of reliability and validity. *Sex Roles, 13,* 343–356.

Gilroy, F. D., Talierco, T. M., & Steinbacher, R. (1981). Impact of maternal employment on daughters' sex-role orientation and fear of success. *Psychological Reports, 49,* 963–968.

Gold, D., & Andres, D. (1978a). Comparisons of adolescent children with employed and nonemployed mothers. *Merrill-Palmer Quarterly, 24,* 243–253.

Gold, D., & Andres, D. (1978b). Developmental comparisons between ten-year-old children with employed and nonemployed mothers. *Child Development, 49,* 75–84.

Gold, D., & Andres, D. (1978c). Relations between maternal employment and development of nursery school children. *Canadian Journal of Behavioral Science, 10,* 116–129.

Gold, D., Andres, D., & Glorieux, J. (1979). The development of francophone nursery school children with employed and nonemployed mothers. *Canadian Journal of Behavioral Science, 11,* 169–173.

Hansson, R. O., Chernovetz, M. E., & Jones, W. H. (1977). Maternal employment and androgyny. *Psychology of Women Quarterly, 2,* 76–78.

Hayghe, H. (1986, February). Rise in mothers' labor force activity includes those with infants. *Monthly Labor Review, 109,* 43–45.

Hefner, R., Rebecca, M., & Oleshansky, B. (1975). Development of sex-role transcendence. *Human Development, 18,* 143–158.

Hock, E. (1980). Working and nonworking mothers and their infants: A comparative study of maternal caregiving characteristics and infant social behavior. *Merrill-Palmer Quarterly, 26,* 79–101.

Hodge, R. W., Siegel, P. M., & Rossi, P. H. (1965). Occupational prestige in the United States, 1925–63. *American Journal of Sociology, 70,* 286–302.

Hoffman, L. W. (1963). Mother's enjoyment of work and effects on the child. In F. I. Nye & L. W. Hoffman (Eds.), *The employed mother in America* (pp. 95–105). Chicago: Rand McNally.

Hoffman, L. W. (1974). Effects of maternal employment on the child: A review of the research. *Developmental Psychology, 10,* 204–228.

Hoffman, L. W. (1977). Changes in family roles, socialization, and sex differences. *American Psychologist, 32,* 644–657.

Hoffman, L. W. (1979). Maternal employment: 1979. *American Psychologist, 34,* 859–865.

Hoffman, L. W. (1980). The effects of maternal employment on the academic attitudes and performance of school-aged children. *School Psychology Review, 9,* 319–335.

Huston, A. C. (1983). Sex-typing. In M. Hetherington (Ed.), *Handbook of child psychology: Vol. 4. Socialization, personality, and social development* (pp. 387–467). New York: Wiley.

Huston-Stein, A., & Higgins-Trenk, A. (1978). Development of females from childhood through adulthood: Career and feminine role orientations. In P. B. Baltes (Ed.), *Lifespan development and behavior* (Vol. 1, pp. 257–296). New York: Academic Press.

Kagan, J. (1958). The concept of identification. *Psychological Review, 65,* 296–305.

Kendall, P. C., Lerner, R. M., & Craighead, W. E. (1984). Human development and intervention in childhood psychopathology. *Child Development, 55,* 71–82.

King, K., McIntyre, J., & Axelson, L. J. (1968). Adolescents' views of maternal employment as a threat to the marital relationship. *Journal of Marriage and the Family, 30,* 633–637.

Lamb, M. E. (1982). Maternal employment and child development: A review. In M. E. Lamb (Ed.), *Nontraditional families: Parenting and child development* (pp. 45–69). Hillsdale, NJ: Lawrence Erlbaum.

Lamb, M. E., Chase-Lansdale, L., & Owen, M. T. (1979). The changing American family and its implications for infant social development: The sample case of maternal employment. In M. Lewis & L. A. Rosenblum (Eds.), *The child and its family* (pp. 267–291). New York: Plenum Press.

Lerner, J. V., & Galambos, N. L. (1985). Maternal role satisfaction, mother-child interaction, and child temperament: A process model. *Developmental Psychology, 21,* 1157–1164.

Lerner, J. V., & Galambos, N. L. (1986). The child's development and family change: The influence of maternal employment on infants and toddlers. In L. P. Lipsitt & C. Rovee-Collier (Eds.), *Advances in infancy research* (Vol. 4, pp. 39–86). Hillsdale, NJ: ABLEX.

Lerner, R. M. (1984). *On the nature of human plasticity.* Cambridge: Cambridge University Press.

Lerner, R. M., & Busch-Rossnagel, N. A. (1981). Individuals as producers of their development: Conceptual and empirical issues. In R. M. Lerner & N. A. Busch-Rossnagel (Eds.), *Individuals as producers of their development: A life-span perspective* (pp. 1–36). New York: Academic Press.

Lerner, R. M., & Hultsch, D. F. (1983). *Human development: A life-span perspective.* New York: McGraw Hill.

Lipman-Blumen, J. (1972). How ideology shapes women's lives. *Scientific American, 226*(1), 34–42.

Maccoby, E. (1958). Effects upon children of their mothers' outside employment. In National Manpower Council, *Work in the lives of married women* (pp. 150–172). Proceedings of a conference sponsored by the National Manpower Council. New York: Columbia University Press.

Macke, A. S., & Morgan, W. R. (1978). Maternal employment, race, and work orientation of high school girls. *Social Forces, 57,* 187–204.

Meier, H. C. (1972). Mother-centeredness and college youths' attitudes toward social equality for women: Some empirical findings. *Journal of Marriage and the Family, 34,* 115–121.

Montemayor, R. (1984). Maternal employment and adolescents' relations with parents, siblings, and peers. *Journal of Youth and Adolescence, 13,* 543–557.

Montemayor, R., & Clayton, M. D. (1983). Maternal employment and adolescent development. *Theory Into Practice, 22,* 112–118.

Mussen, P. H. (1969). Early sex-role development. In D. A. Goslin (Ed.), *Handbook of socialization theory and research* (pp. 707–731). Chicago: Rand McNally.

Owen, M. T., Easterbrooks, M. A., Chase-Lansdale, L., & Goldberg, W. A. (1984). The relation between maternal employment status and the stability of attachments to mother and to father. *Child Development, 55,* 1894–1901.

Pearlman, V. A. (1981). Influences of mother's employment on career orientation and career choice of adolescent daughters. *Dissertation Abstracts International, 41,* 4657A–4658A.

Petersen, A. C. (1984). The early adolescence study: An overview. *Journal of Early Adolescence, 4,* 103–106.

Petersen, A. C., Schulenberg, J. E., Abramowitz, R. H., Offer, D., & Jarcho, H. D. (1984). A self-image questionnaire for young adolescents (SIQYA): Reliability and validity studies. *Journal of Youth and Adolescence, 13,* 93–111.

Pleck, J. H. (1975). Masculinity-femininity: Current and alternative paradigms. *Sex Roles, 1,* 161–178.

Powell, B., & Steelman, L. C. (1982). Testing an undertested comparison: Maternal effects on sons' and daughters' attitudes toward women in the labor force. *Journal of Marriage and the Family, 44,* 349–355.

Powell, K. (1963). Personalities of children and child-rearing attitudes of mothers. In F. I. Nye & L. W. Hoffman (Eds.), *The employed mother in America* (pp. 125–141). Chicago: Rand McNally.

Richardson, R. A., Galambos, N. L., Schulenberg, J. E., & Petersen, A. C. (1984). Young adolescents' perceptions of the family environment. *Journal of Early Adolescence, 4,* 131–153.

Robinson, B. E., & Green, M. G. (1981). Beyond androgyny: The emergence of sex-role transcendence as a theoretical construct. *Developmental Review, 1,* 247–265.

Rosenthal, D., & Hansen, J. (1981). The impact of maternal employment on children's perceptions of parents and personal development. *Sex Roles, 7,* 593–598.

Roy, P. (1963). Adolescent roles: Rural-urban differentials. In F. I. Nye & L. W. Hoffman (Eds.), *The employed mother in America* (pp. 165–181). Chicago: Rand McNally.

Schulenberg, J. E., Asp, C. E., & Petersen, A. C. (1984). School from the young adolescent's perspective: A descriptive report. *Journal of Early Adolescence, 4,* 107–130.

Smith, R. E. (1979). The movement of women into the labor force. In R. E. Smith (Ed.), *The subtle revolution: Women and work* (pp. 1–29). Washington, DC: The Urban Institute.

Spence, J. T., & Helmreich, R. L. (1978). *Masculinity and femininity.* Austin: University of Texas Press.

Stein, A. H. (1973). The effects of maternal employment and educational attainment on the sex-typed attributes of college females. *Social Behavior and Personality, 1,* 111–114.

Stephan, C. W., & Corder, J. (1985). The effects of dual-career families on adolescents' sex-role attitudes, work and family plans, and choices of important others. *Journal of Marriage and the Family, 47,* 921–929.

Stuckey, M. F., McGhee, P. E., & Bell, N. J. (1982). Parent-child interaction: The influence of maternal employment. *Developmental Psychology, 18,* 635–644.

Tangri, S. S. (1972). Determinants of occupational role innovation among college women. *Journal of Social Issues, 28,* 177–199.

Thornton, A., Alwin, D. F., & Camburn, D. (1983). Causes and consequences of sex-role attitudes and attitude change. *American Sociological Review, 48,* 211–227.

Vanfossen, B. E. (1977). Sexual stratification and sex-role socialization. *Journal of Marriage and the Family, 39,* 563–574.

Vogel, S. R., Broverman, I. K., Broverman, D. M., Clarkson, F. E., & Rosenkrantz, P. S. (1970). Maternal employment and perception of sex roles among college students. *Developmental Psychology, 3,* 384–391.

Waldman, E. (1983, December). Labor force statistics from a family perspective. *Monthly Labor Review, 106,* 16–19.

Weeks, M., Wise, G. W., & Duncan, C. (1984). The relationship between sex-role attitudes and career orientations of high school females and their mothers. *Adolescence, 19,* 595–607.

Woods, M. B. (1972). The unsupervised child of the working mother. *Developmental Psychology, 6,* 14–25.

Worell, J. (1978). Sex roles and psychological well-being: Perspectives on methodology. *Journal of Consulting and Clinical Psychology, 46,* 777–791.

Worell, J. (1981). Life-span sex roles: Development, continuity, and change. In R. M. Lerner & N. A. Busch-Rossnagel (Eds.), *Individuals as producers of their development: A life-span perspective* (pp. 313–347). New York: Academic Press.

Yarrow, M. R., Scott, P., de Leeuw, L., & Heinig, C. (1962). Child-rearing in families of working and nonworking mothers. *Sociometry, 25,* 122–140.

7

Maternal Separation Anxiety
Its Role in the Balance of Employment and Motherhood in Mothers of Infants

Ellen Hock, Debra DeMeis, and Susan McBride

I. INTRODUCTION

One clear conclusion from the research on the effects of maternal employment is that the relationships among employment, maternal beliefs, attitudes and practices, and child development are complex and require consideration of many factors. Stolz (1960), in one of the first reviews of the topic, concluded that a striking characteristic of the research on maternal employment was the number of different and often contradictory findings, an observation shared by Hoffman (1974) when she reviewed the literature more than a decade later. Bronfenbrenner and Crouter (1982) made perhaps the most critical observation by stating, "Taken by itself, the fact that a woman works outside the home has no universally predictable effects on the child" (p. 51). The failure to obtain consistent and interpretable results is due in part to the substantial differences among women within each employment status category (Hoffman, 1961, 1984; Lamb, 1982). For example, employed women may differ in their reasons for working, peer and spouse support of their employ-

---

Ellen Hock • Department of Family Relations and Human Development, Ohio State University, Columbus, Ohio 43210-1295.   **Debra DeMeis** • Department of Psychology, Hobart and William Smith Colleges, Geneva, New York 14456.   **Susan McBride** • Graduate School, Wheelock College, Boston, Massachusetts 02215.

191

ment, numbers of hours they are employed, and type of job they hold; the list is endless. Consequently, the simple model of comparing employed and nonemployed women and their children cannot be used to examine the effects of employment, and a more complex model must be proposed (Hoffman, 1984). Researchers must identify the differences that exist within the groups of employed and nonemployed women and determine how these differences impact the effects of employment status (Hoffman, 1961, 1984; Lamb, 1982).

One way to recognize the heterogenity within each group is to conceptualize employment status as representing not only the objective situation of remaining home or being employed but also psychological variables, particularly how the woman regards employment and the homemaker/mother role (Bronfenbrenner, 1961; Yarrow, Scott, DeLeeuw, & Heinig, 1962). Many early researchers recognized the significance of the psychological dimensions of employment status. Siegal (1961), for example, argued that the fit between a woman's motivations, her reference orientations, and what she is doing is more important than her employment status *per se*. Indeed, these early writings (Brieland, 1961; Hoffman, 1961; Stolz, 1960) included calls for more investigations of women's motivations to work and their appraisals of the importance of mothering and employment. Despite these directives, subsequent research generally did not address the importance of psychological factors and was designed to simply regress maternal employment status against a number of child outcome variables (Hoffman, 1974). Attention to psychological dimensions of employment has finally reappeared in more recent writings (Bronfenbrenner & Crouter, 1982; Lamb, 1982; Lamb, Chase-Lansdale, & Owen, 1979) where maternal attitudes toward job and home have been highlighted as the crucial variables in the study of maternal employment. Indeed, maternal attitudes have been hypothesized to be a key variable in mediating the relationship between maternal employment and child outcomes (Hoffman, 1974).

This chapter focuses on the psychological dimensions of employment by examining two factors and their relationships with employment status. More specifically, the chapter includes discussion of maternal separation anxiety, a mother's concern about providing care for her infant and about closeness to her infant, and maternal employment preference, her stated desire to be employed or to be at home. We believe that these factors are a central part of the process by which mothers of infants psychologically balance their perceptions of their own needs with their perceptions of the needs of their child. These factors, in combination with a woman's employment status, will ultimately affect how a woman responds to and experiences motherhood. In the second part of the chapter, we report the results of an exploratory study designed to show how maternal separation anxiety and employment status may influence the type of child care a mother selects for her child.

II. THE IMPORTANCE OF MATERNAL SEPARATION ANXIETY

Each mother who considers employment outside the home must also consider her own feelings about separation from her infant and her beliefs about how nonmaternal care will affect her child. Mothers frequently are in the process of balancing their own needs against their perceptions of their infants' needs. The process is dynamic to some extent. That is, a mother's level of separation anxiety may influence her employment decisions but conversely, her personal needs to fulfill herself through a career may influence her feelings about separation. Also, her anxiety about separation may influence when she returns to work, the type of care she selects for her child, and her child's adaptation to that nonmaternal care setting.

We view maternal separation anxiety as a powerful construct that, in many ways, mediates the impact of maternal employment on the child. At this point in this chapter we will describe the development of our concept of maternal separation anxiety. Following that explication, we will describe our definition of employment preference and then, in Sections IV and V of this chapter, maternal separation anxiety will be discussed as it relates to employment status, employment preference, and to choices about child care.

To guide the development of assessment techniques, a working definition of maternal separation anxiety was generated. Maternal separation anxiety is defined as an unpleasant emotional state reflecting a mother's apprehensions about leaving her child. A mother's expressions include feelings of sadness, worry, or uneasiness about being away from her child. This definition indicates a transitory state of anxiety that is associated with separation events (Hock, 1984).

Maternal separation anxiety is a complex, multidimensional, multidetermined construct. A mother's personality structure, role-related beliefs and cultural background can contribute to the way she feels about separation. The perception of the multidetermined nature of separation anxiety is similar to Bowlby's description of the origins of mothering characteristics.

> What a mother brings to the situation . . . derives not only from her native endowment but from a long history of interpersonal relationships within her

family of origin (and perhaps also within other families); and also from long absorption of the values and practices of her culture. (Bowlby, 1969, p. 342)

Thus, when considering the maternal contribution to the mother–infant separation experience, it is important to understand how the mother's personality and the culture influence her perceptions of separation and, subsequently, her contribution to the separation experience.

The works of Levy (1943) and Benedek (1970) have delineated the intrapsychic forces that determine unusual levels of concern about separation. The contribution of these classic works to our concept of separation anxiety is described in detail elsewhere (Hock, 1984). More relevant to the orientation of this book on maternal employment is the study of how the culture and commonly accepted definitions of the maternal role affect a mother's feelings about employment and employment-related separation.

A. The Sociocultural Influence

Separation anxiety is influenced by prevailing cultural beliefs about the separation of mother and infant. The culture in which the mother lives sets the standards associated with the enactment of the maternal role. Roles dictated by the cultural norms greatly influence how a woman views motherhood and child rearing. The ethnic and cultural setting provide guidelines for acceptable mothering behaviors, specifically with regard to behaviors involving mother–infant separation, including separation by employment, and the use of nonmaternal caregivers. For example, a woman leaving her infant to return to work may experience heightened anxiety if her peers and/or family hold strong beliefs that exclusive maternal care for babies is necessary.

Cultures vary tremendously in what they view as acceptable degrees of mother–infant separation. Frankel and Roer-Bornstein (1982) compared infant-rearing ideologies in two Jewish communities—Yemenites and Kurdishes. These two communities were found to express significantly different beliefs regarding the intimacy of the mother–child relationship. Kurdish Jews were most likely to favor nonmaternal care, whereas Yemenite Jews preferred little disruption to the mother–child interaction.

In past cross-cultural study, Maital (1983) sought to gain greater understanding of the cultural norms influencing mothers' feelings about separation. Maital interviewed 104 urban-dwelling mothers (52 Israeli and 52 American) from intact families with children aged 24 to 32 months. Measures used were the Maternal Attitude Scale (Cohler,

Weiss, & Grunebaum, 1970) and an interview schedule developed by Hock (1978) that yield scores for career orientation, infant discontent, infant separation distress, maternal separation distress, and attitudes toward nonmaternal child care. Results of the Maital study indicated basic cultural differences in maternal separation anxiety with American mothers experiencing greater anxiety than Israeli mothers. American mothers also had greater concerns about nonmaternal child care and would enter their children in preschool at age 3 as contrasted with Israeli mothers' plans to enter their children in preschool at age 2. Maital suggests that American mothers' greater separation anxiety may relate to the greater role conflict American mothers experience.

These studies clearly show that there exist ethnic or cultural differences in beliefs about the necessity of exclusive maternal care or, conversely, in beliefs about how much a mother should be away from her infant. Furthermore, Maital suggests that American women seem to experience more separation anxiety; she hypothesizes that this may be associated with conflicts associated with the maternal role.

B. The American Situation: Maternal Employment

Considering the American situation, there is reason to believe that the current cultural norms, supporting the view that mothers should stay home, create stress for women who wish to rely regularly on nonmaternal care. The most common reason for regular mother–infant separation is employment. Although the majority of mothers now hold paying jobs, many Americans are ambivalent, even critical, of employed mothers.

A recent survey of American attitudes suggests that societal censorship may be a factor that significantly influences mothers' anxiety about separation. In 1982, the Public Agenda Foundation, headed by Daniel Yankelvich, conducted a survey of a representative national sample of employed men and women. The study included an attitude survey of 845 people (The Public Agenda Foundation, 1983), including working men and women without young children and working mothers of children under 12. In response to the statement that, when mothers of children under 6 work, it weakens the family, 54% of the men agreed, 46% of the women agreed, and 43% of the working mothers agreed. In response to the statement that having a mother who works is bad for children under six, 63% of the men agreed, 52% of the women agreed, and 42% of the mothers agreed. From these data, it is clear that, for whatever reason, there exists in our society strong beliefs that families and young children suffer when mothers of young children work out of the home. It is striking that a substantial number of the working mothers themselves believe that what they are doing is bad for their children. Awareness of these attitudes is important to our consideration of maternal separation anxiety because it is evident that as women leave their infants to return to work, they do so in a climate of criticism and doubt. Certainly anxiety about separation from one's infant is heightened in such circumstances.

Thus the traditional cultural belief that a woman's place is in the home still seems prevalent enough to instill doubt in the minds of mothers in our culture who return to work. There is some empirical documentation of the effects that this doubt has upon the working mother's perception of her adequacy as a mother as well as her fear for her child's emotional well-being. Birnbaum (1975) surveyed professional women and found they worried they were not involved enough with their children and felt guilty about not being accessible to them. Poloma (1972) also surveyed career women and found that they felt guilty about work-related separations as well as feeling unable to protect their children. Yarrow et al. (1962) examined child-rearing practices and attitudes in both working and nonworking mothers. Forty-two percent of the working mothers reported dissatisfaction related to the maternal role and worried over whether their working negatively influenced the quality of their child rearing or interfered with their relationships with their children. These studies were conducted on mothers of older children; there is reason to believe that mothers of infants experience even greater feelings of guilt and anxiety. Michael Lamb (1982; Lamb et al., 1979) writes that mothers of young infants may experience more guilt related to employment than mothers of older children even though maternal employment is becoming more common. Lamb states that

> when women fear, and others gloomily confirm, that maternal employment will adversely affect their children's development, employed mothers may feel guilty about their decision to work, especially when that decision appears to have been selfishly motivated rather than economically necessary. (Lamb, 1982, p. 51)

Pederson, Cain, Zaslow, and Anderson (1982) confirm the ambivalence felt by mothers of infants; they report that

> it is likely that the mother's behavior may reflect some conflict and uncertainty over the choice to be in the work force during the infant's first year of life. (p. 218)

C. Maternal Employment: Conflicts about Separation

Despite the apparent conflicts, a substantial number of women are trying to combine motherhood and employment. Their task, however, is not an easy one because these roles are, for the most part, mutually exclusive, and there are no established guidelines for integration of the two roles. Gerson (1985) suggests that one strategy these women use to accomplish their goals is to redefine their traditional beliefs about motherhood. One central belief that must be reformulated is that mothers are their children's sole caregivers and that mother–infant separation should be a relatively infrequent event. For these women who want both jobs and children, concern over separation and nonmaternal care is different from the concern expressed by women who have adopted the traditional motherhood role.

Whether a woman remains home or tries to combine motherhood and employment, she faces a difficult task (Gerson, 1985). Although mothers who stay at home and care for their children are supported by the dominant culture, they are also challenged by currently emerging beliefs that demean the value of domestic work. The phrase *only a housewife* reminds them of the negative view that others hold regarding their choice. On the other hand, women who choose to be employed and raise a family confront the dilemma of how to combine two seemingly contradictory roles. Neither choice, then, provides a safe solution to the problem (Gerson, 1985). Because no societal guidelines exist, each woman must create her answer, and in so doing, deal with the issues of maternal separation. Thus, due to the nature of our current social situation, mother–infant separation is a dominant issue for women.

D. The Development of the Maternal Separation Anxiety Scale

A major step in strengthening the empirical foundation of the concept of maternal separation anxiety was to develop a reliable and valid measure. Guided by the theoretical and sociocultural perspectives discussed here as well as previous empirical work (Hock, 1976, 1980), several content areas were identified to provide an organizational structure for generation of items for the separation anxiety scale. These content areas were expressions of feelings about separation; desire for physical closeness and cuddling; attitudes about the value or importance of exclusive maternal care; and concerns surrounding the issues of employment-related separations.

The task of developing the questionnaire began by generating "agree-disagree" statements that could tap the content of these areas. Sixty-eight items were selected for the initial version of the scale that was called the Maternal Separation Anxiety Scale (MSAS).

An assumption in generating items for the scale was that maternal separation anxiety was a single attribute and that even though the items were drawn from several content domains, a collection of items that had a high average correlation with the total score would be obtained. Alternatively, factor analysis of the scale could reveal that the questionnaire was tapping clearly defined clusters of items, or factors. An assessment of the psychometric properties of the 68-item questionnaire and refinement of the scale was undertaken. The scale was administered to 623 women shortly after the birth of a firstborn child (Time 1). In order to assess the temporal stability of the scores, it was readministered to 400 mothers from the original sample about 8 weeks later (Time 2).

The goal was to develop a shorter, psychometrically sound version of the Maternal Separation Anxiety Scale (MSAS). Item analysis and factor analytic procedures were used to produce a 35-item version. When the 35-item questionnaire was subjected to factor analyses, the results revealed a three factor solution with a simple structure where each item loaded on only one factor. In addition, the low magnitude of the coefficients of the interfactor correlation of the three factors revealed that the factors are independent. The three factors appear to represent three distinct components of maternal separation anxiety; three factors are labeled as follows: Maternal Separation Anxiety (Factor 1), Perception of Separation Effects on the Child (Factor 2), and Employment-Related Separation Concerns (Factor 3).

The first factor is composed of two areas that reflect aspects of maternal anxiety and feelings of guilt resulting from or in anticipation of leaving her child. Anxiety expressed in mothers' beliefs about the importance of exclusive maternal care are also encompassed in Factor 1. A mother scoring high on Factor-1 items believes that the child prefers her and is better off if she is taking care of him or her. Alternatively, those mothers scoring low on Factor 1 report little concern about spending time away from her child and experience fewer feelings of sadness or worry. They do not feel the same level of apprehension about other caregivers and may believe that a baby-sitter is as capable as she is. Examples of items included in this factor are: "Only a mother just naturally knows how to comfort her distressed child"; and "My child prefers to be with me more than anyone else."

Factor 2 corresponds to a mother's beliefs about her child's ability to adapt to and profit from nonmaternal care. Examples of items included in Factor 2 are: "Exposure to many different people is good for my child"; and "My child needs to spend time away from me in order to develop a sense of being an individual in his or her own right."

Factor 3 addresses the balance between maternal role and employment. If a mother believes strongly that outside employment is important, she may find mother–child separations natural (low score) and necessary, whereas women who prefer not to work may find employment-related separations from their children stressful (high score). Examples of items related to this concept include: "I would resent my job if it meant I had to be away from my child"; and "I would not regret postponing my career in order to stay home with my child."

The reliability of subjects' responses to the MSAS at Time 1 and Time 2 were estimated by correlating the responses of the 400 women who completed the MSAS at both times of measurement. The stability coefficients for the summed items of each factor and the total MSAS were high: $r = .73$ for Factor 1; .58 for Factor 2; .72 for Factor 3, and .75 for the total. This was an indication of the substantial retest stability of the MSAS.

Other recently completed studies have used other types of measures of separation anxiety to evaluate the construct validity of the MSAS (Hock, Gnezda, & McBride, 1983). These investigations offer strong support for the validity of this measurement and the robust nature of the construct. Thus maternal separation anxiety is a relevant and meaningful construct, and its manifestation in employed women can help us understand how they balance work and motherhood. We will examine the relationship of maternal separation anxiety to employment after introducing and explaining our definition of employment preference.

III. THE IMPORTANCE OF EMPLOYMENT PREFERENCE

Regardless of employment status, some women are in their preferred role, whereas others are not. Given today's economic conditions, many women are working out of the necessity to supplement the family income. Other women are working for more personal reasons (e.g., a sense of accomplishment) and would choose to work even without the financial need. Similarly, women who are homemakers may choose to be at home because of their strong investment in their role as primary caregiver to their child. Others may feel obligated to remain at home because of the prevailing social norms about motherhood, even though they would rather be employed. The effect of employment status should certainly be different in these various situations.

A woman's employment preference (i.e., her desire to remain at home or to be employed) probably reflects the psychological balance between motherhood and employment. We expected that women who prefer to stay at home should be more invested in the role of mother than those who prefer to be employed. In comparison, mothers who would rather be employed should place a greater value on their careers or jobs than those who would rather be full-time homemakers. A woman's preference, then, should be related to her psychological commitment to and appraisal of the roles of mother and worker. Consequently, consideration of a woman's employment preference may facilitate understanding of (1) her attitudes toward the maternal role, (2) how she implements the maternal role (e.g., the amount of time and commitment she allots to the role), and (3) the influences of her role implementation on her child's development.

The potential importance of employment preference was recognized in early discussions of maternal employment (Brieland, 1961; Siegal, 1961; Yarrow et al., 1962). Siegal (1961) presented the strongest position by stating that a mother's attitudes toward what she is doing are the primary determinants of the impact of maternal employment. This belief in the central role of preference was supported by findings from several studies. Yarrow and her colleagues (Yarrow et al., 1962) reported that preference affected women's child-rearing attitudes and behaviors such that homemakers who preferred to be at home had more satisfying relations with their school-aged children and more confidence in their performance as mothers and scored higher on a scale measuring adequacy of mothering than homemakers who preferred to be employed. Preference also affected employed women's performance of the maternal role; employed mothers who chose to work showed their children more affection and sympathy, disciplined less severely, and felt less hostility during interactions when their school-aged child was noncompliant (Hoffman, 1961). It seems that the women who were in their preferred status, whether at work or at home, felt more satisfied with their lives and were able to respond more positively to all of their roles, including motherhood. Regardless of employment status, then, preference appears to influence how a woman assumes and acts out the maternal role.

Given that maternal employment was not the norm when these studies were conducted, women who wanted to be employed may have been a special and highly unique group of mothers who would be expected to be quite different from those who preferred the more traditional choice. It is questionable, then, whether preference would currently have the same impact because the incidence of maternal employment has increased so dramatically. Mothers who are in the labor force are now the statistical majority, whereas those who remain at home have become the minority (U.S. Bureau of Statistics, 1985). Despite the demographic changes, findings from more recent research indicate that preference still remains an important factor. In general, women who are in their preferred roles, whether homemaker or employee, seem to have higher self-esteem, be more satisfied, and be less anxious or depressed than women who are not in roles by choice (Baruch, Barnett, & Rivers, 1983). Studying a group of women who had graduated from college with honors 15 years earlier, Birnbaum (1975) found that employed women (all of whom chose to work) viewed themselves as more competent, had fewer doubts about themselves as mothers, and placed more emphasis on the fun and pleasure of motherhood than women who remained at home. It is not surprising that these women should respond more positively to motherhood than women who are in conflicted roles and are having difficulty integrating motherhood and employment.

In most of the previous research, the women have been mothers of school-aged children. Yet the most significant recent increase in employment has occurred among mothers of infants (Gamble & Ziegler, 1986); 50% of these women are currently in the labor force. Although limited, some research has been conducted to examine preference as it relates to the effects of maternal employment of mothers of infants. In their study of maternal communication behaviors, Schubert, Bradley-Johnson, and Nuttal (1980) found very few differences among homemakers who preferred to be home, homemakers who preferred to be employed, and employed mothers who preferred employment. Differences existed only early in the interaction and were primarily between homemakers who preferred to be at home and employed mothers. Easterbrooks and Goldberg (1985) studied a grouop of mothers of 10-month-old infants and found that maternal employment status had minimal effects on the qualitative aspects of mothers' behaviors and attitudes. The lack of differences may have occurred because the women were in roles that were consistent with their perceptions of the effects of employment and their employment preferences. Employed mothers expected that employment would have a positive effect on their relations with their infants, whereas nonemployed mothers expected negative consequences. In addition, all of the employed women preferred to work even if there was no financial need. These results clearly demonstrate the need to examine preference in order to understand the effects of maternal employment.

Most research (Hoffman, 1961; Schubert et al., 1980) has obtained a relationship between employment preference and child outcome measures, although the direction of the effect has varied. According to more recent studies, inconsistency between preferred and actual status is associated with more negative child outcomes. For example, Farel (1980) reported that children whose mothers wanted to be employed but were at home had the lowest achievement scores. Similarly, employed women who would rather be at home had less favorable views of their children than those who worked for personal reasons (Alvarez, 1985).

In summary, employment preference may be a critical factor that must be considered in addition to a woman's employment status. In both past and current research, consideration of preference has helped to clarify the effects of employment on a woman's experiences of motherhood and on her child's response to her employment status. The consistency of the results indicates the need for further study of preference and its impact.

Research on the relationship between preference and maternal separation anxiety is quite limited. Gnezda and Hock (1983) reported that preference predicted separation anxiety when the latter was measured at 2 days and 7 weeks postpartum. In a sample of professional women who were mothers of infants, differences in employment preferences were associated with different levels of separation anxiety during the first year of the infant's life. (DeMeis, Hock, & McBride, 1986). In addition, the amount and direction of change in levels of anxiety varied, according to preference and employment status. For example, anxiety increased over the first year for full-time mothers who preferred to be at home but decreased for employed mothers who preferred to be at home.

IV. MATERNAL SEPARATION ANXIETY AND EMPLOYMENT PREFERENCE

A. Purpose

Earlier studies have provided tentative evidence for a relationship between these two psychological dimensions: employment preference and maternal separation anxiety. The current study reported in Section IV of this chapter was a longitudinal study that extended across the first 13-½ months postpartum and used a large sample that was more diverse (i.e., with respect to maternal education, occupation, and socioeconomic status) than those used in previously published studies. The current study was designed to explore in more depth the connection among employment preference, maternal separation anxiety, and employment status.

B. Instruments

1. Maternal Separation Anxiety Scale

This instrument, developed by Hock, Gnezda, and McBride (1983), is a 35-item, self-administered, paper-and-pencil questionnaire. Each item is a 5-point Likert scale ranging from *strongly agree* to *strongly disagree*. The scale is designed to measure maternal separation anxiety that is defined as "an unpleasant emotional state reflecting a mother's apprehension about leaving her child" (Hock, 1984, p. 194) for short-term separations. Principal components factor analysis indicates the scale is composed of three factors that are not strongly related to one another; correlation coefficients are .19 for Factors 1 and 2, .22 for Factors 1 and 3, and .22 for Factors 2 and 3. Formation of three subscales was guided by the factor analytic study, that is, the items associated with each factor were summed to form a subscale. Each of the three subscales assesses a different aspect of maternal separation anxiety and should be viewed as an independent measure. Scores on each subscale ranged from 7 to 35.

(a) Subscale 1. Maternal Separation Anxiety. This subscale consists of 21 items and represents a mother's level of worry, sadness and guilt when separated from her infant, beliefs about the importance of exclusive maternal care (i.e., that a mother is best able to care for her child), beliefs that her child prefers her care and is better off in her care, and beliefs about her child's abilities to adapt to nonmaternal care. Higher scores on this subscale represent more anxiety due to separation and stronger beliefs about the value of exclusive maternal care.

(b) Subscale 2. Perception of Separation Effects on the Child. This subscale is composed of seven items and represents the mother's perceptions of her child's reactions to separation and the positive or negative effects on the child due to separations. A higher score indicates that a mother believes her child is not comfortable with separation and will not benefit from such experiences.

(c) Subscale 3. Employment-Related Separation Concerns. This subscale has seven items and assesses a mother's attitude about balancing the maternal role and career investments that would be associated with mother–child separation. If a mother scores high on this subscale, she is very concerned about leaving her child to work outside the home.

Hock et al. (1983) reported the internal consistency reliability coefficient using Cronbach's Alpha to be .90 for Subscale 1, .71 for Subscale 2, and .79 for Subscale 3. In order to examine the factor stability of the structure, Hock et al. (1983) used a coefficient of congruence to compare the similarity of the factor structure at two points in time, approximately 3 months apart. The coefficients of congruence were Factor 1, 1.0; Factor 2, .987; and Factor 3, .996. Thus, the three-factor structure of the Maternal Separation Anxiety Scale is very stable.

2. Maternal Role Investment Scale

This scale measured a woman's commitment to motherhood as her primary responsibility and the priority that motherhood assumes in her self-concept. It was a modified version of Hock's (1976) Investment in Maternal Role, a semistructured interview rating scale. Interviewers assigned a score from 1 (low investment in the maternal role) to 9 (extremely high investment) based on the mother's responses to four interview questions concerning the meaning and importance of motherhood for her, (e.g., "How complete would your life be if you weren't a mother?"). Interrater reliability ranged from .81 to .98.

3. Career Salience Questionnaire

The scale, which was developed by Greenhaus (1971), assesses the importance a person places on a career for personal fulfillment. The self-administered instrument contains 27 Likert-format items that are designed to tap three broad areas: general attitude about work, the relative imortance of work, and the degree of relevant vocational thought and planning. (The twenty-eighth item, which is a ranking of life priorities concerning different areas of life [e.g., family, career, religion], was not used in this study). The career salience score is obtained by an unweighted summation of the responses (range 27–140). High scores reflect high career salience. Greenhaus reports the coefficient alpha of the scale to be .81 for males and females.

4. Family Information Form

This short, paper-and-pencil form was administered through the mail when the mothers were 8 months postpartum. In addition to questions about plans for future childbearing, the form consisted of questions about employment preference ("If you had a choice of being employed or staying home, which would you choose?") and employment history ("Have you been employed since your baby was born?").

5. Information Form for Employed Mothers

Each mother who had worked since her baby's birth completed this 8-item questionnaire when her baby was 8 months old. The form was designed to gather information about a mother's work history since her baby's birth. More specifically, the questions asked were: (1) when the mother had returned to work; (2) if and when she had stopped working;

(3) her *primary* reason for working (financial need, career interests, boredom at home, social contact, enjoyment of working); and (4) her current employment status (either employed or not employed; part-time versus full-time distinctions were not made). Information about child care arrangements and satisfaction with child care was collected but not used because of problems with the questions. Like the Family Information Form, this form was administered through the mail.

C. Procedure

All primaparous women delivering healthy babies over a 3-month period were first contacted in the maternity wards of three hospitals within 48 hours after their infants' birth. The research project was explained, and written consent to participate was obtained. The research was described as an investigation of mothers' feelings about motherhood over the infants' first year of life. Of particular interest was the woman's commitment to the role of mother and the priority that motherhood assume in her self-concept. In addition, the importance a woman placed on a career for personal fulfillment was explored.

In the maternity ward, research assistants conducted an interview to collect demographic information and to administer the Maternal Role Investment Scale interview. After the interview, the research assistant provided directions for completing the Career Salience Questionnaire (Greenhaus, 1971) and the Maternal Separation Anxiety Scale (MSAS). The mother was thanked for agreeing to participate in the research, and the questionnaires were left to be completed at her convenience. On the following day, the research assistant returned to the maternity ward to collect the questionnaires. Including the 2-day assessment, the MSAS was administered four times; at 7 weeks and 8 and 14 months postpartum the scale was administered by mail. Mothers were asked to complete and return the questionnaire within 1 week. The 7-week assessment was chosen because it coincided with the period immediately prior to the time when most mothers return to employment. Around 8 months infant age, infants begin to develop separation protest, a development that may affect maternal separation anxiety. Finally, the 14-month measurement reflects decisions and feelings that a mother makes at the end of her first year of motherhood.

At both 8 and 14 months, mothers responded to an additional questionnaire about their employment history since their infants' birth and their current preferences to be employed versus being at home with their infant. Those mothers who were employed completed additional questions about their current reasons for working. Other information not used in this study was also collected at those times.

D. Subjects

The subjects of this study were selected from 292 women who participated in a longitudinal study of maternal separation anxiety conducted in a midwestern metropolitan area. Primaparous mothers were first contacted in the maternity wards of three hospitals where they were interviewed at 1 to 3 days postpartum; subsequent data were collected from them through mailed questionnaires at three other times during their infants' first year of life: 7 weeks, 8 months, and 14 months. Women who were Caucasian, married, age 19 or older, and for whom there was complete data for the four assessment periods were considered eligible for this study. (Women were required to be married and over 18 years of age to control for anxiety or stress that may be associated with single and teenage parenthood; the sample was limited to Caucasian women because a representative sample of non-Caucasian women was not available.) The final sample consisted of 130 women who met these selection criteria and had complete data for the four periods of data collection reported in this study. These women averaged 26.4 years of age (SD = 3.4), had completed an average of 14.9 years of education (SD = 2.0), and were in families with an average head of household socioeconomic index of 49.7 (SD = 20.5) that falls in the middle range of the revised Duncan Socioeconomic Index (Stevens & Featherman, 1980). Sixty-three of the infants of these mothers were male (48%) and 67 (52%) were female. Most of the women were employed during their pregnancies, and 56% (N = 73) of the women returned to the labor force during their infants' first year of life. The mean age of the infants at the time the mothers returned to employment was 3.3 months (SD = 1.9; range 1–10 months).

The women were divided into four groups based on their responses to questions about employment preference and status on the Family Information Form and the Information Form for Employed Mothers. The 8-month time period was selected because 97% of the sample who returned to employment during the infant's first year had done so by 8 months postpartum. In fact, the majority of these women had returned by 4 months and thus had several months of experience to consolidate their roles as employed mothers. Mothers were assigned one of two preferences, home or employment, based on their response to the single question on the Family Information Form. Employment status, home or employed, was determined by a mother's answers to the questions,

"Have you been employed since your baby was born?" from the Family Information Form, and, "Are you still employed outside the home?" from the Information Form for Employed Mothers. The classification of women by employment preference and status resulted in the following four groups of women: (1) employment preferred/employed ($N = 41$); (2) employment preferred/home ($N = 10$); (3) home preferred/employed ($N = 32$); and (4) home preferred/home ($N = 47$). The four groups were not statistically different from each other on two of three demographic characteristics (mother's age and head of household socioeconomic status). An analysis of variance did reveal an overall significant group effect for mother's education, $F(3,126) = 3.60$, $p < .01$. Post-hoc analyses revealed the home preference/home group to be significantly less well educated than the employment preference/home group ($M = 14.19$ vs. 15.9 years), the home preference/employed group ($M = 14.19$ vs. 15.34 years), and the employment preference/employed group ($M = 14.19$ vs. 15.15 years). Chi-square analyses revealed no differences in the distribution of male and female infants across groups ($\chi^2 = 1.2$, n.s.).

To further understand the psychological makeup of the four preference/employment status groups of women, they were compared on their ratings of maternal role investment and career salience that were assessed in the maternity ward. A significant group effect for career salience, $F(3,126) = 7.34$, $p < .001$, indicated the need for *post-hoc* analyses. Significant *post-hoc* contrasts were found for home preference/home ($M = 72.8$) and home preference/employed ($M = 74.9$) versus employment preference/home ($M = 85.9$) and employment preference/employed ($M = 81.9$). Thus preference to be employed or to remain at home was the primary indicator of differences in levels of career salience in the four groups. A significant analysis of variance was also found for maternal role investment, $F(3.126) = 3.10$, $p < .05$. Post-hoc analyses indicated significantly different levels of maternal role investment for the home preference/home group compared to the employment preference/employed group ($M = 7.28$ vs. 6.19). In this case, levels of maternal role investment are most clearly understood when *both* employment *preference* and employment *status* are considered and are most distinctly evident when employment preference and employment status are congruent.

For those women who were employed during their infants' first year of life, their primary reason for working also differed according to their preference. Financial need was cited as the primary reason for employment for 88% of the home preference/employed group versus only 54% of the employment preference/employed group. Although only 12% of the home preference/employed group cited valuing their career or liking to work as a primary reason for employment, 46% of the employment preference/employed group did so. Of all employed women, the majority of the mothers (68%) were employed for financial reasons, whereas 32% indicated valuing their career or liking to work.

In summary, the four groups determined by *preference* to be employed or to remain home with an infant and actual employment *status* are similar in terms of demographic characteristics with the exception of the home preference/home group being significantly less well educated than the other three groups. Yet the groups are psychologically different. Women who prefer to be employed have higher levels of career salience than those who prefer to remain at home despite their actual employment status. Maternal role investment is highest in nonemployed women who prefer to be at home and lowest in those who prefer to be employed and are employed.

Although the majority of women are employed for financial reasons, those who prefer to remain at home cite financial need as the primary reason to work more often than those who prefer employment. Thus employment preference is a valuable factor that clearly helps understand psychological differences in women whether or not they are employed.

E. Results

1. Individual Stability and Change

In order to assess the stability of the mother's responses to the Maternal Separation Anxiety Scale over their infant's first year of life, correlation coefficients were computed. Table 1 presents the cross-time stability coefficients for the three subscales of the MSAS over the four assessments. All correlations were significant at the $p \leq .0001$ level. Thus, for all subscales of the MSAS, women who were most likely to score higher on the MSAS at any one time did so at other periods of assessment as well. (The coefficients for Maternal Separation Anxiety and Employment-Related Separation Concerns are higher than those for Perception of Separation Effects on the Child, indicating mothers may be more liable in their responses to this subscale of the MSAS.) However, in general, a high level of stability within individuals in response to the MSAS is evident.

In order to assess changes in mothers' feelings about separation from their infants during the first year, data obtained at the four assessments (maternity ward, 7 weeks, 8 months, and 14 months) was subjected to a 4(Time) × 2(Preference) × 2(Employment Status) ANOVA with time as a repeated measure. The results of these analyses are detailed in terms of each subscale of the MSAS.

Table 1. Cross-Time Stability Coefficients for the MSAS Assessed in the Maternity Ward (T$_1$) and at 7 Weeks (T$_2$), 8 Months (T$_3$), and 14 Months (T$_4$); Infant Age for All Mothers (N = 130)

Maternal Separation Anxiety Scale	(T$_1$ vs. T$_2$)	(T$_1$ vs. T$_3$)	(T$_1$ vs. T$_4$)	(T$_2$ vs. T$_3$)	(T$_2$ vs. T$_4$)	(T$_3$ vs. T$_4$)
I. Maternal Separation Anxiety	.71	.59	.56	.71	.67	.79
II. Perception of Separation Effects on the Child	.62	.48	.39	.56	.52	.57
III. Employment-Related Separation Concerns	.77	.69	.65	.78	.62	.81

Table 2. Means and Standard Deviations for the MSAS over Time for All Mothers (N = 130)

Maternal Separation Anxiety Scale	Maternity ward M	SD	7 weeks M	SD	8 months M	SD	14 months M	SD
I. Maternal Separation Anxiety	21.50	3.2	20.54	3.4	19.95	3.8	19.49	4.1
II. Perception of Effects on the Child	13.93	3.2	14.08	3.2	13.91	2.9	13.79	4.1
III. Employment-Related Separation Concerns	23.39	4.9	24.37	4.4	24.53	4.6	24.47	5.9

(a) Subscale 1: Maternal Separation Anxiety. A main effect for time, $F(3,378) = 15.58$, $p < .0001$, on Subscale 1 indicated that, across all women in this study, maternal worry, sadness, and guilt related to brief separations decreased in a linear trend over the four assessment times during the infants' first year of life ($M = 21.5$ vs. 20.5 vs. 19.9 vs. 19.5) (see Table 2). A second main effect for employment preference also emerged, $F(1,126) = 4.08$, $p < .05$. Inspection of relevant means revealed that women who indicated that they would prefer to be employed expressed less maternal separation anxiety than women who would prefer to remain at home ($M = 19.22$ vs. 21.11). The ANOVA did not reveal other significant main effects or interactions.

These findings suggest that as the infants developed over the first year of life, maternal concerns and worry about leaving their infant (Subscale 1) became somewhat less salient. Yet women who preferred to remain at home with their child expressed more separation anxiety than those who preferred to be employed. The actual employment status of the mother was not a factor in determining differences in levels of maternal separation anxiety as measured by Subscale 1 of the MSAS.

(b) Subscale 2: Perception of Separation Effects on the Child. A significant main effect for employment preference and a time-X employment preference interaction were found for this subscale, $F(1,126) = 17.80$, $p < .0001$ and $F(3,378) = 3.04$, $p < .05$, respectively. Mean scores on this subscale revealed that women who preferred to be employed expressed less concern about the effects of separation on their child than women who preferred to remain at home ($M = 12.84$ vs. 14.63). In addition, the time-X employment preference interaction, $F(1,126) = 4.08$, $p < .05$, shows that over the first year of the infant's

life, the scores of mothers who indicated that they preferred to be employed decreased over time (M = 13.16 vs. 13.23 vs. 12.8 vs. 12.18), whereas those who preferred to remain at home increased (M = 14.44 vs. 14.63 vs. 14.62 vs. 14.84). Thus mothers who preferred to be employed were in general less concerned about the possible negative effect of time away from their child. In addition, as their infant became more socially interactive and less reliant on the mother, these women became even less anxious. On the other hand, women who preferred to remain at home reported generally higher levels of concern about the effects of brief separations on their child and these feelings intensified over the child's first year.

A near-significant main effect for employment status, $F(1,126)$ = 3.78, p = .054, revealed that mothers who actually remained at home during their child's first year of life were less concerned about the negative effects of separation on their child than the women who had returned to employment (M = 13.87 vs. 13.97). Although this analysis approached significance, the corresponding means are not greatly different.

In summary, both employment *preference* and employment *status* influence responses to Subscale 2 of the MSAS that reflect maternal anxiety about the effects of separation on the child. Time has a differential effect on scores, depending on employment preference. No interactions between employment preference and employment were found.

(c) Subscale 3: Employment-Related Separation Concerns. A main effect for employment preference was found for this scale of the MSAS that assesses a mother's attitude about balancing the maternal role and being employed outside of the home, $F(1,126)$ = 71.95, $p < .0001$. Inspection of the means revealed that, not surprisingly, women who indicated a preference to be at home expressed more anxiety concerning issues related to separating from their infants for the purpose of employment than women who preferred to be employed (M = 26.66 vs. 20.36, respectively). This finding is further explained by a significant time by employment preference interaction, $F(3,378)$ = 13.38, $p < .0001$. As can be noted in Figure 1, the scores of the home preference women increased linearly over their child's first year of life, whereas those women who preferred to be employed generally reported a decrease in employment-related concerns about separation.

The interaction of Employment Preference × Employment Status approached significance on Subscale 3, $F(1,126)$ = 3.35, $p < .07$. Post-hoc analyses utilizing Tukey's HSD test with $p < .05$ were computed. Using the appropriate critical value (HSD = 5.43), several comparisons

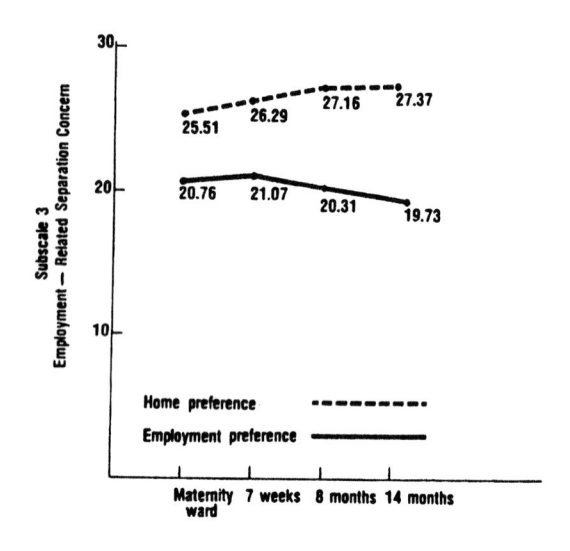

Figure 1. Interaction of employment preference and time with Subscale 3 of the Maternal Separation Anxiety Scale.

were significantly different. The mean of the home preference/home group was significantly higher than either the employment preference/employed or employment preference/home groups (M = 27.46 vs. 20.50 and 19.77, respectively). The home preference/employed group was significantly different only from the employment preference/home group (M = 25.46 vs. 19.77). Thus the women who preferred to remain at home and were doing so reported more employment-related separation concerns than women who preferred to be employed, despite their actual employment status.

Comparisons of mothers who shared the same employment status but had different employment preferences did reveal some differences. Of mothers who remained at home, women who preferred to be at home expressed significantly more anxiety than those who preferred employment. In comparison, the difference between the two groups of employed mothers was not significant. Employment preference, then, was a particularly powerful determinant of variation in Subscale 3 scores; in comparison, actual employment status seemed to exert less of an influence.

A more complicated significant three-way interaction for Time × Employment Preference × Employment Status was also found, $F(3,378)$ = 4.75, $p < .01$. This interaction is depicted in Figure 2; thus only par-

Maternal Separation Anxiety

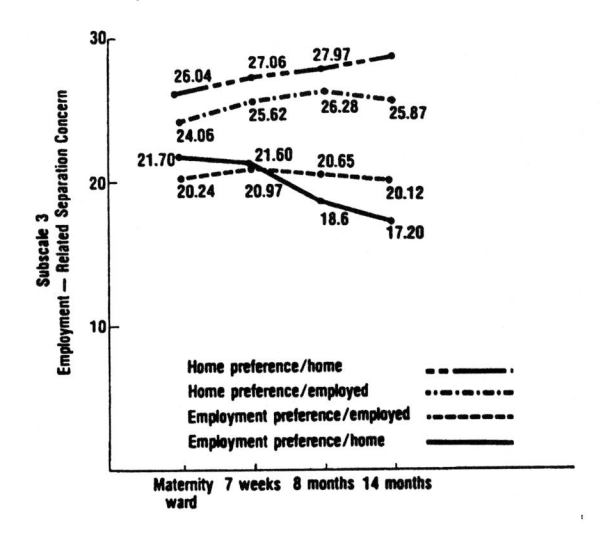

[Figure 2: Plot showing Subscale 3 — Employment-Related Separation Concern across time points Maternity ward, 7 weeks, 8 months, 14 months for four groups:
- Home preference/home: 26.04, 27.06, 27.97, 25.87
- Home preference/employed: 24.06, 25.62, 26.28, 20.12
- Employment preference/employed: 21.70, 21.60, 20.65, 17.20
- Employment preference/home: 20.24, 20.97, 18.6 (and 20.12)]

Figure 2. Three-way interaction of employment preference, employment status, and time with Subscale 3 of the Maternal Separation Anxiety Scale.

ticularly interesting *post-hoc results* will be noted where the critical value (HSD = 2.11) was achieved. Through the first three time periods, employment preference was more important than employment status in determining scores on this subscale. A comparison of the means of groups who shared the same preference but had different employment status revealed no significant differences. However, comparisons between preference groups indicated that home preference mothers scored significantly higher than work preference mothers at 2 days, 7 weeks, and 8 months postpartum. By 14 months, however, all four groups are significantly different from one another. Thus, after the infant's first year, the experience of actually working or staying home with the child as well as employment preference influenced maternal concerns about employed-related separation. The two groups of mothers who remained at home had the extreme scores; mothers who preferred to be at home had the highest scores, and those who preferred employment the lowest of the employed groups; the home preference group was more anxious about employment-related separations than the employment preference group.

F. Discussion

As we examine the process of balancing a mother's needs with those of her child, we see that maternal separation anxiety has an important role. We have studied separation anxiety of women as their infants grow older and as they experience life at home or in the workplace. At the birth of the first child, *preference* to be employed or to remain at home with the child differentiated these women. By 14 months, consideration of employment preference and the mother's actual employment status is critical in predicting how a woman interprets the meaning of mother–infant separation. The four groups that are defined by preference and status (i.e., employment preferred/employed; employment preferred/home; home preferred/employed, and home preferred/home) are different in their concerns about employment-related separation. The effect of this concern on their children is clearly a need for further study. A beginning effort is discussed in the next section that assesses the relationship between maternal separation anxiety and the use of various types of child care.

It is clear from our data on career salience and maternal role investment that the group differences extend beyond issues specifically focused on separation. The group of women who preferred to be at home had a significantly different orientation toward motherhood and jobs than the group who preferred employment. The women with a home preference were highly invested in their role as mother and only moderately interested in jobs and careers. If they were employed, they were working primarily for financial reasons and were relatively unmotivated by personal benefits (e.g., prestige) of their jobs. This group of women, then, defined motherhood as their primary raison d'être and relegated employment to a rather insignificant place in their lives.

The women who preferred to be employed reported a very different relationship between motherhood and employment. These women were strongly committed to their careers and usually worked for personal as well as financial reasons. Yet these women had lower scores on the Maternal Role Investment Scale, indicating that they were not as strongly invested in the role of mother as women who preferred to stay at home. Thus these women who preferred to be employed seemed to define motherhood as only one of their many interests. For them, a crucial task had to be balancing and integrating their roles as mother and as workers.

Not surprisingly, these groups of women developed different attitudes toward maternal separation and nonmaternal care and different perceptions of the effects of separation on the child. However, women in both groups reported attitudes and perceptions that were consistent with the degree to which motherhood and employment were central in their lives. Mothers who preferred to remain at home were more anxious about separation (Subscale 1) at all four times of measurement. During the course of the first year, their scores on Subscale 2 increased, indicating that they became progressively more negative in their beliefs about the effects of separation on the child. Between the maternity ward and 8 months postpartum, their anxiety about employment-related separation also increased. These attitudes toward and feelings about separation seem consistent with their strong investment in mothering.

The women who preferred employment held attitudes toward separation that were most conducive to integrating the roles of motherhood and work. These women had significantly lower scores on Subscale 1, indicating that they were less apprehensive about separating from their infants and leaving their infants with alternative caregivers. In addition, their low scores on Subscales 2 and 3 reflected their beliefs that their children would not be negatively affected by separation and their less intense concern about leaving their infants to work outside of the home. These mothers may have reported less separation anxiety for two alternative reasons. First, these mothers may have established a psychological balance between their own needs and their infants' needs that allowed them to act without guilt and anxiety on their desire to be employed. Alternatively, they may have been denying their concerns about nonmaternal care and separation so that they could consider employment. In either case, these women's lower anxiety about separation is entirely consistent with their less intense investment in the role of mother and their greater interest in employment.

The finding that these two orientations are more strongly related to employment preference than to employment status may seem somewhat surprising. However, in a past study (DeMeis, Hock, & McBride, 1986) of professional women, similar results were obtained, such that preference not status was related to maternal separation anxiety, career salience, and maternal role investment. We hypothesize that the weak association with status results from the variability *within* the groups of employed and nonemployed mothers. As Hoffman (1984) and Lamb (1982) note, differences within the groups may be as great or greater than those between the groups. Variability in attitudes toward the maternal role and employment may be especially large because many women have a status that is inconsistent with their attitudes (e.g., women who prefer to be home but work because of financial needs). Indeed, in the study of professional women, DeMeis *et al.* (1986) found that attitudes of employed mothers who wanted to be home were more similar to those of mothers who chose to and were at home than to those of employed mothers who wanted to work. Thus, formation according to preference may result in more homogeneous groups, particularly in regard to the definition of the maternal role, and consequently lead to a better understanding of how women psychologically balance motherhood and employment.

In summary, it appears that women are constructing at least two very different definitions of motherhood. One group of women perceives motherhood as their central role. These mothers hold a more traditional view in which mothering is such a predominant role that it cannot be "diluted" with activities that require mother–infant separation. Mothers in the second group seem to have developed a less conventional definition, one that allows them to pursue nonfamilial goals simultaneously with being a mother. These women do not perceive mothering as a role that excludes other interests, in particular, employment. They appear to be less convinced that good mothering requires that a mother be constantly available to her infant. These findings are consistent with other findings (e.g., Gerson, 1985) that there is no universal definition of motherhood but that women today are working out their own definitions based on their own unique life circumstances and background.

V. MATERNAL SEPARATION ANXIETY AND CHOICES REGARDING NONMATERNAL CARE

A. Purpose

One of the most significant effects of the rise in employment of mothers of young children is that these children are now spending considerable amounts of time in settings outside the home. In the past, the world of children younger than 3 consisted almost exclusively of home and the people who resided there; movement to the world beyond the family was a developmental transition that occurred during the late preschool and early school years. But as mothers of young children take jobs, they often move their children out of the home and into nonmaternal care at earlier ages. Although most employed mothers use some form of nonmaternal care, they can choose from a wide variety of arrangements. The focus in the second part of this chapter was to examine some of the psychological factors that influence a mother's choice of nonmaternal care.

Many demograhic and structual factors affect a mother's choice of alternative care arrangements. Not surprisingly, one of the primary variables is the cost of the care. Although most parents prefer home care (Belsky, Steinberg, & Walker, 1982; Blum, 1983), few choose it because of its high cost. Other features of the child care setting that determine choice include location, flexibility, and number of hours of operation, relation of the caregiver to the family (Moore, 1982), and curriculum (Belsky et al., 1982). Decisions are also based on familial factors such as the number and ages of children, family income, parental education, and parental experiences in day care when they were children (Clarke-Stewart, 1984). However, an overriding variable is simple availability. The unfortunate fact is that the number of children needing care far exceeds the amount of quality child care, particularly for children under 3. Parents are often forced to choose what is available rather than what is desired or optimal for their child's development.

Beyond structural factors, attitudinal variables may also influence child care decisions. Because nonmaternal care involves leaving the child in the care of another adult, maternal attitudes toward the adequacy of alternative care (Hofferth, 1979) and nonmaternal perceptions of the effects of alternative care on the child should certainly be related to a mother's choice of child care. For example, a woman should be more likely to choose home and less likely to choose group care if she believes that only a mother can comfort a child or that interactions with other children and adults expose her child to objectionable values and attitudes. Use of nonmaternal care should also be related to a woman's investment in the maternal role. The woman who remains at home and has chosen motherhood as her primary role may be more reluctant to place her child in any alternative care, even educational settings such as preschool. Because maternal separation anxiety taps a woman's attitude toward nonmaternal care, her perception of the effects of nonmaternal care and her commitment to the maternal role, the relationship of maternal separation anxiety to choice of type of child care was examined.

A difficulty of the past research has been to create meaningful categories to discriminate among the various forms of nonmaternal care. One of the most frequent schemes is to divide day care into three types: center care, family care in which a woman cares for several children in her own home, and home care in which a sitter cares for the child in the child's home. One drawback to the scheme is that preschool is often not included because it is viewed as an educational rather than a caregiving setting (Blum, 1983). However, employed mothers frequently use preschool as a form of child care. Clarke-Stewart (1984) has created a new scale that categorizes day care, according to several factors: number of hours, number and variety of children, number and variety of adults, and institutionalization. In the continuum of types of care, home with mother and fulltime center care serve as the two end points. Because preschool as well as other less typical forms of care can easily be incorporated into this scale, it avoids the problems of the more traditional scheme.

This investigation, then, represents an exploratory study that examines how maternal separation anxiety and employment status relate to choices about child care. Within the employment group, MSAS scores were correlated to the pattern of child care choices, beginning when the infants were 2 months old. We were particularly interested in the relationship between choice of care and Subscale 2, which is a measure of mother's perceptions concerning whether her child will benefit or not from outside care. We also examined mothers' current choices of child care and relationships with MSAS scores. Separate correlations were computed for employed and nonemployed mothers. For mothers who remained at home, we focused on their use of preschool because it is a form of care used by both groups.

B. Procedures

When the children in the longitudinal study (described in Section IV of this chapter) were 3½ years of age, their mothers were again contacted. At this time, we were particularly interested in the work pattern of the mothers and the type of child care experienced by the children. Additionally, we wondered about the mothers' concerns about separation from their children who were no longer babies but who were preschool-age children. We worked under the assumption that mothers of children of this age would view social experiences outside the home and family as valuable and important to their child's development. However, even mothers of preschool-age children do experience anxiety about separation. In another earlier study of maternal separation anxiety, we found that mothers of 5-year-old children entering kindergarten expressed concern about school-related separation (Martin Huff, 1982). In the current study, we wished to explore the relationship between maternal separation anxiety and choices about nonmaternal care. Mothers completed the same Family Information Form that had been administered at 8 months. The form contained the same questions about current employment preference, current employment status, and employment history since the child birth. Additional questions asked the mother to detail her use and choices of day care (baby-sitter, family day care, day care center, parent. We also readministered the Maternal Separation Anxiety Scale (referred to as the Time 5 MSAS).

C. Subjects

All of the subjects who had participated in the previous data collection phase at 14 months infant age were contacted. One hundred sixty-five questionnaires were mailed. After 2 weeks, a follow-up letter was sent to those mothers who had not returned the questionnaires. This letter explained the importance of the research study and requested their continued participation in the study. One-hundred and forty-four Family Information forms were returned. The attrition was primarily attributable to the lack of current addresses for all of the subjects.

After the Family Information Form was returned, the Maternal Separation Anxiety Scale was readministered by mail. Subjects were instructed to complete and return the scale within 3 weeks. One subject failed to return the MSAS, bringing the sample population to 143 participants.

For purposes of this study, we wished to include only subjects who had been steadily employed since the baby was 6 months of age or steadily at home since the baby was 6 months of age. We selected the subjects in this way because we wished to examine, as an "outcome variable," the number of months a child spent in any one type of care. If a mother dropped in and out of the labor force, cumulative months in child care could reflect her employment status rather than her choice among child care options. In that case, her choices would not be directly comparable to the choices of other mothers who had been steadily employed.

Using only steadily employed or steadily at home women brought the sample size to 107. Seventy-three mothers were employed and 34 were not employed outside the home. Most of the employed women worked close to a full-time work week over the 3-year period. Only 5 working women ever worked less than 15 hours a week.

The employed and home groups were very similar with respect to their demographic attributes. There were no significant differences between the groups in any measured attribute. The mean socioeconomic status of the head of household (Revised Duncan Socioeconomic Index) was 51.51 and 50.90 for the employed and nonemployed groups, respectively. Average mother age was 26.36 and 26.85 years for the employed and nonemployed groups, and average years of education were 14.75 and 14.41 for the employed and nonemployed groups, respectively.

D. Results

1. *Pattern of Child Care Used by Employed Mothers*

The types of child care used by the employed mothers in the first 3½ years of their childrens' lives were tabulated from the mothers' reports on the Family Information Form. On this form, the mothers reported on the predominant type of care for each 6-month interval from 0 to 24 months and each 12-month interval from 24 to 42 months. Choices included by a baby-sitter, in family day care, at a day care center, or by a parent at home. As other studies have reported for infants, the baby-sitter was the most frequently used type of care; 58% of the subjects used this type of care at 12 months child age; however, by 3½ years of age, more children were moved into day-care centers. Use of day-care centers increased at older ages. At 12 months of age, 10% used day-care centers, whereas at 3½ years, 32% of the subjects were enrolled in day-care centers. Group care in someone's home was used by only about 12% of the subjects at any time of measurement.

2. The Relationship of Type of Care to Maternal Separation Anxiety

Correlational analyses were conducted with MSAS scores as predictor variables and the use of a particular type of child care as the outcome measure. The correlational analyses indicated that, among the employed mothers, only the use of day-care centers was significantly related to the mothers' separation anxiety. Two types of analyses were run: one using all working mothers with day care coded as a dichotomous variable, that is, simply "yes" or "no" to reflect whether or not a subject had *ever* used a day-care center. In a second type of analytic approach, only data from subjects who had used day-care centers were entered into the analysis. In this analysis, the number of months that a child spent in a day-care center was the outcome measure.

When the data from all employed mothers were analyzed, with day care coded as a "yes" or "no" variable, it was clear that those who experienced anxiety in terms of their perception of separation effects on the child (Subscale 2), were less inclined to enroll their child in a day-care center. Subscale 2 includes items that ask about how a child will likely respond to nonmaternal care as well as items that inquire about general beliefs that the child can profit (or not) from exposure to many different people. The mothers' responses to Subscale 2 at Time 5 were negatively related to their ever having placed their child in a day-care center, $r = -.23$, $p = .04$. The pattern of findings here suggests that employed mothers who do choose to enroll their infant in a day care setting express lower levels of anxiety on Subscale 2.

The second analytic approach produced similar findings in that higher levels of anxiety were related to fewer months of day-care center care. Among those subjects that did use day care at one time or another, those who expressed more anxiety about balancing work and child care

(Subscale 3) used day care less. For the 27 subjects who had used day care, we found that those with higher Subscale 3 anxiety used day-care centers for fewer months ($r = -.42$, $p = .02$).

3. Current Child Care Choices by Employed and Nonemployed Mothers

In the preceding discussion, we considered the types of child care used by the employed mothers over the entire period of the longitudinal study. In this section, we will focus in greater detail on child care arrangements used at Time 5 in our data collection sequence. In order to examine current child care arrangements, using the Family Information Form, we asked mothers to report on the type of care used in their child's day with the day divided into half-day time periods—morning and afternoon.

(a) Preschool Experiences. From our perspective, we assumed that a mother views a preschool or formal group experience as a positive, valuable experience for a 3-year-old child. We used data from the Family Information Form to study the incidence of group experiences in our study population. Our definition of significant group experience was that the child attended at least 3 half days each week of regularly scheduled group care (i.e., day care center or preschool). Among the nonemployed mothers, only 16% had enrolled their children in a regularly scheduled group program that met at least 3 half days per week. (Forty-two percent had their children enrolled for 1 or 2 half days per week.) The mothers who were employed contrasted markedly with this fairly low use of preschool. Among employed mothers, 58% had their children enrolled in a group program for at least 3 half days each week. (Seventeen percent had their children enrolled for only 1 or 2 half days a week.)

Thus the children of employed and nonemployed mothers were involved in different amounts of group experience, especially when the experience was defined as 3 or more half days a week. When the group experience was defined as 3 or more half days per week, only 16% of the children of nonemployed mothers attended compared to 58% of the children of employed mothers. Clearly, the employed mothers used the time their child spent in preschool as a type of child care while they worked; so the work status differences are not too surprising. The surprising feature to us was the very low enrollment in preschool or other group experiences in the nonemployed group. In order to better understand choices about group experiences, we wished to identify attributes of the mothers, in addition to work status, that could provide insight into their choices about social/educational experiences for their children. The following section reports on our analysis of the relationship of maternal separation anxiety to such choices about group experiences for 3-year-olds.

(b) Relationship between Maternal Separation Anxiety and the Selection of Group Care Experiences for 3-Year-Olds. As we discussed before, many demographic and situational factors influence the type of care selected for children. Yet it is clear that a mother's psychological attributes, that is, her feelings about separation from her child, may also influence the nature and extent of nonmaternal care experiences provided for the child. We sought to better understand how maternal separation anxiety might function to affect choices about social and educational experiences in both the employed and nonemployed groups. In these analyses, we used the MSAS scores from all five times of data collection. The type of care the child experienced was coded as the number of half-day periods currently spent in preschool, at a day-care center, in home-based group care or with a baby-sitter.

(c) The Nonemployed Mothers. Among the nonemployed mothers, the use of preschool was the only type of care reported. We hypothesized that women who were more anxious about separation would be less likely to enroll their child in preschool. Perhaps, out of their own needs for closeness to the child, they would, in their view, perceive preschool as promoting too much autonomy that ultimately would lead to the child's movement away from them, associated with his or her less intense need for mothering.

In order to assess these relationships, the number of half days in preschool was entered into a correlational analysis with the MSAS scores from all five data-collection periods. For these exploratory analyses, we wished to document trends and patterns and so decided to report findings where the p value was $> .05$ but $< .10$. The findings reflected a clear and consistent pattern: higher scores on Subscale 2, Perception of Separation Effects on the Child, were related to *less* use of preschool. The MSAS Subscale 2 scores from Times 2, 3, and 4 where correlated with preschool attendance ($r = -.32$, $p = .07$; $r = -.39$, $p = .03$; and $r = -.33$, $p = .08$ for Times 2, 3, and 4, respectively).

Interestingly, Time 1 scores for Subscale 3, Employment-Related Separation Concerns, was significantly related to preschool attendance in nonemployed women ($r = -.39$, $p = .02$). Thus women who, in the maternity ward, expressed higher levels of concern about leaving a baby to return to work were less likely to enroll their 3-year-olds in preschool. Given the fact that so many demographic and practical factors strongly influence preschool attendance, we were somewhat surprised to find significant correlations with a psychological variable.

Even though significant findings are not obtained for every MSAS measurement time, the pattern is clear. The greater the concerns about separation as measured by the MSAS, the less the use of preschool. Further research should investigate in greater detail the relationship between separation anxiety and child's enrollment in social/educational experiences.

(d) The Employed Mothers. When analyses were conducted to test relationships between use of types of care and the MSAS for the employed mothers, interesting findings emerged. Unlike the preschool findings for the nonemployed group, no MSAS scores were related to preschool attendance in the employed group. In contrast, for the employed group, day-care center attendance was the only type of care significantly related to separation anxiety scores. The use of a day-care center for care of a 3-year-old was negatively related to separation anxiety assessed by Subscale 2 (Perception of Separation Effects on the Child) at three times of measurement. At Times 2, 3, and 5, the correlations with Subscale 2 were $-.26$ ($p = .03$), $-.20$ ($p = .09$) and $.21$ ($p = .06$), respectively. As mentioned before, Subscale 2 items do tap concerns about the child's benefiting from social experiences. It would appear that a mother's concern assessed in this subscale of the MSAS is related to day-care center use. Again, although of low magnitude, this finding reflects a consistent pattern. Children who are enrolled in day-care centers have mothers who report less anxiety on Subscale 2 of the MSAS. Thus, maternal feelings and attitudes are consistently related to choices about types of child care.

E. Discussion

In Section V of this chapter we reported findings from our longitudinal study of 3½ years. In contributing to this volume devoted to the effects of maternal employment on children, we wanted to demonstrate that maternal attributes, other than employment status *per se*, influence children's experiences. How a mother feels about separation from her infant—particularly when she focuses on the effects of separation on the child—may very well mediate the effects of employment status. At a very basic level, a mother's anxiety about separation may influence her decisions about employment. And, certainly, her concerns about separation affect whether or not she prefers to be employed. With respect to our concern for the child's experiences, a woman who is highly anxious about separation may select a different type of care for her child than a woman who is less anxious, and her anxiety may influence her child's adaptation to that care setting.

We know that many factors influence choices about the type of care that is selected for a young child. In the introduction to Section V, we noted several important demographic factors, particularly financial concerns and availability. Given these very salient constraints limiting choices about child care, it is remarkable that a psychological measure like Subscale 2 of the MSAS would be reliably related to choice and extent of use of a particular type of care. The salience of this factor is demonstrated by the fact that it related to choices about group care for both employed and nonemployed mothers. Perceptions about the effects of separation is related to preschool usage by at home mothers and center care usage by employed mothers. Thus, for mothers of 3½-year-old children, issues about separation are strongly related to real-life decisions about group experiences for the child.

Subscale 2, Perception Separation Effects on the Child, was related to employed mothers' use of day care center care in both the analysis of current care practices with the 3½-year-old child and the analysis of the pattern of care from the time of the infant's birth. The less the employed mother's anxiety, the more inclined she was to use a day-care center. The interpretation of this relationship in terms of cause and effect is complex. To begin with, a new mother who has a low Subscale 2 score will be more likely to enroll her child in a day-care center. In addition, she may be more willing to use center care when her infant is young. As a result, she will use center care for more total months than a mother who is more anxious and does not begin to use center care until her infant is older. Alternatively, of mothers who use center care, those with low anxiety may be more satisfied with the care. Because, should the child's experience in the center be positive, her beliefs and feelings are confirmed, she may be more likely to continue using center care. Thus mothers who have used day-care centers for a long time have lower Subscale 2 scores. As we noted in Section IV of this chapter, Scale 2, Perception of Separation Effects on the Child, may be more influenced by actual experiences than Subscale I that appears more traitlike. In any case, regardless of the character of the evolution of the mother's anxiety expressed in Subscale 2, it is clear that employed mothers who have children enrolled in day-care centers are different in terms of their feelings and beliefs than mothers whose children are cared for in other settings.

The major implication to be drawn from the present study is the importance of understanding parental feelings and attitudes when trying to assess the effects of different types of care on children. Our findings support a growing base of evidence that suggests that parental attitudes and emotions are systematically related to attributes of the child care setting (Clark-Stewart & Fein, 1983; Everson, Sarnat, & Ambron 1984; Howes & Olenick, 1986; Roopnarine & Lamb, 1980). Researchers must realize that any child "outcomes" that are found may be due to differences in parental beliefs and attitudes. Maternal separation anxiety, for example, appears to relate to the initial selection of day care center care. We also believe that separation anxiety affects the way a child responds to nonmaternal care. (See Hock, 1984, for a more detailed discussion of the mechanisms underlying the process by which a mother's separation anxiety can influence the child's adaptation to nonmaternal care.)

Thus we urge caution in interpreting findings that show the "effects" of day care on children. In a similar vein, we must be conservative in interpreting findings that suggest that the use of a particular kind of nonmaternal care affects the mother–infant relationship. Our belief is that the mothers who chose certain types of care are different to begin with. In any case, we must be cautious in drawing conclusions about the effects on children of maternal employment and type of child care.

VI. SUMMARY

In order to understand how employment affects the experience of motherhood, we must discover what the mother perceives to be the demands of employment and motherhood and how she feels about those demands. Issues about the effects of maternal employment on the child can be resolved by better understanding the mother's perspective. Women who are mothers of infants are engaged in psychological balancing—the process of balancing perceptions of their own needs with perceptions of the needs of their child. This chapter identifies and focuses on two factors that appear to be critical to the balancing process. We focus on maternal separation anxiety, the mother's concern about providing care and closeness to her infant, and employment preference, her stated desire to be employed or not. These factors are considered in light of the mother's personality, with respect to the social context and as they relate to choices about child care.

Many women who are attempting to combine motherhood and career find that there are no established guidelines for the integration of these two, often conflicting, roles. A woman's employment preference (i.e., her desire to remain at home or to be employed) may actually reflect her position in terms of the psychological balance between motherhood and employment. A woman's employment preference can be perceived as her current posture in the ongoing, dynamic, employment-role-versus-mother-role issue. As such, preference should be related to her psychological commitment to and appraisal of the role of mother and worker.

Our findings reveal that women who prefer employment are psychologically different than those who prefer to be home, regardless of their actual employment status. In other words, there is a qualitative difference in the experience of concern over separation and nonmaternal care in women who prefer employment compared to those who prefer to be at home. Employment preference, not employment status, appears to parsimoniously account for this difference. Mothers in our study who preferred to remain at home were more anxious about separation (Subcale 1) at all four times of measurement. During the course of the first year, their scores on Subscale 2 increased, indicating that they became progressively more negative in their beliefs about the effects of separation on the child. Between the maternity ward and 8 months postpartum, their anxiety about employment-related separation also increased. These attitudes toward and feelings about separation seem consistent with their strong investment in mothering.

The women who preferred employment held attitudes toward separation that were most conducive to integrating the roles of motherhood and work. These women had significantly lower scores on Subscale 1, indicating that they were less apprehensive about separating from their infants and leaving their infants with alternative caregivers. (In addition, their low scores on Subscales 2 and 3 reflected their beliefs that their children would not be negatively affected by separation and their less intense concern about leaving their infants to work outside of the home.) These mothers may have reported less separation anxiety for two alternative reasons. First, they may have achieved a psychological balance between their own needs and their infants' needs that allowed them to act without guilt and anxiety on their desire to be employed. Alternatively, the ego defense mechanism of denial may be in operation; these mothers may be denying their concerns about nonmaternal care and separation in order to be able to deal with issues of employment. In either case, their lower anxiety about separation is entirely consistent with their less intense investment in the role of mother and their greater involvement in employment.

In this chapter, we also examined some of the psychological factors that influence a mother's choice about nonmaternal care. We view maternal separation anxiety as a powerful mediator when examining the impacts of maternal employment on the child. Several patterns emerged in the analysis of our data. Nonemployed mothers who reported higher levels of concern on Subscale 2, Perception of Separation Effects on the Child, and Subscale 3, Employment Related Separation Concerns, were less likely to enroll their 3-year-old child in preschool. Among employed women, higher scores on Subscale 2 were related to less use of day-care center care. Thus, the mothers' issues about separation as assessed by the Maternal Separation Anxiety Scale, were systematically related to their choices about social and educational experiences for their child. In future studies, care must be taken in interpreting the "effects" of employment and type of child care on children. Maternal separation anxiety may mediate the effects of employment and nonmaternal care on the child.

In conclusion, we are once again forced to acknowledge the complexity of the issues associated with isolating the effects of rearing conditions on children. However, as we begin to document relationships between maternal attributes and child care choices, the problem becomes less confusing and more amenable to systematic multivariate analysis. The designs of future studies can incorporate measures that are sensitive to conditions that reflect maternal perceptions and feelings as well as conditions inherent in the child care setting.

REFERENCES

Alvarez, W. (1985). The meaning of maternal employment for mothers and their perceptions of their three-year-old children. *Child Development, 56,* 350–360.

Baruch, G., Barnett, R., & Rivers, C. (1983). *Lifeprints: New patterns of love and work for today's women.* New York: McGraw-Hill.

Belsky, J., Steinberg, L., & Walker, A. (1982). The ecology of day care. In M. E. Lamb (Ed.), *Nontraditional families: Parenting and child development* (pp. 71–116). Hillsdale, NJ: Erlbaum.

Benedek, T. (1970). Motherhood and nurturing. In E. J. Anthony & T. Benedek (Eds.), *Parenthood: Its psychology and psychopathology* (pp. 153–166). Boston: Little, Brown.

Birnbaum, J. A. (1975). Life patterns and self-esteem in gifted family-oriented and career-committed women. In M. T. S. Mednick, S. S. Tangri, & L. W. Hoffman (Eds.), *Women and achievement* (pp. 396–419). New York: Wiley.

Blum, M. (1983). *The day-care dilemna.* Lexington, MA: Lexington Books.

Bowlby, J. (1969). *Attachment and loss (Vol. 1, Attachment).* London: Hogarth Press.

Brieland, D. (1961). Maternal employment: situational and psychological variables. In A. E. Siegal (Ed.), *Research issues related to the effects of maternal employment on children* (p. 489). University Park, PA: Social Science Research Center.

Bronfenbrenner, U. (1961). Some familial antecedents of responsibility and leadership in adolescents. In L. Petrullo & B. M. Bass (Eds.), *Leadership and interpersonal behavior.* New York: Holt, Rinehart & Winston.

Bronfenbrenner, U., & Crouter, A. C. (1982). Work and family through time and space.

In S. B. Kamerman & C. D. Hayes (Eds.), *Families that work: Children in a changing world* (pp. 39–83). Washington, DC: National Academy Press.

Clarke-Stewart, A. (1984). Day care: A new context for research and development. In M. Perlmulter (Ed.), *The Minnesota symposia on child psychology (vol. 17), parent-child interaction and parent-child relations in child development* (pp. 61–100).

Clarke-Stewart, A., & Fein, G. (1983). Early childhood programs. In M. M. Harth & J. J. Campos (Eds.), *Handbook of child psychology* (Vol. II, pp. 917–999). New York: Wiley.

Cohler, B., Weiss, J., & Grunebaum, H. (1970). Child care attitudes and emotional disturbance among mothers of young children. *Genetic Psychology Monographs, 82,* 3–47.

DeMeis, D., Hock, E., & McBride, S. (1986). The balance of employment and motherhood: A longitudinal study of mothers' feelings about separation from their first born infants. *Development Psychology, 122*(5), 627–632.

Easterbrooks, M. A., & Goldberg, W. A. (1985). Effects of maternal employment on toddlers, mothers, and fathers. *Developmental Psychology, 21,* 774–783.

Everson, M. D., Sarnat, L. T., & Ambron, S. R. (1984). Day care and early socialization: The role of maternal attitude. In R. Ainslie (Ed.), *The child and the daycare setting* (pp. 63–97). New York: Praeger Publishers.

Farel, A. M. (1980). Effects of preferred maternal roles, maternal employment, and sociodemographic status on school adjustment and competence. *Child Development, 51,* 1179–1196.

Frankel, D. G., & Roer-Bronstein, D. (1982). Traditional and modern contributions to changing infant-rearing ideologies of two ethnic communities. *Monographs of the Society for Research in Child Development, 47,* (4, Serial No. 196).

Gamble, T. J., & Ziegler, E. (1986). Effects of infant day care: Another look at the evidence. *American Journal of Orthopsychiatry, 56,* 26–42.

Gerson, K. (1985). *Hard choices: How women decide about work, career, and motherhood.* Berkeley and Los Angeles, CA: University of California Press.

Gnezda, M. T., & Hock, E. (1983, August). *Working mothers of infants: Desired work status.* Paper presented at the annual meeting of the American Psychological Association, Anaheim.

Greenhaus, J. H. (1971). An investigation of the role of career salience in vocational behavior. *Journal of Vocational Behavior, 1,* 209–216.

Hock, E. (1976). *Alternative approaches to child rearing and their effects on the mother-infant relationship.* Urbana, IL: Educational Resources Information Center/Early Child Education (ED 122943).

Hock, E. (1978). Working and nonworking mothers with infants: Perceptions of their careers, their infants' needs, and satisfaction with mothering. *Developmental Psychology, 14,* 37–43.

Hock, E. (1980). Working and nonworking mothers and their infants: A comparitive study of maternal caregiving characteristics and infant social behavior. *Merrill Palmer Quarterly, 26*(2), 80–101.

Hock, E. (1984). The transition to day care: Effects of maternal separation anxiety on infant adjustment. In R. C. Ainslie (Ed.), *The child and the day care setting* (pp. 183–203) New York: Praeger.

Hock, E., Gnezda, T., & McBride, S. (1983). *The measurement of maternal separation anxiety.* Paper presented at the meeting of the Society for Research in Child Development, Detroit, MI.

Hock, E., Gnezda, T., & McBride, S. (1984). Mothers of infants: Attitudes toward employment and motherhood following birth of first child. *Journal of Marriage and the Family, 46,* 425–431.

Hoffman, L. W. (1961). Mother's enjoyment of work and effects on the child. *Child Development, 32,* 186–197.
Hoffman, L. W. (1974). Effects of maternal employment on the child: A review of the research. *Developmental Psychology, 10,* 204–228.
Hoffman, L. W. (1984). Work, family, and the socialization of the child. In R. Parke (Ed.), *Review of child development research* (Vol. 7) (pp. 223–282). Chicago: University of Chicago Press.
Hofferth, S. (1979). Day care in the next decade: 1980–1990. *Journal of Marriage and the Family, 41,* 649–658.
Howes, C., & Olenick, M. (1986). Family and child care influences on toddler's compliance. *Child Development, 57,* 202–216.
Lamb, M. E. (1982). Maternal employment and child development: A review. In M. E. Lamb (Ed.), *Nontraditional families: Parenting and child development* (pp. 45–69). Hillsdale, NJ: Erlbaum.
Lamb, M. E., Chase-Lansdale, L., & Owen, M. T. (1979). The changing American family and its implications for infant social development: The sample case of maternal employment. In M. Lewis & L. A. Rosenblum (Eds.), *The child and its family* (pp. 267–291). New York: Plenum Press.
Levy, D. M. (1943). *Maternal overprotection.* New York: Columbia University Press.
Maital, S. L. (1983). An examination of American and Israeli mothers' attitudes and behavior toward preschool entry (Doctoral dissertation, Temple University, 1983). *Dissertation Abstracts International, 44,* 339-B.
Martin-Huff, E. (1982). *Parental and contextual influences over children's early adjustment to kindergarten.* Unpublished doctoral dissertation, Ohio State University, Columbus, OH.
Moore, J. C., Jr. (1982). Parents' choice of day care services. *Journal of the American Academy of Political and Social Science, 461,* 126–134.
Paloma, M. M. (1972). Role conflict and the married professional woman. In C. Safilios-Rothschild (Ed.), *Towards a sociology of women.* Lexington, MA: Xerox College Publications.
Pederson, F. A., Cain, R. L., Zaslow, M. J., & Anderson, B. J. (1982). Variation in infant experience associated with alternative family roles. In L. M. Laosa & I. E. Sigel, (Eds.), *Families as learning environments for children* (pp. 203–221). New York: Plenum Press.
The Public Agenda Foundation (1983). *Survey: Work in the 1980's and 1990's.* New York: The Public Agenda Foundation.
Roopnarine, J. L., & Lamb, M. E. (1980). Peer and parent-child interaction before and after enrollment in nursery school. *Journal of Applied Developmental Psychology,* 1980 1, 77–81.
Schubert, J. B., Bradley-Johnson, B., & Nuttal, J. (1980). Mother-infant communication and maternal employment. *Child Development, 51,* 246–249.
Siegal, A. E. (1961). Characteristics of the mother related to the impact of maternal employment or non-employment. In A. E. Siegal (Eds.). *Research issues related to the effects of maternal employment on children* (pp. 29–36). University Park, PA: Social Science Research Center.
Stolz, L. (1960). Effects of maternal employment on children: Evidence from research. *Child Development, 31,* 749–782.
U.S. Bureau of the Census (1985). *Statistical abstracts of the United States: 1986.* Washington, DC, U.S. Government Printing Office.
Yarrow, M. R., Scott, P., DeLeeuw, L., & Heinig, C. (1962). Childrearing in families of working and nonworking mothers. *Sociometry, 25,* 122–140.

III

Maternal Employment

Integration of Findings, Corporate Applications, and Social Policies

The two chapters presented in this part provide a view of maternal employment in the context of corporate programs and policies (Hughes and Galinsky) and social policies (A. E. Gottfried and A. W. Gottfried). Hughes and Galinsky review literature concerning job and family conditions that influence the balance between work and family responsibilities, present data pertinent to this issue from their own Corporate Work and Family Life Study, and they discuss family-oriented corporate programs and policies.

The final chapter by A. E. Gottfried and A. W. Gottfried provides an integration of findings across the studies focusing on the issues to which this book is addressed. The intent of the authors is to analyze, synthesize, and determine the generalizability of findings across studies, as well as to highlight some of most salient individual findings obtained, and suggest avenues for future research. In the last section of this chapter, implications of these research findings for social policies are advanced.

8

Balancing Work and Family Lives
Research and Corporate Applications

Diane Hughes and Ellen Galinsky

I. CHANGING DEMOGRAPHICS

In a 1951 *Fortune* article, an IBM executive described his company's profamily policy. According to this policy, wives and children of "company men" should be included in the life of the corporation by the provision of country club facilities, picnics and parties, and special children's clubs (Whyte, 1956). Then, the "work–family problem" was viewed primarily in terms of the conflict between the excessive work hours of career-oriented corporate men and the emotional needs of their wives and children. Corporations typically provided social resources for family members (Hill, 1970; Kimmelman, 1969; Whyte, 1956), and beyond that there was little acknowledgment that work could have a profound impact on family life and that family life could likewise have an impact on work.

In the intervening years, between the 1950s and the 1980s, family life has undergone radical changes. In today's world, the work–family problem differs in nature and complexity. These changes are largely a function of the increase in the number of mothers in the work force. The traditional family with a homemaker wife and breadwinner husband is disappearing rapidly. In 1940, only 8.6% of mothers with children

---

Diane Hughes and Ellen Galinsky • Bank Street College of Education, New York, New York 10025.

under 18 were in the labor force. By 1985, 62.1% of these mothers were employed (Bureau of Labor Statistics, 1985; Hoffman, 1982). The percentage of working mothers with children under 3 increased from 35% in 1976 to 41% in 1979 to 50% in 1985 (Kamerman & Kahn, 1981; Bureau of Labor Statistics, 1985). The most dramatic change has been in the labor force participation of mothers with infants, which increased by 95% between 1970 and 1984; 50% of these women are now working (Ad Hoc Day Care Coalition, 1985; Galinsky & Friedman, 1986).

Despite the fact that the majority of mothers are presently employed or looking for work, most jobs are designed as if there were a homemaker to provide support for the working husband. Most employers do not consider the fact that a large percentage of their workers are either parents in dual-earner families or single parents. Therefore, families have had to adapt in order to earn a living and care for their children. The failure of institutions in general and employers in particular to respond to these changes has raised many questions: How have such shifts in family patterns affected working parents and the quality of family life? Do employed mothers experience more negative outcomes than employed fathers and other employed women? What are the antecedents and consequences of work–family conflicts and stress for working parents?

Thus this chapter has several goals. First, it provides an overview of existing research that has addressed these questions. Second, it describes the findings of a recent study, the Bank Street College Corporate Work and Family Life Study (CWFLS) that examines the sources of stress and satisfaction in a sample of corporate employees. Third, it argues that the widely held view that work–family stress is a women's issue rather than a family issue is inconsistent with what we have learned from available research. Finally, it provides a summary of recent corporate work and family programs.

II. OVERVIEW OF THE LITERATURE

Current research on the effects of jobs on individual health and well-being argues that the job is a potential source of stress for workers and their families. Workers must accommodate their schedules to their jobs more so than to their families. Jobs structure time (Piotrkowski, 1979) and determine the availability of workers to participate in family life (Kanter, 1984). Additionally, jobs sometimes generate negative affective states that are brought into the family system and affect interactions among family members (Piotrkowski, 1979).

Researchers who have examined the relationship of specific job conditions such as work hours, work scheduling, job demands, and job autonomy to individual outcomes have generally found significant relationships in terms of the individual's perceptions of work–family interference, feelings of role conflict, role overload, role strain, and feelings of stress and ill-health (Bohen & Viveros-Long, 1981; House, 1981; Karasek, 1979; Katz & Piotrkowski, 1983; Pleck, Staines, & Lang, 1978). Generally, 30% to 40% of a given sample indicate that the job interferes with family life "some" or "a great deal" (Galinsky, Ruopp, & Blum, 1983; General Mills, Inc., 1981; Quinn & Staines, 1977). Lack of time, worker fatigue, irritability, lack of energy, and withdrawal are among the processes most commonly mentioned.

Although the job seems to have a more potent effect on the family than family life does on the job, the most recent research efforts, including our own Corporate Work and Family Life Study, have moved beyond investigating simple univariate relationships between job conditions and family outcomes. To the extent that these interrelationships have been studied, the following review will include both job conditions and family conditions that have been linked to negative outcomes such as work–family interference, stress, and role strain for working parents. Additionally, it will indicate how these factors are experienced differently by employed mothers and fathers.

A. Job Conditions

1. Work Time

Time studies show that when a mother enters the labor force, 40 to 50 hours of combined paid and family work are added to the family system per week (Hunt & Hunt, 1977). Several studies have linked the total hours spent in paid employment to marital and family strain (Pleck, Staines, & Lang, 1980) and to feelings of role overload (Keith & Schaffer, 1980).

Research also suggests that the number of hours worked has important implications for the well-being of the worker's spouse (Burke, Weir, & DuWors, 1979; Keith & Schaffer, 1980; Pleck, Staines, & Lang, 1978). Pleck and his colleagues (1978) found that the spillover of work time into family time was associated with the spouse's experience of conflict between work and family life. Keith and Schaffer (1980) found that the amount of time husbands spent at work was a significant predictor of work–family role strain for wives, although the number of hours the wife worked had no significant relationship to the husband's experience of work–family role strain. Burke et al. (1980) found that the more hours the husband spent at work, the more likely the wife was to feel depressed, worthless, guilty, and isolated, as well as to smoke more frequently. Husband's work hours were also negatively associated with the wife's level of marital and life satisfaction.

A limitation of most studies of work and family life is the failure to consider other job variables that may moderate the effects of the number of hours worked on family outcomes. Though researchers have begun to control for job schedule (Pleck et al., 1978) and job autonomy and demands (Katz & Piotrkowski, 1983), other job variables (such as job insecurity and relationships at work) as well as family variables (such as the spouse's work schedule, the age and number of children, and the reliability of child care arrangements) are also likely to influence the relationship between work hours and family outcomes.

2. Schedule Incompatibility

A critical determinant of the congruence between work and family life is what has been termed *schedule incompatibility* (Staines & Pleck, 1983). The regularity of patterns of work and the flexibility and autonomy the worker has in arranging those hours influence the ease with which working parents are able to coordinate their schedule with those of other family members. In addition, conflicts between an employee's work schedule and the schedule of community facilities frequently result in difficulties in accomplishing personal and family tasks. Thus schedule compatibility has two components: (1) how the worker's schedule matches the schedules of other family members and (2) how the worker's schedule matches the availability of community services. Pleck and his colleagues (1980) found that schedule conflicts were a more critical issue for women than for men.

Conflicts between work and family schedules are intensified for shift workers. Frequently, workers arrange their schedules with one parent working days, the other evenings, in order to rotate caring for their children. Several studies suggest that this arrangement reduces the complexity of coordinating child care but is difficult for the marital relationship because the couple has little, if any, time together (Lein, et al., 1974; Mott, Mann, McLaughlin, & Warwick, 1965; Young & Willmott, 1973).

Differences in the effects of shift work have been found for men and women. In a study by Pleck and Staines (1983), the pattern of wives with nondaytime shift work was associated with greater work–family interference for husbands, whereas the pattern of husbands with greater overtime was linked to higher work–family interference for wives. For all groups, workers with spouses who worked the day shift reported less work–family interference. Additionally, schedule incompatibility was associated with lower family adjustment and overall well-being and with less job satisfaction. The negative impact of shift work seems to diminish when workers select their shifts (De la Mare & Walker, 1968).

The lack of fit between an employee's work schedule and the schedules of community facilities is a source of tension for workers in several ways. Workers, particularly those who are subject to strict time policies, have trouble getting to the doctor, dentist, bank, or dry cleaners. Teacher conferences and school performances usually take place during the workday and, thus, problems occur for working parents. Even the hours of the day care center can promote conflicts. A study by Shinn and her colleagues found that 38% of workers with flexitime programs said that their child care responsibilities prevented them from making more use of flexitime (Shinn, Wong, Simko, Ortiz-Torres, 1986).

3. Job Autonomy and Demands

The possibility that conditions such as job autonomy and job demands may affect workers and their families has received less attention in the literature than conditions such as work hours and schedule flexibility. However, their importance is suggested by both the research on job conditions and individual health and well-being (Karasek, 1979) and by the strong association between schedule inflexibility and work–family interference and stress (Bohen & Viveros-Long, 1981; Katz & Piotrkowski, 1983). Pleck, Staines, and Lang's (1978) measures of work inflexibility (which taps autonomy in terms of the timing and structuring of job tasks) and of work demands were correlated with respondent's reports of work–family interference.

When people have control over the tasks and timing of their jobs, they are more likely to be satisfied with the situation (Mason & Espinoza, 1983), and may be better able to negotiate and manage family and work demands successfully. Katz and Piotrkowski (1983) found that job autonomy and job demands were stronger predictors of family strain than work hours and other important job and family conditions in a small sample of black women.

Karasek's (1979) work underscores the potential importance of considering the interrelationship between these job conditions. In a series of studies on the relationship between job factors and well-being (Karasek, 1979; Karasek, Baker, Marxer, Ahlbom, & Theorell, 1981), the researchers found that mental strain was related to the interaction of job demands and decision-making latitude. The combination of little decision-making power and heavy job demands was a powerful predictor of job dissatisfaction, stress, and negative health outcomes such as heart disease. Unfortunately, these and other studies of job stress in the industrial/organizational field of psychology have rarely considered the effects of such job conditions on the well-being of workers in their families, such as their marital satisfaction.

4. Supervisory Relationship

Studies of job stress have identified the relationship with the supervisor as a moderator between job conditions and individual health and well-being (House, 1981). Repetti (1985) found that having a nonsupportive supervisor at work was predictive of anxiety and depression, independent of self-report bias.

Most studies have focused on the supervisor's work role (e.g. task competence and managerial skills). However, preliminary evidence indicates that an important dimension of the supervisor relationship is the supervisor's sensitivity to the family needs of supervisees. In a study of 5,000 employees, Fernandez (1985) found a significant relationship between stress at home and at work when the boss was not supportive about the employee's child care needs.

Further evidence for the concept of supervisory sensitivity to family needs comes from a prior stage of the Corporate Work and Family Life Study. In a census conducted in 1983 as part of the Bank Street corporate study, employees were asked to select a work condition that had the most negative effect on work life. The supervisor/supervisee relationship was most frequently chosen by respondents (Galinsky, Ruopp, & Blum, 1983). Additionally, in an open-ended question asking for a workplace change to improve both family life and productivity, a sizable number of employees wrote about improving the supervisor/supervisee relationship.

Thus, though the supervisor/supervisee relationship has not been a primary focus in work and family life research to date, its effects are potentially powerful. In terms of work-related support, it seems reasonable to suggest that a tense relationship with the supervisor may lead to negative mood spillover at home. Additionally, a supervisor who is insensitive and inflexible in relation to family needs may exacerbate difficulties in coordinating work and family demands.

B. Family Conditions

1. Family Division of Labor

The family division of household work and child care responsibilities is a critical determinant of the compatibilty between work and family life, particularly for women. In general, women retain the responsibility for overseeing family work (Barnett & Baruch, 1983), and estimates of the employed wife's role overload relative to her husband's range from two to six times (Carlson, 1984; Pleck, 1983). Studies of employed mothers highlight both their guilt feelings about inadequate performance of household roles (Hauenstein, 1976) and the complexity of schedules they must develop to accommodate increased demands in decreased time (Lein et al., 1974). Pearlin (1970) found that housework overload was positively related to depression in employed wives. In a British study, Bailyn (1970) found that the more housework the wives performed, the more likely they were to be dissatisfied with their marriages. Zur-Shapiro and Longfellow (1981) found that a higher level of participation in household work by husbands was associated with lower maternal depression and parenting stress scores for employed mothers.

In contrast, other studies indicate that the perception that the husband is contributing his share of housework and child care may be more critical to working women's health and well-being than the division of labor *per se*. Pleck (1983) reported that the employed wife's level of satisfaction with the husband's performance of family work was a more powerful predictor of her family adjustment and overall well-being than the husband's actual level of family and paid work. Yogev and Brett (1983) also found that husbands and wives were more likely to be satisfied with their marriages if they perceived their spouses as doing more than their fair share of child care and housework, regardless of the actual time spent in such tasks.

2. Child Care

The supply of quality and affordable child care in the United States in no way meets the demand, especially in the areas of infant/toddler and afterschool care (Blank, 1984; Seligson, Genser, Gannett, & Gray, 1983). Recent federal, state, and local budget cuts have further reduced the supply of child care for the children of the working poor who are now more likely to be left home alone or with a sibling or to be in substandard child care arrangements (Blank, 1984; Children's Defense

Fund, 1984). Accordingly, finding child care is one of the most problematic aspects of being a working parent. In a recent study by Emlen and Koren (1984), 75% of the female and 57% of the male employees reported difficulty in locating their current child care arrangement.

In addition to the fact that child care is hard to find, it is expensive. Even though child care workers are among the lowest paid of all workers, child care is often the third to fourth most costly item in the family's budget (Fernandez, 1985; Friedman, 1985; Ruopp & Travers, 1982). Furthermore, it is perceived as a woman's expense that must be justified by comparing her income with the costs of her employment, such as child care, transportation, lunch money, clothes, and the like (Nordberg, 1985).

Most studies of child care, including the most recent government surveys, ask working parents to indicate the one child care arrangement they use for each child, but this kind of assessment presents a very limited picture of the realities most families face. Kamerman (1980) has documented that employed parents develop their own intricate child care system with a number of child care arrangements for each child that may change daily or seasonally. Shinn and Wong (1985) have found that the greater the number of child care arrangements used by a family, the more likely these arrangements were to break down. They also found that the breakdown of child care was a significant predictor of poor mental and physical health. The research of Pleck, Staines, and Lang (1978) found that problems with child care were related to overall work–family interference. Difficulties for working parents in finding and maintaining child care arrangements are likely to increase because there is currently a high turnover rate of child care providers, which has been attributed to the low pay and lack of status in this profession.

Overall, child care remains predominantly a women's issue. Women are more likely to be responsible for locating child care, to work at maintaining the child care package, and to stay home when children are sick (Emlen & Koren, 1984; Fernandez, 1985; Shinn & Wong, 1985). Consequently, women experience more stress in relation to child care then men. In a community survey of 8,121 employees in a variety of occupations, 47% of the women as compared to 28% of the men with children under 12 reported child care stress (Emlen & Koren, 1984).

III. THE CORPORATE WORK AND FAMILY LIFE STUDY

The Corporate Work and Family Life Study at Bank Street College has been designed in response to the dramatic increase of mothers in the labor force. It is a cross-national, action-oriented study that will examine the extent to which changes in the workplace that are worker designed affect the mental and physical well-being of employees. It will address questions that are most frequently posed by corporate decision makers, family advocates, and policymakers:

1. If corporations develop new policies to help workers manage their work and family responsibilities, what is the payoff for the corporation in terms of worker productivity, absenteeism, and the like?
2. What is the payoff for families? Do family-responsive workplace policies affect family relationships?
3. What is the payoff for workers? Do such programs reduce stress and improve health?

We have recently completed analysis of an in-depth questionnaire. These data will provide baseline data against which to measure the impact of a worker-designed work-site intervention that will address workers' work–family needs.

The following section will describe the findings from the questionnaire regarding the differential antecedents and consequences of stress, psychosomatic symptoms, and work–family interference for the employed parents in our sample.

A. Procedures

The Corporate Work and Family Life Study (CWFLS) is part of a larger set of studies on work and family life at several job sites being conducted by Bank Street College of Education in New York. This study was conducted at a large pharmaceutical company in New Jersey that was selected because of its reputation as a trend setter for family-responsive policies and because of a strong interest among decision makers at the company in designing and implementing a worker-designed work–site intervention to address employee's family needs.

The CWFLS was conducted in two divisions at the study site. The divisions were selected on the basis of a companywide census, administered during the initial stages of the study in order to provide a demographic profile of the company's work force. The selection of the division for the study was guided by the need for an adequate sample of married workers, parents, and women in management positions. The two divisions selected (Research and Human Resources) most closely met the sample criteria.

The CWFLS questionnaire was distributed to 1,368 managers, scientists, and clerical/technical workers at the company in January 1985. To ensure confidentiality, CWFLS researchers were sent a list of employees within the two divisions. Each employee was assigned an identification code number that was stamped onto the questionnaire. Questionnaires were placed in sealed envelopes with the respondents' names and distributed through company interoffice mail. Letters of support from management were enclosed with the questionnaire, and follow-up reminders were periodically placed in the company's daily newsletter. Participation in the study was entirely voluntary. Fifty-four percent of the mailed questionnaires were returned ($n = 736$). Four incomplete questionnaires were discarded, resulting in a total sample of 732 respondents.

B. Sample

The full sample of 732 employees consisted of 326 women and 406 men. Twenty-six percent ($N = 188$) of the respondents were in the managerial category (managers or supervisors), 42.3% ($N = 310$) were scientists, and 31.1% ($N = 228$) were clerical/technical workers. As previously mentioned, this chapter will focus primarily on the findings for the working parents with children under 18 in our sample. They consisted of 83 women and 202 men. Because many of our family variables of interest were spouse-related (spouse work hours, spouse participation in child care and housework), 22 single mothers and 9 single fathers have been dropped from the subsample of working parents for the purpose of this analysis. Demographic characteristics of the full and subsamples of working mothers and fathers are presented in Table 1.

C. Measures

The questionnaire consisted of measures of job conditions, family conditions, and individual and family outcomes. Standardized measures were used where possible. When available measures did not meet our requirements for brevity or unobtrusiveness or did not tap the specific constructs we wanted to investigate, we developed measures based on theoretical research literature or on our experience in working with corporations. Means, standard deviations, and Cronbach's alpha coefficients for these measures are presented in Table 2.

1. Job Conditions

Job time was defined as the total amount of time spent at work during an average week. This measure was derived by combining self-report

Table 1. Sample Characteristics for Full Sample and Subsample of Married Parents

	Full sample		Married parents	
	Frequency	Percentage	Frequency	Percentage
Sex				
Male	407	55.5	202	70.9
Female	326	44.5	83	29.1
Marital status				
Never married	138	18.8	0	00
Married	534	72.9	285	100.0
Separated/divorced/widowed	58	7.9	0	00
Parental status				
No children under 18	417	56.9	0	00
Children under 18	316	43.1	285	100.0
Children 13–18	98	13.4	83	29.1
Children 6–12	83	11.3	72	25.3
Children under 6	135	18.4	130	45.6
Race				
White	662	90.3	247	86.7
Black	26	3.5	13	4.6
Other minority	39	5.3	24	8.4
Job position				
Management	188	25.5	101	35.4
Scientist	310	42.3	126	44.2
Clerical/technical	228	31.1	55	19.3
Family income				
Under $30,000	47	6.4	6	2.1
$31–$50,000	170	23.2	71	24.9
$51–$75,000	249	34.0	129	45.3
Over $75,000	144	19.6	67	23.5
Age				
Under 25	60	8.2	2	.7
26–35	233	31.8	89	31.2
36–50	290	39.6	174	61.1
50+	143	19.5	18	6.3
Spouse employment status				
Not employed	160	21.8	94	33.0
Employed part-time	73	10.0	55	19.3
Employed full-time	305	41.6	129	45.3
No spouse	195	26.6	0	00

Table 2. Means, Standard Deviations, and Cronbach's Alpha for Study Variables

	Full sample			Married parents	
	Mean	Standard deviation	Cronbach's alpha	Mean	Standard deviation
Autonomy[a]	2.35	.652	.76	2.27	.628
Supervisor sensitivity[a]	1.62	.594	.91	1.63	.552
Challenge[a]	1.82	.573	.79	1.77	.53
Total work hours	43.93	7.13	—	44.97	7.15
Job security[a]	1.20	.407	.87	1.19	.388
Demands[a]	2.58	.601	.78	2.55	.570
Control over work hours[a]	2.27	1.08	—	2.09	1.02
Spouse housework[b]	3.11	.86	—	3.14	.837
Spouse child care[b]	3.47	.83	—	3.46	.837
Child care reliability	.792	1.96	—	.766	1.81
Spouse work hours	25.77	19.03	—	22.74	19.01
Stress[c]	3.58	.64	.84	3.55	.617
Symptoms[c]	4.27	.466	.88	4.28	.428
Interference[c]	2.71	.90	—	2.50	.86

[a] Low score = greater autonomy, challenge, demands, supervisor sensitivity, control over work hours, and job security.
[b] Low score = greater dissatisfaction with child care and housework.
[c] Low score = greater stress, more frequent symptoms, and greater work–family interference.

data about scheduled work hours and overtime hours. Respondents were asked, "How many hours are you scheduled to work each week at this company, on the average?" Because all but one respondent were employed full-time, there was very little variation in responses, with a range from 38 to 40 hours per week. Respondents were also asked two questions regarding overtime: (1) "Do you work above and beyond your scheduled hours per week?" and (2) "How many overtime/extra hours do you work in an average week?"

Schedule flexibility was defined as the amount of control the respondent had in regards to the hours she or he worked. Respondents were asked, "How much control do you have over the scheduling of your work hours at your company?" (1 = *a great deal*, 4 = *none at all*).

Job autonomy was defined as the possibility for an employee to exercise control over his or her job tasks and the organizational policies that effect the job (Piotrkowski & Katz, 1982). It was assessed by a shortened version of an 8-item index developed by Piotrkowski and Katz (1982) that tapped task independence, closeness of supervision, control over working hours, and control over company policy. Respondents indicated on a 4-point scale (1 = *strongly agree*, 4 = *strongly disagree*) the extent to which statements characterized their present job. The index demonstrated high reliability in a study of 60 working-class women (Cronbach's alpha = .80) and was correlated in the expected direction with job demands (r = .55).

Job demands was defined as the extent to which the job required physical or mental exertion from the respondent. It was assessed by a 6-item index based on items developed by Karasek (1979). Respondents were asked to respond to questions about the pressure of output during the workday on a 4-point scale (1 = *strongly agree*, 4 = *strongly disagree*).

Job challenge was defined as the extent to which the respondent believed she or he had the opportunity for growth and learning in his or her work. Items were based on Karasek's index of job decision latitude as well as on items from the 1977 Quality of Employment Survey. The measure assessed the extent to which the respondent perceived the job to be stimulating, growth producing, and allowed the worker to exercise acquired skills on the job. Respondents rated statements that characterized their job on a 4-point scale (1 = *strongly agree*, 4 = *strongly disagree*).

Job security was defined as the extent to which the respondent believed his or her job was secure. It consisted of two items modeled on questions in the University of Michigan Quality of Employment Survey (Quinn & Staines, 1979): "How likely do you think it is that you will be temporarily laid off from your job within the next year?" and "How likely do you think it is that you will permanently lose your job within the next year and have to look for another one" (1 = *not at all likely*, 3 = *very likely*).

Supervisor sensitivity was defined as extent to which the respondent perceived his or her supervisor to be supportive of the employee in the work role as well as flexible and understanding about the employee's family responsibilities. It was assessed by an 8-item index. The work items were based on the University of Michigan Quality of Employment Survey's measure of resource adequacy that included the supervisor's behavior (Quinn & Staines, 1979). Because previous studies have generally ignored the potential importance of the supervisor's family sensitivity, three items tapping flexibility regarding family demands were developed by the Bank Street research team. Respondents rated these statements about the supervisor on a 4-point scale (1 = *very true*, 4 = *not at all true*).

2. Family Conditions

Age of youngest child was coded as a 4-level variable. Respondent's with a youngest child under 6 were coded as "4." Those with a youngest child between 6 and 12 were coded as "3," whereas those with a youngest child between 13 and 18 were coded as "2." Respondents with no children below 18 were coded as "1."

Spouse participation in housework was defined as the extent to which the respondent felt that his or her spouse was doing an adequate share of household chores (Yogev & Brett, 1983). It was assessed by a single item that asked the respondent to evaluate the division of household work in his or her family (1 = *much less than his/her share*, 5 = *much more than his/her share*).

Spouse participation in child care was defined as the extent to which the respondent felt his or her spouse was doing a fair share of child care (Yogev & Brett, 1983). It was also assessed by a single item that asked the respondent to evaluate the division of child care responsibilities in his/her family (1 = *much less than his/her share*, 5 = *much more than his/her share*).

Spouse work hours was the average number of hours the respondent's spouse spent at work, including scheduled hours and overtime. Respondent's whose spouse's were not employed were coded "0" on this item.

Child care reliability was defined as the frequency with which the respondent's child care arrangements have broken down within a 3-month period (Shinn & Wong, 1985). It was assessed by a single-item question that asked the respondent to report the number of times he or she had to make special child care arrangements because of an ill child, a school vacation, a child care provider who quit, a child care center was closed, and the like.

3. Outcomes

Stress was defined as the extent to which the respondent felt overwhelmed and unable to control the important things in her or his life. It was assessed on a 5-point scale by the 5-item Perceived Stress Scale (Cohen, Karmarch, & Mermelstein, 1983) that asked the respondent to assess how often he or she had experienced a range of feelings in the past 3 months (i.e., "How often have you felt that you were able to control the important things in your life?").

Psychosomatic symptoms was defined as the frequency with which the respondent experienced negative physiological conditions within the past 3 months. We used the 14-item Quality of Employment Survey (QES) Physical Symptoms Checklist (Quinn & Staines, 1979). The respondents indicated on a 5-point scale (1 = *very often*, 5 = *never*) the frequency with which he or she experienced a list of physiological symptoms (i.e., sleeplessness, fatigue and increased smoking, eating or alcohol consumption).

Overall work-family interference was defined as the extent to which the respondent perceived a global interference between work and family life (Pleck, 1983). It was assessed using the 1977 QES single item that asked, "All in all, how much would you say your work and family life interfere with each other?" (1 = *a great deal*, 5 = *not at all*).

D. Methods of Analyses

The analyses for this chapter were guided by several overarching questions. First, we wanted to examine the extent to which the negative outcomes (stress, psychosomatic symptoms, and overall work–family interference) were reported in varying degrees for the men and women and for the parents and nonparents in our sample. Second, we wanted to determine which sets of job and family conditions were significant predictors of negative outcomes, and then, within those sets, which individual job and family conditions were the strongest predictors. We were interested in which family conditions were most influential in relation to other family conditions and which job conditions were most influential relative to other job conditions. Third, we wanted to determine whether job or family conditions explained more variance in outcomes, and whether there was a different pattern of relationships for mothers and fathers. Finally, we were interested in identifying how job characteristics differed, according to gender and job position.

Given the statistical and theoretical interrelationships between dependent measures, multivariate techniques were employed as an initial step in all analyses. Multivariate analyses of variance (MANOVAs) were used to evaluate group differences in dependent measures by gender and parental status. Multivariate multiple regressions were employed to determine the relative importance of individual job and family conditions and the contribution of sets of job and family conditions to stress, psychosomatic symptoms, and work–family interference for our sample of mothers and fathers. Job and family conditions were examined in blocks, using standard simultaneous regression techniques.

Several statistical caveats should be mentioned here. First, because of the large number of potentially important Sex × Family and/or by Job Conditions interactions relative to the sample size, separate analyses were conducted for women ($N = 85$) and men ($N = 202$) within the group of working parents. Second, because there were relatively few missing cases per variable but a large number of variables, missing values were replaced by the mean of the group that the respondent belonged to by gender and job position (e.g., female manager, male scientist) in all univariate regression equations. And finally, the correlations between control variables that are typically used in analyses of this sort (age, race, income, education) and the dependent measures were examined prior to conducting multivariate analyses. Because none of these variables were significantly associated with the independent measures, they were not included in the regression equations so as to limit the number of variables in the model.

E. Results

1. Are Sex and Parental Status Associated with Stress, Psychosomatic Symptoms, and Work–Family Interference?

Multivariate analyses of variance (MANOVAs) were conducted to examine the extent to which there were differences in stress levels, psychosomatic symptoms, and overall work–family interference by sex (two levels) and parental status (two levels). Significant multivariate effects were found for parental status [$F(3,720) = 11.66, p > .001$] and sex [$F(3,720) = 6.65, p > .001$], though no significant interaction effects between sex and parental status were found. Univariate analyses of variance were then conducted to examine the locus of effects.

Women reported significantly higher stress levels than men [women, $M = 3.48$; men, $M = 3.66$: $F(1,722) = 16.16, p > .001$] and more frequent psychosomatic symptoms [women, $M = 4.20$; men, $M = 4.33$: $F(1,722) = 15.78, p > .001$], but there were no significant differences by gender in reports of work–family interference. Additionally, parents with children under 18 reported significantly higher stress levels than nonparents [parents, $M = 3.54$; nonparents, $M = 3.61$: $F(1,722) = 5.12, p > .05$] and greater work–family interference [parents, $M = 2.50$; nonparents, $M = 2.86$: $F(1,722) = 32.92, p > .001$]. There were no significant differences in psychosomatic symptoms for parents and nonparents.

2. Are Family Conditions Related to Stress, Psychosomatic Symptoms, and Work–Family Interference for Employed Parents?

Multivariate multiple regression analyses were conducted to determine the extent to which family conditions were associated with stress, psychosomatic symptoms, and work–family interference for employed parents. Results indicated that there were significant multivariate effects for fathers [$F(12,549) = 1.98$, $p > .05$] and mothers [$F(12,216) = 2.05$, $p > .05$]. Univariate simultaneous regression analyses were conducted to further examine these relationships.

Within the sample of employed fathers, family conditions were significant predictors of stress [adjusted $R^2 = .054$, $F(5,169) = 2.67$, $p > .05$] and approached significance for psychosomatic symptoms [adjusted $R^2 = .03$, $F(5,196) = 2.10$, $p = .066$] but were not significantly related to reports of work–family interference. Examination of the individual predictor variables indicated that only one of the family variables was individually significant in predicting the employed father's reports of stress. When fathers perceived their wives were not doing their share of housework, they were more likely to report higher stress levels [$B = .19$, $sr^2 = .03$, $F(1,194) = 5.49$, $p > .05$]. The shared variance between the set of family conditions contributed another 1% to the explained variance in employed father's reports of stress.

Because the variance explained in employed father's psychosomatic symptoms approached significance, the patterns of relationships of individual predictor variables were examined to identify potentially interesting trends in the data. Again, the husband's report that the wife was not doing her share of housework was marginally associated with the frequency of husband's psychosomatic symptoms ($sr^2 = .020$). Additionally, the frequency of child care breakdown was marginally associated with employed father's psychosomatic symptoms ($sr^2 = .017$).

For employed mothers, the set of family conditions was a significant predictor of work–family interference [adjusted $R^2 = .17$, $F(5,77) = 4.15$, $p > .01$] but was not significant in predicting stress or psychosomatic symptoms. Three variables related to child care were the most important individual predictors of work–family interference for this group. These included the frequency of child care breakdown, [$B = -.26$, $sr^2 = .08$, $F(1,77) = 6.43$, $p > .01$] the perception that the husband was not doing his fair share of child care [$B = .23$, $sr^2 = .06$, $F(1,77) = 4.98$, $p > .05$], and the age of the youngest child [$B = -.26$, $sr^2 = .08$, $F(1,77) = 6.61$, $p > .05$].

3. Are Job Conditions Related to Stress, Psychosomatic Symptoms, and Work–Family Interference for Employed Parents?

Multivariate multiple regression analyses were conducted to examine the extent to which the set of job conditions was significantly related to stress, symptoms, and work–family interference for employed parents. Significant multivariate effects were found for fathers, [$F(21,531) = 5.78, p > .001$] but not for mothers, [$F(21,198) = 1.44, p < .05$].

Univariate multiple regressions indicated that, for fathers, the set of job conditions was significant in predicting stress [adjusted $R^2 = .20$, $F(7,194) = 8.29, p > .001$], psychosomatic symptoms [adjusted $R^2 = .21$, $F(7,194) = 8.60, p > .001$], and work–family interference [adjusted $R^2 = .26, F(7,194) = 10.91, p > .001$].

For mothers, the set of job conditions was significant in predicting stress [adjusted $R^2 = .12, F(7,75) = 2.57, p > .05$] but was not a significant predictor of psychosomatic symptoms or work–family interference.

Three of the seven job-related variables were significant in predicting father's reports of stress. These included job security [$B = -.15$, $sr^2 = .03, F(1,194) = 5.36, p > .05$], supervisor sensitivity [$B = -.18$, $sr^2 = .03, F(1,194) = 5.81, p > .01$], and job demands [$B = .24, sr^2 = .05, F(1,194) = 10.94, p > .001$]. The seven job-related variables in combination contributed an additional 12% to the explained variance in father's stress scores.

Only two of the job conditions were individually significant in terms of father's reports of psychosomatic symptoms. These were supervisor sensitivity [$B = -.25, sr^2 = .06, F(1,194) = 11.26, p > .001$] and job challenge [$B = -.27, sr^2 = .05, F(1,194) = 10.39, p > .01$]. An additional 13% in explained variance was contributed by shared variance in the job conditions.

Finally, the most powerful predictors of work–family interference for fathers were the total job hours [$B = .23, sr^2 = .05, F(1,194) = 10.62, p > .01$], supervisor sensitivity [$B = -.16, sr^2 = .02, F(1,194) = 4.68, p > .05$], job demands [$B = .28, sr^2 = .08, F(1,194) = 15.68, p < .001$], and job challenge [$B = -.22, sr^2 = .04, F(1,194) = 7.34, p > .01$]. The seven job variables in combination contributed another 9% to the explained variance in work–family interference for fathers.

For employed mothers, two of the job-related variables were individually significant in predicting stress. These were supervisor sensitivity [$B = -.28, sr^2 = .07, F(1,75) = 5.73, p > .05$] and job security [$B = -.25, sr^2 = .07, F(1,75) = 5.44, p > .05$]. Although the overall regression equation using job conditions to predict psychosomatic symptoms only approached significance, the standardized regression coefficient for job hours was significant [$B = .25, sr^2 = .06, F(1,75) = 4.34, p > .05$]. The set of job conditions was not significantly related to work–family interference for the employed mothers in this sample.

4. What Are the Relative Importance of Job and Family Conditions in Predicting Outcomes for Employed Mothers and Fathers?

Communality analyses were conducted to determine the relative contribution of job and family conditions in predicting stress, psychosomatic symptoms, and work–family interference for employed parents. In the words of Pedhazur (1982, p. 199),

> Communality analyses is a method of variance partitioning designed to identify proportions of variance in the dependent variable that may be attributed uniquely to each of the independent variables and proportions of variance that are attributed to various combinations of independent variables. The unique contribution of an independent variable is defined as the variance attributed to it when it is entered last in the regression equation.

Here, communality analyses were applied to blocks of family and job conditions. Thus family conditions were entered into the regression equation as a block at the first step. The set of job conditions was entered as a block at step two. The order of entry for sets of job and family conditions was then reversed. The increment in R^2 adjusted for degrees of freedom were examined to evaluate the relative importance of job and family conditions. The increment in R^2 and adjusted R^2 for job and family conditions for each of the dependent measures are presented in Table 3.

Job conditions were more highly associated with all three outcomes

Table 3. Percentage of Variance Explained by Sets of Job and Family Characteristics When Entered into the Regression of Outcomes on Independent Variables at the Last Step

	Stress Men	Stress Women	Symptoms Men	Symptoms Women	Work–family interference Men	Work–family interference Women
Family characteristics						
R^2	.040	.088	.028	.047	.043	.236
Adjusted R^2	.022	.041	.009	.000	.026	.202
Job characteristics						
R^2	.206	.178	.214	.126	.279	.078
Adjusted R^2	.184	.113	.191	.047	.260	.008
Final R^2 (job & family)						
R^2	.270	.281	.265	.182	.326	.291
Adjusted R^2	.224	.158	.218	.042	.283	.169

for fathers than were family conditions and were most highly associated with work–family interference. For mothers, a somewhat different pattern emerged. Job conditions were more highly associated with stress for employed mothers than were family conditions, but family conditions were more important in predicting work–family interference.

5. Are Job Conditions Different for Men and Women?

A two (sex) by three (job category) MANOVA was conducted to examine the extent to which perceptions of job characteristics differed by gender and by job category within the full sample.

Univariate ANOVAs revealed that there were main effects by gender for total job time [$F(1,669) = 7.45, p > .01$], control over work hours [$F(1,669) = 5.82, p > .05$], job autonomy [$F(1,713) = 405, p > .05$], and job challenge [$F(1,713) = 5.95, p > .05$]. There were no significant differences by gender in perceptions of job security, supervisor sensitivity, or job demands.

The analyses also revealed main effects by job category for job hours [$F(2,669) = 28.71, p > .001$], control over work hours [$F(2,669) = 30.94, p > .001$], job autonomy [$F(2,713) = 39.03, p > .001$], job challenge [$F(2,713) = 25.60, p > .001$], and job demands [$F(2,713) = 22.63, p > .001$]. Again, no significant effects by job category were found for job security or supervisor sensitivity.

Significant gender by job category interaction effects were found for control over work hours [$F(2,669) = 3.17, p > .05$], autonomy [$F(2,713) = 6.00, p > .01$] and job demands [$F(2,713) = 4.54, p > .05$]. No significant interaction effects were found for security, supervisor sensitivity, total job time, or job challenge.

In the sample as a whole, women were concentrated in lower level jobs, and these jobs had less desirable characteristics than the jobs predominantly filled by men. For example, women generally had less autonomy in their jobs than men ($M = 2.52$ and 2.21, respectively). The one exception to this trend was that female clerical/technical workers reported more autonomy in their jobs than did their male counterparts (women, $M = 2.75$; men, $M = 2.56$).

In considering job challenge, position was not significant. Women experienced less challenge in their jobs than men, regardless of job position (women, $M = 1.98$; men, $M = 1.70$). Likewise, position did not explain differences in control over hours worked. Across all job categories, women had less control over their work hours than men (women, $M = 2.57$; men, $M = 2.03$).

Finally, we found that female managers and female clerical workers have greater job demands than did their male counterparts, whereas within the group of scientists, males have the greatest job demands. Female managers have the highest job demands of all (Managers—women, $M = 2.24$; men, $M = 2.38$: scientists—women, $M = 2.80$, men, $M = 2.68$: Clerical/technical—women, $M = 2.52$; men, $M = 2.73$).

F. Discussion

The results of our study support the prevalent view that balancing job and family demands is extremely difficult for the majority of parents. The period of time before their children entered elementary school (under 6 years) seemed to be the hardest of all for both employed fathers and mothers.

Our data also supported the assumption that women are more affected then men by the dual roles of worker and parent. In accordance with this view, we found that mothers with children under 18 were more likely to have higher stress levels, suffer from more psychosomatic symptoms, and to have greater work–family interference than their male counterparts.

It is interesting to note that the aspects of work that were most problematic were somewhat different for married men and women with children under 18. For both men and women, having a supervisor who was insensitive to work and family roles was most predictive of stress and, for men only, was associated with more frequent psychosomatic symptoms and greater work–family interference. This variable has not been used in previous research and thus is an important finding. Job insecurity was also significantly associated with reports of stress for both mothers and fathers. However, several other job-related variables were individually significant in predicting psychosomatic symptoms and work–family interference for men but not for women.

A second assumption is that women employees with young children have poorer mental health and physical health because they assume more responsibility for family work and that these tasks, in addition to their responsibilities at work, puts them in jeopardy. Our data indicate that child care, rather than housework, is the critical variable for mothers. When the husband was seen doing less than his fair share of child care, women had higher levels of work–family interference. In fact, an overwhelming trend in our data was the importance of a reliable system of child care in promoting the positive mental and physical health of mothers. The more frequently the child care broke down, the more likely the mother was to have higher levels of work–family interference. Interestingly enough, child care breakdown was also marginally linked to psychosomatic symptoms for fathers. Shinn and Wong (1985) have documented the same negative result in a sample of retail and state workers. Because of the growing instability of child care in this country, the issue of child care will undoubtedly be of increasing concern to business and industry.

Although outcomes for men were not as negative as for women, job conditions were the most salient in predicting these problems. Most crucial were a nonsupportive supervisor, job insecurity, job challenge, and job demands. The family outcomes that were influential were the breakdown of child care (as previously mentioned) and the perception that the wife was not doing her fair share of housework.

A third assumption—based on the fact that women have more problems balancing their dual responsibilities—is that the work–family issue is a women's issue. Again, our data point in a different direction. Although employed mothers have poorer outcomes than employed fathers, employed fathers report more stress than men who are not parents.

Work–family interference is a particularly interesting variable in this regard. For our population as a whole, the gender of the worker was not a significant predictor of interference: 42% of the men and 43% of the women experienced "some" or "a great deal" interference. The younger the children, the larger gap between the mother's and the father's level of interference. With children 5 and under, 68% of the women and 51% of the men had high interference scores, whereas when the children were between 13 and 18, the tables had turned, albeit not very significantly. During those years, men had slightly higher work–family interference: 40% of the men and 37% of the women experienced "some" or "a great deal" interference.

Overall, these figures are quite high. With young children, approximately one out of every two male employees and two of every three female employees were having a hard time managing the dual responsibilities at work and at home. Even when the children were older, approximately two out of every five employees, male and female, were feeling conflicted and torn by all they had to do. The same figures applied for the sample of workers as a whole: Two out of every five men and women could be placed in the high range of work–family interference. Therefore, it is clear that a substantial proportion of all employees—not just women—are affected in multiple ways. Thus, this is not just a women's issue.

A fourth assumption is that responding to the work–family problems of employees is beyond the proper role of the corporation. That assumption developed in a time when the majority of families were single-earner families and wives were at home to provide support for family members. Then, the notion that the worlds of work and family were separate and nonoverlapping was tenable (Kanter, 1977). As a part of the American emphasis on individuality, it was also held that individuals were responsible for solving their own problems in the privacy of their own homes and communities (Lasch, 1978).

In some ways, these views have changed with the changing times. It is more widely accepted that work and family life are not separate but are linked in profound ways (Piotrkowski, 1979). Furthermore, within the mental health field, there is a growing acceptance that all individuals have problems and that it is more effective to prevent rather to remediate (Rappaport, 1977; Valliant, 1977; Weissbourd, 1985). Thus, work–family problems are increasingly seen as the result of the unevenness of social change: families changing faster than societal institutions.

G. Summary

The results of our study revealed several interesting trends. First, women in general report more negative outcomes than men do. They reported higher stress levels and more frequent psychosomatic symptoms. Interestingly, however, we found no differences by gender in reports of work–family interference.

Parents generally reported more negative outcomes than did nonparents. Having a child under 18 was associated with higher stress levels and greater work–family interference.

Although we found that women had poorer job conditions than men did, the set of job conditions was only significant in explaining reports of stress (except the individual variable of job hours) and did not appear to contribute to psychosomatic symptoms or work–family interference for women. In contrast, although men reported more desirable job conditions than women did, these job conditions were highly associated with negative outcomes for men.

The results of our study are exciting in that they demonstrate the importance of job and family conditions for both men and women in predicting measurable negative outcomes. However, it is important not only to emphasize that such relationships exist and can be documented but also to encourage corporations to continue to recognize and address the needs of working parents who are effected in dramatic ways by both their job and their family responsibilities. In the following section, we will discuss corporate responses to changing family needs.

IV. CORPORATE WORK—FAMILY PROGRAMS

Most corporations that have adopted family responsive programs have done so in a way that is nonintrusive. Their policies have been ultimately respectful of the view that the responsibility for solving family problems resides within the privacy of the family. The corporation's role is to offer information and resources that the employee can take advantage of if he or she chooses to do so.

At Bank Street, we have worked with numerous companies during the process of developing family responsive programs. We found corporate rationales generally adhere to the following line of reasoning:

1. The demographics of the work force have changed and will continue to change. Companies are aware of the projection that 66% of all new entrants to the work force will be women; 70% of women in the work force are now in the childbearing age; and 80% of them are expected to have children during their working lives (Galinsky & Friedman, 1986).
2. It is proper for the company to get involved in order to recruit and retain employees, to decrease absenteeism, to maintain or improve productivity, to raise morale, and build a better corporate image. In other words, providing family responsive programs gives the company a competitive edge, consistent with its own bottom-line purpose (Friedman, 1985).
3. The company will therefore develop programs and policies that are responsive to the particular needs of its employees as well as its own corporate culture.
4. These programs provide information or resources for the employee to use. They do not interfere with employee privacy by dictating to the family.

Overall, corporations have begun to get involved in responding to work–family issues that are consistent with their own purposes and prevailing American values.

In 1978, approximately 110 companies had programs focused on the child care needs of their employees. By 1986, that number had increased to 3,000 (Galinsky & Friedman, 1986). Although child care is only one aspect of work–family needs, these figures make it evident that family responsive programs have expanded rapidly, yet at the same time serve only a very small fraction of the workers in the six million companies in America today.

Furthermore, these programs are concentrated in large businesses. If the Small Business Administration's definition of a small business is used—a business employing fewer than 500 employees—99% of all companies fall into this category. Almost half the workers in the United States work for organizations that employ fewer than 100 people, and these workers do not have the benefits and services that are found in the multinational corporations. In fact, in Bank Street's research with factory workers, we find that these workers may not have the right to make and receive personal phone calls, to take paid time off on their wedding day or when one's wife is giving birth.

Friedman (1983) conducted a study in three different communities to examine which companies were more likely to institute family responsive programs. She found that the following conditions were most conducive: (1) a large company; (2) a high percentage of women employees; (3) a product or service that is family-related such as health care; and (4) young, entrepreneurial leadership. Furthermore, she found that programs tended to be clustered in certain parts of the country where the community culture was profamily. In addition, at Bank Street, we have found that the impetus for change comes from one individual or a small group of individuals within the company. Thus there is usually a prime mover who is committed to bring about change on behalf of families (Galinsky, 1987).

In the following section, we will describe the work–family programs that have been developed for employed parents with children 18 and under.

A. Work Hours Programs

1. Flexitime

Flexitime means flexible work hours. It is the most frequent work–family initiative. According to a recent survey designed by the authors for *Fortune Magazine*, 33% of a nationally representative sample had flexitime programs in their companies (Galinsky & Hughes, unpublished data, 1987). With this system, workers choose their own arrival and departure times within the limits determined by the company. Nollen (1982) notes that schedules vary along three dimensions: (a) daily versus periodic setting of the work schedule; (b) variable versus constant length of the work day (i.e., whether employees can credit time from 1 day to the next); and (c) "core-time-there" hours, usually during the middle of the work day, when all employees are required to be present.

2. Compressed Work Week

A compressed work week is a full-time job that is scheduled in less than 5 days per week. It is used by 2.7% of workers (Nollen, 1982).

3. Part-Time Work

Work is considered to be part-time if it is less than 35 hours per week. In 1982, according to Plewes (1984), one in five of all workers, or 18 million people, worked under 35 hours per week, and the majority, or 70%, did so by choice. Seventy percent of all voluntary part-time workers are women.

The most promising innovation in part-time work is called V Time or voluntary reduced work time (*Work Times*, 1986). Under V Time, a worker can reduce his or her work hours by a certain percentage (to 80%, for example) for a limited time period and yet retain seniority and have prorated benefits.

4. Job Sharing

Job sharing means that two people share one position. The two workers divide up the hours worked, the responsibilities, the pay, and the benefits.

5. Personal Days

The purpose of personal excused days is to extend the definition of sick days (i.e., a specified number of paid days for sickness) to paid days that can be taken for personal or family reasons. In some companies, the use of personal days is prescribed (religious holidays, care of sick children, etc), whereas in others, these days can be used at the employee's discretion.

6. Time Bank

Under this program, each employee has a certain number of available paid hours to spend away from work during the year that the employee can take in 2- or 3-hour increments.

B. Work Location Programs

1. Flexiplace

Flexiplace means that the employee can work at home. It is mainly used by executives who work at home or by word processors who have a terminal placed in their homes (Axel, 1985).

2. Van Pools

Some companies ease commuting problems by providing van pools that transport employees to and from work.

3. Relocation Assistance and Counseling

Relocation assistance consists largely of the payment of costs associated with moving: trips to look for housing, temporary living expenses, storage, direct moving costs, and sometimes the purchase of furniture and appliances. In addition, a few companies have set up programs that provide counseling for the relocated family as well as job assistance placement for the spouse.

C. Benefit Programs

1. Flexible Benefits

When considering flexible benefits, it is important to keep in mind the fact that not all workers are covered with a standard benefits package. Although 97% of all workers have individual health insurance with close to three quarters of that coverage paid for by the employer, less than half of American households have family health coverage paid for by the employer (Bureau of Labor Statistics, 1984; U.S. Bureau of the Census, 1983).

Section 125 of the Internal Revenue Code, in 1970, created the possibility of flexible benefits though most have been instituted since 1982 (Friedman, 1985). With a flexible benefit package, an employee can select from a complete or partial menu of benefits those that most fit his or her needs. For example, if one's spouse is covered with health insurance, one can trade off this benefit for such things as cash compensation, dental care, dependent care, or life insurance. Currently, there are 150 comprehensive cafeteria benefit programs (Friedman, 1985).

2. Flexible Saving Accounts (FSA's)

Salary reduction plans such as flexible savings accounts became possible after tax legislation in 1978. Employees reduce their salaries by a certain percentage and then can be reimbursed for certain predetermined expenses such as dental bills or child care expenses with pretax dollars. The money in these accounts must be used up by the end of the year or forfeited. Over 800 companies now have FSAs (Friedman, 1985b).

3. Dependent Care Assistance Plans (DCAP)

Section 129 of the IRS code of Economic Recovery Tax Act of 1981 allows employers to reimburse or pay for employee's child care expenses with tax-deductible dollars. Approximately 150 companies have currently established DCAP programs (*Money*, 1985).

4. Reimbursement Programs/Vouchers

Under reimbursement programs, the company reimburses the employee for a portion or the full cost of child care. These programs are either part of a benefits plan or exist as an additional service. Approximately 25 companies have voucher programs (Friedman, 1985).

5. Parenting Leaves

The Pregnancy Discrimination Act of 1978 has determined that pregnancy must be treated like any other worker disability, that is, if a corporation provides disability benefits, pregnant women must be included.

In addition, five states that mandated disability leaves for childbirth. Kamerman, Kahn, and Kingston, (1983) estimate that under this state and national legislation, only 40% of all working women have the legal entitlement to a leave.

Some companies have expanded their paid disability maternity leave with an unpaid parenting leave that includes fathers and generally lasts for a 3- to 6-month period; others provide some portion of paid leave beyond the disability period. A few companies are experimenting with a part-time transition back to work.

The subject of parenting leaves has become a topic of national debate. Several bills have been introduced in Congress that provide fathers and mothers with a guaranteed 18 weeks unpaid leave at the time of childbirth, adoption, or for the care of a sick child or dependent adult. A recent Supreme Court decision affirmed the right of states to provide job-protected leaves for the disability of pregnancy.

D. Family Responsive Services

1. Employee Assistance or Counseling Programs

Employee Assistance Programs (EAP), or counseling services, were begun to assist alcoholic employees but have now been expanded to include such issues as marital discord, care of aging parents, child care difficulties or other work–family problems. It is estimated that there are currently 5,000 such programs in the country (Leavitt, 1983).

2. Fitness Programs

A number of companies have recently developed programs to promote health and fitness. These consist of health facilities, jogging tracks, exercise courses as well as stop-smoking and weight-loss programs.

E. Child Care Support and Services

As previously stated, the number of corporate initiatives related to child care is increasing. Burud, Aschbacher, and McCroskey (1984) noted a growth rate of 395% between 1978 and 1982.

1. Resource and Referral

Resource and referral (R & R) is the fastest growing child care initiative, with 500 companies offering this service in 1985 (Friedman, 1985b). Resource and referral offers (1) the provision of counseling services to help parents locate child care, judge its quality, and make a selection and (2) the provision of money or resources to increase the quantity and/or improve the quality of the child care supply.

2. Support for Community Child Care

Another form of company aid to child care is the provision of financial support to existing local infant/toddler, preschool or afterschool programs. In some cases, companies give money to a program and, in return, a certain number of slots are held for employees, or employees are given preferential admission.

Another form of subsidy is corporate payment for a number of slots within a program for employees' children. This differs from reimbursement because the financial transaction is between the company and the provider, whereas with reimbursement, the parent pays and is refunded.

A third form of support is supply building. Some companies have taken the lead in increasing services, particularly the development of new family day care homes, afterschool programs, hot or warm lines (telephone services for children when they are home alone), and safe homes (a place for latch-key children to turn to if they are in need of help).

3. On- or Near-Site Child Care

When corporate initiatives for child care are discussed, most people think of a center on the work site as being the preferred choice of parents. Out of 18 proposed benefits in the Quality of Employment Survey of 1977, on-site child care was selected last by respondents (Quinn & Staines, 1979); however, in a large study by Fernandez (1985), workers voiced a preference for on- or near-site child care. In 1985, there were approximately 150 work-site corporate child care centers, 400 centers in hospitals, and 30 public agency centers (Friedman, 1985b).

Companies have gotten involved in child care by (1) subsidizing and managing work-site centers alone or as part of a consortium of companies and (2) contracting with child care professionals or parent employees to develop a child care center and paying all or part of the start-up costs and/or a portion of operating costs.

4. Sick Child Care/Travel Care

A few companies have developed sick child care facilities, or sick bays, as they are called. Children can spend time in these day care facilities when they are recovering from being sick. An alternative sick care program involves a liaison between a company and a local health care facility. The company pays for a portion of the cost of the fees of trained health or child care workers who provide in-home care for the sick children of employees. Approximately 20 companies have sick child care programs (Friedman, 1985).

F. Training Programs

1. Work and Family Life Seminars

Catalyst (1984) estimated that the number of workplaces offering a family life seminars is growing with over 1,000 coporations offering seminars. Although varying in location, format, length, and content, these seminars share a common focus on the work and family concerns of employees (Catalyst, 1984). They are unique in being able to address issues for all employees, from single workers to those with aging parents.

V. CONCLUSIONS

It is interesting to compare the kinds of work–family problems that have been identified by our research and by others, with the range of programs developed by corporations to help employees manage.

Employees usually note that time is one of their most difficult problems. In the CWFLS census conducted at the research site in 1983, employees indicated that the scheduling of work hours was the aspect of their jobs that had the most negative impact on their family life. When asked to select a change that would improve the quality of their family life and maintain or improve their productivity, the first choice of employees in 1983 and again in 1986 was to increase the flexibility of work hours (Galinsky, Ruopp, & Blum, 1983; Galinsky, Hughes, & Shinn, 1986). Both times, this choice was the most likely to be made by women with young children. It is interesting to note that, in our study, the total number of hours worked was predictive of work–family interference for men and for psychosomatic symptoms for women.

Corporations, as the previous description of family responsive programs indicate, have developed numerous programs to improve the flexibility of work hours—from flexitime to part-time work; from personal days to leave policies. Do these help working parents? Here the literature is inconclusive. Although one study, for example, shows that the flexitime increased family time and provided greater ease in making child care arrangements (Winett & Neale, 1981), another study found that flexitime did not reduce the role strain of employed mothers. The group who benefitted the most from this schedule change was workers without children (Bohen & Viveros-Long, 1981).

The issues of job autonomy and job demands have been addressed by the growing use of quality circles and worker participation in decision making (Ouchi, 1981; Peters & Waterman, 1983; Simon & Mares, 1982). The next stage of our research will involve workers in designing a workplace change to improve the quality of family life and productivity and, as such, will be an experiment in increasing job autonomy.

There have been numerous programs to help employees with their child care needs—the provision of resource and referral to locate child care, benefit programs to help pay for child care, and on- or near-worksite child care to provide quality care. In addition, employee assistance programs and workplace seminars are designed to deal with aiding employees in gaining skills and knowledge to find and select child care. In view of the importance of the breakdown of child care arrangements to the health and well-being of employed parents, employer initiatives in child care are a very worthwhile direction for corporations.

The one obvious omission from current corporate family responsive programs is in the area of the supervisory relationship. Our work with corporations has made it evident that a company may have an innovative program, but it is generally up to the supervisor's discretion how, or even if, the employee can take advantage of it. Furthermore, research has pinpointed the supervisory relation as potentially one of the leading causes of anxiety and depression (Repetti, 1985). For our sample as a whole, we found that when an employee had a supervisor who was not sensitive to family as well as work needs, the employee was more likely to be dissatisfied with his or her job and to have higher levels of stress and more frequent psychosomatic symptoms. For employed parents in our sample, an insensitive supervisor was a significant predictor of stress for work–family interference and of psychosomatic symptoms for employed fathers and of stress for employed mothers. Furthermore, when asked to suggest a workplace change to improve the quality of family life and productivity in both the corporate census in 1983 and the questionnaire in 1986, the second choice was to sensitize the supervisor to employee needs. This request was most likely to be made by managers (Galinsky, Ruopp, & Blum, 1983; Galinsky, Hughes & Shinn, 1986). There have been few, if any, workplace initiatives or training programs designed to make managers more aware of the work–family problems of employees. Clearly, this is a very pressing need.

One of the most significant findings in our data is the relative importance of job conditions and child care arrangements in predicting negative outcomes for working parents. These can be changed. A number of companies have taken first steps in doing so. It is a beginning—one that hopefully will spread. Because the majority of women as well as men work in factories or small businesses that have few family responsive services or benefits, we still have a long way to go.

Acknowledgments

We would like to acknowledge the contributions of Marsha Love and Marybeth Shinn to the development of the Corporate Work and Family Life Questionnaire.

REFERENCES

Ad Hoc Day Care Coalition. (1985). *The crisis in infant and toddler child care.* Washington, DC: Author.

Axel, H. (1985). *Corporations and families: Changing practices and perspectives*. New York: The Conference Board.

Bailyn, L. (1970). Career and family orientations of husbands and wives in relation to marital happiness. *Human Relation, 23*, 97–113.

Barnett, R. G., & Baruch, G. K. (1983). *Women's involvement in multiple roles, role strain, and psychological stress*. Working paper 107. Wellesley, MA: Wellesley College Center for Research on Women.

Blank, H. (April, 1984). Testimony of the Children's Defense Fund before the Joint Economic Committee concerning child care problems faced by working mothers and pregnant women. Unpublished manuscript, Washington, DC.

Bohen, H. H., & Viveros-Long, A. (1981). *Balancing jobs and family life: Do flexible work schedules help?* Philadelphia: Temple University Press.

Bureau of Labor Statistics (1985). *Current population survey (March supplement)*. Washington, DC: U.S. Department of Labor.

Burke, R. J., Weir, T., & DuWors, R. (1979). Type A behavior and administrators and wives reports of marital satisfaction and well-being. *Journal of Applied Psychology, 64*(1), 57–65.

Burud, S. L., Aschbacher, P. R., & McCroskey, J. (1984). *Employer-supported child care*. Boston: Auburn House.

Carlson, B. E. (1984). The father's contribution to child care: Effects on children's perception of parental roles. *American Journal of Orthopsychiatry, 54*, 123–136.

Catalyst. (1984). *Work and family seminars: Corporations response to employees' needs*. New York: Author.

Children's Defense Fund. (1984). *A children's defense budget*. Washington, DC: Author.

Cohen, S., Karmarch, T., & Mermelstein, R. (1983). A global measure of perceived stress. *Journal of Health and Social Behavior, 24*, 385–396.

De la Mare, G., & Walker, S. (1968). Factors influencing the choice of shift rotation. *Occupational Psychology, 42*, 1–21.

Emlen, A. C., & Koren, P. E. (1984). *Hard to find and difficult to manage: The effects of child care on the workplace*. Portland, OR: Regional Institute for Human Services.

Fernandez, J. (1985). *Child care and corporate productivity: Resolving family/work conflict*. New York: Lexington Book, D. C. Heath Co.

Friedman, D. E. (1983). *Encouraging employer support to working parents*. New York: Carnegie Corporation of New York.

Friedman, D. E. (1985). Corporate financial assistance for child care. *The Conference Board Research Bulletin, Report #177*. New York: The Conference Board

Galinsky, E. (1987). Corporate policies and family life. In M. Yogman & T. Brazelton (Eds.), *Stresses and supports for families*. Boston: Harvard University Press.

Galinsky, E., & Hughes, D. (1987). [*Fortune Magazine* national survey of childcare and productivity]. Unpublished data.

Galinsky, E., & Friedman, D. E. (1986). *Investing in quality child care: A report for AT&T*. Basking Ridge, NJ: AT&T.

Galinsky, E., Ruopp, R. R., & Blum, K. S. (1983). [The Corporate Work and Family Life Study.] Unpublished data.

Galinsky, E., Hughes, D., Love, M., & Shinn, M., (1985). *The Corporate Work and Family Life Study Questionnaire*. New York: Bank Street College of Education.

Galinsky, E., & Hughes, D. & Shinn, M. (1986). *The Corporate Work and Family Study*. Unpublished paper. Bank Street College of Education, New York.

General Mills, Inc., (1981). *General Mills American Family Report, Families at work: Strengths and Strains*. Minneapolis, MN: Louis Haldi & Associates.

Hauenstein, L. A. (1976, May). Attitudes of married women toward work and family: Comparison by stress level, race, and work status. Final unpublished report 1. NIMH, Rockville, MD.
Hill, R. (1970). What is the role of the executive's wife? *Business Quarterly, 35*(4), 54–59.
Hoffman, L. W. (1982). *Maternal employment and the young child.* Paper presented at the Minnesota Symposium on Child Psychology.
House, J. S. (1981). *Work stress and social support.* Reading, MA: Addison-Wesley.
Hunt, J. G., & Hunt, L. L. (1977). Dilemmas and contradictions of status: The case of the dual career family. *Social Problems, 24,* 407–416.
Kamerman, S. B. (1980). *Parenting in an unresponsive society.* New York: The Free Press.
Kamerman, S., & Kahn, A. (1981). *Child care, family benefits, and working parents.* New York: Columbia University Press.
Kamerman, S., Kahn, A., & Kingston, P. (1983). *Maternity policies and working women.* New York: Columbia University Press.
Kanter, R. M. (1977). *Work and family in the United States: A critical review and agenda for research and policy.* New York: Russell Sage Foundation.
Karasek, R. A. (1979). Job demands, job decision latitude, and mental strain: Implications for job redesign. *Administrative Science Quarterly, 24,* 285–308.
Karasek, R. A., Baker, R., Marxer, F., Ahlbom, A., & Theorell, T. (1981). Job decision latitude, job demands, and cardiovascular disease: A prospective study of Swedish men. *American Journal of Public Health, 71,* 694–705.
Katz, M. H., & Piotrkowski, C. S. (1983). Role strain and depression in two-job families. *Family Relations, 29,* 438–488.
Keith, P., & Schaeffer, R. (1980). Role strain and depression in two-job families. *Family Relations 29,* 483–488.
Kimmelman, B. (1969). Executive wives—The need for a positive company-sponsored approach. California Management Review, spring issue, 7–10.
Lasch, C. (1978). *The culture of narcissism.* New York: W. W. Norton & Co.
Leavitt, R. (1983). *Employee assistance and counseling programs.* New York: Community Council of Greater New York.
Lein, L., Durham, M., Pratt, M., Schudson, M., Thomas, R., & Weiss, H. (1974). Final report: Work and family life, National Institute of Education Project #3-3094. Cambridge, MA: Center for Study of Public Policy.
Mason, T., & Espinoza, R. (1983). *Executive summary of the final report: Working parents project* (Contract No. 4000-80-0107). Washington, DC: National Institute of Education.
Money (1985, May). Going for it all, pp. 108–146.
Mott, P. E., Mann, F. C., McLaughlin, Q., & Warwick, D. P. (1965). *Shift work: The social, psychological, and physical consequences.* Ann Arbor: The University of Michigan Press.
Nollen, S. D. (1982). *New work schedules in practice: Managing time in a changing society.* New York: Van Nostrand Reinhold Co.
Nordberg, O. (1985, February). The cost of child care. *Working Mother,* pp. 53–56.
Ouchi, W. (1981). *Theory Z: How Americans can meet the Japanese challenge.* Reading, MA: Addison-Wesley.
Pearlin, L. I. (1970). *Class context and family relations: A cross-national study.* Boston: Little, Brown.
Pedhazur, E. J. (1982). *Multiple regression in behavioral research: Explanation and prediction* (2nd ed.). New York: CBS College Publishing.
Peters, T. J., & Waterman, R. H., Jr. (1983). *In search of excellence.* New York: Warner Books.
Piotrkowski, C. S. (1979). *Work and the family system: A naturalistic study of working-class and lower-middle-class families.* New York: The Free Press.

Piotrkowski, C. S., & Katz, M. H. (1982). Indirect socialization of children: The effects of mothers jobs on academic behaviors. *Child Development, 53*, 1520–1529.

Piotrkowski, C. S., & Katz, M. H. (1983). Work experience and family relations among working class and lower middle-class families. In H. Z. Lopata & J. H. Pleck (eds.), *Research in the interweave of social roles: Families and jobs* (Vol. 3, pp. 187–200). Greenwich, CT: JAI Press.

Pleck, J. H. (1983). Husbands paid work and family roles: Current research issues. In H. Z. Lopata & J. H. Pleck, (Eds.), *Research on the interweave of social roles: Families and jobs* (Vol. 3, pp. 251–332). Greenwich, CT: JAI Press.

Pleck, J. H., & Staines, G. L. (1983). Work schedules and work family conflict in two earner couples. In J. Aldous (Ed.), *Dual earner families*. Beverly Hills: Sage Publications.

Pleck, J. H., Staines, G. L. & Lang, L. (1978). *Work and family life: First reports on work-family interference and workers formal child-care arrangements from the 1977 Quality of Employment Survey*. Wellesley, MA: Wellesley College Center for Research on Women, Working Papers.

Pleck, J. H., Staines, G. L., & Lang, L. (1980) Conflicts between work and family. *Monthly Labor Review, 103*(3), 29–32.

Plewes, T. (1984). *Profile of the part-time worker*. Part-time employment in America.

Quinn, R. P., & Staines, G. L. (1979). *The 1977 Quality of Employment Survey: Descriptive statistics with comparison data from the 1969–70 and 1972–73 surveys*. Ann Arbor, MI: Institute for Social Research.

Rappaport, J. (1977). *Community psychology*. New York: Holt, Rhinehart & Winston.

Repetti, R. L. (1985). *Social factors in the workplace and mental health*. Paper presented at the 1985 Annual Convention of the American Psychological Association, Los Angeles, CA.

Ruopp, R. R., & Travers, J. (1982). Janus faces day care: Perspectives on quality and cost. In E. F. Zigler & E. W. Gordon (Eds.) *Daycare: Scientific and social policy issues* (pp. 72–101). Boston: Auburn House Publishing Co.

Seligson, M., Genser, A., Gannett, E., & Gray, W. (1983). *School-age child care: A policy report*. Wellesley, MA: School-Age Child Care Project.

Shinn, M., & Wong, N. W. (1985). *The Working Parents Project*. Paper presented at the Annual Convention of the American Psychological Association, Los Angeles, CA.

Shinn, M., Wong, N., Simko, P., & Ortiz-Torres, B. (1986). *Promoting the health and well-being of working parents: Coping, social support, and organizational strategies*. Unpublished manuscript, New York University, New York.

Simon, J., & Mares, W. (1982). *Working together*. New York: Knopf.

Staines, G., & Pleck, J. 1983. *The impact of work schedules in the family*. Ann Arbor, MI: Survey Research Center, Institute for Social Research.

U.S. Bureau of the Census. (1983). *Child care arrangements of working mothers: June 1982* (Series P. 23, No. 129). Current Population Reports, Washington, DC: U.S. Government Printing Office.

Valliant, G. E. (1977). *Adaption to life*. Boston: Little, Brown.

Weissbourd, B. (1985, May). *Families, jobs and the supportive workplace: An overview of current trends, challenges, and creative solutions*. Panel presentation at Regional conference sponsored by Family Resource Coalition and Temple University. Philadelphia, PA.

Whyte, W. H. (1956). *The organization man*. New York: Simon & Schuster.

Winett, R. A., & Neale, M. S. (1981). Flexible work schedules and family time allocation: Assessment of a system change on individual behavior using self-report logs. *Journal of Applied Behavior Analysis 1*, 41–51.

Work Times. (1986). The cutting edge: New York state and alternative work schedules. Vol 4, Number 2.

Yogev, S., & Brett, S. (1983). *Patterns of work and family involvement among single and dual earner couples: Two competing analytical approaches.* Washington DC: Office of Naval Research.

Zur-Shapiro, S., & Longfellow, C. (1981, April). *Support from fathers: Implications for the well-being of mothers and their children.* Paper presented at the Society for Research in Child Development Biennial Meeting, Boston.

9

Maternal Employment and Children's Development
An Integration of Longitudinal Findings with Implications for Social Policy

Adele Eskeles Gottfried and Allen W. Gottfried

Does maternal employment affect children's development? The body of data presented in the preceding chapters provides a foundation upon which to answer this question. In this chapter, results will be integrated to determine generalizability of findings across studies, and some of the most important processes pertaining to the relationship of maternal employment to children's development will be highlighted. Directions for future research and implications for social policy are advanced.

I. CONTEMPORANEOUS AND LONG-TERM RELATIONSHIPS BETWEEN MATERNAL EMPLOYMENT STATUS AND CHILDREN'S DEVELOPMENT

Across studies, the overwhelming finding obtained was that maternal employment status *per se* was not significantly related to children's

---

Adele Eskeles Gottfried • Department of Educational Psychology, California State University, Northridge, Northridge, California 91330. Allen W. Gottfried • Department of Psychology, California State University, Fullerton, Fullerton, California 92634.

development. With regard to contemporaneous findings, children whose mothers are employed or nonemployed develop equivalently in the following areas: infant developmental status (Gottfried, Gottfried, & Bathurst); security of attachment in infancy (Owen & Cox), toddlerhood and kindergarten years (Goldberg & Easterbrooks); cognitive, language, and intellectual development in the preschool through school-age years (Goldberg & Easterbrooks; Gottfried et al.; Lerner & Galambos); problem solving in toddlerhood (Goldberg & Easterbrooks); social reasoning during preschool and social maturity during the school years (Gottfried et al.); emotional expressiveness during kindergarten (Goldberg & Easterbrooks); behavioral adjustment from ages 4 through 7 (Gottfried et al.), academic performance in the early school years (Gottfried et al.; Lerner & Galambos); school motivation (Gottfried et al.); and sex role development in adolescence (Galambos, Petersen, & Lenerz). This impressive array of findings across a broad spectrum of developmental domains and at ages ranging from infancy through adolescence shows that there are no detrimental effects associated with maternal employment *per se*. Children of employed mothers do not suffer decrements in development directly attributable to their mothers' employment status.

A few significant findings were obtained. With regard to temperament, Lerner and Galambos found that children whose mothers were employed were temperamentally easier, although Gottfried et al. found no significant differences in temperament from infancy through childhood due to maternal employment status. Goldberg and Easterbrooks found that kindergarten boys whose mothers were employed and kindergarten girls whose mothers were not employed showed the most adaptability and flexibility (ego resilience). On the other hand, ego control (delay of gratification and appropriate expression of affect) was unrelated to maternal employment status.

The studies in this volume address whether maternal employment status has any long-term or sleeper effects on children's development. Results across studies show that maternal employment status *per se* has no reliable long-term significant relationships with subsequent development across the varied developmental domains studied. The longitudinal effects of maternal employment on subsequent development were analyzed by Galambos et al., Goldberg and Easterbrooks, Gottfried et al., Lerner and Galambos, and Owen and Cox.

Maternal employment status during the child's infancy was not significantly predictive of *any* subsequent measure of development at ages 2, 3.5, 5, 6, and 7 years in cognitive, social, academic, and behavioral domains (Gottfried et al.). Goldberg and Easterbrooks found that maternal employment prior to 6 months in contrast to after 6 months during the child's infancy was not significantly related to quality of toddlers' attachments to either their mothers or fathers when analyzed separately. When attachments to mothers and fathers were combined to form a single measure, toddlers whose mothers resumed work in the latter half of the first year were more likely to have a secure attachment to both parents. Timing of mothers' return to work during infancy (early vs. late) was not related to toddlers' problem solving (Goldberg & Easterbrooks). Owen and Cox found that mothers' employment status when the children were 3 months was unrelated to infants' security of attachment at 12 months, although infants' whose mothers were employed at 3 months and 7 to 12 months showed more resistance in the second reunion in the strange situation. Lerner and Galambos correlated maternal employment status from infancy with temperament and adjustment in adolescence and adulthood. No significant correlations were obtained.

Maternal employment status during toddlerhood was not related to kindergarteners' separation anxiety, ego resiliency, or language ability (Goldberg & Easterbrooks). Predictions from maternal employment status at age 2 to subsequent development at ages 3.5, 5, 6, and 7 years showed virtually no consistent significant differences between the children of employed versus nonemployed mothers with regard to cognitive, intellectual, social, academic, and behavioral development (Gottfried *et al.*). This was also true for predictions of maternal employment status from 3.5, 5, and 6 years to subsequent development across all developmental domains studied (Gottfried *et al.*). Lerner and Galambos found that maternal employment status during the child's preschool period did not significantly predict children's school achievement during later elementary-school years, and maternal employment status during children's school-age period was unrelated to temperament and adjustment in adolescence and adulthood. Galambos *et al.* found that maternal employment status when children were in the sixth grade did not relate to sex role attitudes in the seventh or eighth grades.

Interpreting these longitudinal analyses, it is apparent that maternal employment status, whether measured during the child's infancy, toddlerhood, preschool, or school-age years bears no consistent significant relationship to subsequent development across the varied developmental domains studied. Almost all analyses yielded nonsignificant results. There is no evidence that children are adversely affected by mothers' employment from infancy onward. These data are supported by the results of the contemporaneous findings.

The issue of the role of maternal employment in attachment of infants and young children deserves special mention as it has been the subject of controversy (see review by Goldberg & Easterbrooks). The results of the two studies in this volume dealing with attachment (Goldberg & Easterbrooks; Owen & Cox) both indicate that maternal employment status *per se* is not significantly related to major measures of security of attachment in infancy, preschool, or kindergarten years. This was true for contemporaneous and longitudinal analyses. The timing of employment during children's infancy was related to the number of secure attachments to family members in toddlerhood (Goldberg & Easterbrooks). Children whose mothers resumed work later in infancy had a greater number of secure attachments. An ambiguous finding in this study was that the number of hours that the mother was employed during toddlerhood was related to kindergartners' responses to the Separation Anxiety Test, whereas mothers' hours of employment at kindergarten were unrelated to children's contemporaneous responses on this measure. Moreover, maternal employment status at toddlerhood and kindergarten was *unrelated* to children's responses to the Separation Anxiety Test. Owen and Cox found maternal employment status to be related to resistance behaviors in the second reunion but *not* to security of attachment. Infants of employed mothers showed more resistance but were not significantly less securely attached.

Results of both studies do not provide unequivocal evidence regarding the role of maternal employment in infants' and young children's attachments. Data from both studies do indicate that infants, toddlers, and kindergarteners with employed mothers are capable of, and do form, secure attachments to mother and/or father. It seems advisable for future research to take into account the child's attachments to nonfamily as well as to family members to gain a fuller view of the meaning of such phenomena as having one versus two secure attachments to family members or the meaning of showing resistance at reunion but also having secure attachments. Moreover, the specific family processes relating to attachment should be delineated. For example, birth of another child might relate to children's attachments. A direction for future research in this area, then, is to identify specific family and parent–child interaction variables that relate to security of attachment in the homes of both employed and nonemployed mothers as it is apparent that maternal employment status itself is not a consistent predictor of children's attachment.

II. RELATIONSHIPS BETWEEN MATERNAL EMPLOYMENT STATUS AND FAMILY ENVIRONMENT

Maternal employment status *per se* had some significant direct relationships to the family environment above and beyond social class, family size, and marital status. The findings of Gottfried *et al.* showed that, with regard to contemporaneous findings, educational attitudes regarding the child (aspirations, amount of TV viewing by child and mother, availability of out-of-school lessons), fathers' involvement, and variety of children's experience, were all higher in the homes of employed mothers beyond the control variables cited previously and for both boys and girls. A longitudinal trend emerged at 3.5 years for maternal employment status to be positively related to educational attitudes. From the preschool years on, employed mothers were higher on the educational attitudes factor measured at age 7 as compared to nonemployed mothers.

Other aspects of the proximal home environment also significantly differed between the employed and nonemployed mothers. In infancy, the homes of employed mothers had more adults present, more adults caring for the child, and employed mothers emphasized training the child's developmental dressing and toileting skills to a greater extent. The infants of nonemployed mothers had more regular naptimes, and their mothers visited neighbors more.

On the other hand, there were many areas of home environment that were not significantly related to maternal employment status. Gottfried *et al.* found no significant differences between employed and nonemployed mothers on the HOME at 15 and 39 months, nor did maternal employment status in infancy predict the subsequent 39-month HOME scores. Owen and Cox also found no reliable differences in the HOME scores of employed and nonemployed mothers. Social-emotional climate during preschool, kindergarten, and school-entry years was not related to contemporaneous measures of maternal employment, nor did earlier maternal employment predict subsequent climate at any age (Gottfried *et al.*).

With regard to mother–child interactions other than those measured by the HOME, maternal employment status was unrelated to observations of the responsivity and sensitivity of the mother in relation to her infant at 3 months (Owen & Cox). Maternal employment status in toddlerhood was not related to observations of mothers' supportiveness or helpfulness during a problem-solving task (Goldberg & Easterbrooks). Lerner and Galambos reported no significant differences attributable to maternal employment status on the mother–child interaction variables (assessed during preschool years) of maternal rejection, limit setting, and consistency in disciplining the child.

Across studies, the picture of family environment that emerges is that employed mothers are equally capable of providing a stimulating and nurturing environment as are nonemployed mothers. This is true in infancy through the school years. Hence, children of employed mothers do not experience any decrement in environment. On the contrary, these children may experience some benefits, particularly with regard to educational attitudes from the preschool years onward. The higher educational attitudes of the employed mothers cannot be attributable to SES because it was controlled in the analyses. Perhaps employment itself influences this factor. It may be that employment produces an increased emphasis on education, resulting in higher educational aspirations for the child and less TV viewing.

As shown in the Gottfried *et al.* chapter, the proximal environment is of profound importance to children's development. After analyzing all chapters, it is our view that if maternal employment status has any influence on children's development, its impact is through its relation to the proximal family environment because it is these latter experiences that impinge on or interact with the child to influence development (A. W. Gottfried & A. E. Gottfried, 1984). Inasmuch as most of the relationships between maternal employment status and environment are nonsignificant, then it is consistent that children's development is also not significantly related to maternal employment status. This is indeed the case for the present studies for both contemporaneous and long-term analyses. The long-term impact of higher maternal educational attitudes for employed mothers is currently not known. It is possible that if maternal employment continues to relate positively to mothers' educational attitudes, then eventually children's development that is relevant to educational attitudes may differ in relation to maternal employment status.

Our perspective is also supported by findings of Lerner and Galambos who found that children's difficulty was directly related to an aspect of the proximal environment, mothers' rejection (or conversely mothers' acceptance would be related to children being easy). Mothers' acceptance or rejection was influenced by their role satisfaction (whether employed or nonemployed). Hence, an aspect of children's development—temperament—was related to satisfaction with maternal employment status through the mediating environmental variable of mother–child interaction. Goldberg and Easterbrooks also reported a finding that supports our perspective. Toddlers of employed mothers who received stable alternative care were more likely to have two secure family attachments than those who had experienced a change in the caretaking situation. Hence the environment itself was related to a developmental outcome, not maternal employment status *per se*.

III. EFFECTS OF CONSISTENCY OF MATERNAL EMPLOYMENT STATUS ON CHILDREN'S DEVELOPMENT

The effects of cross-time consistency of maternal employment was examined in studies by Gottfried et al., Goldberg and Easterbrooks, and Galambos, Petersen, and Lenerz. Few significant effects were found across these studies with regard to intellectual, social, emotional, sex-role, academic, and behavioral adjustment areas. Goldberg and Easterbrooks found no significant effects of mothers' change in labor force participation (any change, including entry, termination, part- to full-time employment, or vice versa) on ego control, separation anxiety in kindergarten, or emotional expressiveness, although children's ego resiliency was higher if mothers did not change their labor force participation.

Gottfried et al. found no significant effects of consistency of maternal employment status (consistently employed, consistently nonemployed, or inconsistently employed) across infant developmental status, temperament, cognitive development, language, intelligence, academic achievement and motivation, social development, behavioral adjustment, and environmental measures. There was a trend for the homes of nonconsistently employed mothers to be characterized by less rule orientation and control at ages 3, 5, and 7 years. Children of inconsistently employed mothers had significantly higher WISC-R scores at age 6 and higher preschool achievement (KABC). Galambos et al. found no reliable significant relationship between mothers' employment consistency and adolescents' sex role attitudes and vocational goals from the sixth to eighth grades.

It can be concluded that consistency of maternal employment has little relationship to children's development over a longitudinal period. It was suggested in all chapters that the stability of the environment, rather than that of maternal employment *per se*, would be more important for children's development. This is consistent with conclusions by Baker and Mednick (1984) regarding cross-time consistency of maternal employment in a Danish population.

IV. CHILD'S GENDER AND MATERNAL EMPLOYMENT STATUS

Across the studies in this volume, the evidence did not support a hypothesis in the literature that middle-class boys are more vulnerable to the effects of maternal employment and hence will "suffer" to a greater extent than girls (e.g., Bronfenbrenner, 1986). Overwhelmingly, the outcomes of maternal employment status did not differ for boys and girls. This is particularly important in view of the fact that these findings occurred across all studies and all areas of development. Moreover, the environments provided to the sexes did not differ in relation to maternal employment status.

V. SCHEDULES OF EMPLOYMENT AND MATERNAL OCCUPATION

Overall, the distinction between part- and full-time employment status proved to be nonsignificant with regard to children's development, and this was true for boys and girls. No significant differences between part- and full-time employment status were found by Goldberg and Easterbrooks for security of attachment in toddlerhood and kindergarten, kindergarteners' level of emotional expressiveness, ego control and resiliency, parental child-rearing attitudes, or parents' emotional climate in the home. Gottfried *et al.* found no significant differences between part- and full-time employment status across all measures of development and environment from infancy through the school years. Lerner and Galambos's comprehensive work score (nonemployed, employed part-time, and employed full-time) during the first 5 years of the child's life was not significantly related to mother–child interactions, children's adjustment at ages 3 and 5, or IQ and achievement in elementary school. They did find that children whose mothers had worked more during the first 5 years had easier temperaments. Galambos *et al.* found that analyses that separated full- and part-time employment status did not differ from analyses in which full- and part-time employment were combined.

There was a trend for the number of hours per week mothers worked to be significantly correlated with some child outcome variables. Gottfried *et al.* correlated the number of hours of weekly employment with children's development and home environment at ages 5, 6, and 7. Although the predominance of correlations was nonsignificant, where correlations were significant, they tended to show negative relations between the number of hours of work and development. Greater number of hours of employment was related to lower preschool achievement scores and lower teachers' ratings of reading achievement (age 7). Educational stimulation was lower, but educational attitudes were higher with increasing hours of employment at age 7 (Gottfried *et al.*). Finally, there was more rule orientation and control with increasing hours of employment at age 5. Correlations between hours of employment and all other variables at ages 5, 6, and 7 (IQ, achievement, social development, behavioral adjustment) were nonsignificant. Significant correlations were low to moderate.

Working over 40 hours per week, but not less than that, was related to greater maternal anxiety in infancy (Owen & Cox). It was also found that working longer hours was related to less maternal satisfaction and parental investment, greater career commitment, and more infant resistance at the second reunion (Owen & Cox). However, working longer hours was not related to infants' security of attachment. Findings obtained by Goldberg and Easterbrooks resulted in nonsignificant relations between the number of hours of employment and child outcomes except for the results cited earlier with regard to the Separation Anxiety Test. Overall, the relationships between the number of hours employed and child outcomes were not pervasive, and correlations tended to be low.

Fathers appeared to be affected by labor force intensity. For example, Hughes and Galinsky found that number of hours fathers worked was positively related to *fathers'* work–family interference; fathers' whose wives were employed full-time showed less sensitive behavior toward toddlers than fathers with part-time-employed wives (Goldberg & Easterbrooks).

With regard to occupation, Gottfried *et al.* found positive relationships between maternal occupational status (controlling for fathers' occupational status) and infants' developmental scores, cognitive and intellectual development in the preschool and school-age years, reading and knowledge achievement, and social maturity. Maternal occupational status was positively related to the environmental variables of positive family involvement (ages 3 and 5) and educational attitudes (ages 5 and 7). The number of hours worked weekly was positively and significantly related to maternal occupational status (r's = .21, .27, and .28 at ages 5, 6, and 7, respectively, p's < .05 and .01). Hence, children whose mothers had higher occupational status had higher cognitive, intellectual, and achievement scores and tended to be more socially mature. Mothers of higher occupational status themselves had higher educational attitudes, and their family climate was more positive as well. Longer work hours were also associated with higher maternal occupational status.

Based on these findings, a tentative picture may be advanced. Mothers who work longer hours tend to have higher occupational status and career commitment, and higher educational attitudes with regard to their children. Family climates are characterized by more positive family involvement for mothers of higher occupational status. On the other hand, there may be a tendency for mothers who work longer hours to have higher anxiety, provide less educational stimulation, and impose more rule control. Together, these two trends may balance each other to provide no pervasive net influence on children's development. For example, it may be speculated that higher occupational status and educational attitudes of mothers who work longer hours may facilitate children's development, whereas, at the same time, the lower educational stimulation and higher anxiety associated with longer work hours may provide negative influences. The more negative impact of lower educational stimulation and higher anxiety may be balanced by a concomitantly higher level of educational attitudes, positive family involvement, and maternal occupational status. To the extent that one of these opposing trends is more salient in the homes of employed mothers, then the number of hours of employment could be either positively or negatively related to children's development. For the most part, there was not much significance, hence supporting the tentative view that these two influences tend to balance each other out. Negative correlations between the number of hours of employment and some aspects of achievement (Gottfried et al.) may be due to a specific impact of lower educational stimulation for achievement variables. We are proposing that a network of proximal environmental variables mediates between the number of hours of weekly employment and children's development. A new research question, then, would be to determine the network of variables and their causal relationships between the number of hours of employment and children's development. Fathers' roles in this network of variables needs further investigation as well. We are not advocating any specific amount of hours to be worked per week by either mothers or fathers. Rather, each family must be able to detect and respond to family stress and child outcomes that may result from undue work hours.

VI. MATERNAL ATTITUDES, ROLE SATISFACTION, AND STRESS

There were some interesting findings across studies with regard to maternal attitudes, role satisfaction, and stress. A finding that emerges is that more favorable attitudes toward the dual roles of employment and parenthood, less maternal stress, and more role satisfaction are associated with more favorable family environments and children's development.

Gottfried et al. showed that during the early school years, more favorable maternal attitudes toward the effect of employment on children, toward dual roles, and less stress due to these dual roles was related to children's greater degree of interest and participation in school (ages 5 and 7), reading motivation (age 7), academic achievement at age 7, and the environmental variables of educational stimulation (ages 5 and 7) and maternal involvement (age 7). When mothers held more favorable attitudes, their children had fewer reported behavior problems (ages 5 and 7), and there was more democratic rule regulation in the home. However, the magnitudes of these correlations were low, accounting for no more than 13% of the variance for the strongest correlation.

Regarding maternal anxiety and stress, Owen and Cox found that, although maternal employment status was not related to anxiety state, working more than 40 hours per week was related to greater anxiety. Maternal anxiety among all mothers (whether employed or nonemployed) was related to infant attachment at 12 months with more secure attachments and less infant resistance more likely with lower maternal anxiety.

Hock et al. studied the course of maternal separation anxiety (mothers' anxiety about being separated from their infants) during the child's first year. Their findings indicate that employment preference is a salient variable in regulating levels of maternal separation anxiety during children's infancy. More separation anxiety, anxiety about effects of separation on the child, and employment-related concerns were expressed by mothers who preferred to stay home. Mothers' anxiety regarding the effects of separation on the child increased over the child's first year for mothers who preferred to be home but decreased for mothers who preferred to be employed. By the end of the child's first year, mothers' employment-related separation concerns were related to both employment preference and employment status, with the lowest level of concern expressed by all employed mothers.

Maternal anxiety was related to the type of child care chosen through the child's preschool years (Hock et al.). Employed mothers who expressed greater concerns about the effects of separation on the child and greater employment-related concerns (e.g., balancing work and family) were less likely to use center-based child care during the child's infancy and preschool. Nonemployed mothers with greater concerns about the effects of separation on the child were less likely to send their children to preschool at ages 3.5 more than two half days per week. Interestingly, nonemployed mothers were also less likely to send their children to preschool than employed mothers, resulting in a difference in the types of social and educational experiences for children of employed versus nonemployed mothers. This latter finding seems consistent with the finding of Gottfried et al. that mothers' employment status when the child was 3.5 years predicted mothers' later educational attitudes at age 7. At a very early age, the educational experiences and attitudinal environment of children with employed and nonemployed mothers appear to differ.

With regard to employed mothers' work–family interference, family conditions but not job related conditions were significant factors (Hughes & Galinsky). For men, on the other hand, job conditions related to work–family interference. For both men and women, being a parent was significantly related to more reported stress and more work–family interference. However, both women and men reported equivalent levels of work–family interference. For women, work–family interference was greater when there was more frequent child care breakdown, increased perception that husband did not do his fair share of housework, and having children under age 6. For men, work–family interference was greater when they worked a greater number of hours on the job, when the supervisor was more insensitive to family issues, and with greater job demands and job challenge. Stress itself was predicted by job conditions for women (supervisor sensitivity and job security), whereas both family and job conditions predicted stress for men (job security, supervisor sensitivity, job demands, perception that wife does not do her fair share of housework). These data are important by showing that stress and work–family interference are not restricted to women. Being a parent increases stress regardless of the sex of the parent, and both men and women perceive equivalent amounts of work–family interference, albeit due to different circumstances.

Maternal role satisfaction received partial support as a significant variable. Using a causal analysis, Lerner and Galambos found that when mothers were more satisfied with their employment roles (being employed or nonemployed), they were more accepting (i.e., less rejecting) of their children, and this, in turn, was related to the child's level of difficulty. Children were less difficult when the mother was more satisfied. Hence, their findings support a causal link between maternal role satisfaction, mother–child interaction, and child outcome.

Other studies found ambiguous support for maternal role satisfaction as related to child outcome. Satisfaction with employment status was not significantly related to children's development at age 7 for either employed or nonemployed mothers (Gottfried et al.). Maternal role satisfaction was a causal factor for adolescent girls' but not boys' egalitarian sex role attitudes (Galambos et al.). Employed mothers who were satisfied with their role had daughters with more egalitarian sex role attitudes, whereas the egalitarian sex role attitudes of sons with employed mothers were related to maternal warmth not to mothers' role satisfaction. Owen and Cox found that role satisfaction was not related to security of attachment measures, whereas infant resistance following reunion with the mother was (less resistance with more role satisfaction). They also reported no significant relationships between role satisfaction and mothers' perceptions of infant characteristics when the children were 3 months or with investment in parenthood.

Maternal investment in parenting emerged as a factor related to the degree of career salience of the mother. Mothers who preferred to be home and were home had a higher investment in parenting compared to mothers who preferred to be employed and were employed (Hock et al.). Nonemployed mothers had warmer parenting attitudes than employed mothers (Goldberg & Easterbrooks). Mothers of boys were more invested in parenting than mothers of girls, regardless of employment status (Owen & Cox). Gottfried et al. found that mothers of boys were less likely to be employed during the preschool years, providing additional indirect support for the finding that mothers of boys are more invested in parenthood. On the other hand, employed mothers and mothers who preferred to be employed showed greater career salience (Hock et al.). Investment in parenting was not significantly related to infants' security of attachment, but greater investment in parenting was related to less infant resistance in the second reunion (Owen & Cox). Satisfaction with parenting was not significantly related to children's development for nonemployed mothers, but, for employed mothers, satisfaction with parenting was positively related to children's academic achievement, educational stimulation, maternal involvement, and positive family involvement at age 7 (Gottfried et al.).

Although these data provide important sources for hypothesizing about processes that may mediate between maternal employment and children's development, the data do not yield unequivocal evidence that maternal attitudes, stress, and role satisfaction actually do provide mediational links. The impact of these variables on children's development still needs further determination. It has been assumed that maternal attitudes, stress, and role satisfaction influence the child. However, the child's development may influence maternal attitudes, stress, and role satisfaction. When children are developing more satisfactorily, it is likely that the mothers' sense of satisfaction is enhanced and stress reduced. On the other hand, when a child shows any problem, perhaps one then questions the adequacy of one's role. The bidirectional nature of parent–child influences is recognized as important to the child's development and socialization (e.g., Bell, 1968) and was tested by Lerner and Galambos in this volume. This bidirectional perspective needs to be applied more extensively in maternal employment research. Testing causal models of relationships between maternal employment, child development, and these hypothesized mediating variables needs to be conducted.

The present studies have contributed to our knowledge of the ecology of the home. We can describe the most favorable family setting. This would be one in which mothers are satisfied with their roles (either employed or nonemployed), provide intellectually stimulating and responsive social-emotional environments, experience less stress, have increased father involvement, and for families with employed mothers, parents would experience little work–family interference and have more stable child care arrangements. Clearly, these conditions ought to be related to more favorable child outcomes.

It is also necessary to test causal models regarding the influence of mediational processes in homes where the mother is nonemployed. Certainly, these homes have stresses of their own. For example, in our contemporary society, nonemployed mothers may experience the stress of not being employed, particularly because the majority of mothers are employed. Hock *et al.* have shown that there is a group of mothers who are home but would rather be employed. Perhaps it is the relationship of one's employment status in the context of expectations of one's reference group that provides the setting for employment-related concerns.

VII. OTHER INFLUENTIAL VARIABLES

Using multiple regression analyses, Gottfried *et al.* compared the predictability of maternal employment status with that of family home environment, SES, family size, marital status, and child gender. Home environment and SES were much more pervasive and powerful predictors of development across the extensive range of developmental areas from infancy through the school-age years. Family size was also significant for some variables. It is our contention that maternal employment status is best understood as but one variable in the context of the total family environment (see also Hayes & Kamerman, 1983, regarding support for this perspective). To the extent that maternal satisfaction, anxiety, stress, hours of employment, or occupational status influence the proximal family environment, or are themselves influential aspects of the proximal family environment, then they may impact children's development. In future research, any reported direct effect of maternal employment status on children's development must be examined in relationship to the proximal home environment.

VIII. GENERAL CONCLUSIONS AND FUTURE RESEARCH

The studies presented in this volume attest to the resilience of families and children. Regardless of both mothers and fathers carrying the dual roles of employment and parenting, children's development was not impaired. How does the family balance the needs of all family members? This seems to be the relevant next question to ask and answer for the next round of research on maternal employment (also see Hayes & Kamerman, 1983). It is apparent that the myriad of demands are successfully met in middle-class families.

It may also be concluded from the studies presented in this book that maternal employment is a *family* issue, not just a *women's* issue. The family context changes when the mother is employed. Evidence supporting this point emerges from several studies. Gottfried *et al.* found that when the mother is employed, fathers' involvement in the caretaking, nurturing, and stimulation of their children is higher. Employed fathers experience more stress than employed men who are not fathers (Hughes & Galinsky). Apparently, the presence of children in a family increases the responsibilities of employed fathers as well as mothers. Goldberg and Easterbrooks reported that fathers were more aggravated by their toddler's behavior when their wives were employed and viewed their kindergarten children more negatively if their wives were employed while children were toddlers. If fathers become more involved with their children when wives are employed, then they may become more irritable when they have to deal directly with the everyday events of child rearing.

As the family system changes in relation to maternal employment, for example, fathers becomes more involved, this may be a way in which the family adjusts itself in order to maintain the quality of environment for the children. In our society, this new emergent role for fathers will necessitate that they adjust and become more comfortable with their enhanced family responsibilities.

Regarding future research, two needs are apparent. First, causal models regarding mediating processes must be tested. Bidirectional influences between children's characteristics, maternal employment, and attitudinal and environmental variables must be investigated. Second, the findings obtained in this volume pertain to a wide range of predominantly intact middle-class families. Longitudinal studies must be undertaken with populations of different SES, with a variety of ethnic groups, and with single parents. It is possible that maternal employment status might have different outcomes in these families (e.g., see Cherry & Eaton, 1978).

IX. IMPLICATIONS FOR SOCIAL POLICY

Maternal employment status is a social issue. Articles continue to be published in the public media that deal with effects of maternal employment on children and the family. These articles typically reflect an ambivalence about maternal employment in our society. For example, in a recent article published in *Parents* magazine (Berg, 1986), the title itself addresses society's ambivalence, "Good News for Mothers Who Work." Why do working mothers need good news? Is there an underlying fear that they are harming their children? The author of this article carefully addresses these fears and concludes: "Myth says that a mother who works puts her child at risk, but the fact is that the children of working mothers do just fine" (Berg, p. 103). Regarding our research alone, a preliminary research paper that was presented at the 1985 Convention of the American Psychological Association (A. E. Gottfried, A. W. Gottfried, & Bathurst, 1985) has been cited in over 35 newspaper and magazine articles nationally and internationally. A *Washington Post* article (Squires, 1985) is an example of the significance of this topic to our society. A feature article on maternal employment appeared in *Newsweek* (Kantrowitz, Williams, Pratt, Hutchison, & Rotenberk, 1986). It appears that society is trying to integrate and make sense out of this overwhelming phenomenon of maternal employment.

The first social policy implication, then, is for public dissemination of these results. The public needs to be educated and aware that maternal employment status itself is not a negative factor for children's development. This is an important goal for several reasons. First, many women, who may want to work, may be fearful that their employment may harm their child. The current information would help to alleviate such fears. Second, regardless of an individual family's choice regarding maternal employment, the decision should be based on scientific knowledge. Third, employed women should not be made to feel guilty because children can and do develop well regardless of their mothers' employment status from infancy through adolescence. Fourth, increased knowledge by professionals and lawmakers may play a role in support of family programs that can facilitate children's development. Fifth, professionals who provide services to families (e.g., educators, mental health professionals, pediatricians, and pediatric nurses) need to be aware of the current findings with regard to maternal employment and children's development to be able to objectively work with their clients' needs.

The most profound and immediate family need that emerged from the studies is for stable, quality, child care from infancy throughout childhood. First, the number of caretaking arrangements must be simplified. Goldberg and Easterbrooks reported that maternal satisfaction was lower when there were more child care arrangements needed. Hughes and Galinsky found that child care breakdown was a major source of work–family interference for women but not men. In Gottfried et al.'s research, we surveyed mothers on the child care options that were used and found that most families were using several arrangements, a finding supported by Kamerman (1980). If families use several arrangements, it is more likely that one of those arrangements will breakdown more often (Galinsky, 1986). Second, the importance of an early stable caretaking environment was shown by Goldberg and Easterbrooks. Fewer arrangements would result in more stability. Third, we may need more alternative types of quality child care that match the maternal anxiety needs of the mother, as suggested by Hock et al. Fourth, the caretaking environment should provide a quality proximal environment to facilitate the cognitive and social-emotional development of children (A. E. Gottfried et al.). Society needs to face this challenge. Moreover, child care cannot stop in preschool. School-age children need afterschool care as well (Robinson, Rowland, & Coleman, 1986). Corporations' responses to child care needs of employees are detailed in the Hughes and Galinsky chapter. Government needs to respond to the child care issues of working parents. With more mothers employed, our society has a responsibility to provide affordable, quality child care for parents at all SES levels (Blank, 1986). At present, there is no national policy on child care (Martinez, 1986). Kamerman (1980) identified child care as the cardinal problem for employed mothers. Perhaps providing longer and more nontraditional hours could help to alleviate the numerous arrangements needed by parents for child care. Professional training for child care providers would better assure that a quality environment would be provided to children.

Conditions on the job need to be more responsive to the family responsibilities of both women and men. This is suggested by the negative relationships between the number of hours worked and some aspects of development and environment and by job conditions that related to stress and work–family interference, as reported by Hughes and Galinsky. Leaders in business, industry, and government need to become aware that work and family roles are interrelated (e.g., see Baruch, Biener, & Barnett, 1987) and become more sensitive to the changing roles of fathers in the family. The Hughes and Galinsky chapter details recommendations for increasing employers' responsivity to families.

Research by Gottfried et al. (1985) has already had an impact in the field of law. This latter paper was cited in and provided a foundation for a recent California State Supreme Court ruling (*Burchard v. Garay*,

1986) regarding child custody. The State Supreme Court ruled that a mothers' employment status could not be used to discriminate against her in deciding a child's custody arrangement. Our results regarding the lack of significant direct effect of maternal employment status on children's development provided a basis for this decision.

Maternity policies (Kamerman, Kahn, & Kingston, 1983) are necessary to protect the rights of employed mothers. Factors that threaten mothers' job security, income, or health benefits (Kamerman, Kahn, & Kingston, 1983) could heighten anxiety, stress, or work–family interference. These latter factors might adversely relate to children's developmental outcomes. Because most mothers who resume employment during their child's infancy do so by the time the child is 8 months old (Goldberg & Easterbrooks; Owen & Cox), maternity policies are particularly critical to facilitate mothers' transition into the work force during their children's infancy.

Now that social scientists have collected and put forth these important findings regarding maternal employment and children's development, it is society's responsibility to provide for the needs of all families, using scientific evidence as a basis. The route from scientific knowledge to policy implementation is not direct and requires efforts at a multiplicity of levels (Zigler, Kagan, & Klugman, 1983). We believe that the findings in this volume provide a scientific foundation for the future development of relevant policies and programs. We also hope that the findings give optimism to employed mothers, mothers considering employment, and nonemployed mothers for valuing and feeling confident about their employment-related decisions within the context of their individual family circumstances. The findings are not meant to prescribe whether or not a mother should work. Rather, we hope that the findings will provide a foundation of knowledge to help families make decisions that best fit their needs.

REFERENCES

Baker, R. L., & Mednick, B. R. (1984). *Influences on human development: A longitudinal perspective.* Hingham, MA: Kluwer Academic Publishers.

Baruch, G. K., Biener, L., & Barnett, R. C. (1987). Women and gender in research on work and family stress. *American Psychologist, 42,* 130–136.

Bell, R. Q. (1968). A reinterpretation of the direction of effects in studies of socialization. *Psychological Review, 75,* 81–95.

Berg, B. J. (1986, October). Good news for mothers who work. *Parents,* pp. 103–108.

Blank, H. (1986). The special needs of single-parent and low-income families. In N. Gunzenhauser & B. M. Caldwell (Eds.), *Group care for young children* (pp. 25–35). Johnson

& Johnson Baby Products Company Pediatric Round Table Series, 12. Skillman, NJ: Johnson & Johnson.

Bronfenbrenner, U. (1986). Ecology of the family as a context for human development: Research perspectives. *Developmental Psychology, 22,* 723–742.

Burchard v. Garay, 42 Cal.3d 531; Cal.Rptr., P.2d, (Sept. 1986).

Cherry, F. F., & Eaton, E. L. (1977). Physical and cognitive development in children of low-income mothers working in the child's early years. *Child Development, 48,* 158–166.

Galinsky, E. (1986). Contemporary patterns of child care. In N. Gunzenhauser & B. M. Caldwell (Eds.), *Group care for young children* (pp. 13–24). Johnson & Johnson Baby Products Company Pediatric Round Table Series, 12. Skillman, NJ: Johnson & Johnson.

Gottfried, A. E., Gottfried, A. W., & Bathurst, K. (1985, August). *Maternal employment and children's development: A longitudinal study.* Paper presented at the annual convention of the American Psychological Association, Los Angeles.

Gottfried, A. W., & Gottfried, A. E. (1984). Home environment and cognitive development in young children of middle-socioeconomic-status families. In A. W. Gottfried (Ed.), *Home environment and early cognitive development: Longitudinal research* (pp. 57–115). New York: Academic Press.

Hayes, C. D., & Kamerman, S. B. (1983). Conclusions and recommendations. In C. D. Hayes & S. B. Kamerman (Eds.), *Children of working parents: Experiences and outcomes.* Washington, DC: National Academy Press.

Kamerman, S. B. (1980). *Parenting in an unresponsive society.* New York: The Free Press.

Kamerman, S. B., Kahn, A. J., & Kingston, P. (1983). *Maternity policies and working women.* New York: Columbia University Press.

Kantrowitz, B., Williams, E., Pratt, J., Hutchison, S., & Rotenberk, L. (1986, March 31). A mother's choice. *Newsweek,* pp. 46–54.

Martinez, S. (1986). Child care and public policy. In N. Gunzenhauser & B. M. Caldwell (Eds.), *Group care for young children* (pp. 71–81). Johnson & Johnson Baby Products Company Pediatric Round Table Series, 12. Skillman, NJ: Johnson & Johnson.

Robinson, B. E., Rowland, B. H., & Coleman, M. (1986). *Latchkey kids.* Lexington, MA: Lexington Books.

Squires, S. (1985, August 28). Child development unhampered if mom works. *Washington Post,* Health, p. 7.

Zigler, E. F., Kagan, S. L., & Klugman, E. (1983). *Children, families, and government: Perspectives on American social policy.* New York: Cambridge University Press.

Index

Child care
  availability, 115, 135, 239–240, 253
  corporations, 260, 261–262
  maternal separation anxiety and, 216–225
  social policy, 285
  stability of, 136–137, 253
Child development outcomes
  academic performance, 16–17, 25–31, 34–42, 72, 270
  age of child when work resumes, 136, 145–146
  attachment, 91, 101–103, 108–111, 129–130, 131–132, 135–136, 137, 139, 145, 146, 270, 271–272
  behavioral adjustment, 17–18, 25–31, 34–42, 65–66, 270
  cognitive functioning, 16, 25–31, 34–42, 270
  developmental/environmental relationships, 25–48, 53–54
    summary, 272–274, 282–283
    See also Home environment
  ego control and resilience, 132, 138, 139
  emotionality, 132–133, 138, 270
  identification, 163–165
  infant developmental status, 29, 34, 269–270
  intelligence, 25–31, 34–42, 72, 140, 270
  life-span perspective, 156–158
  maternal employment and
    summary and integration, 269–284
  problem solving, 140, 270

Child development outcomes (*Cont.*)
  school adjustment and motivation, 25–31, 34–42, 138, 270
  sex role, 172, 173, 182–185, 270
  sex typing, 156–163, 171, 175, 176–182
  social competence, 25–31, 34–42, 145–146, 270
  temperament, 29, 34, 36, 38, 62–64, 71, 76–80, 270
  vocational-educational goals, 173, 181
  See also Maternal employment
Corporations, 240–255
  benefit programs, 259–260
  child care support and services, 261–262
  demography, 233–234
  family conditions and, 239–240
  family programs of, 256–262
  family responsive services, 260–261
  job conditions, 237–238, 249–251, 252–253, 254
  schedule incompatibility, 236–237
  stresses in, 246–247, 248
  supervisory relationship, 238
  training programs, 262
  work–family interference, 247, 248–249, 251–252, 253–254, 280
  work hours programs, 257–258

Day care. *See* Child care
Demographic characteristics, 23–25, 60, 61, 95–96, 126, 127–128, 168–170, 206, 233–234, 242–243

289

Employment. *See* Maternal employment

Family context, 67–70, 123, 246. *See also* Home environment
 child outcomes and, 73–76, 80
 continuity and, 124–125
 corporations and, 246
 division of labor and, 68, 239
 longitudinal study of, 123–124
Family size, 23–25, 73, 282
Father's attitude, 68, 75, 76, 81, 141, 142, 283
Father's education and occupation. *See* Demographic characteristics

Gender differences. *See* Sex differences

Home environment, 11–14, 18–20
 attitudes and, 27, 50–51, 53, 273, 274
 cognitive stimulation, 25–47, 273
 contemporaneous analyses, 25–33
 distal and proximal variables, 12–13, 53–54, 55–56, 273, 274, 282
 division of labor, 239
 father involvement, 27, 53–54, 273
 longitudinal analyses, 33–47
 maternal employment and, 13, 26–27, 28–33, 43–47, 55
 maternal occupation and, 49
 as a mediator of maternal employment, 53–54, 274
 parental involvement, 27, 46, 53
 parent–child interactions, 53, 68–69, 73–75, 90–91, 100–101, 107–108, 112–113, 174, 183, 273
 social–emotional climate, 25–47, 273
 stability of, 124–125, 136–137, 145, 149–150
 summary and integration, 272–276
 work schedules and, 49–50, 52
 See also Family context

Maternal attitudes, 51, 53, 55, 81, 130–131, 224
 child care and, 217–218
 dual demands of parenthood and employment, 50, 226, 279, 280
 employment decision, 134–135
 maternal stress, 278–279. *See also* Maternal mental health

Maternal attitudes (*Cont.*)
 parenting attitudes, 50–51, 52, 133, 140, 141, 142
 role satisfaction, 66–67, 89, 96, 104–105, 113–114, 165–167, 174, 183
 investment in parenting, 100, 106–107, 113, 207, 281
 process of influence model, 77–79, 176–180
 sex typing, 165–166, 174, 183
 summary and integration of findings, 278–282
 See also Maternal separation anxiety
Maternal employment
 attitudes. *See* Maternal attitudes
 bidirectional child influences, 283
 California State Supreme Court ruling, 286
 career commitment, 207
 consistency of, 47–48, 52, 54, 172, 275
 contemporaneous analyses summarized, 269–272
 demographics. *See* Demographic characteristics
 development. *See* Child development outcomes
 as a distal and proximal variable, 13
 employment preference, 207
 environment and. *See* Family context; Home environment
 as a family issue, 8, 145, 283
 gender role, 155
 hours of work. *See* Work schedules
 issues addressed in this volume, 6–7
 longitudinal research on, 4, 9, 22
 long-term effects, 33–47, 52, 80, 180–182, 208–216, 269–270
 motivation for, 20–21, 60, 122, 134–135, 199–202
 as a multidimensional variable, 5
 parenting attitudes and. *See* Maternal attitudes
 public dissemination of findings, 284–285
 schedules. *See* Work schedules
 sleeper effects, 53, 122, 142–144, 270
 social policy and, 269–287
 stability and change, 52, 144–145, 146–147, 181–182. *See also* Maternal employment, consistency of

Index

Maternal employment (*Cont.*)
  stress and, 50, 90, 111–112, 115, 234, 255. *See also* Maternal mental health
  summary and integration of findings, 269–284
  See also Maternal occupation
Maternal mental health, 90, 96, 100, 105–106
Maternal occupation, 67, 170, 277
  child development and, 49, 52, 55
  home environment and, 49
Maternal personality, 90
Maternal separation anxiety, 191–229, 279
  culture and, 193, 194–196
  defined, 192
  employment preference, 192, 199–202
  Maternal Separation Anxiety Scale (MSAS), 197–199, 202–205
  multidimensionality, 193
  nonmaternal care, 216–225
  role conflict, 196–197
  significance of, 193–199
  stability of, 208–216
Maternity policies, 286
Mother–child relationship. *See* Home environment, parent–child interactions
Mother's education. *See* Demographic characteristics

Occupation. *See* Demographic characteristics; Maternal occupation

Parent–child interaction. *See* Home environment

Part- vs. full-time maternal employment. *See* Work schedules
Process of influence model, 69–70, 80
  sex typing, 176–180
  temperament, 76–79

Role conflict and strain. *See* Maternal attitudes, role satisfaction

Sex differences, 53, 71, 91, 113
  summary of, 275–276
Social policy, 284–286
Socioeconomic status, 23–25, 29–46, 103, 184, 284
Stress. *See* Maternal attitudes

Transition to parenthood, 92–95, 116, 205–206
  commitment to employment, 96, 205
  investment in parenthood, 106–107, 112
  maternal psychological health, 105–106
  role satisfaction, 113–114

Work conditions, 237–238, 244–245, 285
Work schedules
  child outcomes, 50
  corporations, 235–236, 242, 244, 257–258
  extensiveness of employment, 71, 126, 148, 242
  flexibility, 244
  hours of employment, 49–50, 105, 138, 143, 144, 276–278
  part- vs. full-time employment, 21, 71, 141, 170, 175

Printed in the United States
15625LVS00002B/39